A MEANING PROCESSING APPROACH TO COGNITION

A cognitive psychologist and an industrial design engineer draw on their own experiences of cognition in the context of everyday life and work to explore how people attempt to find practical solutions for complex situations. The book approaches these issues by considering higher-order relations between humans and their ecologies such as satisfying, specifying, and affording. This approach is consistent with recent shifts in the worlds of technology and product design from the creation of physical objects to the creation of experiences.

Featuring a wealth of bespoke illustrations throughout, *A Meaning Processing Approach to Cognition* bridges the gap between controlled laboratory experiments and real-world experience, by questioning the metaphysical foundations of cognitive science and suggesting alternative directions to provide better insights for design and engineering.

An essential read for all students of Ecological Psychology or Cognitive Systems Design, this book takes the reader on a journey beyond the conventional dichotomy of mind and matter to explore what really matters.

Fred Voorhorst received his Ph.D. in Industrial Design Engineering from The Delft University of Technology in 1998. He then took up a position as researcher at the ETH Zürich, before moving to industry where he worked in various sectors such as software, automotive, fashion, and financial, always linking product design, product development, and business development, and preferably exploring the boundaries of the impossible. Whenever possible he would grasp the opportunity to teach on product design in the tradition of ecological perception.

John Flach received his Ph.D. in Human Experimental Psychology from The Ohio State University in 1984. After more than 30 years of teaching and supervising graduate research in universities, he recently joined Mile Two LLC as a Senior Cognitive Systems Engineer. John has written extensively about Cognitive Systems Engineering (CSE) and ecological approaches to human performance and design (including three co-authored books, three co-edited books, and more than 180 archival publications). After many years of talking and writing about CSE and Ecological Interface Design, he welcomes the opportunity to test what he has learned against the challenge of designing practical solutions to contemporary business problems. To learn more about John, check out his Perspicacity blog: https://blogs.wright.edu/learn/johnflach/author/w001jmf/ or his extended bio: http://psych-scholar.wright.edu/flach

RESOURCES FOR ECOLOGICAL PSYCHOLOGY
A Series of Volumes Edited By
Jeffrey B. Wagman & Julia J. C. Blau
[Robert E. Shaw, William M. Mace, and Michael Turvey, Series Editors Emeriti]

LOCAL APPLICATIONS OF THE ECOLOGICAL APPROACH TO
HUMAN-MACHINE SYSTEMS (VOLUME 2)
Hancock / Flach / Caird / Vicente

DEXTERITY AND ITS DEVELOPMENT
Bernstein / Latash / Turvey

ECOLOGICAL PSYCHOLOGY IN CONTEXT
James Gibson, Roger Barker, and the Legacy of William James's Radical Empiricism
Heft

PERCEPTION AS INFORMATION DETECTION
Reflections on Gibson's Ecological Approach to Visual Perception
Wagman / Blau

A MEANING PROCESSING APPROACH TO COGNITION
What Matters?
Flach / Voorhorst

A MEANING PROCESSING APPROACH TO COGNITION

What Matters?

John Flach and Fred Voorhorst

Routledge
Taylor & Francis Group

NEW YORK AND LONDON

First published 2020
by Routledge
52 Vanderbilt Avenue, New York, NY 10017

and by Routledge
2 Park Square, Milton Park, Abingdon, Oxon, OX14 4RN

Routledge is an imprint of the Taylor & Francis Group, an informa business

Library of Congress Cataloging-in-Publication Data
A catalog record for this book has been requested

ISBN: 978-0-367-40428-4 (hbk)
ISBN: 978-0-367-40429-1 (pbk)
ISBN: 978-0-429-35610-0 (ebk)

Typeset in Perpetua
by Apex CoVantage, LLC

TO GERDA SMETS WHO LED US TO A PATH LESS
TRAVELLED. IT HAS MADE ALL THE DIFFERENCE.

CONTENTS

THROUGHOUT THE JOURNEY OF ROBERT PIRSIG AND HIS SON DESCRIBED IN ZEN AND THE ART OF MOTORCYCLE MAINTENANCE, CHRIS WAS PORTRAYED AS A VERY RELUCTANT COMPANION WHO DID NOT "SEE" OR APPRECIATE ALL THE WONDERS THAT PIRSIG WAS EXPLORING DURING THE JOURNEY. HOWEVER, AT THE END OF THE BOOK, THE TENSION IS BROKEN WHEN CHRIS STANDS UP ON THE BACK OF THE BIKE AND FOR THE FIRST TIME IS ABLE TO LOOK OVER ROBERT'S SHOULDERS TO SEE WHERE THEY WERE GOING.

IT APPEARS THAT WHILE ROBERT WAS SEEING A BEAUTIFUL WORLD OF MARSHES, PRAIRIES, MOUNTAINS, AND COASTLINES, CHRIS WAS MOSTLY SEEING ROBERT'S BACK.

IS IT POSSIBLE THAT CHRIS REPRESENTS MOST OF US WHO ARE BEING CARRIED ON A JOURNEY BY EVOLVING TECHNOLOGIES, BUT WHO HAVE NO VISION OF WHERE WE ARE GOING? ARE WE THE RELUCTANT COMPANIONS WHO BEAR THE CONSEQUENCES OF NEW TECHNOLOGIES WITHOUT FULLY APPRECIATING THE POSSIBILITIES?

PERHAPS, PIRSIG'S SAGA IS A CHALLENGE TO ALL OF US, TO STAND UP AND LOOK OVER HIS SHOULDERS TO SEE THE AMAZING POSSIBILITIES THAT TECHNOLOGY OFFERS. PERHAPS, PIRSIG'S MESSAGE IS THAT THE ONLY WAY TO AVOID A KIND OF SCHISM WITH THE WORLD IS TO ACCEPT THAT WE ARE NOT THINGS INDEPENDENT OF NATURE AND TECHNOLOGY. RATHER, WE ARE PARTICIPANTS WHO HAVE AN OPPORTUNITY AND A RESPONSIBILITY TO PARTICIPATE IN CREATING OUR FUTURE.

UNLESS WE LEARN TO ENGAGE WITH AND MAINTAIN OUR 'MOTORCYCLES,' UNLESS WE LOOK FORWARD AND TAKE RESPONSIBILITY FOR OUR FUTURE - WE ARE APT TO FIND OURSELVES TO BE CARRIED ON A VERY UNSATISFYING JOURNEY.

IT IS IMPORTANT TO RECOGNIZE THAT HUMAN 'EXPERIENCE' IS NOT SOMETHING THAT HAPPENS INSIDE A DISEMBODIED MIND. OUR EXPERIENCES ARE GROUNDED IN THE NATURAL WORLD - AND TECHNOLOGIES ARE A NATURAL PART OF THAT WORLD. IN CREATING THESE TECHNOLOGIES - WE ARE SHAPING OUR WORLD AND RECREATING OURSELVES. THIS BOOK REPRESENTS OUR ATTEMPT TO STAND UP AND LOOK OVER THE SHOULDERS OF MANY TEACHERS AND MENTORS TO SEE WHO WE ARE AND WHERE WE ARE GOING.

PREFACE

Why Read this Book?

"We become what we behold. We shape our tools and then our tools shape us."
—Marshall McLuhan

This book is in part inspired by Pirsig's book, *Zen and the Art of Motorcycle Maintenance*, which I have read repeatedly over a span of more than 30 years. During that time I have been teaching in psychology and engineering departments in the field of Engineering Psychology. Essentially, this is studying the performance of humans interacting with complex technologies (e.g., piloting aircraft, minimally invasive surgery, managing emergency operations). This work is motivated by a basic interest in human cognition and by the hope that a better understanding of cognition might lead to practical design improvements (e.g., increased safety).

In the course of this work, I have come to the conclusion that many of the conventional assumptions that have been made about the relations between mind (e.g., mental activity like decision making) and matter (physical activity like vehicle motion) and about the relations between science and art create gaps between cognitive science and engineering/design that are difficult to bridge. In Pirsig's book, and specifically in his Metaphysics of Quality, I have discovered alternatives to these conventional assumptions that I believe may help to bridge or even eliminate some of these gaps.

I have also discovered that these ideas are not unique to Pirsig. These ideas have roots at the beginning of the science of Psychology with people such as William James, Charles Sanders Peirce, and John Dewey. And these ideas are being rediscovered and articulated in new constructs associated with ecological psychology, situated or embodied cognition, cognitive systems engineering, experience design, and the dynamics of self-organization.

Most significantly, I have come to the conclusion that the dynamics of human experience and rationality are best characterized in terms of Peirce's construct of Abduction. This is in contrast to more conventional approaches that use the normative standards of traditional logic as a benchmark for assessing the quality of human thinking and problem solving.

It has been more than 100 years since the establishment of psychology as a science, and the field continues to evolve as cognitive science and neuroscience. However, despite this history, we still know surprisingly little about everyday human experiences and how people use 'common sense' to successfully muddle through life. The goal for this book is to explore the intersections of mind and matter and to offer some hypotheses about 'what matters' to people in everyday life, and about what should matter to scientists and designers who are seeking to design products that improve the quality of that life.

In his book, Pirsig draws a contrast between two types of motorcycle riders. On the one hand are the people who take responsibility for maintaining their own bikes. These people take responsibility and even pleasure in acquiring the tools and skills needed to maintain and repair the bike. On the other hand, there are the riders who enjoy riding the bike, but who take no interest in learning how to maintain and repair the bike. When the bike breaks down, these people are often frustrated by the need to trust the expertise of others (e.g., a paid mechanic) to do the repair.

I take the motorcycle as a token representing all technologies. And I believe that Pirsig is using the relation between people and their bikes as a metaphor for the general relationship between people and technology. All of us are dependent on technologies to some extent in order to get where we want to go (i.e., achieve satisfaction in life). Yet, few of us have any interest in knowing how the technologies that we depend on (e.g., the computer, the internet, the smart phone) work. We tend to look to others (e.g., the geeks) to bail us out when things break down, as they inevitably do.

Pirsig seems to be suggesting that this state of dependence on a technology that we don't fully understand can lead to an existential crisis. This is because the technology is not something 'out there' disconnected from who we are. Rather, the technology is a fundamental part of who we are. Thus, an ignorance about the technologies that we depend on is an ignorance about ourselves. This leads to a schism between our experiences and the reality of who we are—a split between mind and matter that makes it difficult to appreciate what matters.

Another contrast that Pirsig draws is between those who drive the motorcycle—looking forward and determining the future—and those who ride on the back—the passengers, who see only where they've been and who have little say about where they are going.

I take the motorcycle driver as a token representing the innovators who are creating the new technologies (e.g., Steve Jobs). And the passenger is a token for the rest of us, the consumers of the technology, who will be carried along and changed by the technology, but who may have little to say about what road to follow next. There is no choice in this matter; we are all on the same bike. Thus, changes in technologies will change who we are—whether we are passengers or drivers.

This book is written for both the drivers of the motorcycles and the passengers. In particular, there are two types of drivers that I hope to reach with this book. One type of driver is the designer/technologist. These are the people who know how the technologies work and who will have the most direct control over which road we take. The message for them is that it is not enough to know the technology, but they must also be guided by an understanding of other aspects of human experience. They need to make choices that are informed by an understanding of cognition and emotion. It is important for them to appreciate that every new design is a hypothesis about humans—about how they think and what will make them happy!

The other type of driver is the cognitive or social scientist (of which I am one). Our impact on the direction of travel is less direct, but relevant nonetheless. Many designers and technologists will look to us, the social scientists, to help them understand human experience. The message for my fellow social scientists is that we need to understand that every design is a potential test of our theories. Additionally, it is important for us to understand that whether intended or not, our theories will impact the trajectory of technologies. So, we have a social responsibility to frame our theories in terms that make the practical implications of these theories explicit.

The goal is to provide a framework for the two types of drivers, the technologists and the social scientists, to collaborate. This is motivated by the belief that the experience of driving the motorcycle has emergent properties (or in Pirsig's terms: qualities) that cannot be fully appreciated or understood from a perspective that considers the riders as objects independent from the bikes (the conventional social sciences) or from a perspective that considers the bikes as objects independent of the riders (the conventional engineering sciences).

For example, who owns the question "what makes a motorcycle beautiful?" Is this a question for the social scientists or for the engineers/designers? We might even take Don Norman's suggestion and ask "Do beautiful motorcycles work better or lead to better experiences?" This is where science might learn something from the artists. But I suspect that satisfying answers will not be found in either the domain of the social scientist (looking inside the eyes/heads of the riders) or that of the technologists (looking into the guts and forms of the bikes). I believe that both engineering/design and basic science will benefit by closing the gap that currently separates the arts or applied disciplines from the pure or academic disciplines.

But this book is not just for the drivers. One of the themes throughout Pirsig's book is the tension between Pirsig (the driver) and his son (the passenger). Ultimately, the tension is resolved when the son stands up on the back of the motorcycle to look over Pirsig's shoulder and see where the motorcycle is going. A fundamental goal of this book is to allow anyone who is curious about the trajectory of the motorcycle to look down the road, so that they can see and perhaps participate in a dialog with the technologists and scientists to decide in what direction we should be going.

All of us—technologists, designers, cognitive scientists, economists, consumers, etc.—are riding on the same bike. Whether we are innovators, early adopters, or the last to embrace the new technologies, the technologies are changing and will continue to change our lives—to change who we are! We have a choice. We can be the person who embraces the challenges associated with learning the technologies and how they change us. Or we can sit on the back and trust others to create who we will eventually be.

This book is my attempt to extrapolate from Pirsig's Metaphysics of Quality to make some hypotheses about what a pragmatically oriented cognitive science might look like. The goal is to frame a cognitive science that will better address the dynamics of common sense (i.e., abduction) and that will be useful in making decisions about the design and use of advanced information technologies. In a sense, my goal is to bring a bit more art and creativity to cognitive science—to take the science out of the laboratory and ground it in the pragmatics of everyday human experience.

I also hope to bring a bit more science to the art of design innovation. Technologists need to be more mindful of the impact of these technologies on human experiences. As a society, we need to be more deliberate in our choices of what roads we go down. We need to consider both what we can do and what we should do. It is also important that our experiences with practical innovation can feed back to inform basic theories about cognition.

Thus, this is about a new way to think about who we are and who we are becoming. It is a new way that explicitly acknowledges the important role of the motorcycle and the intimate connections between mind and matter that ultimately shape What Matters!

Merleau-Ponty, M. (1945). *Phenomenology of perception*. London: Routledge Classics

Design of the Book

One of the eccentric features of the book is the use of cartoons that are drawn by Fred Voorhorst. This reflects our belief that words alone are not sufficient to tell the story we want to tell. The cartoons help to dampen my tendencies to be the erudite professor! It is sad that today the adjective 'academic' is a pejorative term that typically means 'not relevant to everyday life.' We are hoping that this book will be more than an academic exercise. We want it to be of interest to a broad audience of people who are curious to discover new ways to think about human experience.

Part 1 provides the metaphysical foundations for thinking about what matters. I know you are thinking, here comes the 'academic' mumbo jumbo. However, the goal of this section is to turn philosophy on its head—to shift the focus from searching for 'absolute truths' toward a practical philosophy relevant to everyday living. Chapter 1 considers what a practical reality looks like. Chapter 2 explores the paths to discovering this practical reality. Chapter 3 focuses on the pragmatics of meaning to consider how we learn to see the world as it is. Finally, Chapter 4 introduces three constructs that span the gap between mind and matter to reflect what matters. These constructs are satisfying, specifying, and affording. Each of these constructs reflects relations between mind and matter that are critical to understand the dynamic of successful adaptation.

Part 2 explores the dynamics of the coupling between perception and action. Everyday life is about adapting to the world in order to achieve satisfaction. This is a closed-loop dynamic in which people adjust their actions to be consistent with the demands of situations. At the same time, their actions are reshaping the situations. The goal for this section is to illustrate that the typical scientific language of explanation (i.e., cause and effect) will not work. In a circular coupling, there is no temporal ordering in time that will allow specification of causal relations. The interaction of mind and matter cannot be isolated in time, because the interaction happens over time.

Chapter 5 looks at abduction as a model for the logic of common sense. This is contrasted with classical models of deduction and induction that are framed independently from the context of everyday life. Chapter 6 considers the dynamic of adaptation from the perspective of development and learning. It introduces the construct of self-organization. Chapter 7 considers the dynamic of adaptation from the perspective of control. The focus is on how constraints associated with affording and specifying shape the capacity for satisfying. Chapter 8 considers the dynamic of adaptation from the perspective of observation. The focus here is on how the constraints on affording and satisfying are specified.

Part 3 explores the dynamic of adaptation in the context of everyday problem solving. This section explores how we use experience to guide the choices we make and how we learn from the consequences of those choices. A central theme in this section is that life is not about making the right choices, but rather it is about making the choices right. In other words, achieving satisfaction is not about a decision isolated in time, but about an extended process of muddling through.

Chapter 9 provides a general overview of how people muddle through to make choices work. Chapter 10 contrasts conventional thinking that measures human rationality in relation to the prescriptions of context-free, mathematical logic, with an ecological approach that measures human rationality in relation to the practical constraints of everyday life. Chapter 11 focuses on the constraints of situations and how the representation of these constraints matters for understanding human problem solving. Chapter 12 considers the role of emotion as an intrinsic property of adaptation in everyday life. We make the case that emotions are essential to making choices right.

Part 4 extends the scope a bit and then tries to tie everything together. Chapter 13 explores some alternative ways to visualize the dynamics of experience. State space representations are suggested as a way to represent trajectories over time. A key consideration is to choose an alphabet for specifying functional 'states' of experience. Chapter 15 considers organizational sensemaking. We make the case that the dynamic of adaptation is similar at the organismic and organizational level. Chapter 14 considers the wisdom of experience. In Part 3 we reject the prescriptions of mathematical logic as appropriate norms for rationality. In this chapter we make hypotheses about possible norms for gauging good thinking. In Chapter 16 we sum up the main points and present our hypotheses about the implications for cognitive science and the design of technology.

Writing this book has been a very satisfying journey for me. Whenever I got a new cartoon from Fred, my day was brightened! The cartoons were an important part of the dynamic of writing that in part shaped the cartoons and in part was shaped by the cartoons. The book has turned out quite differently from the book I had in mind when I started. In many respects, the book has self-organized and emerged over time as my thinking was shaped by writing and by living. The hardest part was letting go, because my journey continues and my thinking continues to change.

However, it is necessary that I let go to see if some of the ideas can fly on their own. Now the book is in your hands. I hope that the ideas will be reshaped by your experiences in ways that I can't even imagine. The ultimate success of this book will depend on what you create next. I can't wait to find out!

John Flach

ACKNOWLEDGEMENTS

This book has emerged as the product of interactions with many teachers, students, and colleagues over many years. An important teacher who has influenced both of us is Gerda Smets. Gerda was a pioneer in extending the intuitions of James Gibson and applying them to Industrial Design Engineering. Gerda was way ahead of her peers, and as a result she never got the full credit that she deserves for her positive impacts on both psychology and design thinking. Thus, we have dedicated this book to Gerda.

It is impossible to recognize all the people who have shaped our thinking, but each of us would like to recognize a few key individuals whose impact has been significant. True to form, my acknowledgements will be text and Fred will use images.

I would like to recognize my Ph.D. advisor Richard Jagacinski, who introduced me to the logic of closed-loop systems. This provided a unique lens through which I could appreciate an ecological approach to psychology, which I was introduced to by Dean Owen and Rik Warren. Peter Kugler further expanded my view to consider the dynamics of self-organizing systems. Jens Rasmussen introduced me to the triadic model of semiotic systems, which provided an overarching context to integrate cybernetics and ecological psychology and to explore the implications for designing sociotechnical systems.

Along the way, questions from eager and curious students pushed me to explore alternative ways to represent and illustrate these various perspectives in order to highlight the common threads. Among these students, one student, Kim Vicente, had a particularly strong influence. Kim's questions challenged and pushed me to dig deeper and to explore paths that I would not have found on my own. On these paths, I discovered many colleagues and friends who were struggling with the same challenges. Among these were Matthijs Amelink, Kevin Bennett, Clark Borst, Jeff Caird, Sydney Dekker, Joost Ellerbroek, Chris Hale, Peter Hancock, John Paulin Hansen, Heiko Hecht, Larry Hettinger, Robert Hoffman, Alex Kirlik, Gary Klein, Nancy Leveson, Gavan Lintern, Neville Moray, Max Mulder, Don Norman, Kees Overbeeke, Penny Sanderson, Peiter Jan Stappers, Fumiya Tanabe, Hiroyuki Umemuro, Rene van Paassen, Chris Wickens, Lawrence Wolpert, Dave Woods, and many others. Note that not all of these people would concur with the concepts or endorse the narrative in this book, but all share my curiosity and enthusiasm for learning about how people deal with the complexities of work and life.

At the end of the day, every concept discovered along these paths was tested against the everyday challenges and joys of family life. Thus, my parents and six siblings set the foundation for my search; and my wife Linnea (Bits); my sons John (Turk), James (Peeper), and Joe; my daughters-in-law Sarah, BJ, and Sa; and my grandkids Johnny, David, Ean, Thomas, Ema, and Cooper continue to provide valuable feedback in my struggle to muddle through and make sense of the world.

Multiple people provided editorial feedback that helped to correct many typographical errors in early manuscripts. In particular I would like to thank Yoon Sun Choi at Liberty Mutual Research Institute for Safety and Gavan Lintern, who saved us from making many typos and grammatical errors. Also, the students in Heiko Hecht's Human Factors Seminar at the Johannes Gutenberg University at Mainz provided valuable feedback on an early version of the manuscript.

Finally, I would like to thank Fred for providing the aesthetic context for presenting these ideas. Without the humor and beauty of Fred's images, few would have the motivation or patience to listen to my 'academic' and often pedantic musings. Over the last few years, receiving a cartoon from Fred was often the high point in my weeks. These cartoons not only illustrated what I was thinking but often shaped what I was thinking. The first reaction of almost everyone who has read this book is "Fred's cartoons are awesome." I am looking forward to long-term collaborations with Fred.

John

PRAISE FOR THIS BOOK

THE MOST IMPORTANT PROBLEMS FACING THE WORLD ARE DIFFICULT AND COMPLEX, YET OFTEN DESCRIBED AS SIMPLE, CAUSAL SYSTEMS. NO: IF THEY WERE SIMPLE, THEY WOULD NO LONGER BE PROBLEMS, THEY WOULD HAVE BEEN SOLVED. REAL SYSTEMS ARE MESSY. TO UNDERSTAND THEM REQUIRES A NEW APPROACH.

ONCE WE ARE OUTSIDE THE CONTROLLED ENVIRONMENT OF THE LABORATORY AND INTO THE CHAOTIC INTERACTIONS AND SYSTEMS OF THE WORLD, THE LESSONS TAUGHT BY FLACH AND VOORHORST IN THIS DELIGHTFUL BOOK BECOME CRITICAL. THEY WILL CHANGE THE WAY YOU THINK ABOUT THE WORLD.

DON NORMAN
DIRECTOR, UNIVERSITY OF CALIFORNIA, SAN DIEGO DESIGN LAB
AUTHOR OF "DESIGN OF EVERYDAY THINGS"

WHAT MATTERS? SUGGESTS THAT TRADITIONAL PSYCHOLOGICAL METHODS PROVIDE, "THE WRONG COORDINATE SYSTEM FOR REPRESENTING THE RATIONALITY OF EVERYDAY PROBLEM SOLVING AND DECISION MAKING". TRADITIONAL PSYCHOLOGY SEEKS TO DEMONSTRATE THE ERRORS HUMANS MAKE COMPARED TO MATHEMATICAL LOGIC IN TOY WORLD PROBLEMS DEVOID OF THE RICH CONTEXT PEOPLE USE IN EVERYDAY DECISION MAKING. WHAT MATTERS? PROVIDES A FIRST STEP TOWARDS AN APPROACH THAT ADVOCATES THE IMPORTANCE OF UNDERSTANDING THE IMPACT THAT CONTEXT, ECOLOGY, AND SITUATIONS HAVE. IT SUGGESTS THAT INSTEAD OF TRYING TO CREATE MORE RATIONAL HUMAN BEINGS, WE SHOULD DEVELOP METHODS FOR HELPING HUMAN BEINGS GET BETTER AT "MUDDLING THROUGH".

DR. KYLE J. BEHYMER
HUMAN FACTORS SPECIALIST AT INFOSCITEX CORPORATION

"WHAT MATTERS?" IS AN IMPROBABLE BOOK. TO READ IT IS A PERSONAL EXPERIENCE THAT INCREASES THE NUMBER OF POSSIBILITIES TO THINK ABOUT... HUMAN EXPERIENCE.

PROF. DR. THIERRY MORINEAU
PROFESSOR IN PSYCHOLOGY AND COGNITIVE ERGONOMICS
AT THE UNIVERSITY OF SOUTHERN BRITTANY

IF YOU DO COMPLEX CONSEQUENTIAL WORK, ATTEMPT TO STUDY OR REGULATE IT, THEN "WHAT MATTERS" MATTERS. HEALTH CARE, ENERGY, COMMUNICATION, TRANSPORTATION, SUSTAINING THE ENVIRONMENT; ALL INTRICATE AND DEMANDING, EACH WORLDS UNTO THEMSELVES; YET MIGHT COMMONALITIES TRANSCEND THE DIFFERENCES AT SOME LEVEL? ORIENTED FROM THE PERSPECTIVE OF COGNITIVE ENGINEERING AND USER EXPERIENCE DESIGN, FLACH & VOORHORST'S VOICES RESONATE WITH LEADERS SEEKING TO EMBRACE TENETS OF HIGH RELIABILITY, RESILIENCE AND SUSTAINABILITY.

INSPIRED BY PRISIG'S METAPHORICAL MOTORCYCLE ADVENTURE THE BOOK TAKES A 'SEEMINGLY' MEANDERING JOURNEY THROUGH TWISTS AND TURNS OF SCIENCE AND PHILOSOPHY; WITH THE OBVIOUS BUMPS AND POTHOLES FOR THOSE ACCUSTOMED TO THE MORE 'TRADITIONAL' FORMULAIC QUICK TRIPS THAT ACCRETE DUST ON MANAGEMENT BOOKSHELVES. IN TAKING SUCH A PATH LESS TRAVELED THEY TREAT US TO UNEXPECTED NEW VISTAS EXPANDING AWARENESS OF WHAT IT MEANS TO OPERATE, SURVIVE AND THRIVE IN UNKNOWABLE, UNCONTROLLABLE SPACES THAT ARE AT THE SAME TIME THE REALITIES OF COMPLEX TECHNICAL WORK AND THE WELL SPRINGS OF INNOVATION.

FLACH & VOORHORST GIVE US A REFRESHING NEW CONTRIBUTION TO THE INCREASINGLY IMPORTANT SCIENCE OF HOW PEOPLE DO THE INEXPLICABLE.

W. EARL CARNES
RETIRED SR. ADVISOR HIGH RELIABILITY, U.S. DEPARTMENT OF ENERGY

WHAT MATTERS IS DESCRIBED AS A BOOK ON HUMAN FACTORS ENGINEERING. BUT AS ITS TITLE SUGGESTS, IT IS ABOUT DISCOVERING WHAT MATTERS. THIS BOOK WOULD DO WELL AS A READING IN GENERAL PHILOSOPHY, OR THE HISTORY OF SCIENCE, OR THE PHILOSOPHY OF PSYCHOLOGY, OR ECOLOGICAL PSYCHOLOGY, OR CONTROL THEORY, OR (ESPECIALLY) THE PHILOSOPHY CALLED CONTEXTUALISM. WHILE THE BOOK SETS ONE'S MIND ON A PROPER TRACK IN HUMAN FACTORS ENGINEERING (OR COGNITIVE SYSTEMS ENGINEERING), IT WOULD DO JUST AS WELL AS A READING IN CRITICAL THINKING, PROBLEM SOLVING, AND LOGIC. IT IS RICH WITH EXPLANATORY CARTOONS BY ARTIST FRED VOORHORST, CONTEXTUALIZING EXAMPLES, AND COLORFUL (SIC) YET MEANINGFUL QUOTATIONS FROM SOME OF THE WORLD'S GREAT THINKERS AND SCIENTISTS. A QUOTATION FROM DEVELOPMENTAL PSYCHOLOGIST JEAN PIAGET MIGHT BE JUXTAPOSED WITH A PASSAGE FROM PIRSIG'S ZEN AND THE ART OF MOTORCYCLE MAINTENANCE, OR JUXTAPOSED WITH A CARTOON DEPICTING THE QUANTUM MUSINGS OF PHYSICIST RICHARD FEYNMAN, OR A CARTOON ABOUT THE EDUCATIONAL PHILOSOPHY OF JOHN DEWEY. I'M TEMPTED TO CALL WHAT MATTERS A FIRST ATTEMPT AT MERGING THE TRADITIONAL, LINEAR COLLEGE TEXT WITH THE UNTRADITIONAL NONLINEAR GRAPHIC NOVEL. USING VARIOUS LITERARY TECHNIQUES, ARTISTIC ILLUSTRATIONS, AND CARICATURES OF QUOTABLE SCHOLARS AND SCIENTISTS, FLACH DEFTLY EXPLAINS SUCH ETHERIAL CONCEPTS AS ABDUCTIVE INFERENCE, CLOSED LOOP CYBERNETIC MODELS, AFFORDANCES, AND EMERGENT PROPERTIES, AMONG OTHERS. ADAPTIVE CONTROL THEORETIC MODELS ARE ILLUSTRATED WITH GOOD EXAMPLES, SUCH AS THE EXPLANATION OF LAYERED HIERARCHICAL MODELS BY THE EXAMPLE OF TENNIS PLAY AND THE PROBLEM SOLVING CHALLENGES FACING EMERGENCY ROOM PHYSICIANS. ADDITIONALLY, FLACH DEFTLY DECONSTRUCTS THE PARADIGMS THAT DEFINE HUMAN COGNITION IN TERMS OF LIMITATIONS AND BIASES. WHAT IS PERHAPS MOST REMARKABLE ABOUT WHAT MATTERS IS THAT FLACH PULLS OFF AN INTEGRATION OF HUGE SWATHS OF SCIENTIFIC SCHOLARSHIP, EVERYTHING FROM SEMIOTICS TO FRACTAL GEOMETRY. HE ACHIEVES THIS BY FORGING AN ELEGANT DESCRIPTIVE ACCOUNT THAT MERGES ABDUCTIVE INFERENCE WITH CONTROL THEORY AND METHODS FROM THE EUROPEAN WORK ANALYSIS PARADIGM. THIS REVIEWER APPRECIATES FLACH'S CONTEXTUALIST STANCE: HE ADVOCATES FOR A VIEWPOINT THAT REGARDS HUMAN ACTIVITY AND MENTAL LIFE IN TERMS OF AND/BOTH RELATIVITIES, HUMAN-ENVIRONMENT MUTUALITIES AND DYNAMICS, RATHER THAN IN TERMS OF EITHER/OR DISTINCTIONS, STATICS, AND FORCED CHOICES. FOR READERS WHO ARE WILLING TO GET "HOOKED," I RECOMMEND STARTING BY READING THE FIRST FEW PAGES OF THE PENULTIMATE CHAPTER, ON "PUTTING EXPERIENCE TO WORK." BUT BE PREPARED: NOT EVERYTHING IN THIS BOOK IS A SPOON FEED OF INSIGHTS INTO THE READER'S MIND. A GENUINE APPRECIATION OF THE IDEAS FLACH PRESENTS DOES NOT COME EASY. IT TAKES A DELIBERATIVE MIND, ONE THAT IS WILLING TO SOLVE PROBLEMS. WHAT MATTERS IS BOTH DEEP AND FUN. AS A WORK OF ART, AND A WORK OF SCIENCE, AND AN ACT OF DISCOVERY, IT IS THE SHAPE OF THINGS TO COME.

DR. ROBERT HOFFMAN
SENIOR RESEARCH SCIENTIST AT FLORIDA INSTITUTE FOR
HUMAN AND MACHINE COGNITION

AT LAST

WHEN THE NOBEL PRIZE FOR LITERATURE IS PROCLAIMED BY THE SWEDISH ACADEMY IN OCTOBER EVERY YEAR, IT IS A CUSTOM THAT AT LEAST SOME OF THE JOURNALISTS THAT HAVE GATHERED ON THE DOOR STEP TO THE NOBEL LIBRARY IN THE EXCHANGE IN OLD TOWN OF STOCKHOLM EXCLAIM "AT LAST!" IN ORDER TO CELEBRATE THE NOBEL LAUREATE. I REMEMBER MYSELF REACTING IN THE SAME MANNER WHEN I GOT BENNETT AND FLACH'S "DISPLAY AND INTERFACE DESIGN: SUBTLE SCIENCE, EXACT ART" IN MY HANDS IN 2011. AT LAST, I HAD FOUND AN ELABORATE TEXTBOOK FOR MY STUDENTS IN COURSES AND CLASSES LIKE APPLIED PSYCHOLOGY, COGNITIVE ERGONOMICS, COGNITIVE SCIENCE, HUMAN FACTORS, HUMAN ERROR, HUMAN-MACHINE INTERACTION, INTERFACE DESIGN, SOCIOTECHNICAL SYSTEMS DESIGN AND SAFETY SCIENCE. I FINALLY HAD A TEXTBOOK THAT COVERED IT ALL - THE PHILOSOPHICAL AND THEORETICAL UNDERPINNINGS, THE MANY GOOD DESIGN EXAMPLES AND THE THOROUGH SCIENCE THESE DESIGN EXAMPLES WERE BASED ON.

I WAS WRONG! I MEAN, THE BOOK IS AN EXCELLENT STATE OF THE ART DESCRIPTION OF WHAT WE KNOW ABOUT COGNITIVE ERGONOMICS AND INTERFACE DESIGN. I STILL BELIEVE IT IS THE BEST TEXTBOOK AVAILABLE ON THE SUBJECT. BUT THE PROBLEM IS: THE BOOK IS DAMN TOO GOOD! IT IS HARSH AND DISTURBING FOR STUDENTS THAT HAVE NOT CHOSEN TO STAY IN THE FIELD BUT STILL HAVE TO TAKE THE COURSE BECAUSE IT IS COMPULSORY IN THE CURRICULUM. BUT STILL, IT IS EXACTLY THOSE STUDENTS THAT WE NEED TO REACH, BECAUSE IT IS THEY WHO ARE GOING TO CREATE THE INTERFACES AND INTERACTIONS IN THE FUTURE. IN PARTICULAR, THEY NEED TO KNOW THE REASONS TO WHY INTERFACE AND INTERACTION DESIGN IS A SUBTLE SCIENCE AND AN EXACT ART. THEREFORE, I WAS VERY PLEASED TO SEE AND READ "WHAT MATTERS" BY FLACH AND VOORHORST. WE DESPERATELY NEED TO FIND NEW WAYS TO COMMUNICATE THE REASONS BEHIND DESIGN RULES AND PRINCIPLES. AND THE CARTOONS BY VOORHORST IN COMBINATION WITH THE VERY WELL WRITTEN TEXTS BY FLACH IS A FRESH AND EXCITING WAY TO APPROACH THE NEXT GENERATION OF STUDENTS.

WHAT I PARTICULAR LIKE WITH THE NEW BOOK IS HOW IT CHALLENGES THE ORTHODOX UNDERSTANDING OF WHAT A TEXTBOOK FOR STUDENTS MUST LOOK LIKE. IT IS CERTAINLY THE MOST EXCITING THING I HAVE SEEN IN THE FIELD OF DIDACTICS FOR A LONG TIME. SO FINALLY, I HOPE TO PARAPHRASE THE JOURNALISTS WAITING FOR THE PERMANENT SECRETARY OF THE SWEDISH ACADEMY: WE MAY FINALLY REACH THE STUDENTS WE HOPE FOR.

AT LAST!

PROF. DR. ANDERS JANSSON
PROFESSOR IN HUMAN-COMPUTER INTERACTION,
TECHNOLOGY IN HUMAN REASONING AT UPPSALA UNIVERSITY

RECENTLY A GRAD STUDENT AT OUR UNIVERSITY ASKED IF I COULD RECOMMEND A BOOK FOR SOMEONE LIKE HIM WHO HAD BECOME INTERESTED IN CONTROL THEORY ? YES -THIS FREE BOOK FROM FLACH AND VOORHORST WILL GIVE YOU BOTH THE BASICS AND THE VISIONS ON MEANING, DYNAMICS AND HUMAN THINKING, I GLADLY TOLD HIM. HIGHLY RECOMMENDED FOR BINDING LOTS OF LOOSE ENDS AND FOR BEING FUN TO READ.

PROF. DR. JOHN PAULIN HANSEN
HEAD OF THE HUMAN FACTORS RESEARCH GROUP
AT THE TECHNICAL UNIVERSITY OF DENMARK

GREAT BOOK, A 'MUST READ' FOR ANYONE INTERESTED IN HUMAN FACTORS AND DESIGN. PARTICULARLY IF YOU TAKE A SYSTEMS VIEW.

DR. DAN JENKINS
HEAD OF RESEARCH (HUMAN FACTORS AND INTERACTION) AT
DCA DESIGN INTERNATIONAL

A UNIQUE, ACCESSIBLE EXPLORATION OF THE DEEPER UNDERPINNINGS OF DESIGN AND ENGINEERING THINKING, THIS BOOK TREATS SOME OF THE FUNDAMENTAL CHALLENGES OF HOW WE THINK ABOUT THE WORLD, AND ESPECIALLY HOW WE THINK ABOUT DESIGNING SOLUTIONS TO IMPROVE THAT WORLD. THE AUTHORS BUILD ON A BROAD AND DEEP EXPERIENCE IN THE FIELD, AND MANAGE TO MAKE CONNECTIONS BETWEEN THE EVERYDAY NEEDS OF ENGINEERING SOLUTIONS, AND THE FUNDAMENTAL CHALLENGES IN THE POPULAR THEORIES AND CONCEPTS THAT WE HAVE AS TOOLS FOR THINKING IN THESE MATTERS. READING THIS BOOK SHOULD OPEN YOUR EYES, MAKE CONNECTIONS, SEE SOME BASIC FLAWS IN HOW UNDERSTANDING THE WORLD IS COMMONLY TAUGHT THESE DAYS AND, LAST BUT NOT LEAST, HELP YOU TO GAIN NEW, PRODUCTIVE PERSPECTIVES ON DESIGN THINKING AND ENGINEERING ABILITY.

PROF.DR. P.-J. STAPPERS
PROFESSOR OF DESIGN TECHNIQUES AT
DELFT UNIVERSITY OF TECHNOLOGY

THIS IS NO ORDINARY BOOK. BUT THIS IS THE WAY IN WHICH ALL BOOKS SHOULD BE WRITTEN. TO CHALLENGE, TEASE, CAJOLE AND HUMOUR THE READER INTO THINKING ABOUT WHAT THEY ALREADY KNOW AND EXPERIENCE IN A NEW WAY. IF YOU READ THIS BOOK BE PREPARED TO CHANGE THE WAY IN WHICH YOU THINK ABOUT HUMAN FACTORS AND COGNITIVE SYSTEMS ENGINEERING.

JOHN AND FRED WILL TAKE YOU ON A SEEMINGLY FAMILIAR JOURNEY WITH NEW TWISTS AND TURNS THAT WILL LEAD TO A NEW PLACE IN YOUR UNDERSTANDING OF ALL THAT MATTERS. MANY DIFFERENT FIELDS OF RESEARCH ENDEAVOUR HAVE BEEN BROUGHT TOGETHER INTO AN ELEGANT EXPLANATION OF HOW THE WORLD REALLY WORKS. THE INSIGHTS ARE BREATHTAKING.

THIS SHOULD BE ESSENTIAL READING FOR ALL OF THOSE IN OUR INTERDISCIPLINARY SCIENCE. IT IS SO DELIGHTFULLY SUBVERSIVE, CHALLENGING THE ORTHODOXY, BRINGING THE NEW PARADIGM OF COGNITIVE EXPERIENCE DESIGN INTO THE LIGHT.

PROF. DR. NEVILLE A STANTON, C.PSYCHOL.,C.ENG.
TRANSPORTATION RESEARCH GROUP, ENGINEERING CENTRE OF EXCELLENCE, UNIVERSITY OF SOUTHAMPTON

WHAT MATTERS? IS A WONDERFUL AND HIGHLY INNOVATIVE HUMAN FACTORS BOOK. IT IS A TREASURE COVE OF INSIGHTS THAT WILL GROW ON THE READER. JOHN FLACH AND FRED VOORHORST EMBRACE THE PREMISE THAT IN ORDER TO DESIGN GOOD ARTIFACTS WE NEED GOOD THEORIES RATHER THAN COOK BOOK STYLE RECIPES. THE THEORIES ADVOCATED IN THIS BOOK BRING TOGETHER ECOLOGICAL PSYCHOLOGY AND LINEAR SYSTEMS ENGINEERING. WHAT MATTERS? PROBES INTO THE OTHER, FUNDAMENTAL SIDE OF USABILITY AND WILL HAVE A LASTING IMPACT ON HUMAN FACTORS DESIGNERS.

PROF. DR. HEIKO HECHT
PROFESSOR OF EXPERIMENTAL PSYCHOLOGY
AT JOHANNES GUTENBERG UNIVERSITY AT

"WHAT MATTERS?" - MATTERS. I STRONGLY ADVOCATE THAT YOU READ THIS WORK IF YOU WANT TO UNDERSTAND THE WORLD THAT IS AROUND YOU

PETER HANCOCK
FELLOW OF AAAS, AND UNIVERSITY PEGASUS PROFESSOR, UNIVERSITY TRUSTEE CHAIR, AND PROVOST DISTINGUISHED RESEARCH PROFESSOR AT THE UNIVERSITY OF CENTRAL FLORIDA.

THE SCOPE OF THIS BOOK IS TRULY BREATH-TAKING. 'WHAT MATTERS?' TACKLES AN INCREDIBLE ARRAY OF DOMAINS AND SPECIALISMS (E.G., ENGINEERING, PSYCHOLOGY, PHILOSOPHY, COMPUTER SCIENCE, CYBERNETICS AND SEMIOTICS) IN ORDER TO OFFER A NEW VISION FOR HOW BRAIN, BODY AND TECHNOLOGY FIT TOGETHER WITHIN COMPLEX ENVIRONMENTS.

THE BOOK TO MY MIND, IS A NATURAL SUCCESSOR TO CLASSICS SUCH AS HERB SIMON'S 'THE SCIENCES OF THE ARTIFICIAL', DAVID MARR'S 'VISION' AND THE WORK OF JENS RASMUSSEN ON RISK MANAGEMENT AND HUMAN ERROR. HOW THE AUTHORS MANAGED TO SYNTHESISE THE WORK OF PIONEERS WITHIN THE BROAD FIELDS OF COGNITIVE SCIENCE AND DESIGN (WILLIAM JAMES, CHARLES SANDERS PEIRCE, EGON BRUNSWIK AND ULRICH NEISSER) WITH MORE RECENT WORK IN THE FIELDS OF NATURALISTIC DECISION-MAKING (GARY KLEIN) AND THE PSYCHOLOGY OF HEURISTICS (DANIEL KAHNEMAN, GERD GIGERENZER) IS ASTONISHING!

THE BOOK IS VERY WELL WRITTEN AND FULL OF HUMOUR AND INSIGHT. ANYONE INTERESTED IN THE COMPLEXITY OF THE MODERN DAY TECHNOLOGICAL WORLD WILL FIND SOMETHING OF INTEREST IN THIS IMPORTANT WORK.

DR. PATRICK WATERSON PHD, C-ERGHF, FCIEHF, CPSYCHOL.
READER IN HUMAN FACTORS AND COMPLEX SYSTEMS, LOUGHBOROUGH UNIVERSITY

WHAT MATTERS PROVIDES A GREAT OVERVIEW OF DIFFERENT THINKERS ON PERCEIVING THE WORLD AROUND US IN TERMS OF HUMAN EXPERIENCE, REALITY AND PERCEPTION. THEY ALL PROVIDE THEIR OWN FRAMEWORKS AND IT IS INTERESTING THAT THIS BOOK SHOWS THE RELATIONS BETWEEN THOSE FRAMEWORKS.

DR. FROUKJE SLEESWIJK VISSER
ASSISTANT PROFESSOR HUMAN CENTRED DESIGN
DELFT UNIVERSITY OF TECHNOLOGY

FOR ME, JAMES GIBSON WAS A REVELATION. THIS WAS A DIFFERENT SORT OF PSYCHOLOGY. SUDDENLY, THEORY BECAME MORE THAN JUST A PLAUSIBLE COVER STORY. OVER THE YEARS, MANY OTHERS HAVE BUILT ON GIBSON'S FOUNDATIONAL IDEAS.

NOW, JOHN FLACH AND FRED VOORHORST, IN WHAT MATTERS, HAVE PUSHED THIS ALONG EVEN FURTHER. THEY OFFER A SOLID ADVANCE; CLARIFYING, ELABORATING AND DEVELOPING THIS WAY OF THINKING ABOUT PSYCHOLOGY AS A SCIENCE. THEY HAVE DEVELOPED A UNIFIED STORY, ONE THAT EMPHASIZES THE DYNAMIC CIRCULARITY OF EXPERIENCE WITHIN A TRIADIC SYSTEM OF A STRUCTURED WORLD, OF INFORMATION THAT SPECIFIES THAT STRUCTURE, AND THE MEANING OF THAT STRUCTURE FOR US AS WE ENGAGE PURPOSEFULLY WITH OUR WORLD.

IN BUILDING THEIR STORY, FLACH AND VOORHORST HAVE DRAWN IN ORIGINAL CONTRIBUTIONS OF SEVERAL HISTORICAL FIGURES; A DIVERSE COLLECTION OF PHILOSOPHERS AND SCIENTISTS WHO STEPPED OUT OF MAINSTREAM THINKING TO DEVELOP THEIR OWN ORIGINAL PERSPECTIVE. FLACH AND VOORHORST OFFER US A COHERENT AND COMPREHENSIVE TREATMENT OF BEHAVIORAL SCIENCE; ONE THAT CAN HELP US UNDERSTAND HOW WE ACT AND INTERACT IN OUR WORLD AND HOW WE MIGHT DESIGN TO SUPPORT OUR PURPOSEFUL AND MEANINGFUL ENGAGEMENT WITH THAT WORLD.

DR. GAVAN LINTERN
COGNITIVE SYSTEMS ENGINEER

Part 1

THE METAPHYSICS OF MEANING

1

THE REALITY OF EXPERIENCE

Consider two major innovations that have transformed human experience—the airplane and the graphical user interface. In the case of the airplane, how was it that the Wright Brothers, two bicycle shop owners with minimal formal education, were able to succeed where the more conventional scientists and engineers of the day failed (e.g., Samuel Pierpont Langley and Octave Chanute). In the case of the graphical user interface, how was it that the engineers at Xerox's PARC[1] research center (e.g., Alan Kay, Butler Lampson, Charles Simonyi, Robert Taylor, Charles Thacker) and later Steve Jobs were able to imagine potentials for using computers that the executives at Xerox and many others could not?[2] What about the iPhone? Steve Jobs did not invent any of the technologies that made either the graphical user interface or the smart phone possible, yet he and a few others were able to imagine potentials for integrating these technologies into products that changed human experience in fundamental ways.[3]

An important factor that differentiated these innovators from their peers was the fact that they framed what others saw as problems of technology as problems of human experience. Where Langley was designing an aircraft, the Wright Brothers were exploring the experience of flight, which they understood to center on the ability to *control* the aircraft.[4] They did not ignore the aerodynamic problems associated with generating sufficient lift, but they understood that it was not simply about getting off the ground. The Wright Brothers' patents are not on the aircraft per se, but on the control system. They designed their plane around the piloting function.

When most saw computers as specialized scientific instruments, the engineers at PARC and Steve Jobs were exploring how the power of computers could shape the everyday experiences of managing and exploiting information (in both the office and the kitchen). In both cases, the aircraft and the graphical user interface, the focus on putting the human in control was a critical source of inspiration!

These innovators were able to imagine integrations of technology and human experience that their contemporaries did not. These innovators were able to see past conventional images of mind and matter to more fully appreciate 'what matters.' Thus, an important step toward innovation in the design of advanced technologies is innovation in our understanding of human experience and a deeper appreciation of the relations between mind and matter.

There is no recipe or easy path to innovation. There is no simple explanation for the genius of the Wright Brothers or of the scientists and engineers at PARC. Why aren't the things that appeared quite obvious to these modern eccentrics more obvious to others? Perhaps the conventional ways of thinking about humans (mind) and technology (matter) are obstacles to these insights. Is it possible that contemporary science and engineering are grounded in assumptions and/or traditions

that make it difficult to imagine and difficult to realize the possibilities that these eccentrics were able to imagine and realize? For example, Alan Kay is reported to have said:

> People get trapped in thinking that anything in the environment is a given. It's part of the way our nervous system works. But it is dangerous to take it as a given because then it controls you, rather than the other way around. That's McLuhan's insight, one of the bigger ones in the twentieth century. Zen in the twentieth century is about taking things that have been rendered invisible by this process and trying to make them visible again.[5]

The point of this book is to open your imagination and your heart to consider new ways to think about human experience with the hope that this might open new paths to innovation.

We are quite lucky to be living at a time when the elemental components for a new way to think about 'what matters' are all around us. None of the particular ideas in this book are new, and in fact, many of the ideas have been around for quite some time. However, there is an opportunity to integrate these components, in a smarter more elegant way. The hope for this book is to repackage elements from our sciences of mind and matter into a more coherent narrative about 'what matters.' The challenge is to go beyond the framework of information processing and to consider a framework for meaning processing. The hope is that this integration will be a springboard for creativity in both science and design. To start the discussion, consider some of the most basic assumptions that shape (or bias) our understanding of our world and ourselves.

Meta-Science

> Readers with a background in science and technology may find it implausible that philosophical considerations have practical relevance for their work. Philosophy may be an amusing diversion, but it seems that the theories relevant to technological development are those of the hard sciences and engineering. We have found quite the opposite. Theories about the nature of biological existence, about language, and about the nature of human action have a profound influence on the shape of what we build and how we use it.[6]

Philosophy or metaphysics is the last thing that most STEM[7] students are interested in at the start of their careers. For example, students pursuing careers in the cognitive sciences are anxious to start collecting data to empirically test specific hypotheses about human performance to learn how the mind works. For students in engineering and design, they are eager to start building things to test their intuitions about how technology works and to explore the potential for new innovations. However, whether you mindfully make metaphysical choices or not, your work is guided by metaphysical assumptions about the fundamental nature of reality (i.e., an ontology) and the fundamental limits of your ability to discover that nature (i.e., epistemology).

In the following cartoon, the figure at the intersection of the column and row on the blackboard is given three different interpretations:

the letter "B",
the number "13", or
an "ambiguous" object.

Are any of these interpretations more or less real than the others? Are some of these interpretations *illusions*? What about a person's preference for a particular smart phone, the sense of quality associated with a well-designed hand tool, the frustration associated with a poorly designed web interface, or the emotions elicited by a beautifully designed Zen garden? Are these experiences real? Or are they epiphenomena associated with underlying neural networks?

Conventionally, the interpretations of the two boys in the cartoon have been attributed to illusions, while the interpretation of the teacher has been considered to be a concrete fact—to be *real*.[8] If you are totally comfortable with that, then the point of this book is to disturb that comfort and to challenge some of your assumptions. Consider the possibility that 'B' and '13' are both as real as the teacher's interpretation of an ambiguous figure. The lesson of this example is that context matters with respect to the reality of human experience. Not just the spatial context of the adjoining figures, but also the experiential history of the people with alphabets and numbers (and with illusions). Reality involves the extended experience over space and time, not the isolated ambiguous figure. Each response reflects a different context—but there is no sense in which any of the contexts are more or less real than the others.

If you are not willing to change your assumptions, at least carefully consider the assumptions that underlie your choices. The fundamental hypothesis of this book is that conventional assumptions about *mind* and *matter* have become obstacles to the development of cognitive science and to the practical application of cognitive science to the design of technology. A premise of this book is

William James[9]

that *what matters* is fundamental and that the constructs of an objective *matter* and a disconnected *mind* are abstractions from this fundamental reality.

Ontological Perspectives

> Living a human life is a philosophical endeavor. Every thought we have, every decision we make, and every act we perform is based upon philosophical assumptions so numerous we couldn't possibly list them all. We go around armed with a host of presuppositions about what is real, what counts as knowledge, how the mind works, who we are, and how we should act.[10]

The cartoon on the front plate for this chapter illustrates four different assumptions about the fundamental nature of reality—or, in other words, four different ontological positions. The goal for this chapter is to introduce these different positions, so that you can be aware of the assumptions that are entailed. Hopefully, this awareness will facilitate clarity of thought and will help to cut through some of the fog and friction that make collaboration across disciplines so difficult.

The first three ontological positions are well illustrated by the Venn diagram in Figure 1.1. One circle in this diagram represents mental phenomena—associated with constructs of *Mind*. The second circle in this diagram represents physical phenomena—associated with constructs of *Matter*. The ontological question, in terms of Figure 1.1, is: which parts of this Venn diagram reflect aspects that are fundamental to the nature of reality?

One position is that nature is fundamentally composed of *Matter*. This position is typically referred to as *Materialism*. This ontological position assumes that anything outside the Matter circle is an epiphenomenon that will ultimately be discovered to arise from elements within the Matter circle. Paul and Patricia Churchland represent a modern variation on this view—*Eliminative Materialism*.[11] In this view, the aspects of Mind that fall outside the Matter circle represent a kind of 'folk psychology' that will be found to be unscientific. In other words, this 'folk psychology' is a derivative from more fundamental properties of matter.

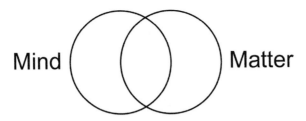

Figure 1.1 Mind or matter, which matters when it comes to a scientific basis for explanation?

Thus, materialists typically search for answers to nature's puzzles in the properties of matter—in the chemical properties of the tea interacting with the biological properties of the brain. For example, many cognitive scientists prefer the label 'neuroscientist,' because they assume that the answers to psychological questions will ultimately be grounded in the properties of the brain (e.g., neural networks). Similarly, many designers and engineers dismiss input from the 'soft' sciences as too 'fuzzy' or as simply a matter of 'taste' or 'marketing.' They prefer to address the 'user experience' in terms of simple empirical questions framed as usability studies in the final phase of the design process.

A second ontological position is that each circle in the Venn diagram represents a fundamentally different kind of phenomenon and that a complete understanding of nature requires an understanding of these two, different realities. In other words, each circle is important. This position is known as *Dualism*, and it is typically associated with René Descartes. The implication of this is that there may be a need for two different kinds of sciences: one, prototypically physics, for dealing with the ultimate reality of Matter; another, prototypically psychology, for dealing with the ultimate reality of Mind. This position asserts that the phenomenon of Mind cannot be reduced to physics and that the phenomenon of Matter has a reality that is independent from that of Mind. This is summarized in the commonly repeated quip attributed to the philosopher George Berkeley: "What is mind? No matter. What is matter? Never mind." This dualistic ontology dominates Western culture.

One of the challenges for a dualistic ontology is to explain the nature of the interactions between Mind and Matter. How does the reality of Mind come to know the reality of Matter? This raises the issue of information processing. How do properties of the physical tea communicate with the

sensory and cognitive systems to produce a 'taste' or a feeling of 'satisfaction'? Does it depend on logic—the world of matter is inferred based on partial cues from experience (e.g., Richard Gregory's Constructivist approach to perception[12])? Or is our knowledge of the material world empirically grounded in the dynamics of perception-action (e.g., James Gibson's Realist approach to perception[13])?

The problem of linking the properties of mind with the properties of matter is typically referred to as the correspondence problem. As Winograd and Flores observe, the 'rationalist tradition' that has shaped cognitive science has tended to sidestep the correspondence problem—that is, assuming correspondence and then focusing exclusively on the 'rules' governing the relations among objects of the mental representation:

> Rationalist theories of mind all adopt some form of 'representation hypothesis,' in which it is assumed that thought is the manipulation of representation structures in the mind. Although these representations are not specifically linguistic (that is, not the sentences of an ordinary human language), they are treated as sentences in an 'internal language'[14]

A third ontological position, typically referred to as Idealism, assumes that reality is based exclusively in Mind. In terms of the Venn diagram, this suggests that there is no reality outside of the circle of Mind. Idealism has historical roots, through Plato to early explorations in mathematics associated with irrational numbers like Pi. An irrational number has no concrete specification, yet it is fundamental to concrete objects like circles. From the idealist position, the concrete circles that we experience in our everyday lives are imperfect realizations of a more basic reality that can only be accessed through mathematics. In Plato's terms, our experiences in the physical world are mere shadows on the cave wall that correspond to a reality based on a rational ideal (e.g., mathematics).

Thus, for the idealist, irrational numbers like Pi, which are impossible to realize materially (i.e., because it would require an infinite number of decimal places), may be more fundamental to reality than the material approximations that we can experience directly. In essence, the rational rules that govern the representations (e.g., mathematical or mental) are considered to be the ultimate grounding for reality.

A modern variant on an idealist view is phenomenology (e.g., Edmund Husserl, Martin Heidegger). Phenomenology focuses on the mind as a fundamental key to reality. Constructs like 'being in the world', 'consciousness,' 'intentionality', 'meaning', 'qualia', or 'throwness' become fundamental constructs to be understood as the basis for our beliefs about the world of matter. The representations in the mind—the sentences of our internal speech—become the most fundamental basis of experience.

Thus, for the phenomenologist the 'taste of the tea' may be more fundamental than the chemical composition of the tea; and in fact, the chemical composition of the tea may only become 'real' relative to the human experience of that composition. As Winograd and Flores observe about Heidegger's ontology:

> The interpreted and the interpreter do not exist independently: existence is interpretation, and interpretation is existence.[15]

Although the idealist ontology may seem anti-scientific at first blush, consider the pragmatic constraints on observation. How is it possible to know a reality of matter that lies outside the scope of Mind? Practically, we can't know what we don't know, so science is limited to what we can bring to Mind, what we can imagine. When it comes down to it, isn't 'science' a system of beliefs or at least a system for testing and establishing beliefs (e.g., hypotheses)? This position conflates the problem of *what is real* (ontology) with the problem of *what can be known* (epistemology) that will be explored more extensively in the next chapter. This position is known as *Pragmatism*. Historically, this position is a precursor to a fourth ontological position suggested by William James. That is the ontological position of *Radical Empiricism*.[16]

This fourth ontological position is more difficult to understand relative to the diagram in Figure 1.1. This view shares some similarities with phenomenology as it is motivated by James' keen curiosity about the basis for human beliefs. In terms of Figure 1.1, it would be tempting to associate *Radical Empiricism* with the intersection of the two circles. This image suggests that the larger parts of the two circles that are outside that sliver are epiphenomena that must ultimately be grounded in properties of the interaction between Mind and Matter.

The problem with the Venn diagram in Figure 1.1 is that William James' expansive ontology that considers both Mind and Matter as parts of a unified ontology is depicted as a narrow view relative

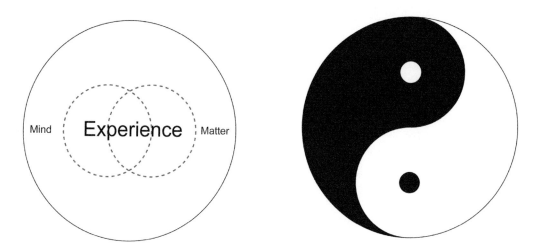

Figure 1.2 Mind and matter, two different depictions that both show two facets of the phenomenon of nature to be understood as components that are integrated within a unified whole of experience.

to the other three positions. It is especially narrow relative to the dominant dualistic ontology that appears to provide the broadest view of nature. In the context of Figure 1.1, the Radical Empiricist ontology seems to exclude significant parts of both Mind and Matter as epiphenomena. But this problem is the result of the culture that we live in. Figure 1.1 started with a dualistic assumption by creating two circles, one for Mind and another for Matter. If you grew up in a Western tradition, you probably accepted this, without question, as the most logical starting point for any discussions of reality.

In fact, you have probably had some exposure to the first three ontological positions (materialism, idealism, and dualism), and they have probably been presented as the only three logical possibilities. That is, ontology is either exclusively based in Matter (materialism); or it is exclusively based in Mind (idealism); or we need independent ontologies for each (dualism). What other possibility is there? Figure 1.2 illustrates a fourth possibility that James imagined. James did not want to deny any aspects of the phenomenon of mind or matter from the sphere of science, but he refused to accept that there were two realities. He resisted the temptation to divide science between the science of mind and the science of matter. He was searching for a unified science that would address Mind and Matter—a science of experience.

Thus, in the earlier cartoon showing the 'ambiguous' figure, consider the possibility that the perceptions of "B" or "13" are not illusions—nor are they purely 'mental' events. Rather, these perceptions are grounded in the larger context of the diagram (including the surrounding figures) and in the larger experiential context that includes the boys' social history with alphabets and numbers. These perceptions are not exclusively matter (e.g., disconnected physical objects), nor are they exclusively mind (i.e., unconstrained by the physical context). These perceptions are emergent properties that reflect constraints associated with both mind (e.g., past experience) and matter (e.g., the physical arrangement on the board).

This point is also illustrated by Weinberg's story about the three umpires and how they called 'balls' and 'strikes' (the previous cartoon). Is there an absolute 'truth' for differentiating balls and strikes that is independent from the experience of the umpires? Or perhaps, the reality of a 'ball' or a 'strike' is in part determined by the umpire? Note that the point is not that 'balls' and 'strikes' are arbitrary choices of an individual, but rather that the awareness of the umpire plays an important role in shaping the pragmatic reality of the situation. That pragmatic reality is what will ultimately determine the success of the umpire and the outcome of the game. No matter what the position of the ball, the umpire's call will determine the batter's fate. But, of course, the umpire's fate is also on the line, and the stability of his situation depends on the correspondence of his calls with the social and physical dynamics of the game. This was the central question for James and the early pragmatists (e.g., Peirce): *How is it our beliefs come to align with the demands of the game of life? How do mind and matter come to a stable relation with respect to what matters?*

For James the division of sciences with some, like physics, focusing on 'objective' properties of matter (e.g., the arrangement of the marks on the board, the trajectory of the ball with respect to the plate) and others, like psychology, focusing on 'subjective' properties of mind (e.g., the relation to the different letter or number contexts, the umpire's call) was a smart tactical choice for managing the complexity of nature. However, he saw this division as a temporary condition for a young science. He assumed that with maturity, the separate lines of investigation (the *sciences* plural) would eventually converge and work together to build a unified singular *Science* to explore the full range of experience (What Matters) that included both 'objective' properties conventionally associated with Matter and 'subjective' properties conventionally associated with Mind.

Certainly, science has matured significantly from the time of William James (1842–1910). However, it seems that it is still far from the kind of convergence that James envisioned. Perhaps it is

even further from that convergence today than in James' day, when it was common for great minds to consider the broader metaphysical implications of their work. Perhaps, this is due to the accumulation of data within specific disciplines. Academic curricula seem to be increasingly burdened by the need to cover the accumulated data, and there seems to be less and less time and opportunity for students to explore across multiple disciplines, much less to get involved in the 'morass' of philosophy. When gaps are discovered between disciplines, there seems to be a tendency to fill the gaps with new even more specialized disciplines.

Despite initiatives from scientific organizations like the National Science Foundation to promote cross-disciplinary collaborations, there seems to be little patience among engineers and scientists to engage with the metaphysical assumptions that shaped and separated the disciplines. Until these assumptions are engaged, it may be impossible to bridge the gulfs that separate the 'hard' and the 'soft' sciences; or the gulfs that separate the 'basic' scientists from the 'applied' scientists; or the gulfs that leave 'theories of cognitive science' disconnected from 'practical problems of designing user experiences.'

The failure to bridge the gap between our minds and the things that matter (e.g., the qualities of life such as goodness) can result in a kind of existential schizophrenia, as insightfully described by Robert Pirsig (*Zen and the Art of Motorcycle Maintenance, Lila*[17]). On the one hand, the products of the hard sciences (e.g., the internet) are becoming an increasingly essential part of our experience, but rather than increasing our sense of connectedness with reality, the result is an increasing sense of disconnectedness (e.g., an alienation from the technologies that we depend upon). While science reveals much about nature, the price of admission to science often is that we leave our values (our sense of morals or goodness) out of the discussion. Thus, we become more knowledgeable but increasingly less intimate. We see more but from an increasingly distant perspective. In the end, we become isolated and lost in a world that is reduced to cold, hard facts, and we lose the ability to judge what is good for us and what is bad. Pirsig's Metaphysics of Quality is a modern variant of James' Radical Empiricism. In Pirsig's metaphysics, *Quality* is a joint function of mind and matter:

> Man is not the source of all things, as the subjective idealist would say. Nor is he the passive observer of all things, as the objective idealists would say. The quality which creates the world emerges as a relationship between man and his experience. He is a participant in the creation of all things. The measure of all things.

(p. 384)[18]

In Pirsig's metaphysics the subjective qualities (e.g., the goodness of the taste) are no longer of a different kind than the objective qualities (e.g., the chemistry of the blend of tea). It is not the case that only one of these is real, and it is not the case that these are parts of two separate realities. No! There is a single reality, a single experience of the tea. The challenge is to find a single science that can provide both the theoretical context for appreciating this 'quality' and a practical context for engineering technologies that will potentially improve the 'quality' of life.

It is probably easier for people struggling with the practical problems of designing technologies that work for people to realize that the problems of user experience span the classical constructs of mind and matter. The recent emergence of Apple to pass Exxon as the most profitable company in the world suggests that intuitions into the user experience can be more valuable than oil. Yet, until the metaphysical contradictions of our ontologies that treat mind and matter as disconnected are faced, the design of quality user experiences will remain the art of geniuses like Steve Jobs and Jony Ive, rather than the product of science-driven, engineering practice.

The goal is not to take the genius out of design but to explore ways to put the power of science behind that genius, and perhaps to explore ways to put the genius of design back into science. Science was never intended to be the authority that defends conventional wisdom; rather it is intended to be the engine of innovation for overturning conventional wisdom in pursuit of deeper insights into the complexities of nature.

This is an exciting time with respect to the questions that early functional psychologists like James raised about the metaphysics of cognition. On the one hand, technological innovations associated with information technologies are increasing appreciation for the fundamental role of humans with regards to making systems work.[19] This is raising many practical questions about the nature of human experience in relation to the design and use of these technologies. On the other hand, developments in the physical sciences associated with chaos and dynamical systems are raising analogous questions about both the dynamics of natural systems (e.g., self-organization) and the nature of scientific explanations (e.g., circular causality). For example, Mandelbrot's fractal geometry suggests that a simple fact like the length of a coastline may depend on the choices that scientists make.[20] As the basic unit of measurement becomes smaller, the length of the coastline increases (approaching infinity as the unit of measurement becomes finer). As with the 'balls' and 'strikes,' it seems that the length of a coastline cannot be decided on purely 'objective' grounds. Ultimately, the scientist has to make the call.

Additionally, empirical work in neuroscience[21] is inspiring new intuitions with respect to metaphysics. Constructs such as embodied cognition are for the first time putting 'flesh' on William James' intuitions and are paving the way for reconnecting mind and matter within the pragmatic dynamics of perception and action in a world that matters.[22]

Thus, this book is an effort to reconsider some of the questions raised by Winograd and Flores about the nature of computers and cognition:

> In the course of developing a new understanding we came across questions that have long been the subject of debate, such as "Can computers think?", "Can computers understand language?", and "What is rational decision-making?" We address these questions not so much to solve them as to dissolve them. They arise in a background of understanding about human thought and language, a background that itself needs to be reexamined and revised. In the end, we are not concerned with providing new answers to questions about technology as they have traditionally been posed. We look towards new questions that can lead to the design and use of machines that are suited to human purposes.[23]

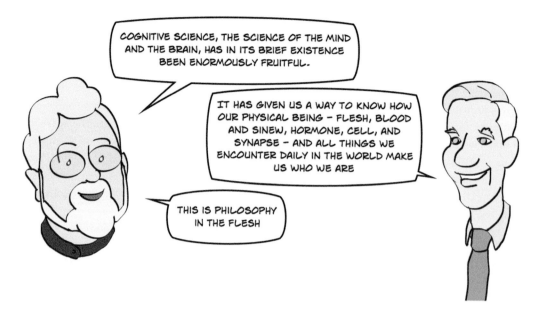

George Lakoff and Mark Johnson[24]

Perhaps, questions raised in this book will help those pursuing careers in cognitive science, cognitive engineering, or experience-centered design to gain new insights into what matters? Perhaps, we can move beyond information processing models of human performance to begin to understand how humans are able to engage with the functionally significant aspects of their ecology. Perhaps, we can begin to imagine how we process meaning.

Notes

1. Palo Alto Research Center.
2. Hiltzik, M.A. (1999). *Dealers of lightning: XEROX parc and the dawn of the computer age*. New York: Harper Collins.
3. Isaacson, W. (2011). *Steve Jobs*. New York: Simon & Schuster.
4. Crouch, T. (1989). *The bishop's boys*. New York: W.W. Norton & Company.
5. Quoted in Hiltzik (1999), p. 83.
6. Winograd, T., & Flores, F. (1986). *Understanding computers and cognition: A new foundation for design*. Norwood, NJ: Ablex Publishing Corporation. (p. xii).
7. STEM—Science, Technology, Engineering & Mathematics.
8. Kahneman, D. (2011). *Thinking fast and slow*. New York: Farrar, Straus, and Giroux.
9. James, W. (1909). *Psychology*. New York: Henry Holt and Company. (pp. 461–462).
10. Lakoff, G., & Johnson, M. (1999). *Philosophy in the flesh: The embodied mind and its challenge to western thought*. New York: Basic Books. (p. 9).
11. Churchland, P.M. (1981). Eliminative materialism and the propositional attitudes. *Journal of Philosophy*, 78(2), 67–90.
12. Gregory, R.L. (1974). *Concepts and mechanisms of perception*. New York: Charles Scribner's Sons.
13. Gibson, J.J. (1979). *The ecological approach to visual perception*. Boston: Houghton Mifflin.
14. Winograd, & Flores (1986), pp. 19–20.
15. Winograd, & Flores. (1986), p. 31.
16. James, W. (1912). *Essays in radical empiricism*. London: Longmans, Green & Co.
17. Pirsig, R. (1974). *Zen and the art of motorcycle maintenance: An inquiry into values*. New York: Morrow, Co.

    Pirsig, R. (1991). *Lila: An inquiry into morals*. New York: Bantam Books.

18. Pirsig, R. (2000). *Zen and the Art of Motorcycle Maintenance*. First Perennial Classic Edition (p. 384).

19. Norman, D.A. (2010). *Living with complexity*. Cambridge, MA: The MIT Press.

   Norman, D.A. (2007). *The design of future things*. New York: Basic Books.

   Norman, D.A. (2004). *Emotional design:Why we love (Or hate) everyday things*. New York: Basic Books.

   Norman, D.A. (1993). *Things that make us smart: Defending human attributes in the age of the machine*. Reading, MA: Perseus.

20. Mandelbrot, B. (1983). *The fractal geometry of nature*. San Francisco: W.H. Freeman.

21. Damasio, A. (1994). *Descartes' error: Emotion, reason, and the human brain*. New York: Penguin Books.

22. Lakoff, G., & Johnson, M. *Philosophy in the flesh*. New York: Basic Books.

23. Winograd, T. & Flores, F. (1986) p. xii–xiii.

24. Lakoff & Johnson, p. 568.

2

PUTTING THINGS INTO PERSPECTIVE

Heinz von Foerster, a general systems theorist, once observed that there are two distinct attitudes toward the world. On the one hand, there are the 'discoverers,' and on the other hand, there are the 'inventors.' The Discovers see themselves as *apart from* the world. They consider themselves to be residents of an independent world whose regularities are 'out there' to be explored and discovered. In contrast, the Inventors see themselves as a *part of* the world. They consider themselves to be participants in a dynamic world whose regularities are continually evolving and being recreated, at least in part as a consequence of their own actions. Foerster notes that he is particularly impressed by the fact that neither of these two groups is aware that they have made a particular choice about how to look at reality. This choice that Foerster is referring to is classically addressed in philosophy as the problem of *Epistemology*.

Where the ontological problem addressed in Chapter 1 considers *what reality is*, the epistemological problem considers *what we are capable of knowing about that reality*. In academic philosophy these are two different questions, but in practice, the choice of *epistemology* is typically intimately related to the choice of *ontology*. For example, those who choose a materialist ontology typically see themselves as Discoverers. For them, the world is out there. For them, it is essential for achieving good science to take an objective stance toward the phenomena of nature. In fact, from this perspective the function of the scientific method is to create this objective distance between the observer and the phenomenon.

Thus, for example, a cognitive neuroscientist might search for the answers to psychology in objective brain structures or in computational models realized as concrete computer simulations,

Heinz von Foerster[1]

or in carefully controlled experimental paradigms designed to minimize demand characteristics.[2] This attitude leads the neuroscientist to be skeptical toward more naturalistic forms of observation, where the scientist often becomes more of an active participant than a passive observer. This attitude also leads to a large gulf between the 'hard' disciplines, where an objective separation is maintained between phenomenon and observer (e.g., neuroscience), and the 'soft' disciplines, where there is a more intimate relation between observer and the phenomenon (e.g., art and design). This attitude also leads to a large gulf between research enterprises (e.g., the *science* of medicine) and fields of practice (e.g., the *art* of healing).

The combination of a materialistic ontology with the epistemological attitude of a discoverer has been dominant in Western attitudes toward the discipline of science. However, it leads to an interesting conundrum. When acting as the scientist, apart from the phenomena, where is the observer standing? Is it really possible for the scientist to stand apart from the natural phenomena that he is studying? Where does the scientist stand? Is there a 'ruler' for measuring the length of the coastline of England that is independent of the observer?

This conundrum leads many people to become open to the possibility of a dualistic ontology. That is, the addition of the possibility of a mind, independent from the world of matter, provides a place for the objective observer to stand! Thus, science and mathematics can be exercises of Mind to understand the world of Matter that is 'out there.' This attitude has generally worked well for the physical sciences. The discipline of objective, empirical science has generated a wealth of discoveries about the independent properties of Matter. This enterprise has been so successful that it has become the *de facto* model of 'science.' A model that has been embraced not only by those seeking to uncover the regularities of Matter, but also by those who seek to discover the regularities of Mind.

While dualism provides a solution to the conundrum about where the scientific observer is standing with respect to the phenomenon of Matter, the problem remains for the phenomenon of Mind. Is it possible to take the objective perspective of a Discoverer when studying the Mind? Where does the scientist of Mind stand? This conundrum led John Watson[3] to redefine the 'science of psychology' from the 'science of mind' to the 'science of behavior.' In objectifying the phenomenon as behavior, it became plausible that the scientist could stand apart from that behavior as a passive observer in order to discover the regularities. Researchers pursuing a science of behavior, such as B.F. Skinner, realized that by shifting their attention to animal behavior (e.g., white mice and pigeons), it would be easier to stand apart from the phenomenon in order to achieve the objective distance essential to the attitude of a Discoverer. Clearly, this program of research has been very successful and has contributed greatly to our understanding of the world.

For many, however, the behaviorist approach was unsatisfying. It seemed too narrow a perspective, even for understanding animal behavior. For example, Edward Tolman[4] showed through a series of clever experiments on maze learning with rats that the learning could not be explained based on simple associations between behavior and reward. As illustrated in Figure 2.1, he showed that when reinforced routes through the maze were blocked, rats chose alternative paths that suggested that they had learned more than a specific route (i.e., a specific sequence of actions). They chose a path that was most nearly associated with the direction to the goal box (C in Figure 2.1), illustrating that they had learned about the layout of the maze and the relative position of the goal box. This led Tolman to posit the construct of a 'mental map' to reflect the fact that the rat had learned more than a simple sequence of behaviors; it had learned something about the general layout of its environment. Tolman's observations and hypotheses were very significant in helping psychology to escape from strict behaviorism to reconsider the possibility of a science of Mind.

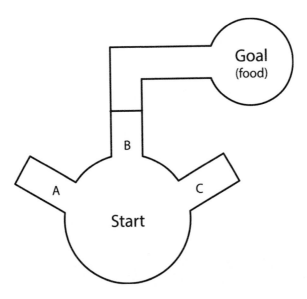

Figure 2.1 This illustrates the logic of experiments to assess whether rats are learning spatial relations when trained in a maze. After being trained to follow path B to attain food reward, that path is blocked. How do rats respond?

The invention and development of the computer through the 1940s and 1950s offered another plausible solution for maintaining an objective Discoverer epistemology with respect to a science of Mind. The computer metaphor allowed Matter to be objectified in terms of 'hardware' and Mind to be objectified in terms of 'software.' With the framework that evolved from this computer metaphor, the phenomenon of Mind could be visualized as objective *information processes*. These information processes (e.g., encoding, memory, decision making) could be tested both empirically in the experimental laboratory and analytically through computer simulations. The computer simulations, in particular, became a benchmark for establishing objective, computational norms or standards against which to 'measure' man.

The computer metaphor reinforced both the plausibility of the Discoverer attitude toward the phenomena of Mind and Matter and the plausibility of a dualistic ontology where Mind (i.e.,

software) could be treated independently from Matter (i.e., hardware). This intersection of a Dualistic ontology and a Discoverer epistemology has been dominant over the last 50 years, and it has led to significant advancement in both science (including the evolution of a new *computer science* to focus explicitly on the properties of computations) and engineering (leading to amazing developments in information technologies). In some ways, developments of information technologies in terms of smart phones and social networks have leapfrogged well beyond the imaginations of even the science fiction writers. For example, compare how smart phones are used today relative to how the 'communicators' were envisioned in the Star Trek series.

Although the computer metaphor has been enormously successful, for some there continues to be something missing with respect to a complete science of Mind. There seems to be both less and more to Mind than the 'cold' computations of logical machines. Initially, researchers focused on the apparent deficits of humans relative to computers. The gulf between the prescriptions of normative logical algorithms and the actual behavior of humans could be attributed to the information limitations of humans, such as the seven-plus-or-minus-two capacity of working memory described by George Miller.[5]

However, as researchers expanded their field of view, from examining performance on relatively simple puzzles and games (e.g., tic-tac-toe, crypt-arithmetic, and checkers) to more complex problem solving (e.g., chess, medical diagnosis; fault diagnosis in nuclear power plants; and management of aviation systems), they discovered that in complex, dynamic worlds, the human can often be more resilient than the logical automatons. It seems that decision making in fields of practice, such as medicine, require nuanced insight that, for now, exceeds the capacity of even very sophisticated computers.

Dissatisfaction with the computer metaphor has led some to look into the brain for a more satisfying understanding of human cognition. Perhaps, the differences between computers and humans reflect fundamental differences in the way these systems are wired [e.g., neural nets versus production systems; or analog systems versus digital systems; or the presence and/or nature of the interplay between 'higher' (logic-based) and 'lower' (emotional-based) centers within brains]. For these neuroscientists, the Discoverer epistemology is maintained, but the 'out there' that they are exploring shifts from a computational object to a biological object.

For some, however, dissatisfaction with the ability of classical scientific programs designed from the Discoverer epistemology has led them to consider an alternative attitude toward observation. It has led them to shift to an Inventor epistemology, where the observer is considered to be inextricably linked to the phenomenon being studied. Whereas the Discoverer seeks to keep an objective distance between the scientist-observer and the phenomenon of study, the Inventor seeks to immerse in the phenomenon. Whereas the Discoverer is skeptical about naturalistic forms of observation, the Inventor is skeptical of controlled, laboratory experiments.

The Inventors fear that essential properties may be lost when a phenomenon is reduced to fit the constraints of the laboratory. They fear that when scientists create objective distance, they are losing sight of essential properties of the phenomenon. Where the Discoverer seeks to explore the phenomenon from the outside, the Inventor believes that there are essential properties that can only be discovered from the inside. Thus, for some, the Discoverer epistemology is unsatisfying, at least with respect to the development of a science of Mind. Rather than treating the Mind as an external object, they have begun to think about Mind as a dynamic process and to think of themselves as participants in this process.

One solution to this dissatisfaction can be the adoption of a dualistic view of epistemology, with a Discoverer epistemology being applied to the phenomenon of Matter (where it has been clearly successful), but an Inventor epistemology being applied to the phenomenon of Mind. This, of course, adds to the gulf between the 'hard' sciences and the 'soft' sciences, since they now are dealing with distinct realities AND applying different epistemologies. The result is not only two different kinds of reality but also two different kinds of science.

An alternative solution is to adopt an Idealistic ontology. If you begin with the assumption that knowing requires intimate interaction of the observer with a phenomenon (i.e., the Inventor's epistemology), then pragmatically speaking there is little value in postulating a world of Matter that lies outside of your capacity to know it. Thus, the Pragmatist position is that we might as well confine our ontology to the things that can be known, at least as far as Science goes.

For example, phenomenology embraces an Inventor's attitude towards the phenomenon of Mind. Thus, the phenomenologist immerses into the mental and emotional aspects of human experience and shifts attention from 'objective' measures grounded in behavior to examine more 'subjective' measures including think-aloud protocols and other expressions of human creativity, such as art and music, that reflect both thoughts and feelings.

It is probably not that surprising to you that those interested in Mind (i.e., the softer sciences) might consider an Inventor alternative to the objective Discoverer epistemology that has been so successful for the physical sciences. But an important motivation for the Inventor epistemology is coming from research in quantum physics. It is true that the Discoverer attitude has been incredibly successful for learning about important properties of matter. However, there are aspects of the physical world where this perspective can lead to puzzling contradictions. John Wheeler's Surprise Version of the 20 Questions game in the following cartoon illustrates the epistemological implications of observations at the quantum level.[6]

In the Surprise Version, the people in the room each independently choose their own words with the constraint that once the game begins, the word that they have in mind must not contradict any previous answers to questions. This may require them to change their word over the course of the game, creating a moving target that is shaped, in part, by the questions asked. Wheeler concludes his story by saying that "In the real world of quantum physics, *no elementary phenomenon is a phenomenon until it is an observed phenomenon*. In the surprise version of the game no word is a word until that word is promoted to reality by the choice of questions asked and answers given. 'Cloud' sitting there waiting to be found as we entered the room? Pure delusion!"

The lesson of the Surprise Version of 20 Questions is particularly relevant to exploring human experience. Just as at the quantum level, the actions of the observer (i.e., scientist) can be a significant source of variance. This impact is typically referred to as the demand characteristics. These demand characteristics (e.g., the awareness of participants that they are being observed) can be important factors in shaping the experience (i.e., performance) that results.

Also, it is important to realize that human actions (e.g., innovative technologies) are shaping the opportunities for experience more globally. For example, new forms of travel and communication greatly extend our abilities to explore the world and to collaborate with people in distant locations. Cell phones have dramatically changed how people coordinate social activities—"Just call me when you get out of class and I will let you know where I am, so that we can meet." Thus, we should not think about human experience as an "object" that exists "out there" independent from the experience of the scientist or designer. To a large extent, the world that we live in is a world that we are creating. *We shape the world and are simultaneously shaped by that world.*

At this point, you might ask yourself, which of the two groups that Foerster described do you belong to? Are you a Discoverer? Or are you an Inventor? Are you a Discoverer, who bets on the

classical scientific methods designed to create an objective distance between observer and phenomenon? Or are you an Inventor who prefers to become immersed intimately into the phenomenon? Is there an alternative?

Just as the two circles in Figure 1.1 set up a dialectic presumption that a phenomenon had to belong to one of two realities, either Mind OR Matter but not both, Foerster's observation sets up a dialectic presumption that one of two epistemological positions, Discoverer OR Inventor, must be chosen. Just as the *Radical Empiricist* ontological position suggests that a single reality may be both Mind AND Matter, a *Pluralist Epistemology* suggests that it is not necessary to stand either outside apart from the phenomenon (as the Discoverer) OR inside as part of the phenomenon (as the Inventor).

Consider the possibility of observing from multiple perspectives. Consider the possibility that neither perspective offers a privileged or complete view of reality, but that each perspective allows valid insights into the phenomenon that are not possible from the other. Consider the possibility that complete understanding requires multiple perspectives—it requires that you take the attitude of the Discoverer AND the Inventor.

Perhaps, a Pluralistic Epistemology is essential for bridging the gulf that separates science from application and that separates research from design. On the one hand, innovation depends on the ability of Discoverers to appreciate the hypotheses generated by the Inventors through naturalistic observations and iterative design and also to appreciate that the success or failure of a design can be a valid and important test of the hypotheses that guided it. On the other hand, innovation depends on the ability of Inventors to appreciate the value of controlled laboratory tests to help partition the complexity of natural phenomenon and to provide the objective distance needed to protect us from potential bias due to infatuation with our own creations.

Consider the possibility that the epistemological positions of Inventors and Discoverers are complements that, when joined in a collaboration of mutual trust and respect, can be far more powerful than the sum of their independent contributions. In other words, consider the possibility that not only does science contribute to application, but application also is an important component of science. Would both science and design be better if scientists were more open to a design perspective and designers were more open to a scientific perspective?

Note that this chapter and the first began with an *exclusionary* dialectical form of argument based on EITHER/OR contrasts and ended with an *inclusional* or *integrative* form of argument based on BOTH/AND integrations. It is easy to get trapped in EITHER/OR arguments that circle endlessly around the same trees without resolution, especially when interacting across disciplines. In fact, academic institutions are typically organized around exclusional arguments.

Exclusional arguments essentially start with two sides with the assumption that one is right and the other is wrong. In principle, these arguments are different than rhetoric, in that the goal is not to win the argument but to find the 'truth'—in essence to eliminate the 'false hypothesis.' However, in practice, winning the argument often becomes more important than collaborating to create a more satisfying understanding of nature.

A consequence of the exclusional approach tends to be reduction of phenomena to fit into controlled experiments (in essence arguments), where it becomes plausible to eliminate the 'false' hypotheses. This also leads to increasing differentiation around the reduced phenomenon and the specialized experimental methods. In this context, there can be an emphasis on experimental paradigms (e.g., Sternberg Task), rather than on exploring natural phenomenon. For example, there is the classic story of the cognitive psychologist who was asked what he studied and he responded, "reaction time." To which his colleague ironically responded, "Oh, I study percent correct." In essence the phenomenon of *cognition* was being trivialized to the level of a single dependent measure. There is a growing sense that the experimental paradigms become the phenomenon of interest. The goal is experimental control, but the result may be trivialization of the phenomenon.

Thus, rather than the convergence that James envisioned for science, we see an increasing divergence into a collection of highly specialized little sciences or paradigms. Students tend to be forced to choose a discipline early, and there is typically little room for electives that allow for the students to explore perspectives outside their specializations. Universities put students into boxes and provide little opportunity for them to learn the languages of other boxes or to appreciate the value of other disciplines.

Perhaps, the most tragic consequence of a world based on dialectical forms of argument, however, is the Schizophrenia that Pirsig described in *Zen and the Art of Motorcycle Maintenance* and *Lila*. The dialectic form dismisses aesthetics, morals, and values as 'biases.' Today, even many scientists who choose an Inventor stance and who choose to immerse themselves in the phenomenon of interest, feel compelled to leave their opinions about quality (e.g., beauty or goodness) on the shelf. These opinions are considered to be 'unscientific.' Universities take responsibility to teach students the 'facts,' but leave the students to their own devices to deal with issues of aesthetics and morals. Challenges like Don Norman's claim that beautiful things work better[7] become difficult for 'science' to consider. Science as framed dialectically only deals with the substance of 'things.' It has little to say about their beauty or their goodness.

The biologist Alan Rayner[8] has suggested an alternative to the exclusional form of argument. He suggests that we might consider reframing some of the arguments in BOTH/AND terms.

This shift in frame can often lead to satisfactory resolutions to many of the arguments that divide disciplines and that keep us from productive collaborations. Instead of standing on the faces of other disciplines, perhaps we could see farther if we stood on their shoulders. More importantly, Rayner's hypothesis (or more accurately his hope) is that the Inclusional framework will help us to explore 'quality' (e.g., goodness) as a valid part of the real world, rather than it being isolated apart from the world as insubstantial (i.e., not real). Can 'meaning' be addressed by cognitive science without considering the aesthetic and moral qualities of human experience? Can a scientist who denies his own aesthetic and moral values fully explore the complexities of Mind and Matter in order to help create a world that Matters—a world that is beautiful and that works better!

Notes

1. Foerster, H. von (2003). *Understanding understanding: Essays on cybernetics and cognition*. New York: Springer-Verlag. (pp. 287–304).
2. 'Demand characteristics' is academic jargon for the impact that the act of observing or being observed has on the patterns of behavior that are exhibited in the experiment. Minimizing demand characteristics is considered to be essential for an objective scientific stance toward the phenomenon.
3. Watson, J.B. (1913). Psychology as the behaviorist views it. *Psychological Review*, 20, 158–177.
4. Tolman, E.C. (1948). Cognitive maps in rats and men. *Psychological Review*, 55, 189–208.
5. Miller, G.A. (1956). The magic number seven, plus or minus two: Some limits on our capacity to process information. *Psychological Review*, 63(2), 81–97.
6. Wheeler, J.A. (1980). Frontiers of time. In G. Toraldi de Francia (ed.) *Problems at the foundations of Physics*. p. 392–398, Amsterdam: North Holland.
7. Norman, D. (2004). *Emotional design: Why we love (or hate) everyday things*. New York: Basic Books.
8. Rayner, A. (2006). Inclusional nature: Bringing life and love to science. http://people.bath.ac.uk/bssadmr/inclusionality/

3

CAN'T YOU READ THE SIGNS?

The French movie "The Diving Bell and the Butterfly"[1] describes the experiences of the writer Jean-Dominique Bauby with Locked-in Syndrome that resulted from a stroke. Locked-in Syndrome refers to a condition where a person has normal mental functioning but has limited or no means to communicate due to impairment of motor systems (e.g., as a result of stroke, degenerative muscle diseases like ALS, or damage to the spinal cord). The movie depicts how Bauby was able to learn to communicate with his therapist using only eye blinks. In fact, they laboriously write the book that the movie is based on via this method.

Imagine the frustration of having a mind full of ideas and feelings, but having severely limited capacity for acting (e.g., a single switch) in response to those feelings (e.g., not being able to scratch your nose when it itches) or limited capacity for communicating with the people around you (e.g., not being able to share your feelings with a friend or to ask for help). Imagine the frustration of Bauby's therapist trying to figure out what the blinks mean. For Bauby and others with Locked-In Syndrome there is only a narrow communication channel connecting their mental life with the material and social ecology surrounding them. This extreme condition highlights the problem of connecting internal 'mental' experiences (e.g., a belief, an intention, or a feeling) with an external physical and social ecology.

In some sense, this is the inverse of the epistemological problem—it is not how a mind can know the world, but *how can a mind make itself known to the world*. Designers of information technologies (including the inventors of languages and alphabets) face a similar problem: how do they express the capabilities associated with these technologies so that they are compatible with the demands of the material and social ecologies that they inhabit—or in other words, so that the

functions that the designer intended for the technology can be realized. For example, how can they let the 'user' know what the symbols express, or when the technology needs its nose scratched, or how can the motorcycle rider diagnose problems with his bike, or how can the characters in the opening cartoon know what the big red button 'means.'

Semiotics: A Dyadic System

This is the problem of 'signs.' What do the blinks mean? What do the tracks on the trail mean? This problem has been formalized as the field of *semiotics*.[2] It is commonly defined as the science of signs. It is historically a precursor to the field of linguistics, which focuses more specifically on languages that were the particular interest of Ferdinand de Saussure.[3] Formal languages often have alphabets or symbol systems that are somewhat arbitrary with regards to any particular meaning (e.g., the connection between the letters d-o-g and a specific animal).

Thus, Saussure framed the semiotic system in terms of a dyad between the signifier (the symbols, or in Bauby's case the blinks) and the signified (which could be either Bauby's or the therapist's interpretation of what it means, but not both simultaneously). For Saussure, the semiotic problem is primarily a problem of interpretation. How does a Mind infer the meaning of a sign or how does a Mind assign meaning to a sign? Or how does a society choose an alphabet, a language, or a grammar? When reference is made to the 'meaning' of a sign in Saussure's semiotic system, one is talking about the 'interpretation' in the mind of a single specific observer (e.g., either Bauby's intention or the therapist's interpretation).

In Saussure's dyadic system, whether a sign is meaningful or not depends exclusively on the interpretation of the person reading the sign. For example, the fresh tracks of a predatory animal are meaningful only if a person knows how to read them. Regardless of any relation to real danger due to the presence of a threat, if the person doesn't know how to read them, then they are meaningless. Similarly, in the dyadic semiotic system, words that are full of meaning to a native speaker of French may be totally meaningless to a native speaker of English. Again, in the dyadic system meaning exists (or not) only in the 'mind' of the observer.

Saussure's system provided the foundations for the field of linguistics, which in turn had a strong impact on the development of cognitive science. Particularly influential was the debate between B.F. Skinner and Noam Chomsky about the acquisition of language. For Skinner[4] learning languages was similar to pigeons learning to press buttons in a Skinner box. Behaviors that are reinforced (e.g., the attention from mother following the sound 'ma') will increase in probability. Further, the behaviors can be shaped through selective reinforcement to become associated with particular stimulus conditions (e.g., 'ma' becomes selectively associated with the presence of mother).

However, Chomsky's[5] arguments, supported by observations of language development, took similar lines to Tolman's[6] observations about maze learning in rats. Chomsky argued that children were not simply learning behaviors, but they were actually learning to apply rules. They were learning about the 'structure' of language, and this learning became evident when they generalized across situations. For example, early in the development process children will often be observed to 'over-regularize.' They might say something like "The gooses goed south for the winter." This pattern suggests that the child is creatively applying rules (i.e., add 's' to create plural, add 'ed' for past tense), rather than simply repeating behaviors that have been reinforced. In a similar way, Tolman's rats chose new paths when the normal route to the goal box was blocked, based on what they had learned about the layout (i.e., structure or pattern) of the maze.

As a result of developments in linguistics and in part due to the influence of Chomsky's arguments, cognitive science has largely been framed in terms of a dyadic, symbol processing

THE ONLY FRAMEWORK FOR THE ANALYSIS OF PERCEPTION AVAILABLE TO MOST PSYCHOLOGISTS IS ONE THAT TAKES PHYSICAL STIMULATION AS THE APPROPRIATE CONCEPTUALIZATION OF THE "STIMULUS"

BEGINNING WITH A CONCEPTUALIZATION OF THE STIMULUS AS PHYSICAL STIMULATION AT THE RECEPTOR LEVEL CREATES ENORMOUS, AND PERHAPS, INSURMOUNTABLE, THEORETICAL AND PHILOSOPHICAL PROBLEMS FOR ANY ACCOUNT OF PERCEPTION BECAUSE FROM THE OUTSET THE STRUCTURAL PROPERTIES OF THE ENVIRONMENT ARE ABSENT

WITH SUCH FORMULATION, PERCEPTION OF ENVIRONMENTAL FEATURES BECOMES, IF NOT MAGICAL, THEN PURE GUESSWORK

Harry Heft[7]

system. In this frame, the fundamental challenge has been to understand how 'meaning' is *constructed* through brain processes to interpret arbitrary signs. Extensive bodies of research on perceptual illusions and decision biases have tended to reinforce the notion that the signs, which are the inputs to this information processing system, are at least somewhat arbitrary with respect to an external ecology (just like formal alphabets or symbol systems). Thus, Richard Gregory and others have framed problems of perception and cognition in terms of information processes to actively construct 'meaning' from impoverished cues (signs) at the sensory surface (e.g., a 2D image on the retina). In this paradigm, the problem of cognition starts with the input of a stimulus (sign) and ends with a response that is, in effect, an interpretation of that sign (e.g., an inference about 3D space). In this dyadic approach to cognition all the action happens 'inside the head' between sensory stimulus and mental interpretation (e.g., to construct a 3D mental model from the 2D retinal cues).

This dyadic frame has also shaped how human factors engineers and designers approach interface design. The interface design problem has been conventionally framed as an 'interpretation' process, and the focus of attention has been to explore the relations between the 'signs' on the interface (e.g., the knobs and dials, and graphical icons) and the 'internal models' in the heads of the intended users. Thus, we have the field of Human Computer Interaction (HCI), where research programs are organized around properties of the interfaces (e.g., alphanumeric representation vs. graphical representations; or integral vs. separable graphical forms; the appropriate uses for color, etc.) relative to the information processing capacity of humans (e.g., analytical vs. spatial reasoning; serial vs. parallel processing; color sensitivity).

The general prescription for design that has resulted from the HCI research program is to design the interface to match the 'mental models' of your intended user population. In other words, use the interface to translate your design intentions into a language that your customers understand. This is commonly summarized in the dictum "Know thy user." This is generally good advice, but beware there may be a catch! For example, Henry Ford is reported to have observed that before the car, few would have asked for it or appreciated the value of it; rather they would have asked for better horses. Similarly, the smart phone was not built to satisfy the 'internal models' of users. Who would have imagined the need for a phone that takes pictures? Or who would have imagined that people would prefer 'texting' to talking? However, it is clear that the expectations and behaviors of users have been shaped by the new possibilities that smart phones offer.

Semiotics: A Triadic System

At the same time that Saussure was laying the foundations for linguistics, Charles Sanders Peirce[8] was also wrestling with the semiotic problem. However, Peirce framed the problem differently. Peirce is considered to be the father of Pragmatism. He was primarily interested in the 'fixation of belief,' or how it was that our beliefs about the world could lead to productive interactions with the world. Thus, in the context of Bauby, Peirce would not be simply interested in Bauby's interpretation OR in the therapist's interpretation of the blink. He would be interested in how well the therapist's interpretation matched with Bauby's intention.

In the example of the predator's tracks, Peirce was interested in both the relation of the tracks to the state of the situation (Is it safe?) and the relation of the tracks to the beliefs of the human observers (I am safe or not). Thus, for Peirce, there were two relations relevant to meaning processing. On the one hand, there is the grounding of the sign with respect to the source (e.g., the state of the ecology). On the other hand, there is the interpretation in the mind of an observer (e.g., the situation awareness). In essence, Peirce was interested in how our beliefs serve the demands for successful interactions in everyday life.

Thus, Peirce framed the semiotic problem as a triadic system that included the source of the sign (e.g., either Bauby's intention or the presence of a dangerous predator), the sign (e.g., the blink or the tracks), and the interpretation (e.g., of the therapist or the person in the woods). Although Peirce was a contemporary of James, who James credits with having an important influence on his views about psychology and philosophy, Peirce's triadic semiotic system had little acknowledged influence on the early development of psychology or cognitive science. However, his work has recently been rediscovered, in part motivated by increasing interest in the design of autonomous robots. Computer scientists working on robots have discovered the importance of 'grounding' the internal logic of the robot (interpretation) in the practical realities of the physical ecology within which it must function. A robot will not function very effectively if its 'beliefs' (i.e., its internal logic) about what different spaces afford do not match well with the realities that it will experience when moving through those spaces.

IF ONLY THE ROBOT WAS PROGRAMMED TO UNDERSTAND THE DIFFERENCES BETWEEN WHAT IS A TREE AND WHAT LOOKS LIKE A TREE. IT JUST STOOD THERE, HOPING THE TREE WOULD GO OUT OF THE WAY BEFORE THE UFO WOULD DEPART. THEN AGAIN, CHANCES HAVE IT THE ROBOT WILL MISTAKE THE SHADOW FOR THE UFO AND STAND THERE WAITING IN THE YARD FOR EVER...

Although Peirce was rarely cited as the source, other psychologists, such as Egon Brunswik,[9] James Gibson,[10] Jacob von Uexküll,[11] and Ulrich Neisser,[12] were dissatisfied with the dyadic basis for cognitive science. The approach they advocated was typically labeled 'ecological' to reflect the missing component of the dyadic symbol processing system—that missing component was the relation between the 'sign' and the functional ecology (or umwelt). Two images of a triadic semiotic system are shown in Figure 3.1.

Brunswik's Lens Model[13] anchors the 'signs' with both the ecology (e.g., this could be Bauby's intention; or the presence of a predator) and with the interpreter (e.g., this could be Bauby's therapist; or the person's belief about whether a predator is near). The mapping from the ecology to the signs reflected the ecological validity, and the mapping from the signs to the belief reflected the interpretation process. The *achievement* of this system (i.e., the accuracy of a judgment with respect to the ecology) depends on both mappings. This achievement is what Peirce was trying

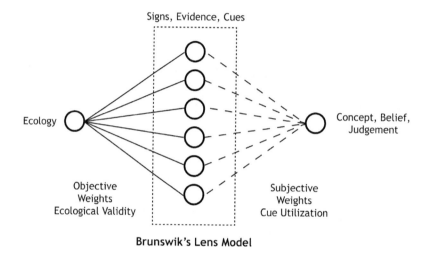

Brunswik's Lens Model

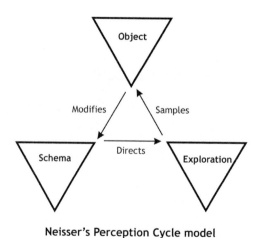

Neisser's Perception Cycle model

Figure 3.1 Two contrasting images of the cognitive (or semiotic) system.

32

to understand, how is it that our internal beliefs about the ecology are able to support harmoni-
ous functional relations with that ecology? How is it that Bauby's therapist can know what Bauby
means? What do the animal tracks mean with respect to whether I am in danger or not? How do
our beliefs guide us toward satisfying experiences?

Neisser's Perception Cycle[14] is another example of a triadic semiotic dynamic that includes the
ecological source (e.g., the object) and the mental model (e.g., the schema). The unique feature
of Neisser's model relative to Brunswik's model is that the 'sign' is modeled as a consequence of
active exploration of the ecology. This reflects Gibson's influence. A fundamental theme for Gibson was that perception and action are dynamically coupled, so that perception both *shapes* action
and *is shaped by* action. Thus, for Gibson, the feet were a critical part of the visual perceptual system
because they allow an animal to move about and explore the environment (e.g., walk around and
see an object from multiple perspectives).

For example, in the case of Bauby, the sign system is a product of an interaction between Bauby
and the therapist. The 'meaning' of the signs is constructed not in either Bauby's mind or in the
therapist's mind, but it is constructed through the interactions between Bauby and the therapist.
In this case, it is constructed through social interaction, but meaning is also constructed through
physical interaction. For example, we manipulate and heft an object to find the right 'fit' so that
it can be carried comfortably. We explore to find what kind of animal 'fits' with the tracks on
the ground. We play with the buttons and triggers on the controller to discover their functions
in the video game. We manipulate a tool like a hammer to discover how to grip and swing it to
accomplish work.

Figure 3.2 contrasts two potential images of the cognitive/semiotic system. The top image
is a strawman image of the conventional approach to cognitive systems motivated by early
work in linguistics and supported by communication and computer metaphors. The bottom
image provides a first look at a triadic image of the cognitive system. This image will be revis-
ited throughout the book, and the labels will vary to emphasize different facets of the triadic
dynamics.

It can be confusing when comparing a dyadic perspective to perception such as assumed by
Richard Gregory[15] with a triadic perspective such as assumed by James Gibson,[16] because both
describe their theories as reflecting "active" perception. The difference is that when Gregory says
'active' he is referring to mental activities to construct an internal image from the impoverished
cues at the sensory surface. Much of the data that is the basis for Gregory's models of perception
are based on passive observation.

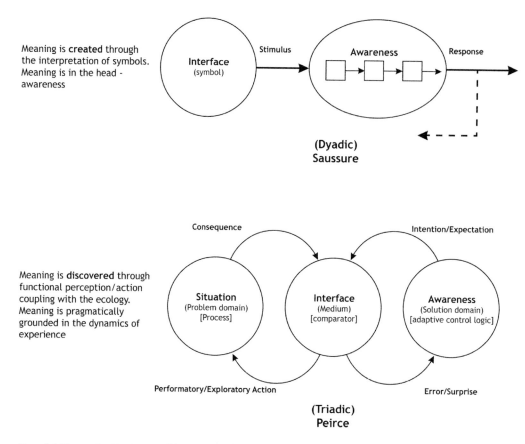

Figure 3.2 Two contrasting images of the cognitive (or semiotic) system.

When Gibson says 'active' he is referring to active exploration of the environment through moving around and manipulating objects. In Gregory's model, ambiguities in the sign (e.g., on a two-dimensional retina) with respect to the source (e.g., a three-dimensional world) are resolved through logical inference. In Gibson's models, these ambiguities are resolved through acting to create more specific information (e.g., moving to create invariant structures in a flowing optical array).

There is also a big gulf between Gregory and Gibson in terms of the assumptions about the nature of information and meaning. From the more conventional perspective represented by Gregory, Gibson's claims that the meanings or affordances of the environment can be 'directly' seen seem quite radical, if not nonsensical—particularly in light of the huge body of literature on perceptual illusions that show that people are not good at making judgments about 'space' (at least in terms of how space is construed by Gregory and others). It seems obvious from Gregory's perspective that people must add something to the impoverished data available to the senses in order to 'infer' the 'true' state of the world, and that these inferences are a necessary prerequisite for successful action in the world.

Wolfgang Langewiesche, author of an insightful account of the art of flying (*Stick and Rudder*[17]) provides an example that clearly illustrates the difference between Gregory's and Gibson's views and that might make Gibson's view far more plausible. Langewiesche (1944) contrasts how a pilot and a passenger might specify the location of an airport that appears in the distance:

> The passenger might say, "The airport is about 3,000 feet below us but still many miles away." The pilot, in his own mind will say the same thing differently, "The field now lies 5 degrees under the horizon." Later the passenger might say, "The height is the same, but the field is much nearer." The pilot will say, "The airport now lies 30 degrees under the horizon." He means that it lies more steeply under the airplane than it did before.
>
> (p. 271)

The passenger is using a rectangular coordinate system (height, distance). The pilot is using an angular coordinate system (degrees relative to the horizon). From the point of view of geometry, both coordinate systems are valid, and it is not problematic to transform from one to the other (i.e., no information is lost). However, is there a sense in which one of these coordinate systems is *smarter* than the other with regards to the semiotic problem of aligning the beliefs with the reality of experience? Langewiesche (1944) explains why the pilot's choice of coordinates is smarter than the passenger's choice:

> Both statements, the passenger's and the pilot's, express the same thing. But here is one difference: the passenger is only guessing. How does he know the distance, and the height? But the pilot is not guessing; although he doesn't know distance and height either, he does know that the field under him lies at that angle; he could even prove it, right from where he sits, by measuring the angle with some suitable instrument, such as a sextant.
>
> (p. 271)

So, one reason that the angular coordinate system is *smarter* is that the angle is well specified locally, as illustrated in Figure 3.3, but the height and distances are not well specified. However, there

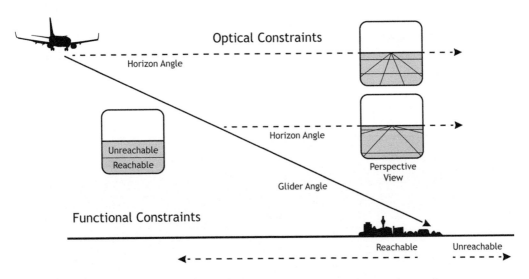

Figure 3.3 The optical constraints associated with angular perspective map directly to the functional constraints associated with glide angle, so that there is an invariant relation independent of height and distance.

is another, much more important difference that makes the angular coordinate system *smarter*. Langewiesche continues:

> And here is another difference: The passenger's statement is useless; the pilot's statement is useful; it is angle, rather than actual height and distance, that matters. Here is why.
>
> In a given ship, of given gliding angle, it is always the same point on the ground you can reach in a glide, regardless of your altitude; the same point, that is, in terms of angle-under-the-horizon. Say your ship's gliding angle is 1:5; this means you can in a glide always reach any point that lies 10 degrees under your horizon, or steeper. This statement (true only in still air) must be thoroughly understood.
>
> (p. 271–272)

> And if you have understood what has been explained concerning angular vision, you will also understand this: How far the glide line lies below your horizon is entirely independent of your height; at any height, the glide line is the same distance (**angular** distance, in terms of degrees) below your horizon. As your height changes in the glide, both the horizon and the glide lines will be at different points on the terrain below you; but the horizon will always be at the same height as your eye; and the glide line will be the same number of degrees below the horizon; and the relation of horizon and glide line will not change.
>
> (p. 273)

This second difference, the degree of specificity with respect to functional distinctions (whether the field is reachable in a glide) is what makes the angular coordinate systems so much smarter than a rectangular system. The invariant mapping between angular position relative to the horizon and functional consequences (i.e., reachability in a glide) is exactly what Gibson[18] meant by optical invariant and direct specification of affordances. Much of the classical research on 'space' perception assumes the traditional rectangular coordinates for judging space, with little consideration of whether that is a good representation relative to the functional problems associated with coordinating action with the world. From the dyadic perspective this is a perfectly reasonable place to start, since it is generalizing from written or spoken language where the signs tend to be arbitrary.

As Langewiesche describes, neither the pilot nor passenger is good at judging position with regard to the rectangular coordinates. However, the pilot, attuned to the angular coordinate

system is able to *see* whether an airport on the ground is *reachable*. However, the passenger using a rectangular coordinate system must somehow *compute* reachability since there is no meaningful one-to-one mapping with any landmark (like the horizon) in his coordinate system. This computation process is further complicated by the fact that the observables or inputs (height and distance) are poorly specified. So, the passenger must compute the solution using noisy data.

Thus, consider the possibility that the real ambiguities that people experience as participants in classical experiments on 'space' perception are not the result of fundamental limits on the information available, but rather they reflect the fact that the problems are posed using representations that do not match the typical demands of experience. The 'illusions' result from the fact that the experimental tasks are designed using an arbitrary, extrinsic coordinate system that has little 'meaning' relative to the functional ecology of the participant. Consider the possibility that the data from these experiments on spatial illusions are a reflection of the assumptions guiding the design of tasks and choice of stimuli, rather than any fundamental limitations of human ability.

There is a growing body of evidence that many of the illusions found in classical experiments disappear when the tasks are reframed in action terms. For example, when participants are asked to grasp an object that is a component of a Müller-Lyer form or similar size illusion (Figure 3.4), the grasp does not reflect the same apparent biases that are found when participants make passive judgments of the sizes.[19] Note that the judgments about the appearances of the size do not change—the objects still appear to be different sizes. However, the appearance has little impact on performance of the grasping task. Thus, the appearance seems to be an epiphenomenon, at least with respect to understanding the functional quality of experience. Similarly, when participants are asked to walk to a visually specified position on the ground with their eyes closed (blind walking paradigm), the errors seen in passively judging 'depth' are no longer evident.[20]

The implications of an ecological approach for design are that the focus is not simply on seeing the Red button, but on understanding the relation between the button and its function. That is, it becomes necessary to consider not only the relation between the observer and the button (i.e., the sign), but also the relation between the button and the opportunities and consequences that it

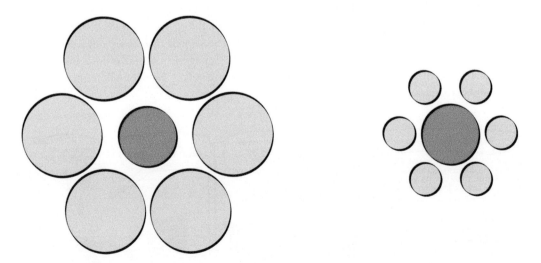

Figure 3.4 When asked to adjust their fingers to pick up the 'coin' in the centers of these figures using the thumb and index finger, the biases that are typical of size judgment do not appear.

affords. The challenge for Ecological Interface Design (EID)[21] is not to simply ensure that the user sees the button, but to ensure that the user sees its function. The challenge in designing an ecological interface is in essence to find the right coordinate system for specifying the affordances. In other words, the challenge is to design a representation so that the possibilities and consequences of action are well specified (so that the user can see what functions are 'reachable').

Here is the catch with respect to more traditional HCI approaches. For a complex control task like operating a nuclear power plant, the operator's mental model may only be partially correct. For example, assumptions or procedures that are valid during normal operations may not be valid during an accident. Thus, an interface designed to match that operator's model may very well reinforce partial or incorrect assumptions about the process. The ultimate goal of EID is not simply to match the operator's model but to shape that model to be aligned with the most valid models of the processes that are being controlled (e.g., models based on scientifically validated analyses of the process that reflect fundamental constraints).

The goal is to help people to better understand the processes that they are controlling so that people not only do the right action, but also so that they are aware of why an action fits the demands of the problem situations. The goal is to shape or *bias* the operator toward beliefs that lead to successful actions. We purposely use the term 'bias' here to suggest that we are not dealing with absolute truths but pragmatic truths. We are interested in shaping beliefs so that the actions based on those beliefs will lead to satisfying experiences (e.g., the beliefs of the pilot will lead to safe and successful performance across a wide range of situations).

ANYONE WHO HAS THE GOOD FORTUNE TO LISTEN TO WIENER AND VON NEUMANN AND ROSENBLUETH AND PITTS WRESTLING WITH THE PROBLEMS OF MODERN COMPUTING MACHINES THAT KNOW AND WANT HAS A STRANGE SENSE THAT THEY ARE LISTENING TO A COLLOQUY OF THE ANCIENTS

BUT THEY WOULD BE THE FIRST TO TELL YOU THAT THEY THEMSELVES ARE DRUNK WITH AN AMERICAN WINE OF AN OLDER VINTAGE: THEY QUOTE LIBERALLY FROM CHARLES PEIRCE AND FROM JOSIAH WILLARD GIBBS, THESE MEN HAVE ALTERED OUR METAPHYSICS BY ALTERING OUR PHYSICS

IT IS EPISTEMOLOGY THAT IS MOST AFFECTED FOR IT IS THE PHYSICS OF COMMUNICATION WHICH IS TODAY RECEIVING AN ADEQUATE THEORETICAL TREATMENT. FOR THE FIRST TIME IN THE HISTORY OF SCIENCE WE KNOW HOW WE KNOW AND HENCE ARE ABLE TO STATE IT CLEARLY

Warren McCulloch (1954)[22]

Notes

1. Bauby, J.D. (1997). *The diving bell and the butterfly*. ISBN 978-0-375-40115-2. New York: Vintage Books.

   Film adaptation in 2007 was directed by Julian Schnabel, written by Ronald Harwood, and starring Mathieu Amalric as Bauby.

2. Deely, J. (2005 [1990]). *Basics of semiotics*. 4th ed. Tartu: Tartu University Press.

3. de Saussure, F. ([1916] 1974). *Course in general linguistics* (trans. W. Baskin). London: Fontana and Collins.

   de Saussure, F. ([1916] 1983). *Course in general linguistics* (trans. R. Harris). London: Duckworth.

4. Skinner, B.F. (1957). *Verbal behavior*. Acton, MA: Copley Publishing Group. ISBN 1-58390-021-7.

5. Chomsky, N. (1959). A review of B. F. Skinner's verbal behavior. *Language*, 35(1), 26–58.

6. Tolman, E.C. (1948). Cognitive maps in rats and men. *Psychology Review*, 55, 189–208.

7. Heft, H. (2001). *Ecological psychology in context*. Mahwah, NJ: Erlbaum. (p. 8).

8. Two key articles by C.S. Peirce are "The fixation of belief" (1877) and "How to make our ideas clear" (1878). These articles are reprinted in Menand, L. (Ed.). (1997). *Pragmatism: A reader*. New York: Vintage Books.

9. Brunswik, E. (1956). *Perception and the representative design of psychological experiments*. Berkeley: University of California Press.

10. Gibson, J.J. (1979). *The ecological approach to visual perception*. Boston: Houghton Mifflin.

11. von Uexküll, J. (1957). A stroll through the worlds of animals and men: A picture book of invisible worlds. In C.H. Schiller (Ed. and trans.). *Instinctive behavior: The development of a modern concept* (pp. 5–80). New York: International Universities Press, Inc., 1957.

12. Neisser, U. (1976). *Cognition and reality*. San Francisco: Freeman.

13. Brunswik, E. (1952). *A conceptual framework of psychology*. Chicago: University of Chicago Press.

14. Neisser (1976).

15. Gregory, R.L. (1974). *Concepts and mechanisms of perception*. New York: Charles Scribner's Sons.

16. Gibson (1969)

17. Langeweische, W. (1944). *Stick and rudder: An explanation of the art of flying*. New York: McGraw-Hill.

18. Gibson, J.J. (1979). *The ecological approach to visual perception*. Boston: Houghton Mifflin.

19. Milner, A.D., & Goodale, M.A. (1995). *The visual brain in action*. Oxford: Oxford Press.

20. Loomis, J.M., da Silva, J.A., Philbeck, J.W., & Fukusima, S.S. (1996). Visual perception of location and distance. *Current Directions in Psychological Science*, 5, 72–77.

21. Bennett, K.B., & Flach, J.M. (2011). *Display and interface design*. Boca Raton, FL: CRC Press.

22. McCulloch, W.S. (1954). Through the den of the metaphysician. *The British Journal for the Philosophy of Science*, 5(17), 18–31.

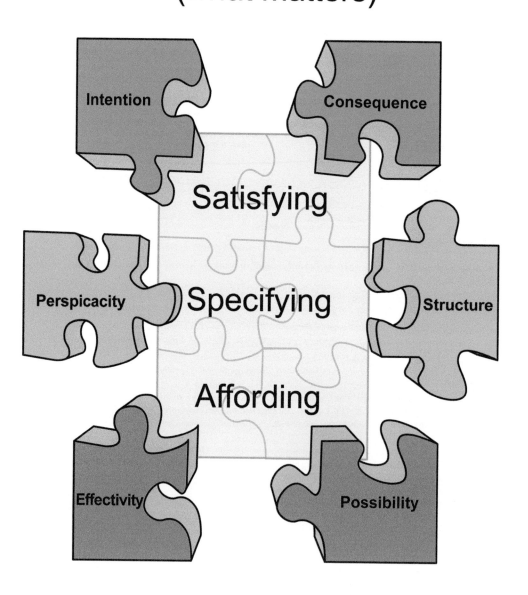

Semiotic Triad
(what matters)

Intention

Consequence

Satisfying

Perspicacity

Specifying

Structure

Affording

Effectivity

Possibility

Agent
(mind)

Environment
(matter)

4

WHAT MATTERS?

Figuring out what matters is not easy! And arguments can be incredibly unproductive because people are speaking based on different ontological assumptions, different epistemological attitudes (discoverers vs. inventors), and different models of the semiotic system. Figures 4.1–4.3 provide a collection of images using block diagram conventions that catalogue some of the many ways that people have parsed human experience.

Figure 4.1 shows four images that suggest open-loop (billiard ball) models of causality. The top-most image represents a classical psychophysical approach as reflected in the work of researchers such as Helmholtz, Weber, and Fechner. These researchers began by examining structure in the physical world (e.g., properties of light, the size and weight of objects) and then tried to infer elemental properties of the mind from relationships to the sensations/responses associated with variation of the physical properties.

Although the work of Helmholtz, Weber, and Fechner predated, and in part inspired, the experimental work of Wundt, historians typically mark the beginning of the science of psychology with the establishment of Wundt's laboratory in Leipzig. The second image reflects the subtle change that might be the motivation for making this distinction. For the psychophysicists, the stimulus was physical (i.e., properties of matter). However, inspired by the philosophy of Hume and others, there was a shift of attention from the physical stimulus to the basic elements of the mental chemistry of association.

Introspection, in which people described their experiences, became the primary methodology. However, it was a very special kind of introspection in which the participants had to be trained to focus on the internal sensations rather than on the external sources of those sensations. This is reflected in Titchener's construct of *stimulus error*. For example, a stimulus error was made if a person described one object as heavier than another, rather than describing the differences in the cutaneous and kinesthetic sensations that resulted from contact with the objects. For Titchener, the stimuli were NOT the objects in the world, but the patterns of sensations that were experienced.

As a result of the empirical/associationist philosophy, experimental psychology could make a clean break from the physical sciences to focus on mental chemistry in which both stimuli and responses were clearly properties of mind. This was also reflected in Ebbinghaus's choice of nonsense syllables for studying memory. Ebbinghaus invented nonsense syllables to minimize confounding associations with the world outside the laboratory in order to better isolate the internal dynamics of mental chemistry. Thus, the experimental efforts that are typically identified as the beginnings of scientific psychology were explicitly designed to treat mind as a purely mental phenomenon with very little regard for a grounding in the external physical world of matter. As a result, scientific psychology has tended to assume Descartes' dualist ontology that separates the reality of mind from

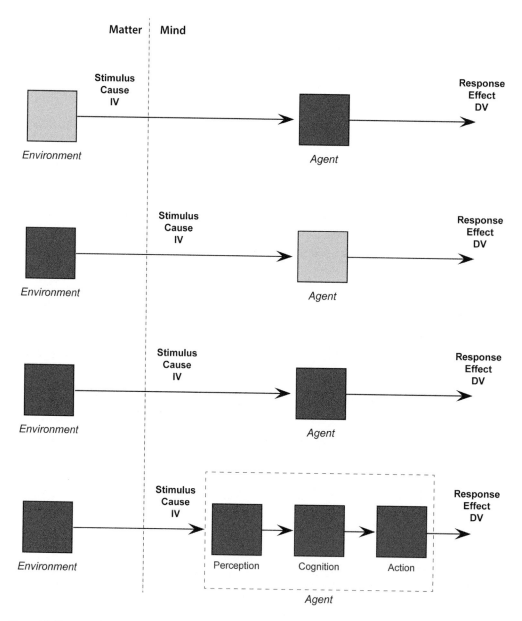

Figure 4.1 Four open-loop, causal models of mind. All four models maintain a clear distinction between mind and matter, and with the exception of the first model, they tend to treat the physical aspects of matter as extrinsic or irrelevant to the dynamics of 'mental chemistry.'

the reality of matter. In fact, the dual nature of mind and matter provided a strong justification for a science of mind (i.e., psychology) distinct from the other 'physical' sciences.

Note that it seems clear that neither Wundt nor Ebbinghaus dismissed the full complexities of human experience. However, in order to establish an experimental science of mind, they made the strategic choice to isolate the mental as much as possible from the physical context. For experimental purposes, they defined the mind as a separate 'system' to be examined independently from the 'confounding' influences of the physical context. James referred to this as "brass instrument" psychology, and he was very skeptical that this approach would 'add-up' to a fuller understanding of human experience (and there is reason to believe that Wundt was also quite skeptical about whether the experimental laboratory could do complete justice to the full scope of human experience). Despite James' reservations, however, most psychologists celebrated and endorsed the strategic choices of Wundt and Ebbinghaus. Thus, today they are widely acknowledged as the fathers of experimental psychology.

The third diagram in Figure 4.1 represents the shift to behaviorism. Watson recognized the difficulties with the construct of *stimulus error*, which depended on the authority of individuals like Titchener to decide what constituted a valid introspection. In an attempt to establish a more objective, empirical basis for experimental psychology, the behaviorists closed the box on the mind to focus on 'objective' properties of behavior. Note, however, that the stimulus remained a property of mind, since the nature of a stimulus (e.g., whether it was reinforcement or punishment) was determined based solely on the impact on behavior (e.g., whether the associated behaviors increased or decreased in frequency).

Although the behaviorists shifted attention from introspection to behavior and although they strongly endorsed the objective methodologies of the experimental physical sciences, they maintained a clear distinction between the content of psychology and the content of the physical sciences. Thus, the gap between mind and matter remained.

The fourth diagram in Figure 4.1 represents the shift from behaviorism to an information processing view of cognition. This view was inspired by metaphors from communications systems and linguistics. Saussure's dyadic semiotic system was instrumental, as were developments in the mathematics of information theory and the evolution of computing machines.

From the information theory perspective, the stimulus was now considered to be a 'symbol,' and the mind was modeled as multiple processing stages that operated on the symbols and transformed them (i.e., recoded them) in order to construct meaning and to guide action. Note that this model remains true to the associative image of 'mental chemistry,' with stimulus and response defined independently from any physical embodiment. With this model, cognition was a disembodied problem of 'symbol processing' or 'software' that could be studied independently from the 'hardware' upon which it operated.

All four models in Figure 4.1 maintain a clear distinction between mind and matter. All are based on billiard ball (or domino) models of causality. And all, but the original model of psychophysics, exclude the physical reality of matter as inconsequential for a science of mind. With the latter three models, Psychology is defined as a science pertaining to aspects of nature that exist in a reality apart from that of the rest of the physical world. This is one reason that there has always been a temptation to isolate 'humans' as special or distinctive from the rest of the natural world (e.g., due to unique reasoning and/or language capabilities).

At the same time that the mathematics of information theory and the first electronic computing machines were being engineered, there were also significant developments in the mathematics of control theory and the development of automatic control systems. This offered an alternative metaphor for psychology—the servomechanism or control system. Unlike the models in Figure 4.10, the servomechanism metaphor challenged conventional billiard ball models of causality with the first analytical descriptions of circular causality, drawing attention to emergent properties of the holistic closed-loop organization (e.g., stability).

However, although the servomechanism metaphor helped to legitimize the use of constructs such as 'goal,' 'purpose,' or 'plans' (that Behaviorists considered to be too intangible for an objective science), overall the construct of circular causality was not fully appreciated by most social scientists. This is suggested by the top model in Figure 4.2.

While feedback loops were added to close-the-loop in the diagrams, the theory and methods of experimental psychology continued to focus on the 'forward-loop' component of the system. The focus tended to be on deriving open-loop transfer functions for the various stages of processing, with the implicit motivation that complete models of the components would 'add-up' to an understanding of the dynamics of the total closed-loop system. Thus, typically the 'mind' was

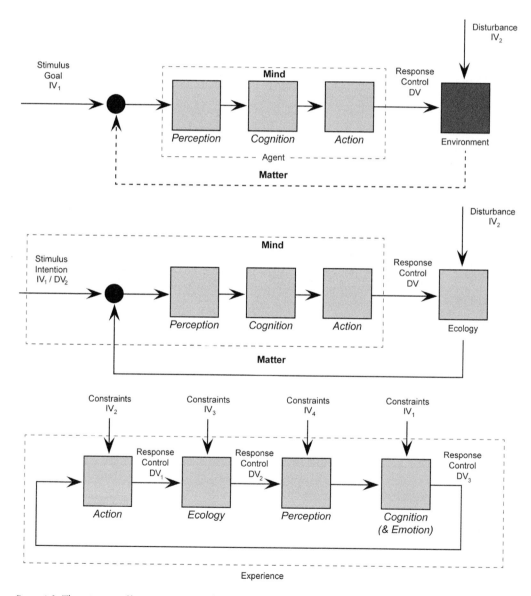

Figure 4.2 Three images of human experience that explicitly recognize the functional coupling of mind and matter.

identified with the 'controller' element that was nested within the larger closed-loop system. The other elements making up the closed-loop system, the 'goal' and the 'environment,' were treated as extrinsic variables (these would typically reflect the independent variables in experiments). Thus, the feedback portion of the diagram was considered to be an extrinsic constraint on the 'controller' (i.e., mind).

Some (e.g., Brunswik, Dewey, Gibson, James, von Uexküll), however, began to realize that stability of the closed-loop dynamic depended on tight coordination between the 'agent' (i.e., controller) and the 'environment' (i.e., the 'plant' or 'ecology'). In order to better understand the coordination at a more holistic level, it became necessary to consider the environment/agent fit. This is the significance of the term 'ecology' (in the second model in Figure 4.2) to emphasize the need to consider the environment in relation to the action capabilities, the goals (and/or needs), and the perceptual attunement of the agent. This inspired Gibson to reframe the approach to visual 'information' in terms of geometric properties of optical flow fields that provided specific information relative to action (e.g., locomotion) in the ecology (e.g., imminence of collision). He also reframed the specification of properties of the ecology in action-relevant terms (i.e., affordances). This was a necessary step in order to understand the dynamics of the closed-loop system where perception and action are intimately coupled as a result of feedback.

Another consequence of a move toward a more ecological perspective (illustrated in the second diagram in Figure 4.2) is that the dynamics of circular causality become more apparent. Thus, the environment (i.e., disturbances) and goals are no longer seen in the context of 'causes,' but are rather seen as 'constraints.' As constraints, they no longer *determine* behavior, but rather they invite or shape behavior. Goals can be viewed as either independent variables (e.g., imposed by the experimenter) or dependent variables (reflecting internal preferences or choices of the agent).

The third model in Figure 4.2 further emphasizes the circular dynamic and the consequential intimate relation between agent and ecology. Note that little changes relative to the other diagrams in terms of the logic of box diagrams. The connections between boxes are essentially the same, with action affecting the ecology, which in turn impacts perception, which informs cognition, which guides action. However, by revising the model to give precedence to action, the ecology now clearly becomes an intrinsic property of the dynamic of experience (i.e., it is embedded within the elements typically attributed to mind).

In this context, action is perceived in relation to the functional consequences in the environment (e.g., affordances), which in turn provides meaningful information, so that the internal cognitive models can learn and adapt as a result of these consequences. This provides one way to think about James' monist ontology of Radical Empiricism. That is, the dichotomy between mind and matter is obliterated, and the 'physical' and 'mental' aspects of experience are seen as conjoint components of a single reality of experience.

Figure 4.3 pushes the case for further integrating mind and matter into a single system. The top diagram suggests that the need for a separate box for the ecology is unnecessary. Instead, the ecological constraints can be distributed across the cognitive functions as in the third diagram. In this diagram, each of the boxes represents a general information processing function that is jointly constrained by properties of agent (i.e., mind) and ecology (i.e., matter). This new view portrays the functionalist perspective (e.g., Peirce, James, Dewey, Angel) in which the conceptual objects are pure functions that involve relations between agent and ecology. The final model in Figure 4.3 provides alternative terms for these basic functions. This is necessary to avoid confusion from the

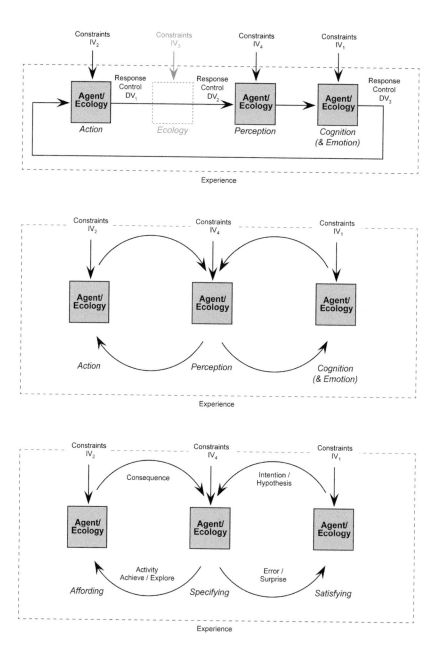

Figure 4.3 Three images of human experience are shown that explicitly recognize the functional coupling of mind and matter, such that each of the basic functions is considered to be dependent on properties of both mind and matter.

classical perspective, where the information processing functions are viewed as components of mind (in the head) without reference to the physical context.

Figure 4.3 suggests an alternative way to parse the problem of human experience that begins with the explicit assumption that the functions of information processing are intrinsically relational. For example, it assumes that perception can only be understood relative to the joint constraints of source (i.e., structure in the world) and receiver (i.e., structure in the head; perspicacity); that action can only be understood relative to the joint constraints of effectors (e.g., legs) and object (e.g., surfaces of support); and that cognition can only be understood relative to the joint constraints of means (e.g., heuristics, hypotheses) and ends (e.g., intentions, consequences).

The parsing illustrated in the bottom of Figure 4.3 also provides a unique bridge between experimental psychology and applications to design. The three functions suggest both the ways that experimentalists can query the system (i.e., classes of independent variables) and the ways that designers can alter the experience dynamic through training and design (i.e., ways to shape performance). Note that in either the case of experimentalists or designers the possible manipulations do not 'cause' behavior, but rather they shape behavior through changing the range of functional opportunities or possibilities. Within the circular dynamic, the classical notion of 'cause' does not make sense. Rather, it becomes necessary to think in terms of 'constraints.'

Although the diagrams in Figures 4.1–4.3 have been presented as a kind of historical progression, it is probably true that all the various perspectives have their proponents among active psychologists today. This is one source of confusion within the field of psychology.[1] A common term like 'stimulus' has a very different meaning across the various modeling perspectives. For the psychophysicist, the stimulus is a physical property of an object, but for others the stimulus might be a sensation, satisfaction of a biological need, a symbol, or an error with respect to a goal.

A Second Perspective

One of the difficulties of the block diagram format for representing the alternative parsing of the problem is the 'negative transfer' that results from experiences with the classical dualistic ontology and its parsing of cognition. Most people who have been trained in more classical paradigms instinctively want to identify some boxes with the mind or agent and other boxes with the environment. The puzzle pieces in the opening plate for this chapter provide an alternative form for visualizing the differences between a monist approach to experience and the conventional dualist ontology.

The left side of the opening picture shows the pieces of the puzzle that are considered by conventional approaches to mind (e.g., Gregory) that are based on a dyadic model of the semiotic problem. In fact, the focus has been primarily on the middle piece (perspicacity—internal logic), with the other two pieces (intention—motivation and effectivity—motor control) being of relatively peripheral interest, because these elements were more closely associated with the physical body, rather than the mind.

One may characterize this approach as focusing on how the internal information processes (the perspicacity piece) connects intention with action (the effectivity piece). For this approach, the right side of the puzzle is of little interest. This approach has assumed a dualistic ontology, separating Mind and Matter as different realities. The sources of information outside the head are typically treated as arbitrary, consistent with Saussure's dyadic model of semiotics.

Thus, *Matter* is left to the physical sciences and *What Matters* is left to domain experts. For design, the focus of classical approaches (i.e., human factors; HCI) has been on generalizations to ensure that the red button in the earlier cartoon (Chapter 3) is easily seen and easily activated. However, this approach has little to offer with respect to what is on the other side of the button.

The focus exclusively on the elements on the left side of the puzzle has been justified with the claim that 'it is the same head.' The implication is that anything we learn about the head/brain, in whatever context, will generalize to other contexts. The implication is that context doesn't matter and that the internal mechanisms of information processing can be understood as independent elements from the ecologies within which they have evolved.

Interestingly, modern Ecological Psychologists (e.g., Michael Turvey[2]) have also assumed an effectively dualistic ontology. However, for them the right side of the puzzle matters, because they have framed the problem of cognition as a closed-loop triadic semiotic system. Thus, in addition to exploring what's inside the head, it becomes important to consider the ecology that the head is inside of. Thus, the construct of affordance was invented by Gibson to characterize both the functional opportunities (i.e., *possibilities*) and *consequences* that an ecology offers to an animal.

Additionally, the information *structure* in the ecology (e.g., in terms of invariants or patterns in optical flow fields) becomes important as the potential information link between mind and matter (e.g., to specify what is reachable). So, the Ecological approach has a more holistic view of the system that includes both Mind and Matter. The ecological approach is based on the strong assertion that context does matter!

Thus, the key difference between Gregory's and Turvey's view has to do with the semiotic systems. Gregory frames the semiotic problem as one of interpreting arbitrary signs or impoverished cues. For Gregory, meaning exists only in the mind of the observer, and there is an implication that the observer is a passive receiver of stimuli, which then are actively processed (i.e., it is an open-loop process).

In contrast, Turvey assumes that the external world is full of meaning, and the meanings are well specified to an observer who is capable of exploring that world. For Turvey perception and action are intimately linked in a closed-loop dynamic that allows the achievement of a skilled fit between situations (matter—the ecology) and awareness (mind).

Despite the differences between Gregory and Turvey with respect to the semiotics, they share an essentially dualistic ontology. This can be a problem and a potential source of many contradictions for exploring problems associated with What Matters. In both cases, there remains the ultimate problem of two realities—one real world that exists out there independently from the observer and another different real world in the mind of the observer.

Although the gap between mind and matter is much bigger in Gregory's approach, there remains a gap for Turvey to cross. In particular, there have been endless debates about the construct of Affordance. Where does it fit into the puzzle? Is an affordance a property of the ecology (matter)? Or is an affordance a property of mind? Peter Hancock once posed the question: "if the hand is in Ohio and the cup is in China does it afford grasping?" Another problem that some have is with the relation between affordances and information. If the cup is on the table within arm's reach, but the lights are out and it can't be seen, does it afford reaching and/or grasping? Thus, there is another dualistic dilemma. What reality does affordance belong to?

An answer to this dilemma is represented as the central portion of the opening plate. This represents a unified ontology of experience where each of the fundamental elements is a joint function of Mind and Matter. Thus, the element of Satisfying is the coupling of intentions and values (Mind) with consequences (Matter). This element helps to answer questions about 'why' an agent is attracted to some things and repelled by others. This addresses the values that motivate and direct action.

The element *Specifying* is the coupling or attunement between the 'objective' information (e.g., geometric structure of optical flow field) (Matter) and the 'subjective' interpretation (e.g., whether a field will be reachable in a glide) (Mind). This element is associated with what an agent can 'see' or 'know' about the state of experience. It provides the 'feedback' that can potentially guide the agent to act in ways that might be satisfying. Constraints associated with specifying play an important role in determining the experience of awareness.

The element *Affording* is the coupling of motor effectivities (e.g., an opposable thumb—agent-based) and the opportunities in the ecology (e.g., the size of the cup—object-based). The affording element provides the means for changing state and thus, sets the constraints on what states can be reached. Thus, the constraints associated with affording help to determine the nature of the situation.

Note that controlled action is a function of all three components—a direction (satisfying), a means for moving (affording), and feedback to discriminate whether motions are in the right direction (specifying). The ability to consistently achieve satisfactory outcomes based on accurate assessment of the situation is what pilots mean when they say that a person has 'good situation awareness.'

Thus, an answer to Peter Hancock's question is that the cup in China affords grasping, but it does not afford reaching, and the information to specify the grasp-ability is not available to the person in Ohio. So, the possibility of grasping exists, but it cannot be realized due to situation and awareness constraints.

As to the cup in the dark, it affords reaching and grasping, but this is not specified visually, though it may be discovered through proprioceptive feedback as a result of exploring the space with one's hands. The key in both instances is the difference between the reality of a possibility (e.g., grasp-ability) and the realization of that possibility (actually grasping the cup). The possibility is associated with one element of what matters, but the realization of that possibility depends on all three elements—whether there is a reason to pick up the cup (satisfying), whether there is capability to perform the action (affording), and whether there is the information to guide effective action (specifying).

The classical ontological positions (materialism, idealism, dualism) disagree about which of the peripheral pieces in the puzzle picture are real elements. However, they all agree that the central elements of the puzzle (satisfying, specifying, and affording) are derivative (i.e., not fundamental elements of reality). The implication of James' Radical Empiricism[3] and Pirsig's Metaphysics of Quality[4] is just the inverse. That is, *the central elements of satisfying, specifying, and affording become fundamental elements, and the peripheral pieces of the diagram are considered to be derivatives from these ontologically basic elements.*

It is possible to take an 'objective' perspective and focus only on the physical aspects of experience, or to consider a more 'subjective' perspective to consider the mental aspects of experience. However, when the pie is cut in either of these ways, the fundamental properties of the reality of experience are lost. The essential elements of satisfying, specifying, and affording are broken. The critical point here is that each of the fundamental elements is a joint function of Mind and Matter. Thus, any separation between Mind and Matter will be problematic for reconstructing a model of human experience.

An analogy with field theories in physics might be appropriate. That is, the satisfying, specifying, and affording reflect the underlying forces that create the fields that shape experience. The pieces on the periphery of the opening puzzle image might reflect isolated 'particles' within those fields. The challenge for those interested in the science of cognition and/or applying that science to designing user experiences is whether to build our ontology around the 'particles' or the 'fields'?

AFTER FEYNMAN LECTURES, P12-9

Feynman, Leighton & Sands[6]

If the goal is to discover 'what matters,' then field theories are to be preferred. Also, the use of *verbs* to specify the fundamental *forces* can emphasize the dynamic, relational aspect of these elements.[5] It is important not to reify 'experience' as an 'object of study.' Experience involves patterns over time. It involves processes of becoming, not a state of being. It is a complex interplay of dynamic 'forces' that interact over time to shape performance.

Figure 4.4 illustrates an alternative to the earlier puzzle image. In Figure 4.4 the elements (or particles) associated with classical approaches to Mind (intention, perspicacity, and effectivity) and Matter (consequence, structure, and possibility) recede into the periphery, and the relational field that joins Mind and Matter emerges into focus. This relational field that reflects both Mind and Matter provides a more productive scheme for considering What Matters.

The elements of this field (satisfying, specifying, and affording) provide the primitives of human experience, and the consequence of breaking these primitives of the field into their component parts is that 'meaning' is destroyed. Thus, satisfying, specifying, and affording are fundamental (ontologically basic) to a science of human experience, and the separate pieces uniquely associated with Mind or Matter (i.e., intention, consequence, etc.) are derivative from these more basic components.

Of course, many interesting questions can be asked about the separate elements of Mind and Matter. However, it is unlikely that questions framed around those separate pieces will ever add up to a satisfying understanding of human experience. On the other hand, questions framed with respect to elements of the central field may lead to more productive thinking about human experience.

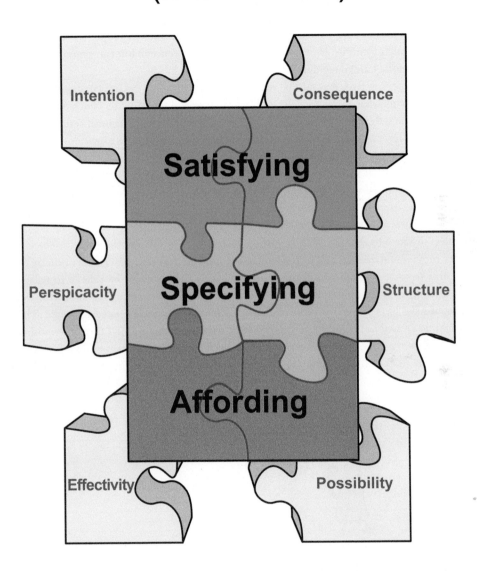

Semiotic Triad
(what matters)

Intention

Consequence

Satisfying

Perspicacity

Specifying

Structure

Affording

Effectivity

Possibility

Agent
(mind)

Environment
(matter)

Figure 4.4 The separate pieces associated with mind (intention, perspicuity, and effectivity) and matter (consequence, structure, possibility) are illustrated as peripheral to the question of What Matters, while the relational properties of the central field (satisfying, specifying, and affording) become the central 'objects' of study.

Approaching the Edge

A mother and her young daughter were approaching the edge of a cliff. As they got near to the cliff the mother started to slow, but her daughter continued toward the cliff without slowing. Fearing for her daughter's safety, the mother reached down to grab her shoulder to slow her down and caution her that they were getting dangerously close. But the daughter looked up at her mother in surprise. She believed that they were still a very safe distance from the edge. She thought her mother was being overly cautious. How can we explain this difference in interpretation of the situation between the mother and daughter?

From the dyadic perspective, it would be reasonable to assume that the information about distance to the cliff is somewhat ambiguous for both the mother and the daughter, since this requires judgment of depth, and they both must infer depth from cues on two-dimensional retinas. So, this suggests that the difference reflects their ability to interpret the ambiguous signs. And further, it would be reasonable to presume that based on more extensive experience (i.e., more knowledge), the mother's interpretation would be more valid than the daughter's interpretation. In this case, the differences are localized within the heads. The mother's 'head' contains knowledge about judging distance and the dangers of cliffs that her daughter's may not.

Figure 4.5 suggests an alternative hypothesis. How close is dangerously close to the edge? Is there a critical distance to the edge with regards to the danger of falling off? Is that distance the same for the mother and daughter? If not, what factors might determine the critical distance?

Suppose that *too close* is a function of the center of mass—which might be related to balance. Suppose that falling over the cliff typically happens only when, if a person might stumble forward, their center of mass passes over the edge of the cliff. Center of mass is related to height. Thus, *too close* might be related to height. Note that at a spot where a stumble could carry the mother's center of mass over the edge, the daughter is far from such danger. The distance that *affords* safety is different for the mother than for the daughter. Thus, the differences in judgments about safety

Figure 4.5 What is too close? How is it specified?

do not necessarily reflect differences in knowledge, but rather real differences in terms of What Matters. Real differences in terms of what will *satisfy* the goal of 'a safe distance.'

Also note that due to the common relation to height, visual angle potentially provides an invariant relation with *too close*. It is possible that too close can be directly specified in the optic array. Thus, it is possible that both mother and daughter are appropriately tuned to the information. Both may be equally capable of validly judging what too close is for themselves. But perhaps, they are not as well able to judge for the other.

This example provides yet another context to think about Gibson's concept of affordance (in this case, the negative affordance of falling off the cliff) and his theory of direct perception. The hypothesis is that too close is the affordance and that this affordance can be directly specified in terms of an optical angle.

The broader implication is that too close is part of the *deep structure* in relation to the problem of safely moving through the environment. It is part of the deep structure, because it is related to the functional aspect of the task (e.g., safety) in a meaningful way. On the other hand, the linear distance to the edge would be part of the surface structure, since it has no direct invariant relation to any functionally significant aspect of the problem. In other words, the answer to 'how far is dangerous?' will always be, 'it depends.' In this context, trying to relate a fixed distance to safety would be the mistake of a novice physicist—one who does not understand the deep structure (i.e., functional significance) of the problem and who is using an inappropriate coordinate system.

More importantly, note that the affordance of falling off, the information to specify too close, and the value of safety do not exist if you isolate the observers from the situation. These are not properties of the cliff, and they are not properties of the observers. These are properties of the experience! These are relations that couple the observers and the ecology. Thus, the fundamental elements of affording, specifying, and satisfying are lost when the problem is decomposed around the separate mind/matter components.

Consider the possibility that the reality of experience consists of these three fundamental elements—satisfying, specifying, and affording. Consider the possibility that these three elements are the dimensions of the field of experience. Thus, the implication for designers is that if you want to shape the quality of human experience, you should be targeting these dimensions. What are the needs that I hope to address with this product (satisfying)? What are the functional possibilities that I hope to realize with this product (affording)? How can the alternative possibilities be clearly specified relative to the users' needs (specifying)?

In sum, the point is that the elements of human experience are neither Mind nor Matter. Yet, they are both Mind and Matter! For any of the classical ontological positions (materialism, idealism, or dualism), this is a contradiction. This also creates an epistemological problem for the discoverer—where can I stand in order to separate the point of observation from the phenomena that is being observed? The implication is that you can't escape human experience in order to discover it. There is no privileged perspective.

Thus, multiple perspectives are required in order to converge on a full understanding of the phenomenon. Each perspective is biased. Yet, each perspective offers unique information that may not be available from other perspectives. Finally, this has important implications for how we choose to bound the "system" for purposes of modelling and observation. The conventional dyadic approach to information processing is simply too narrow a perspective. This perspective misses important constraints that contribute to shaping the human experience. The triadic approach provides a more holistic view of the phenomenon and a more complete view of the full semiotic dynamic.

The ending cartoon is a variant on the old story about the blind men and the elephant. Each blind man is feeling a different part of the elephant, and thus each has a very different notion of what an elephant is. Thus, there are many different ways to see an elephant, so it is difficult to get a complete picture from any single position. The challenge is to develop theoretical constructs that allow constructive integration across these diverse perspectives. Satisfying, affording, and specifying might be useful constructs for achieving this goal. In essence, satisfying, affording, and specifying are REAL, and the classical distinctions (intention, consequence, perspicacity, structure, effectivity, possibility) are derivatives or abstractions from this reality.

This is a radical inversion of classical assumptions about the ontological basis of reality. There are elementary properties of *What Matters* that are joint functions of *Mind and Matter*. These elementary properties of the experiential field (satisfying, specifying, and affording) provide a way to partition the phenomenon so that the functional dynamics of experience are preserved. This leads to more coherent scientific narratives about human experience, and it leads to more innovative ways for thinking about the design of human/technology systems.

Notes

1. Gibson described some of the alternative ways that psychologists use the term *stimulus* in 1960.

   Gibson, J.J. (1960). The concept of stimulus in psychology. *American Psychologist*, 16, 694–703.

   Gibson, J.J. (1979). *The ecological approach to visual perception*. Boston: Houghton Mifflin. (pp. 9 & 33).

2. Turvey, M.T. (1992). Affordances and prospective control: An outline of the ontology. *Ecological Psychology*, 4(3), 173–187.

3. James, W. (1912). *Essays on radical empiricism*. New York: Longmans, Green & Co. Available through the Gutenberg project, www.gutenberg.org/ebooks/32547

4. Pirsig, R. (1974). *Zen and the art of motorcycle maintenance: An inquiry into values*. New York: Morrow, Co.

   Pirsig, R. (1991). *Lila: An inquiry into morals*. Bantam Books.

5. Fredrick Bartlett also preferred using verbs to describe fundamental cognitive phenomena (e.g., remembering rather than memory).

6. Feynman, R.P., Leighton, R.B., & Sands, M. (1963). *The Feynman lectures on physics*. Reading, MA: Addison-Wesley.

Part 2

THE DYNAMICS OF CIRCLES

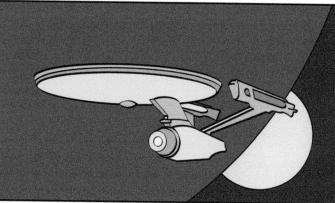

5

ABDUCTION

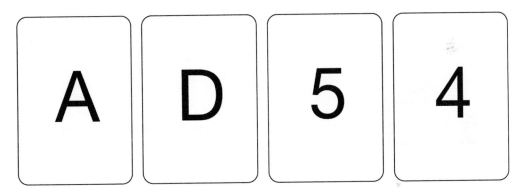

Figure 5.1 The Wason stimulus.

Figure 5.1 shows four cards used in what is typically referred to as the Wason task (after the researcher who first used this task).[1] Each card has a number on one side and a letter on the other side. The task is to determine whether the following assertion is true or false with regards to these four cards, by turning over the minimum number of cards:

If a card has a vowel on the letter side, then it has an even number on the number side.

So, which cards would you turn over?

Now consider another problem: in this case you are the proprietor of a bar and you must be careful to follow the local laws with regards to the legal age for drinking. In your area the law is that it is illegal to serve alcohol to anyone under 21 years of age. This can also be framed as a formal rule:

If drinking alcohol, then over 21 years old.

Figure 5.2 shows a table of patrons. For two of the patrons you know their age, but not what they are drinking; for the other two you know what they are drinking but not their age. What inquiries would you need to make in order to ensure that this is a legal table?

Although the contexts are different, from the perspective of formal logic these two problems are identical or isomorphic. This formal isomorphic structure is illustrated in Figure 5.3, which represents the problems in the form of a tree diagram of the relations implied by the if, then rules.

Figure 5.2 Is this table legal?

With the tree diagram in Figure 5.3, it should be a bit easier to see that the correct answer to the first problem is that the cards that need to be turned over to test the rule are A (to see whether an even number is on the other side) and 5 (to see whether a consonant is on the other side). Note that there is no value in turning over the 4, because as illustrated in the tree diagram, a 4 can have either a vowel or a consonant on the other side without violating the if-then rule. Similarly, it is obvious that to test whether the table is legal, you need to know how old the person drinking beer is and you need to know what the younger boy is drinking, but there is no need to inquire about what the person over 21 is drinking.

While these two problems are isomorphic with respect to the rules of formal logic, they do not appear to be identical with respect to human experience. For most people, the first problem is a difficult one. Many people choose to turn over A and 4. On the other hand, most people find the second problem to be relatively easy. Few would feel a need to find out what the person over 21 is drinking.

The fact that two problems that are isomorphic with respect to the rules of formal logic evoke very different responses from people suggests that factors not relevant to formal logic are relevant to human performance. Another way to say this is that for human performance 'context' matters.

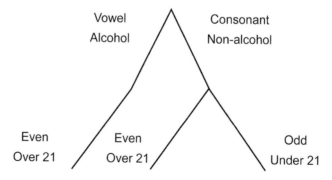

Figure 5.3 A formal diagram illustrating the if, then structure underlying the two problems illustrated in Figures 5.1 and 5.2.

On the other hand, the rules of formal logic are independent of context. Yet another way to say this is that the 'mind' is designed to cope with open-systems, whereas formal logic is framed in terms of closed-systems.

It is interesting to speculate about what makes the second problem (i.e., the bar context) easier than the first (i.e., the original Wason task). Is it because the first problem is more abstract and the second problem is more concrete? Is it that people have lots of experience with bars and drinking laws?

Maybe it has to do with pragmatic reasoning in relation to the social dynamic of cooperation or permission.[2] In a cooperative system, people give up some of their individual rights for the good of the social unit. This requires some degree of trust—you expect that the sacrifices are shared by everyone. Everybody gives up a little, and in return they reap the benefits of cooperation. However, some people cheat—that is, they don't make the sacrifices (don't follow the rules) and still try to get the benefits of the cooperation. In other words, these people take advantage of others around them.

It has been hypothesized that due to this social dynamic, it is important to be able to detect the cheaters (to not be a chump and let people take advantage of your trust). Thus, the hypothesis is that as social creatures, people have become attuned to detecting cheaters (in other words, they have developed a *permission schema*). The prediction is that people should be skilled at these judgments whenever they are framed in a pragmatic context such as social permission. Cosmides and Tooby (1997)[3] write:

> People who ordinarily cannot detect violations of if-then rules do so easily and accurately when that violation represents cheating in a situation of social exchange (Comides, 1985, 1989; Comides & Tooby, 1989, 1992). This is a situation in which one is entitled to a benefit only if one has fulfilled a requirement (e.g., "If you are to eat those cookies, then you must first fix your bed"; "If a man eats cassava root, then he must have a tattoo on his chest"; or more generally, "If you take benefit B, then you must satisfy requirement R"). Cheating is accepting the benefit specified without satisfying the condition that provision of the benefit was made contingent upon (e.g., eating the cookies without having first fixed your bed).
>
> When asked to look for violations of social contracts of this kind, the adaptively correct answer is immediately obvious to almost all subjects, who commonly experience a

"pop out" effect. No formal training is needed. Whenever the content of a problem asks subjects to look for cheaters in a social exchange—even when the situation described is culturally unfamiliar and even bizarre—subjects experience the problem as simple to solve, and their performance jumps dramatically. In general, 65–80% of subjects get it right, the highest performance ever found for a task of this kind. They choose the "benefit accepted" card (e.g., "ate the cassava root") and the "cost not paid" card (e.g., "no tattoo"), for any social conditional that can be interpreted as a social contract, and in which looking for violations can be interpreted as looking for cheaters.

Rationality

The diagram in Figure 5.3 is framed in terms of the rules of deduction. This diagram illustrates the form of an 'if-then' rule (If A, then B). The formalisms of deduction tell us what specific events will be true, if the rules (the premises) are true.

The prototype for deduction is the syllogism, for example:

Major Premise:
If Turk cuts the grass, Dad will pay him $5.00.

Minor Premise:
Dad pays Turk $5.00.

Conclusion:
Turk cut the grass.

The deduction model of rationality provides the criteria for determining whether this is a valid syllogism or a valid argument. Does the conclusion necessarily follow from the premises? What do you think, is this a valid syllogism or not? If you are not sure, perhaps Figure 5.4 will help. It is invalid—that is, you can't conclude that Turk cut the grass if Dad pays him $5.00 — Dad might just be a very generous father.

The Wason task can also be viewed through the lens of induction as well.[4] A good way to demonstrate the induction perspective is to present a class with the following problem: "I have a rule in mind for generating strings of three numbers. I will give you an example of one of the strings

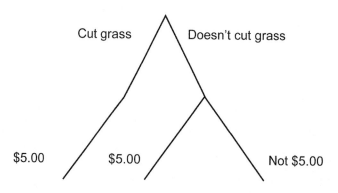

Figure 5.4 Can you conclude that Turk cut the grass, if he gets $5.00?

generated from this rule. Then, you can propose other strings (i.e., do experiments), and I will tell you whether they are consistent with the rule or not. Your job is to continue to do experiments until you can guess the rule. The first example of a string that fits the rule I have in mind is: 2, 4, 6."

Posed with this problem, the most typical first response from the class is "8, 10, 12." To which the answer is, "yes, that is consistent with the rule." Often this is followed by a few other examples of what they now think the rule is: "20, 22, 24" or "100, 102, 104." To each of these 'experiments' the answer is "yes, these are all consistent with the rule." Now some of the students are very confident that they have discovered the rule. They make the guess that "The rule is a sequence of consecutive even numbers." But they are told that this is not the rule. And thus other experiments are required: "1, 2, 3." "Yes, this is consistent." "6, 4, 2." "No, this is not consistent." Eventually, they discover the rule, which is *any sequence of increasing numbers.*

The lesson of this example is that according to the prescriptions of induction it is possible to falsify a rule, by finding a contradiction. But even with a large number of confirmations, the rule is not proven. Note that the hypothesis of a sequence of consecutive even numbers is not 'tested' by a response such as "8, 10, 12." To test this hypothesis, you need to present an alternative such as "1, 2, 3"—that is, a counterexample. The response of "yes" to this string disproves the hypothesis, while the response of "yes" to the string "8, 10, 12" does not prove the rule.

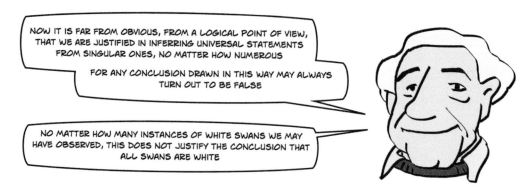

Citation from Karl Popper[5]

This is an important lesson for experimental scientists, since science is often framed as an inductive problem—that is, to infer general laws (i.e., rules) from observations of particular cases (e.g., experiments). Experiments never "prove" hypotheses, but they can disprove hypotheses.

Thus, science progresses by eliminating wrong hypotheses, not by proving hypotheses.[6] The beliefs of scientists are the hypotheses that stand up to the tests of the experiments—but no matter how many tests are consistent with a belief, hypotheses are never 'proven.' According to the logic of induction, for the scientist, beliefs should always be tentative.

In this context, the response of turning over the "4" in the Wason task is considered to be evidence of a "confirmation bias." That is, as with the previous example, people are doing a test to confirm the rule, rather than to contradict it. This is a "bias" in the sense that it is a deviation from the prescriptions of inductive reasoning.

It is important to realize that induction and deduction are two sides of a single coin. That is, deduction starts with the tree diagram specified by the major premise, and specifies which observations will follow from this rule. Induction starts with the observations and tries to infer the underlying tree diagram.

The conventional wisdom typically accepts the prescriptions of induction and deduction as the ideals for human rationality. However, the research shows that these ideals are seldom realized. According to conventional wisdom, this is presumably due to information processing limits (e.g., biases).[7] So, it is not a stretch to say that the conventional theories of thinking are a bit like the old models that showed the sun and planets revolving around the earth—that included many corrections to account for the deviations from the expected ideal trajectories. However, might it be possible that human thinking does not revolve around classical logic, as its core?

Black Ravens and Republican Women

Ray Nickerson[8] suggests a couple other variants on the basic Wason task that might help us to better understand the factors that are influencing performance with regard to rational strategies for testing hypotheses in everyday life. The first example is related to what philosophers refer to as Hempel's paradox of the ravens.[9] In Hempel's paradox the hypothesis to be tested is the claim that "All ravens are black" or, in other words, "If raven, then black."

Nickerson summarizes Hempel's Paradox of the Ravens as follows:

> Hempel pointed out that the assertions "All ravens are black" and "All nonblack things are non-ravens" are logically equivalent, each being the contrapositive of the other. Any evidence that strengthens belief that one of them is true should strengthen belief that the other (equivalent) one is true as well. By the rule that a case of a hypothesis supports that hypothesis, the observation of a white shoe should increase our confidence in the truth of the second assertion. And given that two statements are equivalent, we have no choice, Hempel argues, but to take the same observation as confirmatory evidence also for the claim that all ravens are black.[10]

Does it make sense to you that the observation of a white shoe (or a red herring[11]) would be relevant to testing the hypothesis that 'all ravens are black.' The hypothesis about ravens can be visualized in the same form as the Wason task, as illustrated in Figure 5.5. However, there is a subtle distinction with respect to the original Wason problem. The Wason problem is generally presented to test the assertion only about the four cards presented. However, the Raven problem is framed in terms of generalizing to the full population of ravens.

Which problem is more representative of the problems most generally faced in everyday experiences with hypothesis testing? Could it be that people are misunderstanding the Wason problem, and they are considering whether the rule applies to the full deck of cards? That is, they are testing the proposition that 'All cards in a larger deck with a vowel on one side have an even number on the other.'

To test this proposition, might it make sense to focus your search on all the cards that have vowels on one side? Note that in the case of the legal table problem, the limited scope of the problem is more clearly evident (i.e., the question applies not to finding any illegal drinking, but specifically to that table).

One factor that might be relevant to judging whether this is a smart choice might be the number of cards with vowels on one side relative to the number of cards with odd numbers on one side.

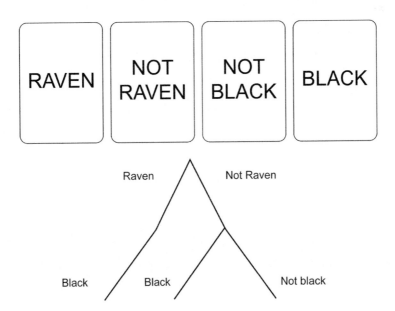

Figure 5.5 (top/bottom) The hypothesis: If raven, then black. The diagram illustrates this hypothesis in terms of deductive inference. How would you go about testing whether this hypothesis is true?

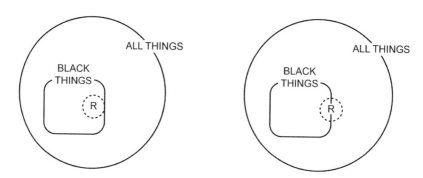

Figure 5.6 The hypothesis: If raven, then black or equivalently: All ravens are black. The diagram illustrates this hypothesis in terms of a Venn Diagram. This boils down to testing whether the subset Ravens (R) is fully contained within the subset Black Things. How would you go about testing whether this hypothesis is true?

Figure 5.6 provides another way to think about the hypothesis about ravens. Figure 5.6 uses a Venn diagram representation. In this context, the set of ravens is represented as a small set within the larger set of all things. Within the set of all things there is also a smaller set of things that are black, but many more things are nonblack.

In the context of Figure 5.6, the question is whether or not the subset of ravens is completely contained within the set of black things, or not. If you were looking to see whether there was a 'counterexample' to disconfirm the hypothesis that 'all ravens are black,' would you start by sampling all the nonblack things to see if any of them were ravens? Or would it be more practical to focus your attention on the ravens, to see if one of them might be nonblack?

Nickerson suggests another counterexample to illustrate the relevance of the set of possibilities on the evaluation of a hypothesis:

> Suppose one knew the US senate to be composed at a particular time (say at the opening of the 104th congress 1995) of 47 Democrats and 53 Republicans, and of 92 males and 8 females, but that one did not know the parties to which individual senators belonged. Consider the two following claims:
>
> All Republicans in the US senate are males. (If X is a Republican US senator, X is male.)
> All females in the US senate are Democrats. (If X is a female US senator, X is a Democrat.)

Figure 5.7 illustrates this hypothesis in the same format as the Wason Task, with the number of cases associated with each category above the card. What would be the most efficient strategy for testing these equivalent hypotheses with respect to the population of 100 senators? Would you query all 100 senators? Only the 53 Republicans to see if any of them are women? Only the 92 men to verify that 53 of them are Republicans? Only the 47 Democrats to see if you could find all eight women? Or would it be more efficient to simply query the eight women?

If people behaved as suggested by the original results of the Wason task, the prediction is that they would most likely sample Republicans and males (or female and democrats, if the second form is used).

Do you think this is likely? What strategy seems most rational to you?

In this countercase, querying the eight females would clearly be the most efficient search strategy. But does the efficiency of sampling matter to people?[12] Nickerson cites several examples of empirical studies that support the argument that it does.

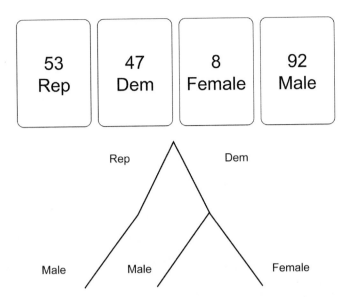

Figure 5.7 (top/bottom) The hypothesis: If Republican, then Male. The diagram illustrates this hypothesis in terms of deductive inference. The numbers above each card indicate the number of items in each category. How would you go about testing whether this hypothesis is true?

The potential impact of the environmental context on human judgment was clearly recognized by Einhorn and Hogarth.[13] Figure 5.8 is Einhorn and Hogarth's way to represent the role of the 'environment' on the process. They write:

> The crucial aspect of the diagram is that judgments and actions are taken within particular task environments. . . . By "task environment" is meant such factors as base rates, selection ratios, treatment effects, uncertainty of the task, sequential versus simultaneous presentation of information, completeness of judgment-action combinations, and so on. It is the combination of judgments, actions, and environments that produce outcomes.
>
> (p. 409)

They continue:

> Furthermore, in the absence of adequate control or understanding of environmental factors, inference regarding causal relationships between judgments-actions and outcomes is problematic.
>
> (p. 409)

Searching for Life in the Universe

Consider one more example illustrated in Figure 5.9. In this case, you are the chief scientist for NASA, and an important scientific hypothesis for you to test is the hypothesis that water is a necessary condition for life. This can be stated formally as:

> If life, then water.

So, where should you send your expeditions?

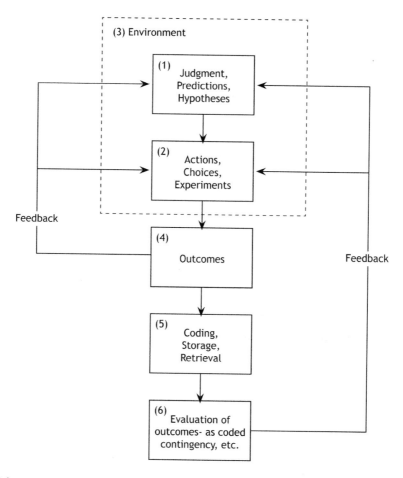

Figure 5.8 Schematic representation of the role of the environment in shaping judgment and action. (adapted from Einhorn & Hogarth, 1978; Figure 6.)

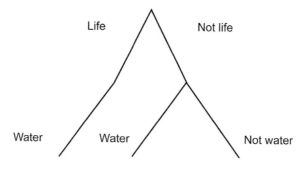

Figure 5.9 The hypothesis that water is a necessary condition for life.

The structure of the underlying syllogism is exactly the same as that for the Wason task. This means that if your goal is to test the truth of the hypothesis, then you need to go to planets where there is life, to see if there is also water; and you should go to the planets without water, to see if there is life.

However, there is no value in going to planets that have water. Even if you visited a hundred planets with water and find life, that would not prove the hypothesis. However, if you visit a single planet without water and find life or a single planet with life and no water, this would prove the hypothesis wrong.

On the other hand, what if your goal is not to test the validity of your hypothesis, but rather, what if your goal is to find life? Wouldn't it be best to search for life in those places that you believe it is most likely to be? Wouldn't it make sense to let your best hypotheses about where life might be guide your search process?

This is essentially the position of Charles Sanders Peirce (remember the guy who introduced the triadic approach to semiotics?) with respect to human experience and thinking. The essence is that thinking is designed for adapting to the demands of everyday life. This has nothing to do with the philosophical abstractions of 'truth' or 'validity.' It has everything to do with making choices that are successful (e.g., enhance survival).

According to the norms of induction and deduction, the 'validity' of a hypothesis is judged based on the structure of the argument alone. However, Peirce suggested *abduction logic* as an alternative to these formal logics. In an abduction system a belief is judged as a function of whether the actions guided by that belief consistently lead to satisfying results. In other words, the test of an idea is *pragmatic*. It is NOT based on abstract mathematical or analytic principles, but it is based on the concrete consequences of the actions that it motivates (e.g., finding life).

Formal induction and deduction systems are abstractions! That is, it doesn't matter whether the syllogism is about getting paid for cutting grass as in the earlier example, or whether the syllogism is framed in terms of unspecified variables, such as:

If A, then B
A
therefore, B.

Another way to say this is that formal logic is a closed-system—it is defined independently from any specific context. Thus, a theory of cognition based on the prescriptions of induction or deduction naturally leads to a dualistic view about mind and matter. Mind is the realm of logic, and it

operates independently from the context of the world of matter. This leads to a focus on awareness, independent from a theory of situations (i.e., ecology or context).

Abduction, on the other hand, offers an eco-logic, in which thinking is evaluated relative to its coupling with the ecology or the world of matter. The test of thinking is successful action or successful adaptation to the ecology.

So, if human experience is based on abduction logic, then the 'confirmation bias' simply reflects the generalization of this eco-logic to puzzles that it was not designed to solve. Some people may approach the Wason task as a challenge to find vowels, so they look where the hypothesis suggests that they find vowels. When the task is to look for cheaters—the strategy works fine—no bias is evident.

Similarly, the search for nonblack ravens or for female republicans is guided by rational considerations relative to the space of possibilities.

Finally, it seems quite rational to frame the NASA mission in terms of using our best understanding of nature to help find life in the universe. As to the syllogism about cutting grass—people would probably be interested in knowing more about the context. Is Turk reliable? How strict are his parents?

Again, note that from the perspective of formal logic, this context is irrelevant. But of course, in everyday life, context is almost always relevant.

Development and Learning: Assimilation and Accommodation

Another perspective to consider with respect to abduction is that it is fundamentally a learning (or adapting) system, rather than a logical system. An abduction system develops and refines beliefs through a trial-and-error process. In general, this learning system will typically start with a naive belief about a situation, and through interaction or iterative-actions it will gradually tune the beliefs in ways that lead to increasing correspondence with the situation over time (improved fitness or greater stability).

Piaget[14] described this learning process in terms of two coupled dynamics: assimilation and accommodation. *Assimilation* is a process of integrating new situations within 'schemas' (hypotheses or beliefs) that have been developed based on prior experience. So, for example, when we start college, we approach the classes guided by the expectations that we developed based on our experiences in high school. Beliefs (or schemas) that have led to success in the past guide actions in the new situations.

In the specific context of the Wason task described earlier, differences might be explained by the framing of the problem. If the problem is framed in a permission context, then people can generalize their experiences developed in similar social contexts (i.e., permission schemas), and thus they solve it correctly. However, when the problem is framed in a more abstract context (e.g., Figure 5.1), then the relevance of the social experiences is not obvious, and the appropriate experiences are not applied.

Accommodation is a process of differentiation, in which our beliefs are refined to meet the needs of specific situations. For example, after some time in college you realize that some of your expectations were wrong, and you begin to differentiate your expectations about how to succeed in college from your expectations about how to succeed in high school. The accommodation dynamic reflects a kind of negative feedback—that is, the abduction system adjusts its beliefs as a function of the difference between what it expected (hypotheses) and the actual consequences that occurred. In a negative feedback control system, this difference is typically referred to as 'error.'

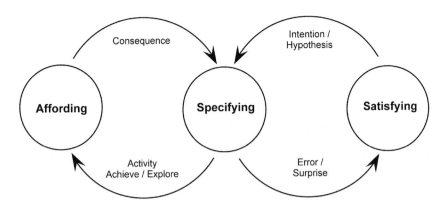

Figure 5.10 Abduction as a closed-loop coupling between the elements of experience

In the context of abduction, Peirce referred to this difference as 'surprise.' In any case, the abduction system is typically designed so that over time, error (or surprise) is reduced. Thus, beliefs are changed to be more in line with the actual consequences, or actions are adjusted so that consequences change to be more in line with the beliefs. This 'cybernetic' aspect of abduction systems will be discussed in much more detail in later chapters.

It is important to appreciate the circular nature of this dynamic. Assimilation is the source of the current beliefs that guide the next action. The consequences from that action drive the accommodative processes that lead to new beliefs or more finely differentiated expectations (schemas). These in turn drive the assimilative processes that guide the next actions. Thus, beliefs are shaping actions while the consequences of actions are shaping beliefs. This is a truly circular causality where every element is both cause and effect.

Figure 5.10 illustrates the abduction dynamic as a triadic semiotic system coupling the basic elements of experience (satisfying, specifying, and affording). The labels on the arrows illustrate that this system is simultaneously a 'control' system (e.g., assimilation) and an 'observer' system (e.g., accommodation).

As a control system, the system adjusts performatory actions based on the differences between actual and intended consequences (i.e., error feedback) guided by schemas (beliefs) derived from previous experience.

As an observer system, the system adjusts expectations (beliefs or schemas) based on the difference between actual and hypothesized consequences (i.e., surprise) that result from exploratory actions. Note that this is a fully enclosed system—there are no extrinsic inputs. The whole of reality, including Mind and Matter, is integrated within this dynamic since each of the elements is a joint function of Mind and Matter.

The functionalist philosopher/psychologist John Dewey also highlighted the 'double movement' implied by this circular dynamic:

> There is a double movement in all reflection: a movement from the given partial and confused data to a suggested comprehensive (or inclusive) entire situation; and back from this suggested whole—which as suggested is meaning, an idea—to particular facts, so as to connect these with one another and with additional facts to which the suggestion has directed attention.[15]

Dewey associated this double movement with a coupling between inductive processes—the generation of a tentative belief—and deductive processes to test that belief. This makes sense in that the inductive process integrates past observations to form a hypothesis (e.g., if I do the things that led to success in high school, then I will be successful in college). It goes from the particulars (i.e., past experiences) to the universals (i.e., beliefs). The deductive process evaluates this universal (the hypothetical belief about a situation), relative to the particular consequences of actions based on that belief (the beliefs about academic success are tested against the consequences obtained in the current context of college).

Although Dewey uses the terms induction and deduction, it seems clear that he is not arguing that thinking operates according to the classical norms for that logic. That is, that the structure of the argument is critical. Conventional views of cognition tend to suggest that the proper 'ordering of thought' in human cognition and behavior reflects the logical rules that order action. In other words, thinking directs action. However, Dewey wrote that:

> All people at the outset, and the majority of people probably all their lives attain ordering of thought through ordering of action.

He continues:

> Adults normally carry through some occupation, profession, pursuit; and this furnishes the continuous axis about which their knowledge, their beliefs, and their habits of reaching and testing conclusions are organized. Observations that have to do with the efficient performance of their calling are extended and rendered precise. Information related to it is not merely amassed and left in a heap; it is classified and subdivided so as to be available as it is needed. Inferences are made by most men not from purely speculative motives, but because they are involved in the efficient performance of "the duties involved in their several callings." Thus, their inferences are constantly tested by results achieved; futile and scattering methods tend to be discounted; orderly arrangements have a premium put on them. The event, the issue, stands as a constant check on the thinking that has led up to it; and this discipline by efficiency in action is the chief sanction, in practically all who are not scientific specialists, of orderliness of thought.[16]

Thus, it seems clear that Dewey is saying that the test of an idea is not the form of the argument but the "results achieved." Thus, order emerges as a result of the consequences associated with previous actions. Constructs like ecology or *umwelt*[17] reflect the constraints that Dewey associates with the *profession*. This is where actions translate to consequences. This can also be termed the 'situation.' Currently, the term 'situated cognition' is being used by many to emphasize the role of the ecology in shaping thinking.[18]

In essence, abduction logic is a kind of learning by doing, where hypotheses are generated as a result of assimilation of past experiences (e.g., schema or beliefs), tested in the context of actions, and revised through accommodative processes associated with the feedback from those actions.

This dynamic is akin to natural selection, where past experience is the source of genetic variation (i.e., beliefs, ideas, hypotheses) and future experience provides the selective forces that determine which of these variations will survive. Also note that, as with natural selection, there is no need to hypothesize an external agent (i.e., intelligent design—homunculus) to account for the patterns (e.g., organization) that emerge.

Circular Coupling

It would be tempting to conclude, in opposition to the conventional wisdom (i.e., that thinking or awareness shapes action), that in actuality action in the ecology shapes thinking. That is, to conclude that our thinking is molded to fit the profession or ecology. However, that conclusion is inconsistent with the circular dynamic. It assumes that the ecology is a static thing, out there, to which people adapt. However, professions and more generally ecologies are not static. They are constantly changing or evolving as a consequence of the interactions with people (e.g., consider the possible human contributions to global warming). The abduction system is a dynamic, circular process with every element changing AND being changed by the others.

Gregory Bateson[19] illustrates this circular dynamic in terms of the adaptive relation between horses and savannas. For most people it is obvious how the horse has adapted to fit the savanna environment (e.g., long legs and flat hooves to facilitate mobility, teeth shaped to eat grass and grain, etc.). However, it is not so obvious that savannas have evolved as a result of interactions with horses (e.g., hooves pack the ground, teeth cut the grass, horse manure fertilizes the grass and promotes growth, etc.).

Thus, horses and savannas participate in shaping each other. Just as the stability of the horse depends on the resources of the savanna, the stability of the savanna depends on the resources provided by the animals that populate it. Changes to one will potentially result in changes to the other. This coupling in ecological systems is often illustrated in terms of predator-prey dynamics.

Peirce and Dewey are describing an evolutionary learning process, where strategies (beliefs) and actions that lead to order and stability are reinforced (or selected), and strategies and actions that lead to chaos and instability are extinguished (or become extinct).

The terms 'reinforced' and 'extinguished' are used to emphasize the connection with operant learning theory. The idea that behavior is shaped by its consequences is perfectly consistent with the hypothesis that thinking reflects an abduction logic. The distinction, however, is that one does not have to adopt the conclusions of the extreme behaviorists, which denies the phenomenon of mental life. Rather, it can be said that beliefs are shaped by consequences.

However, remember that consequences are also being created and shaped by beliefs. Also, it is important to note that the consequences that motivate this dynamic are not necessarily only

reward and punishment in the classical sense; simply satisfying curiosity may be sufficient motivation to propel the dynamic forward.[20]

The ultimate flaw in the behaviorist position as in conventional cognitive science is the stimulus-response image of causality that dominates both positions. In pursuit of causal explanations, the behaviorists chose to deny or at least trivialize the role of mind or awareness in the dynamic of human experience. Similarly, the cognitivists chose to deny or at least trivialize the role of the ecology in the dynamic of human experience. These different positions break the loop in different places, but both break the loop in order to force human experience into a causal scheme (i.e., a billiard ball model).

Peirce's triadic semiotic system along with the logic of abduction begins to provide a system for representing James' 'experience' as a fundamental reality emerging from the dynamic coupling between mind and matter. Breaking the coupling, either conceptually or practically (in the design of experiments), risks destroying the phenomena of experience. More contemporary terms that are being used to emphasize the coupling between mind and matter include 'embodied cognition'[21] and 'evolutionary psychology.'[22]

Summary and Overview

Induction and deduction models of rationality are designed to be context independent. That is, the rules are general principles that apply to any context. The validity of a deductive or inductive argument can be specified based only on the form of the argument itself. There is no need to consider correspondence with any extrinsic domain of application. This is emphasized by the fact that the logical calculus can be framed completely in terms of abstract variables (e.g., If A, then B; A, therefore B).

Framing questions of mind in terms of this abstract calculus implies that the dynamics of mind are also independent from the ecologies that they inhabit. This view fits well with the dyadic semiotic model, discussed in Chapter 2 as the semiotic basis consistent with the computer (symbol processor) metaphor of mind.

In contrast, abduction logic is framed in terms of the pragmatic relations between an agent and its environment. In an abduction system, the validity of a belief (hypothesis or proposition) is tested against the consequences of actions based on that belief. Beliefs that lead to satisfying consequences are retained and beliefs that lead to surprises are revised.

Note that in an abduction system there is no absolute truth or absolute criterion for validity as in a deductive system. In abduction systems beliefs are never completely verified (although the agents may sometimes exhibit great confidence in these beliefs).

Thus, this view shares much with Popper's view of Critical Rationalism. As Miller[23] observes, the critical rationalist approach emphasizes "guesswork as the way knowledge grows" (e.g., in Peirce's terms 'hypothesis;' in Piaget's term 'assimilation') and emphasizes "criticism as the way it is controlled" (e.g., in the feedback that is a natural consequence of acting on our beliefs). Miller continues that "rarely, of course, do we know that we are right; but we don't need to know it if we are."

An abduction system frames beliefs in terms of past experiences—thus, it is vulnerable to the Black Swan phenomenon.[24] An abduction system guesses about the world based on experiences in that world. This system will be surprised when the past (i.e., experience in a world of white swans) does not specify the future (i.e., the appearance of a black swan—a rare event).

The abduction system will also be vulnerable to 'butterfly effects.' That is, there will always be a limited horizon to the ability to specify the future; there will always be phenomena that are outside of our awareness (factors beyond the last decimal place in the 'mental' model) that will limit the ability of an abduction system to have absolute certainty about the future.

Additionally, because of the closed-loop dynamic, the abduction system will be vulnerable to attribution errors and confirmation bias to the extent that hypotheses may impact how the feedback resulting from interactions with the ecology is evaluated. For example, in the case of attribution errors, people may reduce surprise by discounting information that contradicts an assessment based on a first impression about another person (i.e., a belief or hypothesis)—and thus may miss the opportunity to correct an error and to better tune their beliefs to the ecology.[25]

Thus, for an abduction system, the future is always uncertain, not because God plays dice with the universe, but due to the limits/bounds of experience. This is in contrast with the conventional information processing approach that emphasizes the limits of the information processing channel (e.g., limited memory capacity, limited attention span) as the primary bounds on human rationality.

The ultimate limits are not on the internal computational process, but rather on the experience. As experience is accumulated, an abduction system is expected to become increasingly well-tuned to its ecology. In fact, Ericsson and Charness (1994)[26] conclude, based on a review of the literature on human expertise, that "acquired skill can allow experts to circumvent basic capacity limits of short-term memory and of the speed of basic reactions, making potential limits irrelevant" (p. 731).

In other words, the bounds on human thinking are not fixed computational limits, but rather they reflect the degree (and perhaps type) of experiences. This gives new meaning to Simon's construct of bounded rationality. The bounds on cognition are properties of the overall dynamics of experience, NOT simply limits of internal mechanisms of awareness.

Increased correspondence between beliefs about the ecology and the pragmatic constraints of that ecology is expected in the long run. However, as noted previously, in the short run this system is vulnerable to being trapped in sub-optimal beliefs (e.g., local minima) reflecting such phenomena as confirmation bias and attribution errors.

Stability in an abduction system is not dependent on following prescribed rules of rationality, but on a kind of muddling through, which means being open to experience and learning from each surprise (e.g., mistake). Where logical systems provide norms for *making the right decisions*, abduction systems describe how people act to *make decisions right* through active adaptation to change and through managing unanticipated variability. As we will see more clearly in later chapters, to be stable, an abduction system must balance learning from the past against a healthy awareness of the uncertainties of the future.

Basically, an abduction system is a learning machine. Ideas that fit the demands of everyday life, that lead to satisfying outcomes, are reinforced (strengthened, confirmed, selected), and ideas that lead to unsatisfying outcomes are revised or changed (extinguished, become extinct, are adapted), generally in ways that improve the fit to the demands of life (i.e., in ways that increase stability).

It is important to note that we are talking about 'ideas' being reinforced, not simply 'behaviors' being reinforced. The point is not to choose between mind OR matter as the causal agent, but rather the point is to bring mind AND matter together into a unified meaning processing system. The point is to address what matters with respect to creation of and adaptation to opportunities to produce stable relations between Mind and Matter.

The term abduction is old, but it is a concept that was lost amid several paradigmatic revolutions in the field of psychology—first the rise of behaviorism and then the cognitive revolution with the associated computer metaphor of mind. Despite the obvious differences in these two approaches, both shared the goal of explaining human experience using the language of causation. Circularity is a problem for both approaches. Although the term was lost, the gap left by the absence of this

concept was recognized by many. For example, Walker Percy[27] writes about the gap between the mind sciences and the physical sciences:

> I refer to this gap in scientific knowledge as an incoherence . . . we are not talking an ordinary area of ignorance which is being steadily eroded by advancing knowledge. . . . No, the gap is incoherent and intractable. . . . It is not like tunneling under a river from both sides and meeting in the middle. It is more like ships passing in the night.

In the previous chapter on Semiotics there was an illustration of how measuring human performance against classical models of extrinsic space (rectangular coordinates) may lead to false inferences about the nature of human experience. In this chapter, this notion is generalized beyond simple perception to more cognitive aspects of performance.

The fundamental point is that abstract mathematical logic (induction, deduction) may be a poor reference for gauging human rationality, because it is not grounded in the practical realities of human experience. In essence, mathematical logic provides the wrong coordinate system for representing the rationality of everyday problem solving and decision making.

Certainly, humans are capable of appreciating the mathematics of classical logic. However, everyday rationality is not measured against absolute truths or the syntax or form of the argument (i.e., internal consistency). Everyday rationality is measured against the practical consequences of hypotheses and beliefs.

The ultimate test is not the absolute truth of a hypothesis. The ultimate test is the quality of experience that results from behaviors guided by that hypothesis or belief. The test is not whether an idea is crazy (i.e., departs from prescriptions of logic), but whether it works!

In an abduction system, whether it works is the ultimate test of what matters. In relation to the NASA version of the logical puzzle, the challenge is to find life in the universe, not to find absolute truth.

The implication for design is that designers need to consider the dual movement of assimilation and accommodation. The assimilation dynamic can be leveraged by creating new technologies that are consistent with the expectations developed through interactions with older technologies (e.g., locating the print function under the "File" menu).

The accommodation dynamic requires that designers consider the best ways to shape expectations of the users to be consistent with the novel demands of new situations (i.e., to teach the operators about the functional constraints). This has been articulated in terms like direct manipulation and direct perception.[28] The common thread is the direct coupling of perception and action so that the interface provides constructive feedback for learning about the process or problem that it is representing

This requires that interface designers ground their designs in the intrinsic logic (i.e., the eco-logic) of the problem or work domains that they are designing for, NOT in abstract mathematical notions of rationality. For example, in designing decision support for fault diagnosis in nuclear power control rooms, the key to effective interfaces will not be found in the 'head' of the operators or in the norms of classical logic, but rather in a deep understanding of the dynamics of the physical processes. Thus, *work analysis* to uncover the intrinsic logic of a particular domain becomes critical to innovative design.[29]

The key for effective decision support will be to represent the relevant affordances (e.g., what states are desirable and reachable) in relation to the relevant values (e.g., production and safety goals).

In designing graphical interfaces to complex technologies like nuclear power plants, the challenge is to find a graphical coordinate system that lets the operators 'see' and learn about the states relative to functional properties, in the same way that the pilot described by Langewiesche (in an earlier chapter) was able to 'see' locations on the ground relative to the functional capabilities of the aircraft.[30]

The first step is to understand the functional capabilities of the system (e.g., the glide capability of the aircraft), and the second step is to find a way to specify those capabilities using a coherent and comprehensible system of signs (e.g., a configural graphic) that will allow the operators to directly 'see' and learn about the actual states of the plant relative to the intended states.

Reprise

One of the clear implications of Peirce's triadic semiotics and abduction is that context matters. Thus, it may be valuable to consider the larger context of Peirce's work on abduction and semiotics. Louis Menand[31] provides this context in his book *The Metaphysical Club*. He describes the common attitude that shaped the work of Peirce and his fellow pragmatists (Holmes, James, and Dewey):

> what these four thinkers had in common was not a group of ideas, but a single idea—an idea about ideas. They all believed that ideas are not "out there" waiting to be discovered, but are tools—like forks and knives and microchips—that people devise to cope with the world in which they find themselves. They believed that ideas are produced not by individuals, but by groups of individuals—that ideas are social. They believed that ideas do not develop according to some inner logic of their own, but are entirely dependent, like germs, on their human carriers and the environment. And they believed that since ideas are provisional responses to particular and unreproducible circumstances, their survival depends not on their immutability but on their adaptability.[32]

As we continue the exploration of human decision making and problem solving, the *discoverer* versus *inventor* distinction discussed in Chapter 2 should become readily apparent. On the one hand,

DOUBT IS AN UNEASY AND DISSATISFIED STATE FROM WHICH WE STRUGGLE TO FREE OURSELVES AND PASS INTO THE STATE OF BELIEF; WHILE THE LATTER IS A CALM AND SATISFACTORY STATE WHICH WE DO NOT WISH TO AVOID, OR TO CHANGE TO A BELIEF IN ANYTHING ELSE.

THE ESSENCE OF BELIEF IS THE ESTABLISHMENT OF A HABIT; AND DIFFERENT BELIEFS ARE DISTINGUISHED BY THE DIFFERENT MODELS OF ACTION TO WHICH THEY GIVE RISE.

Charles Sanders Peirce[33]

work by people such as Amos Tversky and Danny Kahneman[34] reflect the discover attitude that attempts to measure performance against fixed, extrinsic standards (e.g., logical and economic prescriptions for optimal choice). On the other hand, work by people such as Peter Todd and Gerd Gigerenzer[35] reflect the inventor attitude that attempts to measure performance against intrinsic, situated standards associated with pragmatic ends. These reflect fundamental metaphysical choices that will not be resolved empirically. This difference is not in the phenomena—but in the choice of where to stand as an observer.

Again, it is not necessary to reject the discoverer perspective. However, it is important to legitimize the inventor perspective. Both perspectives offer insights into human experience. Our goal is to integrate these two perspectives and to build a narrative about human experience around the invariants that are independent of perspective.

Notes

1. Wason, P.C. (1968). Reasoning about a rule. *Quarterly Journal of Experimental Psychology*, 20, 273–281.
   Wason, P.C. (1969). Regression in reasoning? *British Journal of Psychology*, 60, 471–480.
2. Cheng, P.W., & Holyoak, K.J. (1985). Pragmatic reasoning schemas. *Cognitive Psychology*, 17, 391–416.

   Cosmides, L. (1989). The logic of social exchange: Has natural selection shaped how humans reason? Studies with the Wason selection task. *Cognition*, 31, 187–276.

   Cosmides, L., & Tooby, J. (1992). Cognitive adaptations for social exchange. In J. Barkow, L. Cosmides, & J. Tooby (Eds.). *The adapted mind: Evolutionary psychology and the generation of culture* (pp. 162–228). New York: Oxford University Press.

3. Cosmides, L., & Tooby, J. (1997). Evolutionary psychology a primer. Online Publication. Center for Evolutionary Psychology, University of California, Santa Barbara. www.psych.ucsb.edu/research/cep/primer.html
4. Wason, P.C. (1960). On the failure to eliminate hypotheses in a conceptual task. *Quarterly Journal of Experimental Psychology*, 12, 129–140.

5. Popper (1959), p. 4.

6. Popper, K.R. (1959). *The logic of scientific discovery*. New York: Basic Books.

7. Kahneman, D., Slovic, P., & Tversky, A. (Eds.). (1982). *Judgments under uncertainty: Heuristics and biases*. Cambridge: Cambridge University Press.

8. Nickerson, R.S. (1996). Hempel's paradox and Wason's selection task: Logical and psychological puzzles of confirmation. *Thinking and Reasoning*, 2(1), 1–31.

9. Hempel, C.G. (1945). Studies in the logic of confirmation (I). *Mind*, 54(213), 1–26.

10. Nickerson (1996), p. 2.

11. Poundstone, W. (1990). *Labyrinths of reason*. New York: Doubleday.

12. FYI, here is a list of female senators in 1995: Dianna Feinstein (D), Barbara Boxer (D), Carol Moseley-Braun (D), Nancy Landon Kassenbaum (R), Olympia Snowe (R), Barbara Mikulski (D), Patty Murray (D), Kay Bailey Hutchison (R).

13. Einhorn, H.J., & Hogarth, R.M. (1978). Confidence in judgments: Persistence of the illusion of validity. *Psychological Review*, 85(5), 395–416.

14. Piaget, J. (1973). *The child and reality* (trans. Arnold Rosin). New York: Grossman Publishers.

15. Dewey, J. (1991). *How we think*. Amherst, NY: Prometheus Books. (p. 79).

16. Dewey (1991), p. 41.

17. Uexküll, J. (1957). A stroll through the worlds of animals and men: A picture book of invisible worlds. In C.H. Schiller (Ed.). *Instinctive behavior: The development of a modern concept* (pp. 5–80). New York: International Universities Press, Inc.

18. Suchman, L.A. (1987). *Plans and situated actions: The problem of human-machine communication*. Cambridge: Cambridge University Press.

    Hutchins, E. (1995). *Cognition in the wild*. Cambridge, MA: MIT Press.

19. Bateson, G. (1972). *Steps to an ecology of mind*. San Francisco: Chandler.

20. Pink, D.H. (2009). *Drive: The surprising truth about what motivates us*. New York: Riverhead Books.

21. Clark, A. (1997). *Being there: Putting brain, body, and world together again*. Cambridge, MA: MIT books.

22. Cosmides, & Tooby (1997).

23. Miller, D. (Ed.). (1985). *Popper selections*. Princeton, NJ: Princeton University Press. (p. 10).

24. Taleb, N.N. (2010). *The black swan: The impact of the highly improbable*. New York: Random House.

25. Ross, L. (1977). The intuitive psychologist and his shortcomings: Distortions in the attribution process. In L. Berkowitz (Ed.). *Advances in experimental social psychology*. Vol. 10. New York: Academic Press.

26. Ericsson, K.A., & Charness, N. (1994). Expert performance: Its structure and acquisition. *American Psychologist*, 49(8), 725–747.

27. Percy, W. (1991). *Signposts in a strange land*. New York: Farrar, Straus. (pp. 275–276).

28. Norman, D.A., & Draper, S.W. (Eds.). (1986). *User centered system design: New perspectives on human-computer interaction*. Hillsdale, NJ: Erlbaum.

    Shneiderman, B. (1992). *Designing the user interface: Strategies for effective human-computer interaction*. Reading, MA: Addison-Wesley.

29. Vicente, K.J. (1999). *Cognitive work analysis: Toward safe, productive, and healthy computer-based work*. Mahwah, NJ: Erlbaum.

30. Bennett, K.B., & Flach, J.M. (2011). *Display and interface design: Subtle science, exact art*. Boca Raton, FL: CRC Press.

31. Menand, L. (2001). *The metaphysical club*. New York: Ferrar, Sraus, and Giroux.

32. Menand (2001), pp. xi–xii.

33. Peirce, C.S. (1877). The fixation of belief. *Popular Science Monthly*, 12, 1–15.

34. Kahneman, Slovic, & Tversky (Eds.). (1982).

35. Todd, P.M., Gigerenzer, G., & the ABC Research Group. (2012). *Ecological rationality: Intelligence in the world*. New York: Oxford University Press (on page 87).

6

THINKING IN CIRCLES

As intellectual beings, we presume the existence of meaning, and its absence is an anomaly. . . . All knowledge, all science, thus aims to grasp the meaning of objects and events, and this process always consists in taking them out of their apparent brute isolation as events, and finding them to be parts of some larger whole suggested by them, which, in turn, accounts for, explains, interprets them; i.e., renders them significant.[1]

Minds make motions, and they must make them fast—before the predator catches you, or before your prey gets away from you. Minds are not disembodied logical reasoning devices.[2]

As the question of What Matters is explored, the system image that is beginning to form is of a triadic semiotic system, where what matters is an emergent property of the closed-loop coupling between mind (awareness) and matter (ecology). Peirce has characterized this coupling in terms of an abduction logic in which hypotheses (or guesses) based on past experiences are tested pragmatically using the concrete feedback from actions guided by those hypotheses. Piaget described the triadic semiotic in terms of the dynamics of assimilation (i.e., generalizing based on schemas constructed from previous experience) and accommodation (i.e., adapting based on feedback).

In essence, Peirce and Piaget are describing a process of learning from mistakes. Thus, let's begin this chapter by considering a particularly interesting and important learning challenge—learning to walk. The point of the examples in this chapter is to begin to illustrate the implications of a closed-loop coupling between Mind and Matter relative to What Matters. In particular, we want to illustrate how explanations that seem plausible based on the logic of simple causality may prove inadequate for understanding the self-organizing dynamics of circular systems.

Classically, human motor development has been modeled as a progression from automatic, reflexive responses to stimuli toward more selective, voluntary responses. In the case of walking, two reflexes were particularly interesting: the stepping reflex and the kicking reflex.

The stepping reflex is a tendency for an infant who is being suspended vertically (e.g., being supported at her armpits) to move her legs in an alternating fashion similar to that of adult "stepping" or walking behavior. Alternatively, the kicking reflex is a tendency for an infant who is lying on her back to "kick" her legs in an alternating fashion.

In terms of the relative patterns of the two legs, the stepping and kicking reflexes appear very similar. However, developmental psychologists had identified these as distinctive reflexes due to their developmental history.[3] The stepping reflex is present at birth, but tends to completely disappear a few weeks after delivery and then reappears at about 10 to 12 months, just prior to the time that most infants take their first steps. That is, if you suspend a 3-month-old infant from its armpits, it is likely that the legs will simply hang down with no evidence of stepping. The kicking reflex, on the other hand, does not disappear but persists over this same period of development.

Because of the different development histories, the "stepping" and "kicking" behaviors were attributed to distinct reflexes (i.e., distinct internal programs). It was thought that the disappearance of the stepping reflex resulted from selective internal inhibition of that reflex. This was thought to be a precursor for voluntary control. That is, it was hypothesized that the first step in gaining control over the reflex was to be able to turn it off (i.e., inhibit it). This first step then progressed to an ability for voluntary control in which the reflex could be turned on and off in a controlled fashion—thus, the basis for voluntary walking.

When Ester Thelen[4] began to investigate the development of walking, she started by comparing the EMG signals associated with the two distinct reflexes (i.e., stepping vs. kicking). EMG measures the electrical signals that are assumed to be associated with communications between the "brain" and the muscles. The expectation was that since the internal control mechanisms for these two reflexes were distinct, the patterns of EMG ought to be distinct. However, the results of these measurements showed that the EMG patterns were as similar, if not more similar, as the movement patterns. As she continued to investigate this phenomenon she noted several interesting patterns that suggested the classical explanation might be wrong.

Thelen observed that there was a correlation between the length of the period between the disappearance and reappearance of the stepping reflex and weight gain. The periods tended to be longer for infants who gained more weight and shorter for infants who gained less weight. She also noticed that during the inhibition period the stepping behavior would reappear when the infants were suspended in water. Finally, she noticed that when infants in the inhibition period were suspended on a moving treadmill, many of them would step in an alternating pattern consistent with

A) REFLEX STEPPING PHASE

B) INHIBITORY OR STATIC PHASE

C) TRANSITION PHASE, WITH ACTIVITIES SUCH AS STOMPING OF FOOT, REAPPEARANCES OF STEPPING MOVEMENTS

D) DELIBERATE STEPPING PHASE WIYH ERECT POSITION

E) INDEPENDENT STEPPING PHASE, FOLLOWED BY F) HEEL-TOEWALKING, AND FINALLY G) ADULT PATERN OF WALKING WITH SYNCHRONOUS SWINGING OF THE ARMS WITH OPPOSITE LEG

normal adult walking. In fact, she found that when she split the treadmill so that the speeds were different for the two legs, the infants' behavior adapted appropriately—resulting in a stepping pattern coordinated with the two speeds. So, the pattern of coordination seemed to emerge in some contexts earlier than it did in other contexts. Can you guess the answer to the mystery of the disappearing stepping reflex?

Thelen's hypothesis was that the disappearance of the stepping reflex is due to the fact that in the first year of life the infant's weight gain tends to outpace the development of her muscles. After a few weeks, the legs are simply too heavy to lift when the baby is suspended in a way that requires her to overcome the full force of gravity. However, when the baby is oriented in a way that reduces the impact of gravity (e.g., lying on her back or supported by the buoyancy of water), then the muscles are sufficient to drive the motion. On the treadmill, much of the energy for driving the steps comes from the treadmill motion. So, here is a very nice illustration of how context matters!

With Thelen's hypothesis, the differences associated with the stepping and kicking reflexes are explained without posing different internal mechanisms or programs (i.e., distinct reflexes). Rather, her explanation poses an interaction between internal constraints and the environmental context (e.g., the orientation to gravity) to determine the pattern of behavior (e.g., the disappearance of the stepping behavior and the persistence of the kicking behavior).

In this sense, the behaviors are emergent properties of a complex human-environment coupling. The behaviors are not completely determined by either distinct internal programs (awareness) or by environmental stimuli (ecology), but rather they emerge as a result of the coupling.

The story of the stepping reflex is important for two reasons. On the one hand, it illustrates how easy it is to invent a plausible explanation for a phenomenon in terms of hypothetical brain mechanisms (i.e., inhibition). On the other hand, it shows the need to expand our frame for explanation to include properties of the physical ecology (e.g., gravity).

Conventional View of Computation

There is a strong tendency for conventional approaches to cognition to posit centralized control mechanisms in the brain that 'direct' action in a top-down hierarchical fashion. This reflects a kind of 'clockwork' logic that fits with conventional views of causality and leads naturally to a tendency to look for the 'causes' of behavior in the centralized control agency. For example, consider Steven Pinker's explanation of why Bill gets on the bus:

> This insight, first expressed by the mathematician Alan Turing, the computer scientists Alan Newell, Herbert Simon, and Marvin Minsky, and the philosophers Hilary Putnam and Jerry Fodor, is now called the computational theory of mind. It is one of the great ideas in intellectual history, for it solves one of the puzzles that make up the 'mind-body problem': how to connect the ethereal world of meaning and intention, the stuff of our mental lives, with a physical hunk of matter like the brain. Why did Bill get on the bus? Because he wanted to visit his grandmother and knew the bus would take him there. No other answer will do. If he hated the sight of his grandmother, or if he knew the route had changed, his body would not be on that bus. For millennia this has been a paradox. Entities like "wanting to visit one's grandmother" and "knowing the bus goes to Grandma's house" are colorless, odorless, and tasteless. But at the same time they are causes of physical events, as potent as any billiard ball clacking into another.
>
> The computational theory of mind resolves the paradox. It says that beliefs and desires are information, incarnate as configurations of symbols. The symbols are the physical states of bits of matter, like chips in a computer or neurons in the brain. They symbolize things in the world because they are triggered by those things via our sense organs, and because of what they do once they are triggered. If the bits of matter that constitute a symbol are arranged to bump into the bits of matter constituting another symbol in just the right way, the symbols corresponding to one belief can give rise to new symbols corresponding to another belief logically related to it, which can give rise to symbols corresponding to other beliefs, and so on. Eventually the bits of matter constituting a symbol bump into bits of matter connected to the muscles, and behavior happens. The computational theory of mind thus allows us to keep beliefs and desires in our explanations of behavior while planting them squarely in the physical universe. It allows meaning to cause and be caused.[5]

Although an explicit goal of Pinker's book is to avoid the homunculus problem by linking computational theories of minds with the dynamics of natural selection, when I read this passage I can't

help but see the image of a little general (homunculus) in the control room of the brain sending down commands to the body: 'go to grandmother's house.'

While there are hints of the circularity, overall the emphasis seems to be on how the bits of matter constituting the symbols magically bump into bits of matter connected to muscles to cause behavior. The image seems to be of a centralized control system sending instructions to the body, like a puppeteer pulling the strings on a puppet. The image is of a computer program specifying the actions of a clockwork machine. Within this image 'meaning' is considered to be part of 'the ethereal world.'

For us, this is a very unsatisfying solution to the mind-body problem. There is a clear implication here of two separate realities—the physical reality of the body and the ethereal reality of 'mind and intention.' There are the vestiges of a dyadic semiotic model—with reference to symbols—and there is a clear assumption of a linear, billiard ball type of causality.

Thelen's explanation for the development of walking, however, suggests a different style of control. Rather than a hierarchical control system, one gets the impression of a more distributed type of control that has become associated with complex dynamical systems. For example, recent approaches to the design of walking machines have adopted a 'passive' type control. That is, in contrast to earlier attempts that were based on 'programs' that specified the coordination between the limbs (e.g., gait transitions), the new solutions let the coordination emerge as the result of the physics of the limbs and joints.

It turns out, there is no need to micro-manage the coordination—even changes from one gait to another can be produced as a result of interactions at the periphery reflecting pendulum dynamics—there is no need for an internal program.

Whenever we observe structured behaviors, it is tempting to assume that there is some 'program' or 'plan' to account for this structure. For example, in Pinker's example of Bill going to see his grandmother, the behavior is explained as being 'caused' by internal instructions. This tends to suggest an internal homunculus pulling the strings of the body (i.e., causing actions), and it is difficult to imagine any other way to explain the behavior.

However, Kugler and Turvey[6] (1987) provide an alternative metaphor in which structured behavior emerges without the benefit of an internal plan or program. The metaphor that Kugler and

Turvey used is the nest-building behavior of a population of social insects. These insects, such as African flying termites, cooperate to build elaborate nests that in proportion to the size of the insects are much larger than even the tallest of human-made architectures. The problem to be explained is how does this cooperation come about? From an information processing perspective, the question might be framed as "where is the plan?" and "how is the plan communicated among the many insects?"

Let's begin with Kugler and Turvey's description of the phenomenon:

> The nest-building behavior consists of a number of qualitatively distinct phases of construction. In the first phase, building materials are carried into the site and deposited randomly. This phase comes to an end with the emergence of preferred sites that number far fewer than the number of original deposits. The second phase is associated with the material build-up of the preferred deposit sites until they take on the shape of pillars. When the pillars achieve a certain size and are separated by a critical distance, a third phase of construction emerges. The third phase is characterized by the mutual "curvature" of two neighboring pillars toward a "virtual midpoint." This phase is complete when the two pillars meet at the virtual midpoint, forming an arch. A final phase is marked by the completion of a dome that extends from the tops of the arches. The completion of the dome marks the end of the building cycle. The cycle can be repeated on the top of the dome beginning with the random deposit phase.[7]

Kugler and Turvey were able to account for the nest-building behavior without reference to any "internal plans" or "blueprints" for the nests. Rather, in their model, the nests will emerge as the result of interactions between two simple processes, one a simple mechanism within individual insects and the other, the physical processes associated with the dispersion of an odor. The specific odor of interest is the scent of a pheromone contained in the building material deposited by the insects.

The mechanism within an individual insect can be summed up with two simple rules: when ready to deposit material 1) move in the direction of the strongest pheromone scent and 2) deposit where the smell is strongest (this is similar to the behavior of dogs who tend to sniff the scent of other dogs' deposits and who have a preference for making their marks on top of the deposits from previous dogs).

How do the nests "emerge" from the interactions between the insects and the pheromone odor? In the first phase, the insects fly around ingesting the raw ingredients for the building material. At some point, the animal becomes sated and the first rule kicks in. If the animal is not within range of the pheromone scent, then a deposit is made at whatever random position the insect currently occupies. However, if the animal is in range of the pheromone scent, then it tracks that scent until it peaks, and then according to the second rule deposits the material at that peak in the pheromone field, which would typically be on top of a previous "fresh" deposit.

If there are only a few insects relative to the size of the space that they occupy, then the probability that an insect will be in range of the pheromone odor from a fresh deposit when it gets the urge to make a deposit is very small. The result is a random scattering of deposits.

However, as the density of insects increases, the probability that the insect will be within range of the odor of a previous fresh deposit increases. Under these conditions multiple deposits at the same site become more probable. With each new deposit at a site the strength of the pheromone field for that site will increase (the deposit site grows and stays fresh).

This is an example of positive feedback. With each new deposit, the probability of further deposits increases in an iterative fashion. The result of this positive feedback is that certain sites

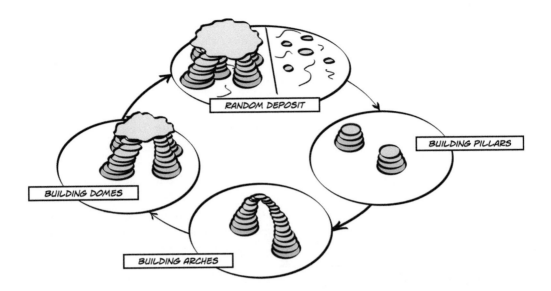

emerge as "strong attractors" in the behavioral field. At this point, the system is in the second phase described by Kugler and Turvey (1987), the pillar-building phase.

As the pillars grow, the pheromone fields associated with each pillar strengthen and expand. As a result of this expansion, the fields of pillars that are close together begin to interact. That is, the pheromone gradient between the pillars becomes stronger than the gradient on the outsides of near pillars. This is because the odors from the two pillars combine within the regions between the pillars. The result of this interaction causes a bias in the growth of pillars. It becomes more probable that insects will be captured by the pheromone fields between the pillars than the fields outside this region. This bias leads to pillars that tend to grow toward each other. These interactions drive the third phase described by Kugler and Turvey (1987), the arch-building phase.

If you follow the logic of Kugler and Turvey's model, then you should be able to anticipate the transition to the dome-building phase. When two pillars meet to form an arch, the peak in the pheromone fields will now be at the point of the freshest deposits—where the pillars meet. These points become the new attractors. These attractors may interact with other attractors (nearby pillars and or arches), and this leads to the dome-building phase—the insects are captured by the fields between interacting attractors, and the result is that deposits are added in a way that creates connections between them.

The end result of the process described by Kugler and Turvey will be a nest with multiple levels supported by arched pillars. Note that all nests constructed as a result of this process will be similar in their general form, but they will also be distinctive—in that no two nests would be likely to have all their pillars in exactly the same relative positions. This is because the placement of the pillars originates from an essentially random initial placement of deposits, and the emergence of attractors in this field depends on the essentially random motion of the insects as they forage for raw materials. It is also important to note that the shape of the nests depends both on the simple habits of the insects (their minds) and on the dispersion properties of the pheromone (the matter), but the shape (what matters) is determined by neither. This is what we mean when we say that the shape emerges or that it is an emergent property of the system.

In terms of the dependence of the nests on the insects' habits and the dispersion properties of the pheromone, it is interesting to speculate on the impact of variables that might affect these— variables that might be considered include the insects' diet (which might affect their capability for locomotion, the frequency of deposits, as well as the intensity of the pheromone produced) and the weather (wet or dry, the presence of prevailing winds, etc.).

For example, in the presence of a prevailing wind, it might be reasonable to suspect that the pillars would tend to lean in the direction of the prevailing wind, since the pheromone odor would be expected to be more intense on the downwind side of a fresh deposit. The result of this might be nests that are aerodynamically adapted to the wind conditions.

From an information processing perspective, it would be very tempting to attribute this adaptation to specialized knowledge (e.g., implicit aerodynamic models) built into the internal programs of the insects. Kugler and Turvey's model, however, requires no specialized knowledge within the insects to account for this adaptation. What do you think might be the result of a change (increase or decrease) in the intensity of the pheromone concentration in the building materials on the shape of the nests produced according to the process described by Kugler and Turvey?

Kugler and Turvey (1987) describe the nest-building 'system' as a complex system. This simply means that important aspects of the behavior of this system (i.e., the shape of the nests) cannot be explained based on an independent analysis of the "parts" of the system (insects and/or environment). These behaviors depend in an important way on interactions or couplings among the components. In other words, these behaviors are emergent properties of the whole system.

The process described by Kugler and Turvey is typically referred to as self-organization. This is just yet another way of saying that the organization, order, or patterns in the behavior are not imposed by some extrinsic agent (like a program). Rather, these patterns emerge as an intrinsic property of interactions among the components.

Note that even though a program might be considered internal (i.e., stored somewhere in the head), it is still an extrinsic agent relative to the patterns of behavior that it specifies. That is, there is always an implied programmer. Also, note that there are simple programs in the heads of the insects in the Kugler and Turvey model. However, these programs do not specify the patterns of behavior at the level of the shapes of the nests.

In contrasting the information processing framework with the complex systems framework, the issue is not whether or not there are internal constraints (i.e., reflexes, rules, expectations, e.g., a desire to see your grandmother). The key to the debate is the degree of specificity of those programs.

From the dynamical systems perspective, the problem with classical information processing approaches based on a computer metaphor is that they typically try to fully specify patterns of behavior in terms of internal programs or computations with little or no consideration for the contributions of environmental factors to shaping the patterns. Of course, just the opposite was true for the behaviorist perspective that only considered environmental factors and tended to minimize the potential impact of internal constraints. Neither the information processing nor behaviorist perspectives recognized the closed-loop coupling between mind and matter and the extent to which emergent properties depend on the dynamics of this coupling.

Again, both the classical computational view of mind and the behaviorist perspective that it replaced tended to be searching for explanations that fit a billiard ball model of causal relations as illustrated in the earlier passage from Pinker. In the termite nest example, causation is circular; that is, the actions of the insects shape the pheromone field, while simultaneously that field is shaping the actions of the insects. The actions and the pheromone field are both simultaneously cause and effect. There is no sense in which either is logically or causally prior to the other. This is a self-organizing system.

The Cybernetic Hypothesis

> Then Rosenblueth let loose a radical idea he and his colleagues were just begin-
> ning to flesh out in Cambridge. In their work on problems of communication and
> automatic control, Rosenblueth said, they had identified a new realm of orderly
> processes observable in nature and the human world. These new communication
> processes were not governed by the traditional logic of linear, cause-and-effect rela-
> tions that had driven the scientific method since its inception. They were governed
> by a new logical principle Rosenblueth called "circular causality"—after the circu-
> itous feedback loops Wiener and Bigelow had tapped and harnessed in their device
> for predicting the future positions of fast-flying airplanes.
>
> The new causality was one in which living things and machines alike behaved with
> purpose. It was a sizeable leap, from machines that took aim at targets to creatures
> and machines with aims of their own, and the first formulation in scientific terms of
> the strange circular logic of feedback that lay at the root of all intelligent behavior.[8]

The quote from Conway and Siegleman describes a presentation by Arturo Rosenblueth at a Macy Conference in May 1942. This small conference was attended by neuroscientists such as Warren McCulloch and Rafael Lorente de No and anthropologists Gregory Bateson and Margaret Mead. The series of Macy conferences that followed are generally regarded as some of the first steps (along with Chomsky's work in linguistics mentioned in the previous chapter) in the cognitive revolution to replace behaviorism as a dominant paradigm for thinking about human behavior.

A significant event in the evolution of the cognitive paradigm was the publication of Miller, Galanter, and Pribram's book, *Plans and the Structure of Behavior*,[9] in 1960. In this book, they intro-duced the Cybernetic Hypothesis to psychology—"namely, that the fundamental building block of the nervous system is the feedback loop" (p. 26–27). The Cybernetic Hypothesis has had a huge impact on our images of information processing.

The Cybernetic Hypothesis provided an alternative framework for addressing the nature of the coupling between stimulus and response that seemed to be trivialized in the dominant Behaviorist view—where responses were reflexive reactions to stimuli (i.e., the billiard ball model of causality). It provided a format to address the intimate coupling identified earlier by Dewey (1896), who saw stimulus and response as components of a coordinative system:

> The stimulus is that phase of the forming coordination which represents the conditions which have to be met in bringing it to a successful issue; the response is that phase of one and the same forming coordination which gives the key to meeting these conditions, which serves as instrument in effecting the successful coordination. They are therefore strictly correlative and contemporaneous.[10]

Most importantly, the Cybernetic Hypothesis provided a framework for addressing the issue of intent or purpose that had been ignored by Behaviorists. As Miller et al. noted, terms like intent are critical to understanding "what makes . . . actions meaningful" (p. 59). It was clear, from the start of the cognitive revolution, that understanding the dynamics of closed-loop systems would be critical to a science of meaning processing.

Thus, a result of the Cybernetic Hypothesis was that feedback loops are now included as critical components in our image of a cognitive system. Despite the impact of the Cybernetic Hypothesis on the images, however, the logic of circular causality has generally not been fully appreciated by cognitive science—where billiard ball models of causality still dominate (both in theory and in the experimental methods).

In fact, cognitive science methods tend to be designed to break the loops between perception and action. Cognitive science tends to be organized around open-loop components within the information processing system. Even today, it is quite rare to find any research that embraces the feedback loop as the fundamental unit of analysis. In fact, it is quite rare to find any evidence in academic programs in social sciences of any serious effort to teach or learn about the dynamics of closed-loop systems.

The goal for the next few chapters is to introduce the logic of feedback systems as an important model for understanding human experience. We will consider the problem of control in relation to simple servomechanisms. We will consider the problem of observation in relation to the problem of detecting signals in noise, and we will link these together in the context of the problem of adaptive control, where control theory merges into dynamical systems and complexity theory.

The Control Problem

Figure 6.1 illustrates how the components of a control system map onto an abduction logic and triadic semiotic. The Satisfying component of the system is identified as the Pilot. It is the source for intention (goals) and values. This represents the constraints on what the system chooses to do or should choose to do in order to thrive (e.g., the criteria for a safe landing).

The Affording component of the system is identified as the Plant or the process being controlled. This represents the constraint on what the system can do (e.g., performance envelopes reflecting biological and physical constraints on the body or vehicle being controlled).

The Specifying component of the system provides the interface between the Pilot and the Plant that provides the means for coupling perception (e.g., feedback from instruments and optical flow) and action (e.g., manipulation of body or, in an aircraft the throttle, stick, and pedals). It

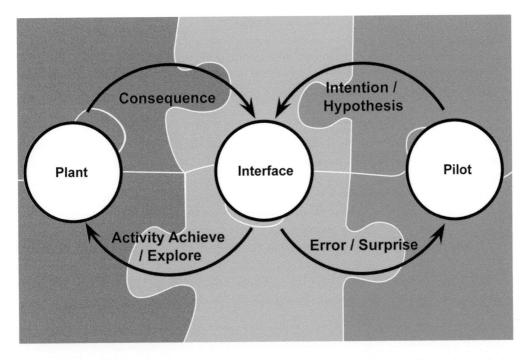

Figure 6.1 Illustrates the parallels between an abduction engine and a feedback control system. If designed properly, this system will tend to reduce errors, or in other words will pursue the intentions (i.e., goals).

serves both as the display or comparator (relating the consequences to the intentions—error) and the control effector (relating intentions of the pilot to actions of the plant—control).

The central feature of any control system is the comparator. This is where the current state of the process is fed back and compared with a goal state. Typically, this comparison involves the subtraction of the current state from the goal state to yield an error signal. This subtraction is the signature of a negative feedback system.

If designed properly, negative feedback control systems will generally act to reduce the error. That is, the control actions will be contingent on the error, such that they will counteract or reduce the current error. Or in other words, the negative feedback system will pursue the goal. Thus, the negative feedback system, or servomechanism, gave social scientists a framework for thinking about purposive behavior.

In the social sciences, there is a tendency to treat 'feedback' as the explanation for purposive or goal-directed behavior. But note that in the preceding paragraph there was an important qualification to the claim that negative feedback systems will reduce error or pursue a goal—that is: 'if designed properly.'

What does it mean for a servomechanism to be 'designed properly'? This is the central issue for the field of Control Theory—to study the conditions that determine the stability and efficiency of alternative solutions to the control problem.

A key to appreciating coordination within closed-loop systems, or to appreciating the dynamics of circles, is to understand that feedback does not guarantee that error will be reduced or that goals will be followed. An improperly designed servomechanism will not necessarily converge on the goal. For example, as Wiener[11] (1948/1961) wrote:

> under certain conditions of delay, etc. feedback that is too brusque will make the rudder overshoot, and will be followed by a feedback in the other direction, which makes the rudder overshoot still more, until the steering mechanism goes into a wild oscillation or hunting, and breaks down completely.[12]

In fact, the unstable behavior of the control loops that Wiener and Bigelow observed motivated the interactions with Rosenblueth (neuroscience). Wiener (1948/1961) writes:

> However, an excessive feedback is likely to be as serious a handicap to organized activity as a defective feedback. In view of this possibility, Mr. Bigelow and myself approached Dr. Rosenblueth with a very specific question. Is there any pathological condition in which the patient, in trying to perform some voluntary act like picking up a pencil, over-shoots the mark, and goes into an uncontrollable oscillation? Dr. Rosenblueth immediately answered us that there is such a well-known condition, that it is called purpose tremor, and that it is often associated with injury to the cerebellum.

Wiener continues:

> We thus found a most significant confirmation of our hypothesis concerning the nature of at least some voluntary activity. It will be noted that our point of view considerably transcended that current among neurophysiologists. The central nervous system no longer appears as a self-contained organ, receiving inputs from the senses and discharging into the muscles. On the contrary, some of its most characteristic activities are explicable only as circular processes, emerging from the nervous system into the muscles, and re-entering the nervous system through the sense organs, whether they be proprioceptors or organs of the special senses. This seemed to us to mark a new step in the study of that part of neurophysiology which concerns not solely the elementary processes of nerves and synapses but the performance of the nervous system as an integrated whole.[13]

Although feedback is typically assumed as an important attribute of cognitive systems, it is rare to find any discussions in this literature about the factors that bound the stability of feedback control systems. There tends to be an implicit assumption that 'stability' is not a problem for cognitive systems. It is a bit ironic that social scientists look to the servomechanism as an explanation for stable goal-directed behaviors—when a critical link for connecting early work on control mechanisms to neuroscience was the similarity between breakdowns in both systems. Again, social science programs typically offer NO training or exposure to the analytical tools for dealing with stability in closed-loop systems. The next chapter will provide a brief introduction to stability to illustrate the problem of reasoning about the behavior of a circular system with the billiard ball logic of causality.

Notes

1. Dewey, J. (1991). *How we think*. Amherst, NY: Prometheus Books. (pp. 117–118, emphasis added).
2. Clark, A. (1997). *Being there: Putting brain, body, and world together again*. Cambridge, MA: MIT Press. (p. 1).
3. McGraw, M.B. (1945). *The neuromuscular maturation of the human infant*. New York: Columbia University Press.
4. Thelen, E., & Smith, L.B. (1994). *A dynamic systems approach to the development of cognition and action*. Cambridge, MA: MIT Press.
5. Pinker, S. (1997). *How the mind works*. New York: W.W. Norton. (p. 25).
6. Kugler, P.N., & Turvey, M.T. (1987). *Information, natural law, and the self-assembly of rhythmic movement*. Hillsdale, NJ: Erlbaum.
7. Kugler & Turvey (1987), p. 67.
8. Conway, F., & Siegelman, J. (2005). Dark hero of the information age. In *Search of Norbert Wiener the father of cybernetics* (pp. 132–133). New York: Basic Books.
9. Miller, G.A., Galanter, E., & Pribram, K.H. (1960). *Plans and the structure of behavior*. New York: Henry Holt & Company.
10. Dewey, J. (1986). The reflex arc concept in psychology. *Psychological Review*, 3, 359–370. (p. 368).
11. Wiener, N. (1948/1961). *Cybernetics: or control and communication in the animal and the machine*. Cambridge, MA: MIT Press.
12. Wiener (1948/1961), p. 7.
13. Wiener (1948/1961), p. 8.

7

CONTROLLING

The cartoon to open this chapter shows different kinds of 'walking machines,' where each machine is a combination of a child and some type of 'technology' (e.g., ice skates, high heels, etc.). It should not be surprising to anyone that to achieve stability with each of the different technologies, the child will have to use a different type of coordination pattern. In essence, for each whole system to function as a stable form of locomotion, the child will have to adapt in a different way. In other words, the child will need to become a different type of mechanism (i.e., in control theoretic language the child will have a different 'transfer function' for each context). The goal for this chapter is to demonstrate this intuition using formalities associated with control theory.

The examples used in this chapter are of very simple control systems, but they may be difficult for most social scientists who might be unfamiliar with the analytic language of control theory. This is unfortunate. Will this technical material enhance the pedagogy or will it be an obstacle? For some this may be a hill too hard to climb. However, for others this may be the nudge they need to begin exploring control theory more deeply.

Anyone who is seriously interested in the behavior of dynamical, closed-loop systems can benefit from some exposure to formal control theory. Exposure to the formal theory will help you to gauge both the value and the limitations of control metaphors for providing insights into human experience.

Stability Dynamics: A Simple Example

Figure 7.1 shows a relatively simple example of a negative feedback system consisting of a time delay, gain, and integrator in the forward-loop. With appropriate parameters for the time delay (100 ms) and gain (1), the step response of this simple circuit will provide a good approximation to human performance in a simple positioning task (e.g., a Fitts Law task[1]). This circuit is sometimes called a velocity control system since the velocity of the approach to the target is proportional to the size of the error.

Figure 7.1 illustrates a typical response of this system to a step input (i.e., the target shifts from one value to another in a discrete step). The step response for this system would be a rounded step output that converges asymptotically on the new target position specified by the step input.

How would the step response of this system change if the gain parameter were adjusted?

Given the fixed time delay of (100 ms), what would happen if we adjusted the gain for this system to be different from 1?

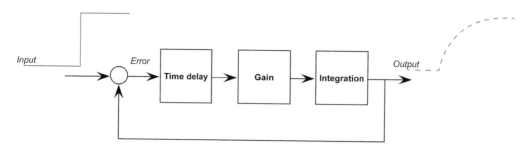

Figure 7.1 A simple feedback (time delay = .1 s, gain = 1) system with a step input. How will the Output response vary as a function of the Gain parameter? Under what conditions will the Output converge to match the input?

Is a gain of 1 the ideal gain for achieving a one-to-one match between the input and the output? Suppose we increased or decreased it by a factor of 10, what would the effect on the response of the circuit be?

1. Would the size of the output step be changed proportionally with the increase or decrease in gain?
2. Would a gain of .1 result in a response that asymptotes on a step at one-tenth the height of the input?
3. Would a gain of 10 result in a response that asymptotes on a step that is 10 times the height of the input?

You might try to imagine how the output for this system would change with a change in gain from 1 to a gain of 10 before you continue reading.

Those not familiar with closed-loop systems (almost everyone) are surprised to learn that in this closed-loop system the gain does not determine the size of the output signal, but rather it determines the speed at which the output will converge toward the input. The gain determines the sensitivity to error.

Very low gains will result in a "sluggish" response to the change in target position (i.e., the system will be slow to correct errors). The output will eventually reach the changed target position, but it will take a relatively long time to get there. As gain is increased (i.e., sensitivity to error is increased), the speed of corrections will increase.

However, at some point the higher gains will cause the response to overshoot the changed target position, before gradually converging back to the target. At still higher gains the output will oscillate around the changed target position before settling down, and at still higher gains the oscillations will actually grow over time—so that the output diverges, never settling down on the target.

The case where high gain leads to diverging oscillations is what Wiener was referring to as 'excessive' feedback, and this pattern of diverging oscillations is the type of behavior observed in some movement disorders (e.g., purposive tremor associated with cerebral palsy). It also appears occasionally in complex human-machine systems (e.g., high performance aircraft), where it is typically referred to as pilot-induced oscillations.[2]

Figure 7.2 illustrates the range of output behaviors as a function of the gain parameter. It should be clear from this illustration that feedback alone does not guarantee that the output will converge to the target. This is one of the fundamental issues of Control Theory—to identify those special conditions that lead to stable control—or more generally to study those factors that determine the boundaries of stable control. In natural closed-loop systems (with inevitable time delays) there will always be a speed-accuracy trade-off. That is, there will always be a limit to how fast a goal can be reliably approached (i.e., a limit to the gain).

In general, the range of stable gains will depend on the size of the time delay. As time delays increase, the upper bounds on gains that will produce stable control will get lower. That is, with longer time delays the system will need to be less aggressive (more conservative, more cautious, less sensitive) in responding to errors in order to avoid oscillatory or unstable responses.[3]

In designing automatic control systems, much of the attention is given to minimizing unnecessary time delays and then determining an appropriate gain for the forward loop—in order to ensure a relatively fast but stable response to errors.

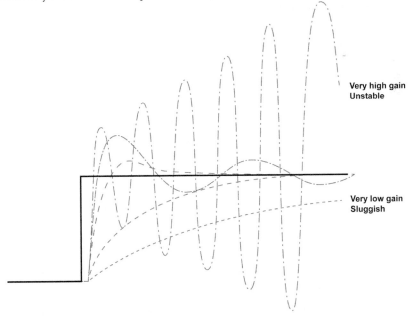

Figure 7.2 This diagram illustrates a range of outputs for the control system illustrated in Figure 7.1 as a function of the gain parameter. For very low gains, the response will 'sluggishly' converge to the target. For very high gains, the response will become unstable with oscillations that diverge from the target. At intermediate gains, the response will range from relatively rapid convergence to the target without overshoot to converging oscillations as gain is increased within this range.

In human-machine systems the gain is typically a joint function of the control interface (e.g., the gain setting for the mouse on a computer) and the human (e.g., the scaling of the manual response to observed error).

You may notice this when you use a computer system that has the mouse gain set differently than on your own computer. If the gain is higher, you may find yourself initially over-correcting and oscillating around the target before finally capturing it. If the gain is lower, then the new system will feel sluggish. However, it will typically not take you long to recalibrate to the system gain and to make adjustments so that the combined gain (Human + Plant) results in reliable target acquisition.

It is very difficult to infer the dynamics (i.e., the stability properties) of the simple system illustrated in Figure 7.1 using simple cause-effect reasoning. When I (the first author) began working with control systems in graduate school, I can remember struggling to try to trace the error around the circuit in order to predict the behavior of this system. It simply will not work!

The appropriate analytic language for describing this simple system is differential equations. See Jagacinski and Flach (2003)[4] for an introduction to the logic of simple control systems. With control systems (and differential equations) the focus shifts from operations on 'points' (isolated in time) to operations on functions (i.e., patterns over time).

The main point of this example is to illustrate that feedback does not explain stable goal-directed behavior. The ability of a negative feedback system to produce an output that follows a goal depends on it being tuned appropriately. In the case of this very simple circuit, the tuning depends on the gain relative to the time delay.

In fact, all natural closed-loop systems will exhibit a speed-accuracy trade-off. That is, there will generally be a limited range of gains that result in satisfactory stable performance. When gain is too low, the response will be sluggish (too slow). When gain is too high, the response will be unstable (overshooting and oscillating around the intended target). The discipline of Control Theory provides analytic tools to help designers choose the right gain to achieve robust solutions to control problems (e.g., in the design of autopilots).

The other point to consider is whether there is any way to infer the dynamics of stability using a classical billiard ball model of causality. Again, you can try chasing the error signal around the circle to see if you can discover the actual dynamics of this simple system. However, it is unlikely that this will lead to a satisfying solution.

The Frequency Domain

In analyzing the stability of closed-loop systems, engineers find it particularly useful to examine the open-loop frequency response. The open loop response is the combined response of the elements in the forward loop (that is, from the error as input to the output). For linear systems, the combined response of the elements to a sine wave at a specific frequency will be a sine wave at that same frequency. However, depending on the nature of the elements, the sine wave can be altered in terms of amplitude and phase.

The open-loop frequency response of the system in Figure 7.1 for three different sine waves is illustrated in Figure 7.3: at the lower frequency (.1 radians/s) the output sine was amplified; at the intermediate frequency (1 radian/s) the output sine wave was equal in amplitude to the input sine wave; and at the higher frequency (10 radians/s) the output sine wave was attenuated. Note that all three sine waves are also shifted in phase.

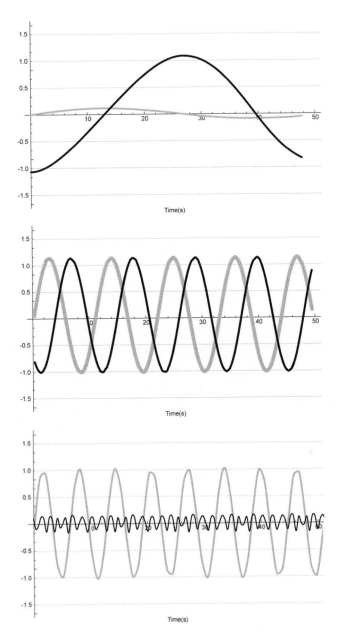

Figure 7.3 (top/middle/bottom) The open-loop sinusoidal response for the system in Figure 7.1 at three different frequencies. The input signal is in grey and the output signal is in black.

Figure 7.4 illustrates the open-loop gain (or amplitude response) and the open-loop phase response as a function of log frequency using a format known as a Bode diagram. The horizontal axis is the frequency of the input sinusoid in radians/s.

The top function shows the amplitude ratio (in db) between the input and the output. At the point where the gain function crosses the horizontal axis (at 0 db), the amplitude or gain ratio is 1 (i.e.,

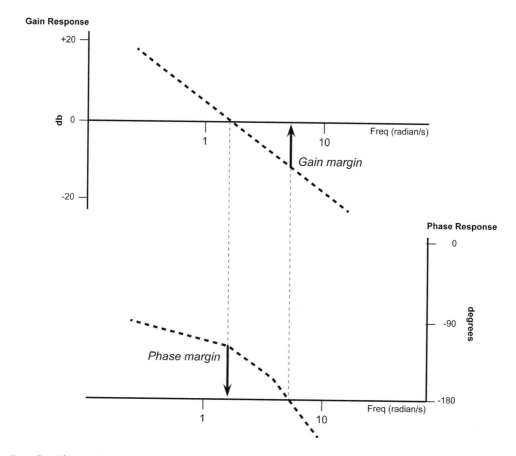

Figure 7.4 The open-loop frequency response for the system illustrated in Figure 7.1. The Bode format shows Amplitude ratio (gain) and Phase Shift as a function of input frequency.

the output sine wave will be at the same amplitude as the input sine wave). This point is referred to as the crossover frequency. For frequencies below the crossover frequency the gain ratio will be greater than 1 (the output sine wave will be amplified relative to the input sine wave in the open-loop response—will be tracked well in the closed-loop response); and for frequencies above the crossover frequency the gain ratio will be less than 1 (the output sine wave will be attenuated relative to the input sine wave in the open-loop response—will be filtered in the closed-loop response).

For the closed-loop system, the crossover frequency reflects the bandwidth. That is, for those frequencies below the crossover frequency, the output of the closed-loop system will follow the inputs very closely (i.e., these signals will be tracked well) due to the high open-loop gains. For those frequencies above the crossover frequency, the closed-loop system will not follow the inputs well (i.e., these signals will be filtered) due to the low open-loop gains.

Thus, the system illustrated in Figure 7.1 is typically referred to as a low-pass filter. This system will follow or 'pass' the low-input frequencies so that they appear in the output (i.e., are tracked well) and will tend to attenuate or filter out the higher input frequencies that will not appear in the output (will not be tracked well).

The open-loop response in Figure 7.4 provides useful information about the stability limits of the closed-loop system in Figure 7.1. For the closed-loop system response to be stable, the open-loop gain MUST pass through zero db before the phase shift passes through -180 degrees. Otherwise, the system will exhibit the unstable oscillations that are similar to the motor ataxias that stimulated the collaboration between Wiener and Rosenblueth.

Thus, typical indexes of stability are the gain margin (i.e., how far below 0 db the gain response is when the phase response crosses -180 degrees) and the phase margin (i.e., how far above -180 degrees the phase response is when the gain crosses through 0 db). A well-designed control system will have an open-loop response with positive gain and phase margins.

The Crossover Model: An Empirical Example

Research by McRuer and his colleagues and others[5] to model the human pilot provides an empirical example to illustrate a control theoretic framework for evaluating human performance and human machine systems.

Figures 7.5, 7.6, and 7.7 illustrate the logic and results of McRuer and Jex's research using a simple compensatory tracking task, where the task of the operator was to use a joystick to keep a cursor on a center mark on a CRT display. The task required that the operator 'compensate' for a disturbance signal (composed of a sum of sinusoids) that would move the cursor off the mark.

Figure 7.5 illustrates the experimental manipulations. In this experiment, the independent variable was the plant (i.e., simulated vehicle or process) dynamics; the dependent variables were the human control action and the plant response; and the 'stimulus' was a quasi-random disturbance (i.e., sum of sine waves) that the human needed to compensate for in order to keep the cursor centered in the display (i.e., to stay on course or minimize deviations from the center mark).

This arrangement allowed assessment of the transfer function of the human, as the relation between the displayed error and the control response; and also the transfer function of the system (human + plant) as the relation between displayed error and the plant response.

The critical experimental manipulation in the study was the plant dynamics. Three different plant dynamics were used:

1. A *position control* in which the plant was simply a proportional element or gain. In this case, a step change in control position resulted in a proportional step change in the plant position (e.g., 1-degree displacement in stick position resulted in a 10-pixel change in cursor position). This is analogous to a position-sensitive computer mouse controlling a cursor on the screen.

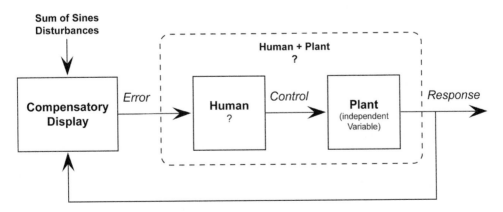

Figure 7.5 Illustrates the experimental task used in the McRuer and Jex (1967) studies of human tracking. Plant dynamics was a variable, and the goal was to assess the human transfer function.

2. A *velocity control* in which the plant was a gain and an integrator. In this case, a step change in control position resulted in a proportional change in the plant velocity (e.g., 1-degree displacement of the stick position resulted in a cursor velocity of 10 pixels per sec). Some controllers for scanning documents use this type of control, where the scan rate is proportional to displacement of the control icon.

3. An *acceleration control* in which the plant was a gain plus two integrators. In this case, a displacement in control position resulted in a proportional acceleration (e.g., 1-degree displacement of the stick position resulted in an acceleration of 10 pixels per sec^2). This is roughly analogous to the initial response of pressing the accelerator in a car. Although the acceleration of the car would not remain constant for a fixed displacement, as it would for the simple acceleration control used in these experiments.

The different plants are illustrated in Figure 7.6 using a sketch of their open-loop frequency response using the Bode plot format described in the previous section and the Laplace transform[6] of the transfer function.

The upper graph in each box plots the logarithm of the output-to-input amplitude ratio on the vertical axis vs. the sinusoidal frequency on the horizontal axis (using a log scale). This is an index of the gain—or the bandwidth of the system—showing the range of frequencies that the system is particularly sensitive to (those where gain is above 0 db). Gain above 0 db indicates that signals at that frequency will be tracked well (i.e., compensated). Gain below 0 db indicates that signals at that frequency will not be tracked or compensated.

The lower graph in each box plots the input-to-output phase lag on the vertical axis vs. the sinusoidal frequency on the horizontal axis. The phase lag is an index of the delay in reacting to

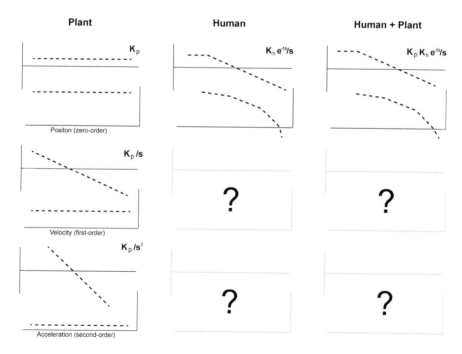

Figure 7.6 This figure provides a partial illustration of the logic of McRuer and Jex's (1967) research program to model the human pilot.

the error. Together, the amplitude and phase pattern represent a 'model' of the processes inside the 'black box.' The key is to understand that unique patterns in the Bode space are associated with unique transfer functions for the element being modeled.

In addition to the different plant dynamics, Figure 7.6 shows human performance for the position control condition and system performance (human + plant) using the open-loop transfer function response (in the Bode format).

Using the Laplace domain, the performance of the human plus plant is simply the product of the two transfer functions. One of the advantages of the Bode format is that the transfer functions are graphically additive since the plots use a log/log space. The logarithms of successive amplitude ratios (upper graphs) and the successive phase lags (lower graphs) are each additive for these linear approximations to behavior.

The pattern for the gain indicates that the human + plant will track the low frequencies well (because gain for those frequencies is above 0 db), but will track the higher frequencies poorly (with gains below 0 db). In this case, the human + plant have the characteristics of a 'low-pass filter' similar to that for the system illustrated in Figure 7.1.

Before the results for the other conditions are presented, we ask the reader to try to generalize from the results of the position control problem to the other two conditions.

Using the billiard ball logic typically associated with causal reasoning, it would be tempting to treat the transfer function of the human obtained in the position control condition as representative of the human processing mechanisms. In this case, the open-loop response suggests that the human is essentially a lag (an approximate integral processor) with a time delay or, in other words,

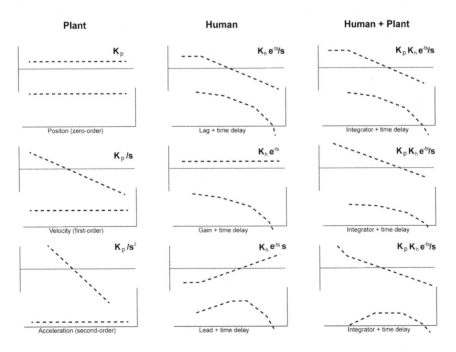

Figure 7.7 This figure summarizes the conditions (plants) and results (human and system response) for compensatory tracking experiments (after McRuer and Jex, 1967). The Human + Plant has a relatively invariant form (Integrator + Time Delay) where the amplitude ratio (upper graph in each box) crosses over the horizontal frequency axis.

Max Wertheimer and Kurt Koffka[7]

a low-pass filter. Based on what we know about the information processing limits of humans, this seems like a quite reasonable general model.

Thus, it is tempting to assume that the human transfer function would take the same form for the other two experimental conditions. In other words, the expectation is that the patterns in the middle column, representing the human transfer function, would be similar across the conditions, and that the functions in the far right column would be essentially the sum of the parts (i.e., the product of the individual transfer functions). In other words, the frequency response characteristics obtained for the human using the position plant should generalize to the other experimental conditions.

Figure 7.7 illustrates the actual results obtained. First, note the distinct qualitative changes in the Bode response for the human component. In the position control condition, the human would be modeled as a lag (an approximate integrator) and a time delay. However, in the velocity control condition, the human response suggests a model consisting of a gain and a time delay (responding to all frequencies, rather than emphasizing the low frequencies). In the acceleration control condition, the human response suggests a model consisting of a lead (an approximate differentiator) and a time delay (responding primarily to high frequencies, while deemphasizing the low frequencies). The transfer function for the human is NOT invariant.

This represents a fundamental flaw in the logic of dyadic approaches to cognition that attempt to model human performance independently from the problem context. The pattern of performance shown in Figure 7.7 provides clear evidence that context matters!

The human transfer function varies depending on the dynamics of the plant being controlled. In terms of the opening cartoon, the child must be a different type of machine (i.e., a different transfer function) in order to achieve stable locomotion with each different device (i.e., plant).

Although the transfer function for the human varies from condition to condition, the open-loop transfer function for the human plus the plant is the simple product of the transfer functions of the components, and most importantly, its form is invariant in the region where the amplitude ratio function in the upper graph crosses over the horizontal axis, which corresponds to zero decibels or a unity amplitude ratio. This invariance is often referred to as the McRuer Crossover Model.

Perhaps you recognize the invariant form for the human + plant system. This is a form that meets the stability requirements described in the previous section. High gain at the low frequencies means that signals in those frequency ranges will be tracked well, but to meet the stability requirements the gain passes through zero db before the phase shift passes through -180 degrees. Thus, the invariant pattern represents the necessary conditions for satisfactory control. The human transfer function adapts so that in combination with the plant dynamics the forward loop (i.e., human + plant) will satisfy the demands for stable control!

In closed-loop systems, constraints at the system level constrain the 'shapes' of the components. So, although the whole is in some sense a function of the parts—*the parts do not determine the whole*. In fact, just the opposite is true. The parts must change or adapt to satisfy constraints on the whole, or otherwise the system will be unstable (i.e., it will not survive). This is an important challenge for reductionist approaches to cognition. The dynamics of stability are an emergent property of the whole that cannot be found in the components. However, that global emergent property is, in fact, a determining factor in shaping the behavior of the components.

Thus, the dyadic relation between the human and the interface can only be understood in the context of the more holistic triadic semiotic system that includes the ecological constraints (in this case, the plant) as an intrinsic component of the system. In essence, the stability constraints reflect holistic properties of the experience that constrain the properties of the components. These ecological constraints are fundamental, not derivative!

Note the similarities between the adaptive tracking and the earlier termite nest-building example. Like the simple preferences of the termites, there is a constraint at the level of the human—a time delay is an invariant property of the human transfer function (although the duration of that delay may not be strictly invariant across conditions). However, like the termite example the global properties of the 'system' are not determined by those constraints. Rather, in both cases there are properties of the whole (the shape of the termite nest and the stability of the tracking) that are 'emergent.' That is, these properties cannot be found in the parts. In both cases these emergent properties reflect 'system level' constraints that in large part determine the shape of the component elements.

Of course, the value of considering the parts or elements in relation to functional wholes was recognized by psychologists from the earliest days. Ehrenfels[8] originally motivated the idea of gestalt qualities using the example of melody in music. A melody retains its unique quality when transposed to different keys or played on different instruments. Thus, the quality of melody is an emergent property that remains invariant over changes of the elemental notes.

Further, one might say that the quality of specific notes is determined by their fit within the melody. This contrasts with the conventional reductionist view that the melody is the sum of the individual notes. But of course, the fact that the melody does not depend on any specific note creates a problem for this conventional view.

Figure 7.8 illustrates the Gestalt psychologist Kurt Lewin's[9] construct of field theory, in which human experience is described as an emergent property of the interaction between the individual and the situation. Note the similarities with Neisser's Perception Cycle (Chapter 3) and with our illustration of the Abduction dynamic (Chapter 5). Once again we see the circular organization and the role of concrete experience (pragmatics) in shaping the emergent concepts (beliefs) that in turn are 'tested' through future actions.

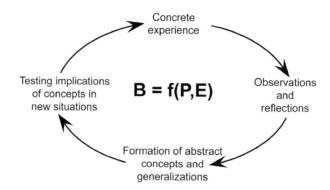

Figure 7.8 Kurt Lewin described human behavior as a joint function (emergent property) of the person and the environment [B = f(P,E)].

Getting off the Ground[10]

On October 7, 1903, Samuel Pierpont Langley catapulted his Great Aerodrome with Charles Manly on board from the roof of a houseboat anchored in the Potomac River. This was a first, highly publicized attempt at powered flight. It failed. A second attempt was made on December 8th, and again the Aerodrome immediately crashed into the Potomac. Fortunately, Manly escaped without serious injury. After the second failure, an editorial in the *New York Times* suggested that it would be one million to ten million years before man would fly. However, just nine days later, on December 17, 1903, the Wright Brothers made their first successful flight at Kitty Hawk, North Carolina. Why did the Wright Brothers succeed where all others had failed?

While Langley had built an engine and wings to meet the requirements for manned flight based on his careful models, he neglected the human-machine interface. The flight on October 7th was Manly's first experience in an aircraft—and an aircraft with a minimal control system!

Here was a classical case where the 'human factor' was an afterthought. Langley focused on wings and engines, but gave little consideration to the problem of control. He had models for the wings and engines, but he didn't have a model for how the aircraft would be piloted, placing his faith in Charles Manly to make this Aerodrome work once the vehicle was in the air.

In 1899, when the Wright Brothers began their explorations into flight, they were quite surprised to learn that there was little work to address the problem of balance and control. Most assumed that an aircraft would be steered with a rudder, much like a boat. Few before the Wrights realized that for a coordinated turn, it would be necessary to bank the aircraft.

From the start, the Wrights focused on the control problem. First, they discovered through observations of bird flight and intuitions from controlling bicycles how to use roll to effect a coordinated turn, then they developed the control system (i.e., wing warping) and spent an extensive amount of time training themselves to use the control system using kites and gliders. It was only when they had mastered the control problem that they turned their attention to designing an engine. Their most important patents are on the control system, not on the aircraft per se.

There were of course many important factors contributing to the first successful flight (e.g., discovering errors in previous lift tables). However, perhaps the thing that differentiated the Wrights from all others was their focus on the control problem and the resulting 'human-centered' approach (designing a control system and training piloting skill as an essential part of the engineering problem).

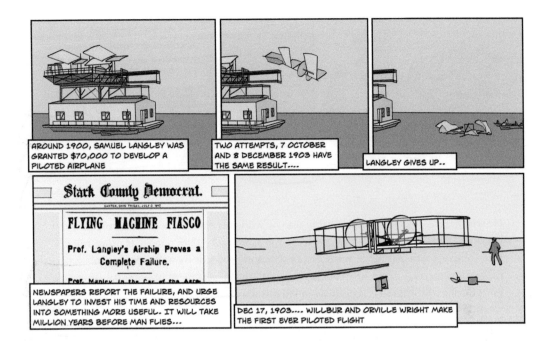

AROUND 1900, SAMUEL LANGLEY WAS GRANTED $70,000 TO DEVELOP A PILOTED AIRPLANE

TWO ATTEMPTS, 7 OCTOBER AND 8 DECEMBER 1903 HAVE THE SAME RESULT....

LANGLEY GIVES UP..

Stark County Democrat.

FLYING MACHINE FIASCO

Prof. Langley's Airship Proves a Complete Failure.

NEWSPAPERS REPORT THE FAILURE, AND URGE LANGLEY TO INVEST HIS TIME AND RESOURCES INTO SOMETHING MORE USEFUL. IT WILL TAKE MILLION YEARS BEFORE MAN FLIES...

DEC 17, 1903.... WILLBUR AND ORVILLE WRIGHT MAKE THE FIRST EVER PILOTED FLIGHT

It is tempting to see parallels between the Wrights' approach to flight and the Xerox PARC approach to computing.[11] A significant part of the success of the first personal computers designed at PARC reflected the attention given to making functionality more accessible through innovations at the interface. The focus on putting control into the hands of users has created a company that is now the most profitable company in the world.

Where others were focusing on circuit boards and code, Apple was focusing on the user experience. Where Langley focused on wings and engines, the Wright Brothers focused on the pilot experience. Note that the engine and wings (and circuit boards and code) have to be right for the system to work, but getting these right is not sufficient! Or perhaps more precisely, it is impossible to define 'right' (or good) without considering the larger problem associated with piloting (i.e., the functional user experience). A holistic perspective framed around the full experience seems to be critical for innovation.

A final important point with regards to the control problem is that, in finding the appropriate solution to the inherent speed-accuracy trade-offs involved in closed-loop control (i.e., finding a good or satisfying solution), the goal is rarely to minimize error. It is important to realize that it is not "error" per se that determines the quality of the control dynamic, but rather the consequences of error.

In most natural contexts, the consequences of error are not proportionally related to the errors. For example, in driving, deviations that are within the 'lane' have very little consequence, compared to deviations that take you into the line of oncoming traffic. A good control system is not designed to eliminate all errors, but rather to minimize those errors that have large negative consequences.

Also, as we will see in the next chapters, errors can have positive consequences in that they provide information about the situation dynamics that may help the system adapt in order to avoid potentially disastrous consequences, and perhaps also to take advantage of potentially positive opportunities. This is a key property of Taleb's construct of antifragile:

He who has never sinned is less reliable than he who only sinned once. And someone who has made plenty of errors – though never the same more than once – is more reliable than someone who has never made any. Evolution proceeds by undirected, convex bricolage or tinkering, inherently robust, i.e., with the achievement of potential stochastic gains thanks to continuous repetitive, small mistakes.[12]

(p. 74)

Antifragile systems are systems that thrive on variability (e.g., small errors). The information associated with this variability becomes the source for learning or improving fitness in an uncertain, changing environment. The pursuit of innovation in design may depend on making errors and learning from each one.

The point of this chapter is to suggest that control theory provides a particularly useful perspective on the triadic semiotic dynamic. The most important lesson of control theory is that there are constraints at the systems level (e.g., stability) that are fundamental. These constraints cannot be discovered through analysis of isolated components. Further, the components themselves are shaped by the larger ecological context.

Thus, to understand the various forms that the components take, it might be better to look to the larger context, rather than breaking the components into more elementary parts. The point is that the circular semiotic dynamic is a fundamental element. Any reduction below that level may destroy essential properties of the phenomenon of experience that cognitive scientists hope to understand and that designers hope to influence.

From a pedagogical perspective, using simple classical control systems rather than more obviously psychological phenomena may not be the best way to illustrate this. However, the goal in doing this is to suggest that the qualities associated with the dynamics of circles are derived from basic systems principles that are independent of the particular substances that compose the circles.

The dynamics of stability are invariants that apply to electrical circuits, hydraulic circuits, mechanical circuits, biological circuits, and cognitive circuits. The question for cognitive psychologists is not whether control theory applies, but whether cognitive phenomena involve closed-loop dynamics (e.g., feedback).

If cognitive phenomenon involves closed circuits, then there is little room for debate about whether the principles of dynamic systems theory apply. If psychology is to become part of the larger singular SCIENCE that William James' imagined, then it must be framed in a way that is consistent with the larger systems perspective. Otherwise, it will remain one of the plural, little sciences that will never add up to a complete understanding of human experience.

Notes

1. Crossman, E.R.F.W., & Goodeve, P.J. (1983). Feedback control of hand-movement and Fitts' law. *Quarterly Journal of Experimental Psychology*, 35A, 251–278.

   Jagacinski, R.J., & Flach, J.M. (2003). *Control theory for humans: Quantitative approaches to modeling performance*. Mahwah, NJ: Erlbaum.

2. McRuer, D.T. (1995). Pilot-induced oscillations and human dynamic behavior. NASA Office of Scientific Management, NASA Contrator Report 4683.

   These are link to videos of two different PIO accidents with the Swedish Gripen Aircraft.

   www.youtube.com/watch?v=wxX4QvLylLY

   www.youtube.com/watch?v=mkgShfxTzmo

3. Jagacinski, R.J. (1977). A qualitative look at feedback control theory as a style of describing behavior. *Human Factors*, 19, 331–347.
4. Jagacinski & Flach (2003).
5. McRuer, D.T., & Jex, H.R. (1967). A review of quasi-linear pilot models. *IEEE Transaction on Human Factors*, 8, 231–249.

   Kleinman, D.L., Baron, S., & Levison, W.H. (1971). A control theoretic approach to manned-vehicle systems analysis. *IEEE Transactions in Automatic Control*, AC-16, 824–832.

6. The Laplace form is commonly used by engineers to describe the transfer functions of control system elements. A distinct advantage of the Laplace domain is that calculus functions such as integration, differentiation, and convolution can be accomplished using algebra. Note that the response of the human + plant in Figure 5.7 is simply the product of their component Laplace transforms.
7. Wertheimer, M. (1938). Gestalt theory. In W.D. Ellis (Ed.). *A source book of Gestalt Psychology*. London: Kegan Paul, Trench, Trubner. (p. 1–11)

   Koffka, K. (1935). *Principles of Gestalt Psychology*. New York: Harcourt, Brace. (p. 22).

8. Ehrenfels, C. (1937). On gestalt qualities. *Psychological Review*, 44(6), 521–524.
9. Lewin, K. (1951). *Field theory in social science: Selected theoretical papers* (ed. D. Cartwright). New York: Harper & Row.
10. Crouch, T. (1989). *The bishop's boys: A life of Wilbur and Orville Wright*. New York: W.W. Norton.

    Freedman, R. (1991). *The Wright brothers: How they invented the airplane*. New York: Holiday House.

11. Hiltzik, M.A. (1999). *Dealers of lightning: XEROX parc and the dawn of the computer age*. New York: Harper Collins.
12. Taleb, N.N. (2012). *Antifragile: Things that gain from disorder*. (p. 74) New York: Random House.

8

OBSERVING

This chapter will examine closed-loop circuits from a different angle. Whereas control looks at the circuits as a means for reaching and maintaining a goal, observation looks at these same circuits from the perspective of making judgments about the world. That is, these circuits can be a means for filtering out the 'noise' in order to accurately judge (perceive) the state of the world (e.g., determining the average height of a population based on samples or observations).

In control or observer systems the comparator is the point at which the output is fed back and 'compared' with the input to compute an error (or surprise) signal. In typical engineered control systems such as that illustrated in Figure 7.1, the system is designed so that the comparator simply involves subtraction of one signal from another to get a third signal. That is, all signals are in a comparable currency (e.g., electrical current) that allows subtraction of one (i.e., the feedback) from another (i.e., the target or goal) to get the third (i.e., the control signal). But this is rarely true in everyday life.

Consider the novice pilot learning to land. The goal might be a particular approach path or simply a soft contact at a particular region of the runway. The feedback would be in the form of optical flow through the windows and/or information presented on the cockpit instruments (e.g., airspeed). These two very different types of signals must somehow be compared in order to specify appropriate movements of the controls (e.g., stick, throttle, rudders).

How does the pilot know whether she is on the right track to satisfy her goal of a soft landing? If she is off track, how does she know what control action or combination of actions (e.g., adjusting the throttle or stick or both) will correct the error?[1]

It should be clear that for the pilot and more generally for most cognitive or biological control systems, the signals involved in the comparator process may be in diverse forms or currencies,

as illustrated in the opening cartoon. Thus, comparing feedback to intentions in order to specify actions is not a trivial process. In fact, this is a central issue for control theory—to determine the dimensionality of the state space or, in other words, to identify what variables must be fed back in order to guide action in a particular situation (e.g., as a function of different vehicle dynamics).

This is also probably the central issue for skill development—attuning to the feedback that specifies the appropriate actions with respect to the opportunities and consequences.[2] In Gibsonian terms, this is the problem of specification of affordances.[3] In the earlier example of judging position on the ground from Langewiesche, a key advantage of the angular coordinate system is that it allows direct comparison of position on the ground relative to the possibilities of landing. In other words, the currency of optical angle helps to simplify the comparator problem.

Figure 8.1 shows a simple feedback system to illustrate the comparator problem from the perspective of the observer problem. This system has a gain and two integrators in the forward loop. Consistent with the discussion in Chapter 7, the Gain determines the sensitivity to error. Because of the two integrations in the forward loop, the output from the Gain element determines the acceleration of the output. This is a dynamic that is consistent with many movement tasks (e.g., vehicle control or body movement) in a world governed by inertia. For example, the initial response of deflection of the accelerator or brake is a change in velocity (i.e., acceleration or deceleration) of your car.

What do you suppose that the response of this system would be to a step input, and how might this response change as a function of the lone parameter in the forward loop—the Gain?

Is there any Gain value that will result in an asymptotic approach to the step change in the target?

Somewhat surprisingly in the context of naive discussions of feedback systems, the answer is "No." Here again is a situation that illustrates that feedback is not sufficient to ensure convergence with the input. In fact, the response of this system to a step input is a sine wave output. The speed of oscillation of this sine wave (i.e., its frequency) is determined by the value of the Gain parameter. A higher Gain produces a higher frequency response. There is NO value of Gain that will lead to convergence of output with the input target!

Figure 8.2 shows an alternative system that includes feedback of both the output position and the output velocity. This system can result in an output that will converge to the input target, if the feedback of position and velocity are combined with the appropriate weights.

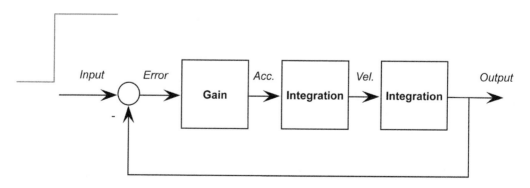

Figure 8.1 A second-order control system in which the Gain determines the acceleration of the response (output).

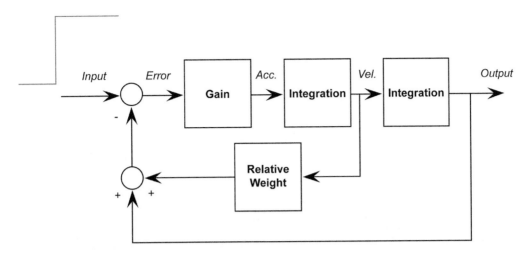

Figure 8.2 Stable goal following can be achieved in a second-order system if feedback includes both position and velocity of the output.

Heavy relative weight on the velocity component will lead to 'sluggish' or conservative approaches to the target. Less relative weight on velocity will lead to more aggressive approaches—with a damped oscillation at very low weights and, as described earlier, a non-converging oscillation at zero weight on velocity.

Depending on the relative weights on position and velocity, this system will achieve a similar range of responses to that described for the low-pass filter in Chapter 7 (from sluggish to oscillatory). Knowing what variables to attend to is an important component of the observer problem—and of course is a property that will differentiate experts from novices with respect to skill. A general implication of the behavior of the systems illustrated in Figures 8.1 and 8.2 is that for control of an inertial system (e.g., a car) position feedback alone is insufficient. The system must have feedback about both position and velocity in order to control the vehicle.

For example, in order to stop the car in front of an obstacle on the road (e.g., stopped line of traffic), a driver must take into account both distance to the obstacle and the speed of approach. Current research suggests that for visual control of locomotion, this information is specified in terms of angular relations, as in the earlier piloting example.

The angular extent (e.g., the projected visual angle of the taillights of the preceding vehicle) and the angular velocity (e.g., rate of expansion of the projected angle) of the object in the visual flow field provide the essential state information about the imminence of collision.[4]

In most natural situations, cognitive systems must deal with many different potentially useful sources of feedback that may or may not be relevant to meeting a particular functional objective. Differentiating the diagnostic feedback (i.e., the signals) from the non-diagnostic feedback (i.e., the noise) is thus an important concern in the design of an effective control/observer system (or semiotic system).

The challenge that intrigued Wiener and Bigelow as they struggled with the design of systems for guiding artillery during World War II was not the design of simple servomechanisms, as is part of social science lore. Rather, the key problem was to predict the future states of the aircraft. Wiener[5] writes:

> Our actual collaboration resulted from another project, which was likewise undertaken for the purposes of the last war. At the beginning of the war, the German prestige in aviation and the defensive position of England turned the attention of many scientists to the improvement of anti-aircraft artillery. Even before the war, it had become clear that the speed of the airplane had rendered obsolete all classical methods of the direction of fire, and that it was necessary to build into the control apparatus all the computations necessary. These were rendered much more difficult by the fact that, unlike all previously encountered targets, an airplane has a velocity which is a very appreciable part of the velocity of the missile used to bring it down. Accordingly, it is exceedingly important to shoot the missile, not at the target, but in such a way that missile and target may come together in space at some time in the future. We must hence find some method of predicting the future position of the plane.

This problem of determining the state of a system (either now or in the future) is typically referred to as the observer problem. In the specific context of anti-aircraft guidance, the problem of predicting the path of the aircraft might be characterized as discriminating the signal (e.g., past and current states that are relevant to the future states) from the noise (e.g., past and current states that are not relevant).

In the absence of the evasive maneuvers the path might be predicted based on a smooth extrapolation from the current states of motion (e.g., position and velocity). However, an anti-aircraft system guided by such extrapolations might easily be evaded by a smart pilot. That is, for a craft directed by a smart pilot, a system whose guess about the future state of the aircraft was based on a simple extrapolation of the path from current states would almost always guess wrong due to the evasive maneuvers of the pilot.

As a practical matter, effective control will almost always involve anticipating or predicting future states. For example, to hit a baseball you have to 'guess' where the ball will be at the time your bat gets to the hitting zone. To hit a receiver racing down field, the quarterback ideally would like to 'lead' the receiver, throwing the ball to the point that the receiver will reach without breaking stride.

Signal Detection

The observer problem is typically introduced in the cognitive sciences in terms of signal detection theory, as illustrated in Figure 8.3. For example, remember the first time your parents left you alone at home, perhaps to babysit for your younger siblings? Part of your job was to listen for any invaders that might be a danger to you or your siblings.

This required that you discriminated the normal sounds of the house and neighborhood at night (i.e., the noises) from the sounds that an invader might make (i.e., the signal). Note that in terms

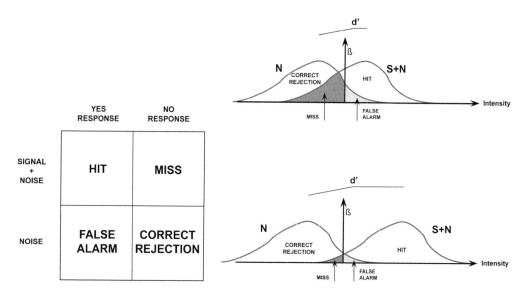

	YES RESPONSE	NO RESPONSE
SIGNAL + NOISE	HIT	MISS
NOISE	FALSE ALARM	CORRECT REJECTION

Figure 8.3 a / Figure 8.3 b Illustrates the problem of signal detection.

of the loudness of the sounds, there might be large overlap between the normal creaks of the house and ambient neighborhood noises and the sounds that a stealthy invader might make. Was that sound a burglar or was it a cat in the alley? Should I call my parents or not?

In signal detection theory, the discriminability of signal and noise is parameterized with d' and the decision rule for identifying a signal is parameterized with the value beta. Together, these two parameters will determine the performance of the observer in terms of the number of hits (i.e., detecting a burglar when one is present), misses (e.g., failing to detect a burglar in time to protect the home), false alarms (e.g., calling the parents to come home when in fact no burglar is present), and correct rejections (e.g., ignoring the normal house creaks because there is no threat).

The d' parameter reflects the difficulty of the discrimination due to the similarity between signal and noise as a function of the sensitivity of the perceptual system. The beta parameter reflects higher cognitive processes that might be associated with both the expectations about the world (e.g., whether you believe a burglar is likely) and with the relative values and costs associated with the various possible outcomes (e.g., hits versus false alarms). Ideal Observer Theory provides analytical means to chose a beta parameter to maximize performance relative to particular value systems.

Note that signal detection theory assumes a triadic perspective on the semiotic problem. That is, the discriminability of signal and noise (d') will depend both on properties of the receiver (the agent) and on properties of the signal source (the ecology). For example, how stealthy the burglar might be. The optimality of the choice of a decision criterion (beta) will depend on an external criterion or value system (e.g., the payoff matrix), which may reflect both internal preferences of the agent (e.g., embarrassment associated with false alarms) and external consequences in the ecology (e.g., whether the burglar is armed).

It is important to emphasize that the quality of the Observer will be a function of the consequences of the errors as reflected in a payoff matrix. As with control systems, it is not necessarily about eliminating errors, but rather about minimizing the costs of those errors.

Figure 8.4 maps the observer problem onto the triadic components of the abduction logic or triadic semiotic system. In fact, the observer problem is almost directly analogous to the abduction problem as formulated by Peirce. That is, the problem of abduction is how biological systems ground their beliefs about nature (i.e., estimations or predictions of the state of the world) based on experience (i.e., integration of noisy past observations).

In essence, the past is a noisy signal with respect to inferring the current state or predicting the future—just as the trajectory of the aircraft is a noisy signal with respect to where it will be when the missile arrives. This is the central problem of cognitive systems—to generalize, based on past experiences, in order to respond more effectively to a somewhat uncertain future. In other words, to apply what you have learned in the past toward achieving future goals.

Figure 8.4 shows an observer linked to a signal source through a comparator. The observer samples the signal source in order to test hypotheses (i.e., to compare the current state with

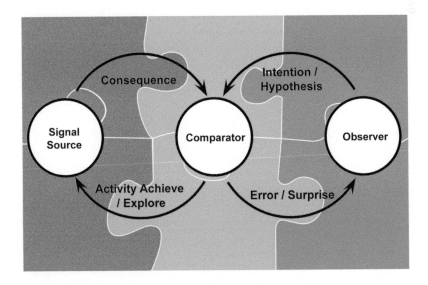

Figure 8.4 Illustration of the observer problem in the context of an abduction system.

predictions). The difference between the actual state and the prediction is labeled surprise, and this surprise is fed back and integrated to make future predictions or hypotheses. Thus, the observer tests beliefs about the world by comparing predictions about that world with the outcomes from empirical experiments (samples).

Iterative Application of Bayes' Theorem

The signal detection problem is typically framed in terms of a single observation—is that sound a burglar? However, in most natural situations, information is acquired over time. That is, you might hear a sound that gets your attention. A second sound might lead to an increased suspicion that someone is breaking into the house. Confidence in this suspicion may grow or fade as a result of additional observations.

Bayes' theorem provides an analytic prescription for adjusting probability estimates on the basis of new information. The iterative application of Bayes' theorem can be illustrated using the classical Book Bag and Poker Chip problem.[6] In this problem there are two identical book bags filled with red and blue poker chips. One bag (the Red Bag) contains 70 red chips and 30 blue chips. The other bag (the Blue Bag) contains 70 blue chips and 30 red chips. One of the two bags is picked randomly. Then chips are sequentially sampled (with replacement) from the bag, and the task is to estimate the probability that the Red Bag was chosen.

Obviously, before any chips have been chosen, the probability that the Red Bag was chosen is 50% (i.e., the initial hypothesis or the prior probability). However, if the first chip chosen is red, how much should your estimate be revised (i.e., what would be the posterior probability)? If this chip was replaced and a second sample also produced a red chip, what would your new estimate be of the probability that the Red Bag was chosen? And what if three red chips in a row were chosen?

Table 8.1 provides the information needed to compute the likelihood of the Red Bag given that a red chip was chosen. The relevant data is in the row associated with choosing the red chip. The cell under the column Red Bag gives the probability of a red chip, given the Red Bag, and the cell under the column Blue Bag gives the probability of a red chip, the Blue Bag. The probability that it is the Red Bag is simply the probability of red chip given the red bag, divided by the sum of the probabilities for the red chip given all possibilities (Red Bag + Blue Bag).

The posterior probability would be:

$.35/(.35+.15) = .70$

This process can be applied iteratively to compute the posterior odds in the case where a second red chip is drawn. In this case, the Prior Odds on this iteration would be the Posterior Odds from

Table 8.1 Cells show the various probabilities for the various possibilities in the Book Bag and Poker Chip Experiment.

Events	Red Bag	Blue Bag
Red Chip	p(RC|RB)*p(RB) 0.7*0.5=0.35	p(RC|BB)*p(BB) 0.3*0.5=0.15
Blue Chip	p(BC|RB)*p(RB) 0.3*0.5=0.15	p(BC|BB)*p(BB) 0.7*0.5=0.35

the first iteration. The .5 probability that the Red Bag was chosen in the first cell would now be .7. Thus, the value in that cell would be .7 × .7. The prior probability for the Blue Bag, after drawing a previous red chip, would be .03. The value in that cell would be .3 × .3.

The new posterior probability would be:

$$.49/(.49+.09) = .84$$

Figure 8.5 shows how the estimate of the probability that the Red Book Bag was chosen would increase with each consecutive selection of a Red Chip. The data in Figure 8.5 reflect the performance of an Ideal Observer with respect to the Book Bag and Poker situation.

When humans are asked to make estimates in this task, they tend to be far more conservative in revising their hypotheses, relative to the prescriptions of Bayes' theorem.[7] One hypothesis to explain this reaction is that the conservative behavior of humans reflects an intrinsic information processing limit.

Alternatively, a second possibility (that will be explored further in the next chapter) is that the Book Bag and Poker task is not representative of the natural context of human experience, so that the conservative behavior reflects an over-generalization from smart strategies developed in more typical situations. The Book Bag and Poker task again reflects a closed system in which the possibilities are countable. That is, we know the exact number of chips and the exact number of book bags, thus we know the denominator for computing the probabilities. In everyday life, we almost never know all the possibilities (again consider Taleb's Black Swan[8]). In this case, exact probabilities are

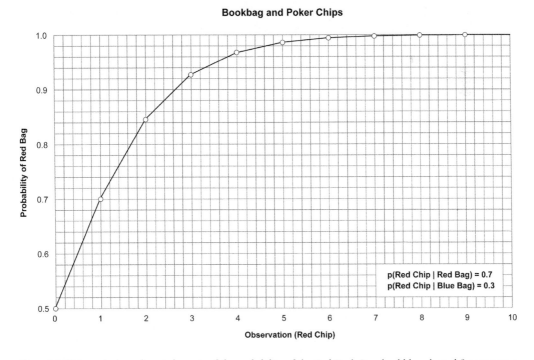

Figure 8.5 This graph shows how judgments of the probability of the Red Book Bag should be adjusted for successive samples of Red Chips as prescribed by Bayes' Theorem.

not computable, and a conservative or cautious strategy for changing hypotheses may be wise.[9] We will come back to this example in the next chapter.

Bayes' theorem provides a simple observer model that is consistent with the closed-loop dynamics of an abduction logic that iteratively revises its beliefs (e.g., hypotheses) about the world, based on experience (e.g., samples). Recently, there has been increasing interest in using Bayesian logic for building computational simulations of mental processes.[10]

Estimation

Figure 8.6 illustrates a simple circuit (identical to the circuit in Figure 7.1) from the perspective of the observation problem. In this case, the signal is a step response, however, the observed input is a noisy signal (step input + random noise). This system also involves negative feedback, where the estimate or prediction based on earlier inputs is fed back and compared to a current observation. The difference between the prediction and the observation is labeled as surprise. This circuit, if appropriately tuned, will act to minimize the surprise. That is, predictions will be adjusted based on differences with the current observation so that over time surprise will be reduced.

Based on what you learned in Chapter 7, how do you think the gain parameter will impact performance? That is, if the goal is to minimize the impact of noise on observations (to filter the noise), would higher or lower gains be preferred?

Figure 8.7 illustrates the response of this simple observer as a function of the gain parameter (with zero time delay). The dashed step function represents the signal. The solid line represents the observations (signal + noise).

As you can see, when the gain is very low the noise is effectively filtered out of the response. In the early phase, the prediction is essentially the mean of the signal + noise function, resulting in an elimination of the random noise and an accurate estimate of the signal. However, with low gain the system is very slow to respond when the signal actually changes (the step transition).

When the gain is very high this simple observer will respond very quickly to the change in the signal associated with the step transition. However, the high gain will cause it to chase the noise—it will respond quickly to any variation (whether due to noise or actual change in signal). The challenge of Ideal Observer Theory is to find the appropriate gain—one that will find a satisfactory balance between filtering noise and following real changes in the signal.

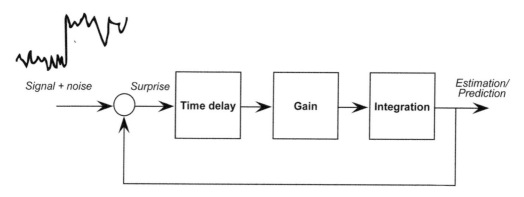

Figure 8.6 A simple observer system.

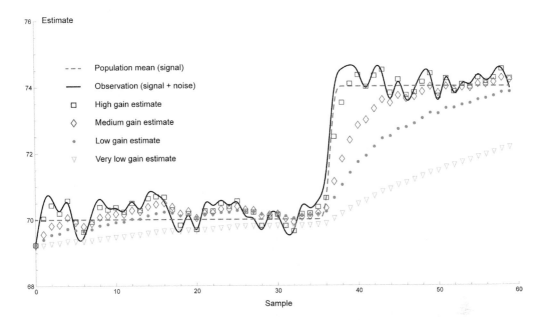

Figure 8.7 Response of a simple observer as a function of the gain parameter. Low gains will effectively filter out noise, but will be sluggish in responding to real changes (the step transition). High gains will respond quickly to real changes (the step transition), but will tend to chase the noise.

This example again illustrates the bounds that shape the observation process. The ideal or optimal solution to the observer problem depends on the larger context of the problem—the holistic, triadic semiotic dynamic. In particular, it depends on the costs of following the noise (i.e., false alarms) relative to the costs of a sluggish response to real change (i.e., misses).

Setting the gain for the observer is analogous to setting the beta in the discrete signal detection problem. However, the observer brings in the dynamics of change over time into the picture. For example, consider the problem of not simply detecting a burglar, but making the judgment about potential changes in your local neighborhood.

Does a recent series of local burglaries reflect a change in the neighborhood (perhaps, it is time to consider moving), or is this just an anomaly (i.e., the neighborhood remains relatively safe on average). Or in a basketball game, does a sequence of consecutive successful shots indicate that a player is "hot" or "in the zone" or is it simply consistent with expectations based on the player's average shooting percentage?

Summary

In everyday life, the information available to us for controlling actions is not necessarily in a form that allows direct comparison with our goals, intentions, or values. In the context of economic decisions, Dan Ariely[11] observes that, "we don't have an internal value meter that tells us how much things are worth." Thus, we have to estimate the values needed from the information available.

Ariely provides several examples of how our choices can be 'biased' as a function of the information available to us. For example, restaurants can boost revenues by including a high-priced entrée on their menus. Although people rarely choose this higher-priced entrée, they will pick the second highest priced option more frequently—presumably because it seems to be a relatively good value. In effect, the 'value' of a menu option, compared to our goals to have a 'good' meal, involves a relative estimate based on the other options on the menu.

For biological and cognitive systems, the problems of control and observation go hand-in-hand. For example, a decision about moving to a new neighborhood (i.e., a control action) might depend on the ability to judge whether the safety of the current neighborhood is changing (i.e., an observer problem). For engineered control problems, the observer and control problems are typically solved in the design process.

The engineer decides based on an analysis of the controlled processes what 'state' variables to measure and how to weight these measures to filter signal from noise (the observer problem) and to satisfy functional values and objectives (e.g., a payoff matrix) (the control problem). The control and observer problems are typically solved "off-line" and then implemented in terms of the parameters (e.g., gains) in a specific control solution.

However, for biological systems, many of the control and observation problems must be solved "on-line." That is, the child learns to walk by walking, to roller skate by skating, to play an instrument by playing, etc. In other words, it is only in the process of solving the control problems that the data available for tuning the gains to find a stable or robust solution to the observation and control problems can be discovered.

For safety-critical systems (e.g., aircraft, nuclear power plants, surgery) it can be quite risky to learn by doing. Thus, in these systems it becomes important to tune the 'system' through carefully designed training programs, typically involving simulations or graded stages of exposure to minimize the possibility of catastrophic failures early in the learning process. For example, the Wright Brothers learned to fly through a graded series of exercises using kites and gliders before they attempted the more dangerous task of powered flight. Similarly, surgeons usually are trained through a graded series of exposures to increasingly more difficult and risky procedures.

In using graded or part-task training to build up to the challenges of a complex domain, it becomes important to make sure that the simplification or partitioning of the tasks are done in ways that preserve the relevant 'state' variables of the process, so that the rules and strategies developed in the training scenarios will result in rules and strategies that will be effective in the target work domains.[12]

Simulators are often used in some of these safety-critical domains to allow people to fail without the risk of catastrophic consequences. From the perspective of control and observation, the point

of the training is to help the participants to identify the appropriate 'state variables' (i.e., the deep structure of the problem) and to discover the appropriate weighting of those variables (i.e., the gains or betas) that will lead to effective decision rules.

Thus, successful training protocols should be designed to include scenarios that make the deep structure salient to the participants, and to provide constructive feedback for tuning the decision rules to reflect the appropriate domain values (e.g., the payoff matrix). In doing this, a major factor is the degree to which the scenarios used in training are *representative* of the situations that the trainees will face in their everyday work domain.[13]

While training is used to shape people's internal models, these models can also be shaped directly through interface design. In essence, the implications are that the interface should make the relevant state variables and the relevant decision rules 'visible' and 'salient' through the design of representations.

Thus, the same types of analyses that control engineers apply in the design of automatic control systems should be applied in the design of interfaces. All the important state variables should be identified and included, and the configuration and salience of these variables should 'bias' the operator toward decision rules (e.g., relative gains or weights) or strategies that lead to robust control.

For example, for controlling second-order systems, as illustrated in Figure 8.1, an effective interface involves a 'quickened' display. That is, the position and velocity feedback are combined into a single point that reflects a satisfactory weighting of position and velocity. With this display, by responding to the position of the cursor, the person is actually responding to a pre-weighted integration of position and velocity, as required for stable control (Figure 8.8).[14]

The quickened display reflects a very simple control problem. For more complex problems the challenge is to identify the relevant 'state' variables and the potentially effective control strategies. This is the point of cognitive work analysis—to uncover the deep structure of the problem domain so that interface and training systems can be designed to meet the requirements for stable observation and control.[15] When the critical variables are perceptually salient in the representation, the right strategies will often be the intuitively most natural choice for operators.

John Dewey

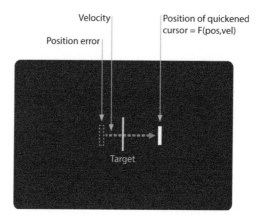

Figure 8.8 Quickening can be a very effective display for compensatory tracking with a second-order plant (acceleration control or inertial system control). The quickened display shows the cursor as a pre-weighted sum of position and velocity error. In responding to the quickened cursor position, the tracker would be effectively responding jointly to position and velocity error. Thus, it reflects the critical states of the inertial system (see Figure 8.1).

In linear control systems it is analytically possible to treat the observer problem and the control problem sequentially.[16] It is also quite convenient for both pedagogical and practical purposes to decompose the system into separate 'stages' of information processing (observing, deciding, etc.) and to consider the constraints and ideals for each component in isolation. However, the control solutions generated through this approach will be bounded by the assumptions made about each component.

If the assumptions do not match well with the demands of the ecology, then there is a significant possibility that these control solutions will be suboptimal at best, or catastrophically unstable in the worst-case scenario. This will be particularly true if the systems include nonlinear components—where a small change in one component can result in dramatic performance consequences.

How is it possible to design a control solution to be successful in a future context that the designer is uncertain about? Practically, in order to control or shape the future, it is necessary to anticipate it.

The challenge to design control systems (i.e., combinations of observers and controllers) that will adapt to maintain stability in the face of situations that may change in ways not anticipated at the design stage brings us to the problem of adaptive control considered in the next chapter.

Notes

1. Amelink, H.J.M., Mulder, M., van Paassen, M.M., & Flach, J.M. (2005). Theoretical foundations for total energy-based perspective flight-path displays for aircraft guidance. *International Journal of Aviation Psychology*, 15, 205–231.

   Flach, J.M., Jacques, P., Patrick, D., Amelink, M., van Paassen, M.M., & Mulder, M. (2003). A search for meaning: A case study of the approach-to-landing. In E. Hollnagel (Ed.). *Handbook of cognitive task design* (pp. 171–191). Mahwah, NJ: Erlbaum.

2. Gibson, E.J. (1969). *Perceptual learning and development*. New York: Appleton-Century-Crofts.

   Ericsson, K.A., & Charness, N. (1994). Expert performance: Its structure and acquisition. *American Psychologist*, 49(8), 725–747.

3. Gibson, J.J. (1986). *The ecological approach to visual perception*. Hillsdale, NJ: Erlbaum.

   Gibson, J.J. (1966). *The senses considered as perceptual systems*. Boston, MA: Houghton Mifflin.

4. Lee, D.N. (1976). A theory of visual control of braking based on information about time-to-collision. *Perception*, 5, 436–459.

   Stanard, T., Flach, J.M., Smith, M.R.H., & Warren, R. (2012). Learning to avoid collisions: A functional state space approach. *Ecological Psychology*, 24(4), 328–360.

   Smith, M.R.H., Flach, J.M., Dittman, S.M., & Stanard, T. (2001). Monocular optical constraints on collision control. *Journal of Experimental Psychology: Human Perception and Performance*, 27(2), 395–410.

   Flach, J.M., Smith, M.R.H., Stanard, T., & Dittman, S.M. (2004). Collision: Getting them under control. In H. Hecht & G.J.P. Savelsbergh (Eds.). *Theories of time to contact*. Advances in Psychology Series (pp. 67–91). North-Holland: Elsevier.

5. Wiener, N. (1948/1961). *Cybernetics: Or control and communication in the animal and the machine*. 2nd ed. Cambridge, MA: MIT Press. (p. 5).

6. Phillips, L.D., Hayes, W.L., & Edwards, W. (1966). Conservatism in complex probabilistic inference. *IEEE Transactions on Human factors in Electronics*, HFE-7: 7–18.

7. Phillips, Hayes, & Edwards (1966), pp. 7–18.

8. Taleb, N.N. (2010). *The black swan: The impact of the highly improbable*. New York: Random House.

9. von Winterfeldt, D., & Edwards, W. (1986). *Decision analysis and behavioral research*. New York: Cambridge University Press.

10. Tenenbaum, J.B., Griffiths, T.L., & Kemp, C. (2006). Theory-based Bayesian models of inductive learning and reasoning. *Trends in Cognitive Sciences*, 10, 309–318.

11. Ariely, D. (2008). *Predictably irrational: The hidden forces that shape our decisions*. New York: Harper Collins.

12. Flach, J.M., Lintern, G., & Larish, J.F. (1990). Perceptual motor skill: A theoretical framework. In R. Warren & A.H. Wertheim (Eds.). *Perception & control of self-motion* (pp. 327–355). Hillsdale, NJ: Erlbaum.

13. Flach, J.M., Schwartz, D., Bennett, A., Behymer, K., & Shebilsi, W. (2010). Synthetic task environments: Measuring macrocognition. In E. Patterson & J. Miller (Eds.). *Macrocognition: Metrics and scenarios: Design and evaluation for real world teams* (pp. 201–284). Aldershot, England: Ashgate.

14. Bennett, K.B., & Flach, J.M. (2011). *Display and interface design: Subtle science, exact art*. London: Taylor & Francis.

15. Vicente, K.J. (1999). *Cognitive work analysis. Toward safe, productive, and healthy computer-based work*. Mahwah, NJ: Erlbaum.

16. Pew, R.W., & Baron, S. (1978). The components of an information processing theory of skilled performance based on an optimal control perspective. In G.E. Stelmach (Ed.). *Information processing in motor control and learning* (pp. 71–78). New York: Academic Press.

Part 3

THE PRAGMATICS OF PROBLEM SOLVING

9

MUDDLING THROUGH

The book bag and poker chips experiment, discussed in relation to Bayes' theorem in Chapter 8, provides a good place to start thinking about more complex decision making and problem solving in the face of uncertainty.

To remind you, one of two bags was chosen. One bag has 70 red chips and 30 blue chips and the other has 70 blue chips and 30 red chips. Chips are drawn one at a time and the task is to judge the probability that the red (or blue) bag was chosen. Bayes' theorem provides a good candidate for a computational model of this task—since all the information to determine the probabilities needed to apply Bayes' theorem is given in the problem.

However, an important issue to consider is whether this task is a good representation of decision making in everyday life? For example, would this task be representative of the task of a physician trying to diagnose and treat a patient? Or of a businessman trying to choose an investment? Or of an intelligence analyst trying to anticipate terrorist threats? Or of a family buying their first home? Or of a couple deciding whether to start a family?

Here is our idea for a more representative version of this task:

> A bag is chosen from among many bags—you don't know exactly how many. You know a little about some of the bags. For example, you know there is one bag with all blue chips, but that most of the bags contain various numbers of various different colors, some including blue. For most of the bags you don't know how many chips they contain and you don't know how many different colors there are, much less the distribution of colors in every bag. Now suppose that one bag is chosen and then a blue chip is chosen from the bag. What is the probability that it was the bag with all blue chips? What is the probability that it is a bag with mostly blue chips? What is the probability that you drew the only blue chip in the bag?

For this example, Bayes' theorem is not of much help, since you don't have the information needed to do the computations. The contrast between the classical bookbag and poker chip experiment and this example illustrates the difference between a closed system and an open system, or what Herbert Simon and Allen Newell called a well-defined problem versus an ill-defined problem.

Bayes' theorem works for the closed system or well-defined problem—in the classical problem all the information needed for the computations is available. In essence, the field of possibilities is fully specified. Thus, there is no need to consider the larger context.

However, in the alternative version and in most natural situations, the field of possibilities is almost never completely specified. There are always possibilities beyond the horizon of the immediate situation (or experience) that could be significant (e.g., black swans). These problems reflect

> IN SHORT, WELL-STRUCTURED PROBLEMS ARE THOSE THAT CAN BE FORMULATED EXPLICITLY AND QUANTITATIVELY, AND THAT CAN THEN BE SOLVED BY KNOWN AND FEASIBLE COMPUTATIONAL TECHNIQUES

> PROBLEMS ARE ILL-STRUCTURED WHEN THEY ARE NOT WELL-STRUCTURED. IN SOME CASES, FOR EXAMPLE, THE ESSENTIAL VARIABLES ARE NOT NUMERICAL AT ALL, BUT SYMBOLIC OR VERBAL.... SECOND, THERE ARE MANY IMPORTANT SITUATIONS IN EVERYDAY LIFE WHERE THE OBJECTIVE FUNCTION, THE GOAL, IS VAGUE AND NON QUANTITATIVE... THIRD, THERE ARE MANY PRACTICAL PROBLEMS – IT WOULD BE ACCURATE TO SAY 'MOST PRACTICAL PROBLEMS' – FOR WHICH COMPUTATIONAL ALGORITHMS SIMPLY ARE NOT AVAILABLE

> IF WE FACE THE FACTS OF ORGANISATIONAL LIFE, WE ARE FORCED TO ADMIT THAT THE MAJORITY OF DECISIONS THAT EXECUTIVES FACE EVERY DAY – AND CERTAINLY A MAJORITY OF THE MOST IMPORTANT DECISIONS – LIE MUCH CLOSER TO THE ILL-STRUCTURED THAN TO THE WELL-STRUCTURED END OF THE SPECTRUM

Herbert Simon[1]

what Simon and Newell called ill-defined problems, and they are the type of problems that people are challenged with daily.

The alternative version of the book bag and poker chip experiment is very similar to an example that Peirce[2] used to introduce the logic of abduction and to compare it to deductive and inductive arguments in terms of different permutations of the same three terms. In this context, Peirce suggested that we could frame a valid deductive argument about the chips as follows:

Major Premise:
All the chips in this bag are blue.

Minor Premise:
These chips are from this bag.

Conclusion:
These chips are blue.

Peirce described the inductive form of the argument that could be made as follows:

Observation 1:
These chips are from this bag.

Observation 2:
These chips are blue.

Generalization:
All the chips in this bag are blue.

Note that the two observations in this second example do not prove that all the chips are blue. As long as there were chips left in the bag (e.g., when choosing with replacement), no number of blue chips would prove that all the chips in the bag were blue.

So, the generalization is supported by the observations, but not proven—according to the prescriptions of induction. However, as more and more blue chips are chosen, it would be reasonable for confidence in the generalization to increase, just as it is reasonable to expect that the Sun will rise in the east tomorrow.

This is shown quantitatively with the steeply increasing probability function shown for the Bayes' theorem solution to the standard problem in Chapter 8. Note though, that one inconsistent observation (i.e., a non-blue chip) would be sufficient to disprove the generalization.

Pierce suggested that there was another interesting permutation of these three sentences:

Known fact:
All the chips in this bag are blue.

Observation (surprise):
These chips are blue.

Hypothesis:
These chips are from this bag.

This third arrangement, Pierce argues, is most representative of the context of common everyday reasoning. That is, we start with some knowledge about the world, but not complete knowledge (e.g., we know about some of the chips in some of the bags, i.e., that there are many different colors and that most of the bags are made up of mixed colors, but that at least one bag has all blue chips).

Then some event attracts attention (e.g., a pile of chips all of the same color blue). This would be a surprise in a world of many different colored chips, where most of the piles encountered might be a random mix of the colors. As a surprise, it would beg for some explanation. How did this come to be?

Thus, evoking a hypothesis. Aha! This surprise would be resolved, if these chips were all drawn from the bag that I know contains only blue chips! This hypothesis is held as a belief, until a better explanation is discovered. Perhaps you learn that Mary loves the color blue and that she is collecting blue chips—Aha! Perhaps Mary created this pile.

An important difference between the deductive form of logic versus induction and *abduction* is that deductive logic is analytical and evaluative. That is, it is designed to evaluate observations relative to a preexisting rule or law (which is accepted as truth). The deductive form starts with an established fact or known truth (i.e., the major premise), as the context of observations.

Induction and abduction on the other hand are both generative. That is, they are designed to generate hypotheses about possible general laws from observations. They are more forward looking, and as a consequence the evidence involved is more tentative. The ultimate test of the hypothesis is in the future. In essence, both induction and abduction are means for predicting the future, rather than evaluating it.

However, the formal rules of induction make the measure of a hypothesis the form of the argument, whereas abduction explicitly makes the measure of a hypothesis the future consequence of a belief. With abduction, the hypothesis is 'tested' against future experiences (e.g., learning that Mary is collecting blue chips) or against the consequences of actions guided by that hypothesis.

Note that the situation of the chips and bags is much different than the situations typically considered in the context of skill-based control. For example, when you are surprised by the response of the brakes in a car (e.g., in a strange rental car, or due to a change in the road surface such as black ice), you typically get immediate, fairly unambiguous feedback from action on the brake to help you to calibrate your hypothesis about how to manage the braking.

In this case, there will be strong evidence (and perhaps selective pressure or significant negative consequences) against false beliefs. However, in the case of the chips and bags, there is a rather tenuous relation between the hypothesis and the evidence or feedback. For example, there is neither time nor capacity to search all the bags and enumerate all the chips. You do not have direct access to the evidence needed to directly test your hypothesis about where the chips came from.

In many natural contexts, the uncertainty is unresolvable. For example, in the case of medical decision making there may NOT be an opportunity for a strong test of a hypothesis/belief relative to the functional context.

Did the patient recover because of the treatment or in spite of it?

The doctor may never have a definitive answer to this question. Similarly, in the context of attribution, it may be difficult to definitively attribute specific behaviors of other people to either their personalities or situational factors.

If it is true that most of the problems of life are ill-structured, that is, that they are complex and rife with uncertainty, then *is it possible to make 'good' or 'right' decisions?* Perhaps, in these complex situations success may depend on *making the decision right* (or making the decision work), rather than on *making the right decision*.

In complex situations, the problem may be more analogous to adaptive control (i.e., making continual adjustments to incrementally satisfy the functional goals—muddling through), than the problem of discretely choosing a right option from a fixed set of alternatives. The loose coupling between a 'right' choice and a successful adaptation was illustrated by Karl Weick[3] (1995) using the following story (illustrated in the opening cartoon):

> The young lieutenant of a small Hungarian detachment in the Alps sent a reconnaissance unit into the icy wilderness. It began to snow immediately, snowed for 2 days, and the unit did not return. The lieutenant suffered, fearing that he had dispatched his own people to death. But on the third day the unit came back. Where had they been? How had they made their way? Yes, they said, we considered ourselves lost and waited for the end. And then one of us found a map in his pocket. That calmed us down. We pitched camp, lasted out the snowstorm and then with the map we discovered our bearings. And here we are. The lieutenant borrowed this remarkable map and had a good look at it. He discovered to his astonishment that it was not a map of the Alps, but a map of the Pyrenees.

Weick concludes that this story suggests the possibility that *"when you are lost, any map will do."* He continues:

> The soldiers were able to produce a good outcome from a bad map because they were active, they had a purpose (get back to camp), and they had an image of where they

were and where they were going. They kept moving, they kept noticing cues, and they kept updating their sense of where they were. As a result, an imperfect map proved to be good enough. The cues they extracted and kept acting on were acts of faith amid indeterminacy that set sensemaking in motion. Once set in motion, sensemaking tends to confirm the faith through its effects on actions that make material what previously had been merely envisioned.

(p. 55)

Charles Lindblom[4] (1959), in his classic paper "The Science of 'Muddling Through,'" comes to a conclusion similar to that of Peirce and Weick.

Lindblom noted that for complex policy decisions, the comprehensive evaluations that are suggested by normative models of decision making are typically impossible:

> Although such an approach can be described, it cannot be practiced except for relatively simple problems and even then only in a somewhat modified form. It assumes intellectual capacities and sources of information that men simply do not possess, and it is even more absurd as an approach to policy when the time and money that can be allocated to a policy problem is limited, as is always the case.
>
> (p. 79)

Lindblom offered a more heuristic program of incremental adjustment as a more realistic alternative to the classical, normative approaches to policy making. He called this heuristic, trial-and-error process: 'muddling through.'

Twenty-years after his classic paper, Lindblom[5] (1979) comments:

> Perhaps at this stage in the study and practice of policy making the most common view . . . is that indeed no more than small or incremental steps—no more than muddling—is ordinarily possible. But most people, including many policy makers, want to separate the 'ought' from the 'is.' They think we should try to do better. So do I. What remains as an issue, then? It can be clearly put. Many critics of incrementalism believe that doing better usually means turning away from incrementalism. Incrementalists believe that for complex problem solving it usually means practicing incrementalism more skillfully and turning away from it only rarely.
>
> (p. 517)

In the next chapter we will draw a stronger contrast between those who look to the 'ought' for a measure of humans and those who choose to measure humans against the 'is' as reflected in practical decision making in naturalistic contexts.

However, for this chapter, we will consider some tentative images for 'muddling through' that are motivated by developments in control theory and field observations of expert problem solving.

Self-Organization or Adaptive Control

As metaphors for cognitive systems, the simple controller and observer models (including the iterative application of Bayes' theorem) have the same problem as raised for the conventional logic-based explanations of human behavior illustrated with the Pinker example. These simple systems are mechanisms, and there is an implicit homunculus who is solving the design problem (choosing the right gains).

For control and observer mechanisms, the stability and the signal to noise problems are solved by the engineers or designers based on *a priori* analyses of the control situations.

The challenge for cognitive science is to discover how biological and cognitive systems solve these problems in the context of contemporaneous engagement. How do these systems simultaneously wrestle with and solve the problems associated with control (e.g., finding the right gain for correcting errors) and observation (e.g., distinguishing between the error signal and the noise) theories?

How do they determine the denominators for computing probabilities?

How do they deal with unresolvable uncertainties that make the application of normative decision rules suspect?

Figure 9.1 provides one perspective on the abduction system that illustrates that the control and observation problems are intimately linked in cognitive systems. Cognitive systems typically must infer the situation dynamics (solve the observer problem) while trying to simultaneously achieve some goal or satisfy some practical need (solve the control problem).

For example, an action such as pressing the brake in a new rental car is simultaneously directed at accomplishing some goal (e.g., to stop the car at a specific place), and it is a test of a hypothesis or belief about how the brakes work (based on previous experiences with other cars). This duality between observation and control (between perception and action) is fundamental to the dynamics of cognitive systems.

The cognitive system must play both the role of the control system and the control engineer (i.e., the observer). While it tries to control the situation, it must evaluate its own performance and adjust its parameters (e.g., gains) in ways to ensure stability with regards to satisfying intentions.

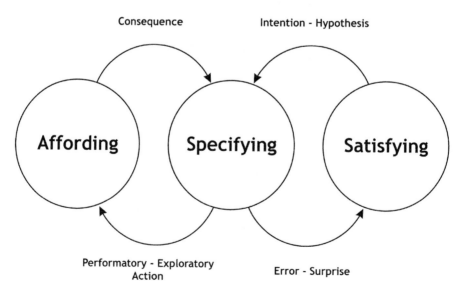

Figure 9.1 The abduction system must simultaneously solve the observation and the control problems. Thus, every link has a dual function in order to couple perception and action.

Note that phenomenologically when the brakes behave as expected (little surprise), it feels like control (simple error nulling). However, when the brakes do not behave as expected (big surprise), the situation feels more like problem solving (the observer problem). This idea of a control system that adjusts its own performance is typically referred to as adaptive control.

The need for cognitive systems to be both controller and observer, the need to function both as real-time controller and as an engineer (observer/designer), leads to what Weinberg and Weinberg (1979) call the *Fundamental Regulator Paradox*.

To put this into the context of abduction, one might say that the success of a cognitive system is to satisfy intentions (e.g., goals, needs, etc.), and it does this by minimizing errors. However, abduction systems learn from errors. So, the better job the abduction system does, the less opportunity it will have to learn. The paradox is that to learn from errors, you have to first make errors.

Weinberg and Weinberg[6] (1979) illustrate the Fundamental Regulator Paradox with the problem of driving over changing surfaces. For example, you might consider the case of black ice. Is the road ahead simply wet, or is it ice?

A good driver might 'test' whether the driving situation has changed by introducing small 'jiggling' actions on the steering wheel to potentially cause a small amount of skidding. The consequences of the jiggling are errors with respect to the intention of staying centered within the lane, but these consequences are information about the potential changes in the situation.

A novice driver, who does not test the situation through jiggling, may not discover the change in the situation until she is in an uncontrollable skid.

In essence, the jiggling is one way that adaptive systems try to avoid being trapped in local minimum solutions [in the neural-net or parallel distributed processing (PDP) literature this might be analogous to the technique of simulated annealing—essentially shaking things up to avoid being trapped in a local minimum]. The information created by the exploratory jiggling may lead the driver to change to a more cautious driving mode, thus leading to a more stable control system.

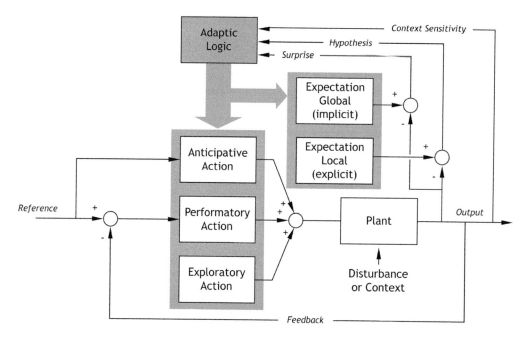

Figure 9.2 This diagram combines an inner (control) loop with outer (adaptive or metacognitive) loops to illustrate three styles that engineers use in the design of adaptive control systems.

Figure 9.2 illustrates a functional decomposition of the adaptive control problem in relation to three different ways that an engineer might introduce outer loops to achieve stable adaptive control.

In Figure 9.2, the thin (wire) arrows represent the flow of signals or information that is then acted on or processed according to the workings of each box (i.e., the transfer function—e.g., control Gains). However, the fat arrows that close the outer loops are signals that change the properties of the boxes (e.g., change the control Gains or the Expectations within the boxes).

Note that the inner loop includes three modes of action: performatory actions are intended to reduce error; exploratory actions are intended to test hypotheses; and anticipative actions reflect direct action to achieve a goal.

The anticipative path is an open-loop response that reflects direct responses to the reference (i.e., not dependent on error feedback). This open-loop path from the reference or goal could reflect actions that are shaped by previous experience with the plant dynamics (e.g., what has often been called a mental model or schema). That is, these are pre-programmed or automatic responses in anticipation of a consequence, rather than in response to error feedback.

This is typically referred to as 'ballistic' control [suggesting that once the action is released (fired), it will be completed without opportunity for correction via feedback]. Motor control research is often framed in terms of ballistic (automatic) versus continuous feedback control, as two incompatible processes. However, it is possible that these reflect two components of a more complex adaptive control system, as illustrated in Figure 9.2.

Note that although three separate paths are included in the inner loop, a single action may fulfill any or all of these three roles at any moment.

For example, the intention to brake might elicit a ballistic response (based on your expectations about how the car will behave). However, this response is also a test of your internal model. Since internal models will rarely be perfectly tuned to the situation, the response might get you into the 'ballpark' of your goal, so that the small errors that result can be corrected via the feedback loop. Or if the resulting errors are large (e.g., if conditions have changed so that your internal model is incorrect), then the surprising results of this 'test' will be information for adjusting the internal model via the outer loops.

The outer loops represent three styles of adaptation. The first style of adaptation is a direct function of the changing context, as illustrated in the outer-most loop (context sensitivity). For example, the aeronautical engineer might compute the appropriate autopilot gains for different altitudes and pre-program these different Gains into an automated control system. The Gains would be changed as a function of a direct measure of the appropriate context variable (e.g., the altitude). This is typically called Gain Scheduling.

In human performance, this path may be representative of the phenomenon of context sensitivity. That is, the strategy for controlling action or the expectations of the human agent (e.g., internal schema) may change as a function of the perception of the situation. For example, a smart driver may have different internal models for driving in different weather conditions. In this case, he doesn't need to test whether the dynamics have changed (e.g., dithering the steering wheel), rather the simple observation of snow may result in the adoption of a more cautious driving strategy.

The next outer loop (hypothesis) in Figure 9.2 reflects conscious exploration of the dynamics through exploratory actions. In engineered systems this might involve a low-amplitude test signal that is constantly input to the plant (i.e., dithering). This input is designed to have minimum consequences relative to the performance objective (e.g., to produce minimal error so that the car stays within the lane). However, the changes in the properties of the output from this signal can be information relevant to detecting changes in the plant dynamics. Deviation in the output related to the dithering can be fed back and used to adapt the control gains (and the expectations).

As noted earlier, skilled human drivers use a similar strategy to test for possible changes in the driving dynamics due to changing road conditions. The reference signals for this loop are labeled 'local expectations' to indicate that this loop reflects explicit tests of local hypotheses. In this loop the human agent is acting as a test signal generator and observer—in order to detect changes that might be relevant to control (stability).

Perhaps play serves a function that is akin to the role of dithering in the hypothesis loop. That is, the function of play is to introduce variations that provide the information needed for adapting the control system more globally, so that it will be better tuned to respond in a wide range of situations that are important to ultimate success of the system (e.g., survival). So, for example, doing donuts (intentionally created skids) in an open parking lot after the first snow may be an effective way for the cognitive system to adapt to future driving conditions. In essence, play is an invitation to explore beyond the bounds of local minima, in order to search for more globally resilient solutions to control problems.

The innermost of the outer loops (surprise) represents an approach to adaptive control that engineers call 'model reference' control. With this style of adaptive control, a normative model of the plant dynamics can be simulated in parallel with the actual performance.

For example, this model might be a simulation of aircraft performance at some nominal altitude. Expectations based on the normative simulation can then be compared with the actual behavior of the vehicle, and deviations from expectation can be fed back to adapt the control strategy (and the expectations). Note that this does not require explicit test signals (e.g., dithering). The evaluation is based on the plant response relative to the expectations for the normal context—that is, on the match to expectations.

As alluded to earlier, the engineer's 'simulation' may be somewhat analogous to what cognitive scientists refer to as expectations based on knowledge or a mental model. This 'model' reflects integrated experiences from the past that provide a backdrop that experts can use to assess situations (e.g., your expectations about how the brakes in the rental car should respond).

In some cases, this 'internal model' operates implicitly—so that experts may not become aware of the expectations until there is a mismatch. And even when the mismatch is noticed, the feedback may only be experienced as a vague sense that something is not normal. Thus, this might be associated with intuitive aspects of expertise.

Overall, the outer loops in Figure 9.2 may provide a constructive way to think about the general phenomena of metacognition; that is, self-awareness or our ability to monitor and critique our own performance. This is another layer of closed-loop, iterative processing in which the processes are simultaneously shaping their responses and being shaped by those responses. Again, this reflects the self-organizing aspect of muddling through. These systems are capable of learning from their mistakes—and of course this includes the implication that these systems do make mistakes.

Adaptive control systems where outer loops change parameters of inner loops are inherently nonlinear and thus are vulnerable to the potential instabilities of nonlinear dynamics. The stability of these systems becomes a much more difficult analytic problem for control theory, particularly considering that all three outer loops may be acting simultaneously. Like abduction, these systems can be trapped in local minima (e.g., converge on a degenerate model of the plant; superstitious behavior), and they are vulnerable to butterfly effects (e.g., a small change can cascade resulting in dramatic effects with regards to stability).

Hierarchical Control Systems

Note that in generalizing the observer/control logic to the performance of cognitive systems (e.g., Figure 9.2), the box labeled 'plant' represents the problem to be solved. In the context of many of the examples used to illustrate control systems, this represents the physical dynamics of a vehicle (e.g., body, aircraft, or automobile) that is being controlled.

However, in many cases, the control problem will involve the dynamics of larger sociotechnical systems that are far more complex, involving the need to satisfy many criteria and requiring consideration of many 'states' in addition to the physical properties of the vehicle. For these more complex problems, it may be useful to unpack the 'plant' with respect to multiple levels of control and observation.

For example, in evaluating pilot performance, it may be important to evaluate not only the pilot's ability to 'steer' the aircraft, but also the pilot's decision making with respect to choices about what goals to pursue (e.g., does he choose to deviate from the original flight plan to avoid potentially dangerous weather situations or perhaps to compensate for earlier delays in order to meet the goals of an on-time arrival?).

In order to better represent the full complexity of cognition, it may be useful to expand the traditional servomechanism metaphor to better reflect multiple layers of the cognitive problem.

William Powers developed a general control theoretic model of human performance that is based on a hierarchy of nested control systems.[7] The multiple layers in this hierarchical system are linked such that outer control loops specify the goals for inner loops. Thus, for example, a pilot's goals relative to satisfying safety and efficiency demands might specify the targets for the piloting loop (e.g., flight paths).

Figure 9.3 illustrates a hierarchical control model for playing tennis. This model includes three nested loops, where each loop reflects control with respect to different aspects of the overall problem (i.e., sub-plants) associated with playing winning tennis.

The inner loop reflects the problem of hitting the tennis ball. In this context, the 'plant' represents the problem of controlling the racket/body in order to hit the ball to the right place.

The middle loop represents control with respect to the game of tennis. This loop deals with the tactical constraints of the game (e.g., the factors that determine what shot selections will increase

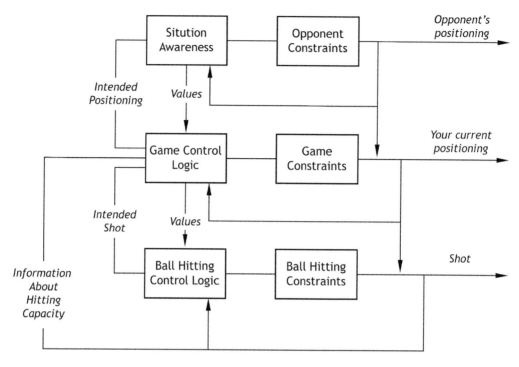

Figure 9.3 This illustrates three layers in a hierarchical control system for winning at tennis.

the likelihood of winning the point). It controls positioning of the player (being in the best position to prepare for the next shot), and one output is specification of the 'right place' to hit the ball, which will be the 'target' for the inner racket control loop.

The game tactics loop may be nested within an outer loop that involves responding to the dynamics of a particular opponent. That is, the strengths and weaknesses of a specific opponent might provide a larger context for choosing the game strategy (e.g., more aggressive, offensive strategy involving attacking the net; or more defensive strategy involving controlling the baseline) that sets the targets for the game tactics—'where to be' and 'where to hit the ball'—that, in turn, sets the targets for the ball hitting loop.

Note that there are three paths from each outer loop to the loop nested within it. The first coupling, as emphasized by Powers, is that the outer loop may specify the goals or targets for the inner loops. Thus, the tactics of tennis will specify the target for the ball hitting control. Similarly, in the case of aviation, decisions related to safety will determine what particular paths a pilot will choose to follow.

Additionally, the outer loop may specify values that set the context for choosing the parameters for inner loop control. These values are not typically specified in the control diagrams, but such values are reflected in the cost functions (e.g., payoff matrixes in signal detection) that are the basis for choosing 'optimal' or 'satisfactory' control solutions. For example, the value functions would reflect the preferences relative to speed-accuracy trade-offs related to the gain parameter for control.

Finally, actions in the outer loops will reflect the contextual changes (i.e., disturbances) that the inner loop must compensate for in order to meet the goals. In the context of the tennis example, the game dynamics loop will determine position on the court, which in turn will set up the physical constraints (i.e., the approach to the ball) that must be adjusted for in order to hit the ball to the intended place.

Hierarchical control systems will also involve couplings from the inner loops to the outer loops. For example, decisions about appropriate game tactics for winning tennis may depend on a player's assessment of her own hitting ability. A player who has a strong baseline game, but who is not confident in hitting overhead volleys, might prefer a more defensive tactic. Thus, choices in outer loops may depend on the ability to observe and make judgments about stability/variability associated with inner control loops.

A common error of novice players is to make tactical choices that are not commensurate with their ability level. That is, they may create unforced errors by trying to hit winners that they don't have the skills to make consistently.

In the early specification of his Perceptual Control Theory (PCT), Powers presented strong hypotheses about specific layers of control in cognitive systems. This led to significant debate, and in fact one of the early criticisms of Powers' approach involved the 'stopping rule' for adding on layers of control. In some cases, this was associated with the infinite regress problem associated with homunculus-based models of control.

However, in light of the idea of fractals, mentioned earlier in relation to the problem of measuring a coastline, it seems that the infinite regress problem may be a generic problem of complexity. The implication is that there is no absolutely correct number of control levels. The choice of the layers must be determined by the scientist/designer/analyst with respect to the pragmatics of her goals. For example, it is certainly possible to add inner and outer loops to this tennis example.

The problem of hitting the tennis ball can be decomposed into loops associated with the different motor components (e.g., leg/body positioning, swing control). Similarly, it would be possible to imagine outer loops to reflect questions about 'why' someone is playing tennis to begin with

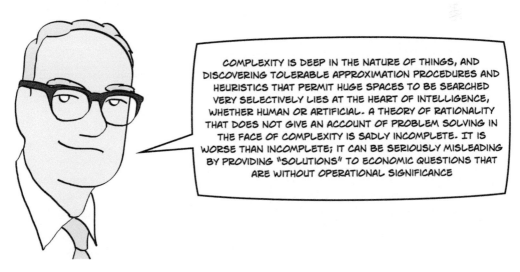

COMPLEXITY IS DEEP IN THE NATURE OF THINGS, AND DISCOVERING TOLERABLE APPROXIMATION PROCEDURES AND HEURISTICS THAT PERMIT HUGE SPACES TO BE SEARCHED VERY SELECTIVELY LIES AT THE HEART OF INTELLIGENCE, WHETHER HUMAN OR ARTIFICIAL. A THEORY OF RATIONALITY THAT DOES NOT GIVE AN ACCOUNT OF PROBLEM SOLVING IN THE FACE OF COMPLEXITY IS SADLY INCOMPLETE. IT IS WORSE THAN INCOMPLETE; IT CAN BE SERIOUSLY MISLEADING BY PROVIDING "SOLUTIONS" TO ECONOMIC QUESTIONS THAT ARE WITHOUT OPERATIONAL SIGNIFICANCE

Herbert Simon[8]

(e.g., is it a recreational or professional activity?). Also, it is easy to imagine that the individual tennis playing system might be nested within larger sensemaking systems (e.g., part of a team, or a league, or a sports culture).

Thus, there is no 'control system' in any absolute sense. Identifying the control system is a decision that researchers must make. This decision will be informed based on metaphysical assumptions (e.g., ontological and epistemological choices) and pragmatic goals.

Finally, it should be apparent that as we increase the number of variables that must be fed back and as we add outer loops that change inner loops, the complexity of the computations involved expands rapidly, thus raising questions with respect to the capacity to model this system using any analytical models of rationality or of control. Perhaps for this reason, those following Powers' approach tend to be quite skeptical about analytical models of control systems, preferring to use simulations as the basis for modeling nested control hierarchies.

Naturalistic (Intuitive) Decision Making

Gary Klein's[9] program to study decision making in naturalistic situations provides an alternative perspective on both adaptive control and on the nature of human decision making.

This program of research was in part motivated by the question of whether the *biases* observed in well-defined laboratory decision tasks, such as those conducted in the Tversky and Kahneman tradition (that will be examined in the next chapter), would be characteristic of decision making by experts facing ill-defined problems in their natural work domains.

Klein began by studying firefighters. This was a population who often were called to make decisions in potentially life-threatening situations (and conveniently, it was a population that was readily accessible). Would the experts be somewhat less likely to show the biases that were commonly found when college sophomores were tested on toy puzzles (e.g., gambles) in a laboratory?

Does experience or *expertise* matter?

Not surprisingly, Klein did discover that expertise matters, but not in the way he initially anticipated. When he began talking to firefighters about how they made decisions, where a decision involved a choice between several alternatives, the response was that this rarely happens. In fact, a common response was essentially, *"we don't make decisions, we put out fires."*

As Klein writes:

> I knew that the firefighters couldn't make their decisions by systematically comparing all of the possible ways to put out a fire because there wasn't enough time. I expected that they would only come up with two leading options, and compare these to each other. I was wrong. The firefighters, especially the more experienced ones, some with over twenty years of experience, usually just considered a single option.[10]

Klein developed the Recognition-Primed Decision (RPD) model to represent the processes that he observed in naturalistic decision-making contexts (Figure 9.4). The RPD model suggests that rather than comparing alternatives, people typically choose one alternative (i.e., hypothesis) based on their assessment (or recognition) of the situation.

This hypothesis may be further evaluated through mental simulation (e.g., by imagining the consequences of the choice, such as how the fire would respond to a particular decision about where

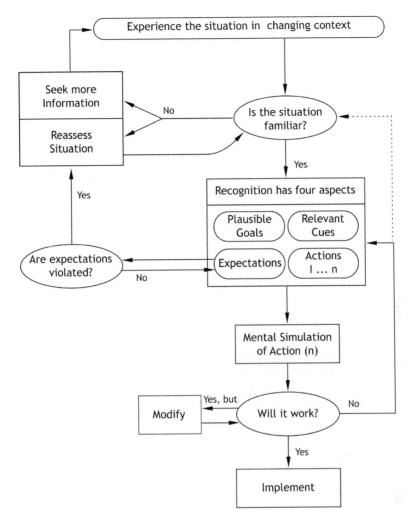

Figure 9.4 Klein's complex version of the recognition-primed decision model. Used by author's permission.[11]

to direct the hoses). If the imagined consequences satisfy the functional goals, then the actions associated with that option are implemented.

If the evaluation of the situation proves problematic (e.g., it is completely unfamiliar, there are inconsistencies with expectations, or there are no viable options), then more data will need to be collected.

However, if satisfactory hypotheses are suggested by the situation assessment, then these are evaluated individually until one is judged to lead to a satisfying outcome. That is, the alternative hypotheses are not compared—as suggested by classical decision theory. Rather, one option is further elaborated (what Dunker described as progressive deepening), and this option is either accepted as the path for action, or rejected. If rejected, then the next option is considered. The

options are not tested relative to the other options, but they are tested, one by one against the demands of the situation (will this work?), and the first option that satisfies those demands will be acted on.

While the diagram of the RPD model is more detailed than our generic diagram to illustrate abduction (Figure 9.1), it should be clear that the RPD model is an alternative representation of a pragmatic, abduction logic. This is an adaptive control system that generates hypotheses based on situation assessment and then tests the hypotheses against the demands of a situation.

An important distinction between the RPD model and classical models of decision making is that the RPD model emphasizes an intimate relation between perception (observation) and decisions. This is partially consistent with the dynamics of circles.

What the RPD model in Figure 9.4 fails to include, however, is the feedback from an implemented action back into the evaluation process. The RPD model closes the loop around mental simulations, but it does not close the loop around action. Thus, this model tends to isolate decision making (i.e., mind) from the larger pragmatic context of testing actions (and the beliefs and decisions guiding them) relative to their consequences (i.e., matter).

The RPD model focuses on choices (i.e., 'making right decisions'), rather than on the broader spirit of adaptive control, which is more about 'making decisions right.' We hypothesize that in situations that do not involve high risks, the options will often be tested by directly acting on them, rather than through mental simulations. That is, we wonder whether the prominence of mental simulations for the RPD model is a reflection of the high-risk contexts which Klein has studied.

Also, it is interesting to note that the patterns associated with recognition-primed decision making are very similar to the patterns that Adrian de Groot[12] had observed with expert Chess players. De Groot noted that Grand Masters tended to consider far fewer options and to explore those options in greater depth than less skilled players.

A critical difference between experts and novices was that the options that the Grand Masters considered tended to be among the best, suggesting that the Grand Masters were better at recognizing the best options. A Grand Master once replied to the question of "how many options he considered before making a move?" with the response, "Just one, but it's the best one."

Klein's observations of experts in a wide range of fields has confirmed many of de Groot's intuitions about expertise and decision making.

The Logic of Circles

The Cybernetic Hypothesis was very important historically in expanding our view of psychology beyond simple behaviorism to include problems associated with cognition (e.g., such as the role of intentions in shaping behavioral trajectories). However, the fundamental insight associated with the Cybernetic Hypothesis and confirmed by observations of naturalistic decision making is that biological systems have a circular organization that cannot be ignored and that cannot be addressed using the conventional logic of billiard ball causality. This insight has had limited influence on the field of cognitive psychology.

Experimental and theoretical work in cognitive science still tends to be organized around the same image of causality that proved so valuable to classical physics and to Behaviorists. Thus, the information processing system is typically viewed as a sequence of independent information processing stages, where the response of one stage is the stimulus for the next.

The goal for this chapter and the previous ones was to provide some indication of how the logic of circles is fundamentally different from the logic of billiard ball collisions (i.e., the stimulus-response model). In an abduction system there is no sense in which any signal can be identified exclusively as either stimulus or response.

For a cognitive system, what it sees shapes how it acts, while simultaneously how it acts shapes what it sees. As Gibson[13] (1966) noted, the abilities to walk around and move our head are as fundamental to how we see the world as the sensory mechanisms (i.e., the eyes). And as Powers (1973) emphasized with the term *"Perceptual Control Theory"*, what is being controlled is defined in terms of the comparator (i.e., the perception of what has happened, relative to what was intended), NOT in terms of the action.

In fact, control means getting the same outcome, through varying actions to meet the demands of different contexts or situations. A control system will rarely accomplish the same goal in the same way. Although a pilot might consistently fly the same approach path, the activities of adjusting the controls will be different each time, reflecting the unique conditions (e.g., winds) associated with each approach. The pilot controls the 'path' or consequences, not the activities on the stick and throttle.

Alicia Juarrero[14] (2002) noted that a wink is fundamentally different from a blink. A wink reflects a level of organization that is fundamentally different from the simple reflex of a blink. This organization reflects an intentional dynamic that is organized to satisfy specific functions. Even though cognitive science has shifted the locus of cause to mental sources (e.g., internalized

speech), for the most part, the field has been attempting to explain winks, using a causal logic that was designed to explain blinks.

In using simple control and observer mechanisms to illustrate the dynamics of circles, there is a danger of trivializing the complex dynamics of natural cognitive systems. In most natural contexts, cognitive systems involve multiple competing goals, linked by multiple interacting information loops (e.g., neural networks) involving nonlinear elements. This is truly a complex, "loopy" system. The insect nest-building example (described in Chapter 6) is a much more realistic metaphor than any simple servomechanism or observer. The simpler control mechanisms, however, can be important pedagogically in order to illustrate the limits of conventional causal logic.

Figure 9.2 provides a functional description of the adaptive control system that decomposes the problem in a way that reflects alternative engineering solutions. However, this decomposition is certainly not a representation of the organization of nervous systems.

In conclusion, the point is to provide further evidence that cognitive systems require a fundamentally different model of causality than the one that has been the basis for much of classical science. The language of cause-effect and the reductionist experimental methods associated with it do not provide an adequate language for describing or discovering the dynamics of living systems.

Cognitive systems involve a relatively tight coupling of perception and action and a relatively tight coupling between situations and awareness. This coupling can never be understood as the sum of main effects from studying perception and action independently. This coupling can never be understood as the sum of main effects from studying awareness and situations independently.

Let's go back to Pinker's[15] example of Bill taking the bus to see his grandmother. To say that Bill's behavior is caused by a desire to see his grandmother trivializes the dynamics of this system. Bill's behavior emerges as a complex interaction of properties of awareness (e.g., Bill's preferences and desires), properties of the situation (e.g., attributes of his grandmother and the transportation system), and properties of the information that links situation and awareness (e.g., bus schedules).

These complex interactions unfold over a long history of interactions (e.g., between Bill and his grandmother and between Bill and the transportation system). This history of interactions has shaped Bill's awareness and his ecology (e.g., the relation to his grandmother). Again, to reduce these dynamic patterns over time to a simple cause (i.e., *Bill wanted to see his grandmother*) frames the problem in a way that ignores potentially interesting aspects of human experience (e.g., higher-order control loops) that might be important for understanding why Bill chooses to visit his grandmother at this particular time.

More importantly, no matter how complex the model computations that link the mental event to the physical event, if the computations are designed around an image where the mental event causes behavior, then the computational model misses the fundamental intuition underlying the Cybernetic Hypothesis. That is, the logic of circles (the logic of life) is fundamentally different from the logic of reflexes or rule-based causal chains.

Circles muddle through!

Dewey[16] (1896) recognized that simple reflex models of causality would not be adequate for understanding human experience long before Wiener and his colleagues began to develop the mathematics of control theory:

The discussion up to this point may be summarized by saying that the reflex arc idea, as commonly employed, is defective in that it assumes sensory stimulus and motor response as distinct psychical existences, while in reality they are always inside a coordination and have their significance purely from the part played in maintaining and reconstituting the coordination; and (secondly) assuming that the quale of experience which precedes the 'motor' phase and that which succeeds it are two different states, instead of the last being always the first reconstituted, the motor phase coming in only for the sake of such mediation. The result is that the reflex arc idea leaves us with a disjointed psychology, whether viewed from the standpoint of development of the individual or in the race, or from that of the analysis of mature consciousness. As to the former, in its failure so see that the arc of which it talks is virtually a circuit, a continual reconstitution, it breaks continuity and leaves us nothing but a series of jerks, the origin of each jerk to be sought outside the process of experience itself, in either an external pressure of 'environment,' or else in an unaccountable spontaneous variation from within the 'soul' or the 'organism.' As to the latter, failing to see the unity of activity, no matter how much it may prate of unity, it still leaves us with sensation or peripheral stimulus; idea, or central process (the equivalent of attention); and motor response, or act, as three disconnected existences, having to be somehow adjusted to each other, whether through the intervention of an extra-experimental soul, or by mechanical push and pull.

(pp. 360–361)

In this context, one has to wonder whether the only change from behaviorism to the information processing model was to shift the origin of the 'jerk' from the 'environment' to somewhere inside the organism. There is little evidence that the larger implications of the coordination described by Dewey and developed more completely in the Cybernetic Hypothesis and models of Self-Organization (e.g., illustrated earlier with the termite metaphor, but also commonly associated with neural networks) have had much impact on computational theories of mind.

In contemporary models of information processing, the elements associated with sensation, perception, attention, cognition, and motor control are still often treated as independent main

effects in a simple causal chain, and there remains a very strong temptation to frame the narrative around agents (homunculi) in the head.[17]

Finally, it is important to note that in adaptive systems, error with respect to expectations is the information that supports learning. An adaptive system is a system that learns from its mistakes. It is interesting to consider the incremental muddling approach from the perspective of Taleb's construct of 'antifragile.'[18]

Taleb's construct suggests that the ability to learn from variability associated with either errors from expectations or from intentional experiments (e.g., play) is what allows the system to improve its fitness, increasing receptivity to new opportunities (positive Black Swans) and increasing robustness with respect to changes that might otherwise threaten stability (negative Black Swans).

In this context, the incrementalist approach reflects caution with respect to the possibility of negative Black Swans, blended with exploration (i.e., muddling) generating the variability that opens the possibility to discover positive Black Swans. Relating back to Weick's example illustrated in the opening cartoon, in everyday life we never have a completely accurate map. Past experience can be a valuable tool to help us orient to current situations (i.e., assimilation), but the future will never be exactly like the past, so we have to be prepared to adapt to the inevitable changes (i.e., accommodation). As Taleb notes:

> the random element in trial and error is not quite random, if it is carried out rationally, using error as a source of information. If every trial provides information about what does not work, you start zooming in on a solution—so every attempt becomes more valuable, more like an expense than an error. And of course, you make discoveries along the way.[19]

Notes

1. Simon, H.A., & Newell, A. (1958). Heuristic problem solving: The next advance in operations research. *Operations Research*, 6(1), 1–10.
2. Peirce, C.S. (1878). Deduction, induction, and hypothesis. *Popular Science Monthly*, 13, 470–482.
3. Weick, K.E. (1995). *Sensemaking in organizations*. Thousand Oaks, CA: Sage Publications.
4. Lindblom, C.E. (1959). The science of 'muddling through'. *Public Administration Review*, 19(2), 79–88.
5. Lindblom, C.E. (1979). Still muddling, not yet through. *Public Administration Review*, 39(6), 517–526.
6. Weinberg, G.M., & Weinberg, D. (1979). *On the design of stable systems*. New York: Wiley.
7. Powers, W.T. (1973). *Behavior: The control of perception*. Hawthorne, NY: Aldine.
8. Simon, H.A. (1978). Rationality as process and product of thought. *The American Economic Review*, 68(2), 1–16. (p. 11).
9. Klein, G. (1989). Recognition-primed decisions. In W.B. Rouse (Ed.). *Advances in man-machine systems research* (pp. 47–92). Greenwich, CT: JAI Press.

   Klein, G. (2003). *Intuition at work*. New York: Currency/Doubleday.

   Zsambok, C.E., & Klein, G. (Eds.). (1997). *Naturalistic decision making*. Mahwah, NJ: Erlbaum.
10. Zsambok, & Klein (Eds.). (1997), p. HV.
11. Klein, G. (1993). Naturalistic decision making: Implications for design. State of the Art Report (SOAR). Wright-Patterson, AFB, OH: Crew Systems Ergonomics Information Analysis Center. (p. 34).
12. deGroot, A. (1965). *Thought and choice in chess*. The Hague, Netherlands: Mouton Press.
13. Gibson, J.J. (1966). *The senses considered as perceptual systems*. Boston: Houghton Mifflin.
14. Juarrero, A. (1999). *Dynamics in action: Intentional behavior as a complex system*. Cambridge, MA: MIT Press.

15. Pinker, S. (1997). *How the mind works*. New York: W. W. Norton.
16. Dewey, J. (1896). The reflex arc concept in psychology. *Psychological Review*, 3, 357–370.
17. Kahneman, D. (2011). *Thinking fast and slow*. New York: Farrar, Straus and Giroux.
18. Taleb, N.N. (2012). *Antifragile*. New York: Random House.
19. Taleb (2012), p. 71.

10

HEURISTICS

Biases or Smart Instruments?

> The theory of heuristic search, cultivated in artificial intelligence and information
> processing psychology, is concerned with devising or identifying search procedures
> that will permit systems of limited computational capacity to make complex deci-
> sions and solve difficult problems. . . . When a task environment has patterned struc-
> ture, so that solutions to a search problem are not scattered randomly throughout it,
> but are located in ways related to the structure, then an intelligent system capable
> of detecting the pattern can exploit it in order to search for solutions in a highly
> selective way.[1]

In the previous chapter, we introduced Herbert Simon's distinction between well-defined and
ill-defined problems. In essence, ill-defined problems, which are the most common in everyday
life, are problems that are too complex to solve using analytical approaches. The opening quote
to this chapter, also from Herbert Simon, suggests that an intelligent approach to solving these
complex (ill-defined) problems is to use 'heuristic' search that leverages structure intrinsic to the
task environment.

Webster's Dictionary[2] defines *heuristic* as follows:

> involving or serving as an aid to learning, discovery, or problem-solving by experimen-
> tal and esp. trial-and-error methods . . . ; also: of or relating to exploratory problem-
> solving techniques that utilize self-educating techniques (as the evaluation of feedback)
> to improve performance.

The parallels between this definition of heuristic and the earlier discussions about abduction, the
logic of circles, and the significance for understanding adaptive systems should be apparent. However, over the last few decades, the term 'heuristic' has taken on a different connotation with those
who study human decision making.

This is the result of an extensive program of research conducted by Amos Tversky and Daniel
Kahneman[3] to compare human decisions with the prescriptions of normative statistical and economic models. In essence, this research began with the question about whether people are good
intuitive statisticians? In particular, they had noticed, based on their own experiences and later
confirmed by empirical research, that people tended to be overly influenced by observations based
on small samples. For example, people (including experienced mathematical psychologists) were

overconfident that the results of an experiment based on a small sample would be successfully replicated with a larger sample.

One manifestation of this 'error' in judgment is the *Gambler's Fallacy*. Consider the following sequence of outcomes (H—heads; T—tails) from flipping a fair (unbiased) coin:

H T H H H H H __ __ __

Imagine the next three flips of this coin and write down what they might be in the blanks.

Now, consider some other situations—an average shooter hits six shots in a row in a basketball game; a top baseball player goes five games without a hit; or a roulette wheel hits red seven times in a row. These situations attract attention because they are surprising—that is, they violate our expectations. Thus, they beg for explanation. They elicit *hypotheses*—the basketball player has a *hot hand*; the baseball player is in a *slump*. In the case of the roulette wheel, one might hypothesize that the wheel is rigged, or if one believes it is a fair wheel, then one might hypothesize that *black* is *due*. Each of these examples illustrates the dynamic of *abduction*.

What was your response to the coin-flipping question: T T H, or T H T? It is very likely that your first imagined flip was tails and that at least one more of the other two flips was a tail. Why?

Tversky and Kahneman[4] used the term *representativeness heuristic* as a general label for these types of 'errors' or 'biases' in human judgment. The hypothesis underlying the representativeness heuristic is that most people have an image of how a roulette wheel (or any random process) behaves. For example, if you ask a class of undergrads to imagine flipping a fair coin 10 times, writing down the result of each flip, most students will generate a sequence with approximately the same number of heads and tails, with few sequences of more than three of the same outcome in a row, and with no simple pattern such as alternating sequences.

Thus, a sequence of seven reds on the roulette wheel does not match expectations for how a random process behaves. For this reason, it is disturbing (i.e., it creates tension or attracts attention and calls for some resolution or explanation). Two likely explanations might be that either it is not a random process (i.e., the wheel is rigged) or *black* is *due* (i.e., to help even the distribution).

Of course, in the very long run, the expectation is that the numbers of red and black will even out (given a fair wheel). However, attributing properties that will be true in the long run to smaller samples is conventionally considered to be an *error* or *bias* in judgment, because it is a misunderstanding of statistics.[5]

The cases of the basketball and baseball players are examples of what is commonly known as the *hot hand phenomenon*. This reflects a common belief about sports—that performance of athletes is typically characterized by streaks (i.e., the success on one shot or at-bat will be influenced by the outcome of the previous few trials). For example, Gilovich interviewed basketball fans about their beliefs regarding sequential dependence among shots:

> Their responses revealed considerable agreement: 91% of the fans believed that a player has a "better chance of making a shot after having just made his last two or three shots than he does after having just missed his last two or three shots"; 68% of the fans expressed essentially the same belief for free throws, claiming that a player has "a better chance of making his second shot after making his first shot than after missing his first shot"; . . . 84% of the fans believed that "it is important to pass the ball to someone who has just made several (two, three, or four) shots in a row."
>
> (p. 297–298)[6]

Gilovich et al.'s analysis of shooting behavior of professional basketball players suggests that, contrary to these beliefs, the probability of making a shot is statistically independent from the previous shots. That is, whether a shooter has made his last one or two shots does not change the probability that he will make his next shot. Thus, at least for premiere athletes, a sequence of shots, like a sequence of coin flips, appears to be statistically independent (at least by some criteria).

If this is in fact true, then the best guess about the likelihood of making the next shot is the shooter's average. In other words, knowing the outcome of the last two shots is no more valuable for predicting the next shot than knowing the results of the last two coin flips is valuable for predicting the next coin flip.[7]

Perhaps, one of the more striking empirical results from the Tversky and Kahneman research program involved another heuristic—the Availability Heuristic. This reflects the impact of memory on estimates of the state of the world. In one experiment, they first had people observe and record the result of spinning a wheel to get a random number. In fact, the wheel was rigged to stop on either 10 or 65. Then they asked two questions:

Is the percentage of African nations among UN members larger or smaller than the number you just wrote?
What is your best guess of the percentage of African nations in the UN?

Surprisingly, the judgments were biased by the supposedly arbitrary random numbers that were presented. Those who saw the 10 estimated the percentage to be 25%, and those who saw 65 estimated the percentage to be 45%. Thus, even though there was no reason to associate the numbers from the spin of the wheel with the questions, the numbers that were in memory at the time of the questions influenced the judgments.

Another example of the availability heuristic that can easily be replicated in classroom demonstrations involves estimating the number of males or females on a list of people. The critical manipulation is to include a number of celebrities of the same gender on the list. The gender that includes the celebrity names will generally be estimated to be more frequent, or people judge that

it will be more probable for a random draw to pick that gender, than the other gender (even when it is actually less frequent).

Again, the explanation is that the familiar celebrity names will be more easily remembered. Thus, the participants in this demonstration are using ease of recall (i.e., availability) as an index of frequency or probability. People seem to act on the implicit assumption that events that are easily remembered or that easily come to mind are more common or more likely than other events.

As with the representative heuristic, the availability heuristic suggests that judgments about situations are based on factors (e.g., ease of recalling or generating alternatives) that would not be considered in logical or economic models of rationality.

Kahneman and Tversky[8] have been consistent in pointing out that heuristics are often useful. For example, in many cases availability or ease of recall may be highly correlated with frequency. However, a fundamental aspect of their work is to measure human performance against the standards of normative prescriptions for rationality. For them, deviations from the prescriptions of normative statistical or logical models are 'sins' or 'irrational' behavior, and an at least implicit motivation for their work is to heighten awareness about the biases, in hopes that they can be corrected. For example they write:

> The true believer in the law of small numbers commits his multitude of **sins** against the logic of statistical inference in good faith. The representation hypothesis describes a **cognitive or perceptual bias**, which operates regardless of motivational factors. Thus, while the hasty rejection of the null hypothesis is gratifying, the rejection of a cherished hypothesis is aggravating, yet, the true believer is subject to both. His intuitive expectations are governed by a consistent **misperception** of the world rather than by opportunistic wishful thinking. Given some editorial prodding, he may be willing to regard his statistical intuitions with proper suspicion and replace impression formation by computation whenever possible.[9]
>
> (p. 110, emphasis added)

The impact of Tversky and Kahneman's program of work is that the term *heuristic* has now become associated with the constructs of error or bias. As they acknowledge:

The main goal of this research was to understand the cognitive processes that produce both valid and invalid judgments. However, it soon became apparent that "although errors of judgments are but a method by which some cognitive process are studied, the method has become a significant part of the message."

(p. 124)[10]

Additionally, what has been lost in Kahneman and Tversky's research program is the association between human decision making and the closed-loop dynamics that couple perception, action, and beliefs about the world that intrigued the earlier functional psychologists such as Peirce and Dewey. Their empirical work is almost exclusively based on open-loop puzzles where the experimenters control the information (i.e., the stimulus) and participants simply make a choice (i.e., response).

Perhaps, it is unfair to attribute this to Kahneman and Tversky, but the program of research that they have inspired has tended to be organized around the *errors* as the *objects of study*. This is analogous to research programs in perception that have been organized around *illusions*.

Thus, the concern raised earlier with regards to space perception may also be relevant here. That is, perhaps the errors reflect the paradigmatic choices of researchers who may be inviting participants to use a coordinate system that is not representative of the dynamics of experience (e.g., remember Langewiesche's example of judgments about distant points on the ground).

An alternative approach is to organize the theory and research around the associated functional dynamics of memory retrieval, situation assessment (observation), action (control), and reflection, and the coupling among these functions as reflected in a triadic semiotic system using abduction logic. In this context, the 'biases' may be symptoms that provide potential insight into the underlying dynamics. However, when these *symptoms* become the phenomena of study that theory begins to take on a naive *cause-effect* flavor that has the potential to miss most of the interesting dynamics of everyday human experience.

There is no denying the elegance of the empirical research program of Kahneman and Tversky. However, there is growing concern that they may have been asking the wrong questions. Or, in other words, there is growing concern that they may have framed the questions in the wrong coordinate system. Observations, such as those of Klein discussed in the previous chapter, raise concern that the problems that the Kahneman and Tversky program set in their studies may not be representative of everyday rationality and decision making.

Fast, Frugal Decision Making

Tversky and Kahneman's work is guided by an implicit belief that the normative models represent standards for correctness or success that people should aspire to (i.e., the 'ought' that Linblum referred to). There is a normative imperialism or idealism that may be justified for the well-structured problems typical of their experimental contexts. However, there is doubt about whether these normative ideals can be used effectively for ill-structured problems typical of everyday life. In contrast to the program on decision biases, de Groot and Klein's observations suggest that what experts do in many natural contexts is quite different than what is prescribed by the normative economic models.

155

The behavior of the experts looks more like skillful muddling than like systematic application of normative logic. This leads many to question whether the assumptions underlying the normative prescriptions are justified in the context of the complexities of everyday experience. Are they justified in the context of the alternative example to the book bag and poker chip situation described in the previous chapter?

Gigerenzer and others[11] offer an alternative to the Tversky and Kahneman perspective on heuristics. Rather than characterizing heuristics as being a negative consequence of internal information processing limits, Todd and Gigerenzer (2003) describe heuristics as an adaptive fit, where people leverage regularities/constraints in the problem ecology to improve the efficiency of performance. This seems to be more in line with the opening quote from Simon and the definition of heuristics at the start of this chapter.

Todd and Gigerenzer (2003) describe the contrast between conventional perspectives on heuristics/bounded rationality as either optimization under constraints or as perceptual illusions with their alternative perspective on an adaptive ecological rationality:

> The . . . preceding perspectives see bounded rationality in a rather negative light, as something that usually keeps us from being truly optimal or properly rational. This arises in part because the internal and external constraints on decision makers are seen as being unaligned and hence often at odds—accordingly, if we had greater memory or better computational ability, perhaps, then we might not need to pay the costs for searching for extra information. But this opposition between internal and external bounds need not be the case (and, for systems that have adapted their internal structure to the external world over time, typically would not be the case). Instead . . . bounded rationality can be seen as emerging from the joint effect of two interlocking components: the internal limitations of the (human) mind, and the structure of the external environments in which the mind operates. This fit between the internal cognitive structure and the external information structure underlies the perspective of bounded rationality as ecological rationality—making good (enough) decisions by exploiting the structure of the environment.
>
> (pp. 147–148)[12]

In contrast to Klein's focus on decision making in natural contexts, Gigerenzer and his colleagues have focused on exploring some of the complexities (unresolvable uncertainties)

associated with ill-defined problems in relation to more controlled laboratory tasks and quantitative simulations.

For example, in one task, the participants were presented pairs of cities and they were asked to indicate which was larger. The results suggested that the 'availability heuristic' (using recognition in memory) can be quite useful in this context. They found that in judging the sizes of pairs of German cities, American students outperformed German students. It seems that American students used a recognition heuristic—if they recognized one of the cities, then they judged that city to be larger. It turns out that this heuristic can be quite effective for contexts where there is a relatively high correlation between recognition and the criterion being judged. For German students, this heuristic was less useful, since many other factors, other than size, affected recognition.[13]

The recognition-heuristic might be envisioned as a component of a noncompensatory decision process that is somewhat analogous to Klein's RPD model. The first step in evaluating a pair of cities is the recognition test. If one is recognized but not the other, then choose that city (ignoring any further information). If both or neither is recognized, then other information might be considered. For example, does one of the cities have a sports franchise? If yes, pick that city. This process could proceed in an iterative fashion, where the next iteration is only considered if a decision is not possible based on the earlier cycles.

This process can be formalized in a lexicographic decision rule. A lexicographic decision rule begins by comparing alternatives relative to the most important attribute, eliminating any alternatives that are not satisfactory with respect to that attribute. It then proceeds with the next most important attribute, continuing until all but one alternative is eliminated.

For example, in searching for a new home, the alternatives may first be narrowed based on price (affordability). All homes above a certain price might be eliminated. A second attribute might be commuting distance. All options beyond a criterion commute time to work might then be eliminated. A third attribute might be number of bedrooms. Homes with less than a certain number of bedrooms might be eliminated from consideration. This process would proceed, until the number of alternative homes was reduced to a single choice (or at least to a small, manageable number of options).

It should be obvious that the lexicographic decision rule requires simpler comparisons (ordering options on only one attribute at a time), relative to a compensatory rule that requires simultaneous consideration of all the attributes of all the alternatives. Thus, it is potentially 'fast and frugal' relative to the cognitive demands of a process that considers all the information.

However, somewhat surprisingly, a lexicographic-type process may also be more accurate or at least as accurate as more cognitively intensive processes that consider and weigh all the information available. This will be particularly true when there is one or a few attributes that are highly diagnostic and/or when the signal values of attributes are highly correlated (they are redundant), but when the noise (uncertainty) associated with each attribute is unique. In these cases, consideration of less-diagnostic attributes can contribute more noise than signal to the process (i.e., increasing uncertainty, rather than reducing it).

A decision maker that selectively focuses on a single (or a few) particularly diagnostic cues may be both faster and more accurate than a decision maker that attempts to take all the data into account before making a choice. Thus, a heuristic that uses structure of the task to narrow the number of attributes/options to consider (as suggested by the opening quote from Simon) may be much smarter with respect to solving ill-structured problems than one that relies on more complete statistical models. Such heuristic solutions might be particularly 'smart' when the complexity/uncertainty is great and the window of opportunity for making the right choice is limited (i.e., there is time pressure).

Other noncompensatory decision rules include conjunctive and disjunctive rules. With a conjunctive rule, attributes for a single option are considered. If all attributes exceed predetermined criteria for satisfaction, then that option is selected. If not, the next option is considered.

For example, you buy the first house that you find that is affordable, close enough to work, with an adequate number of bedrooms. The conjunctive rule seems more consistent with Klein's observations of naturalistic decision making, because with this process alternatives are considered one at a time, until a satisfactory alternative is discovered.

Gert Gigerenzer[14]

A disjunctive rule is similar, but the criterion for choice is that at least one of the attributes has to be satisfactory. While the noncompensatory processes cannot guarantee that the 'best' option will be chosen, these processes greatly simplify the demands on computational resources (e.g., memory) and the result will typically be satisfactory (if not optimal). But for ill-structured problems the concept of *optimal* may be a mythical ideal that is practically unrealizable.

Both the research program of Tversky and Kahneman and the program of Gigerenzer and the ABC group consider the information processing limits of humans (e.g., in terms of memory and computational capabilities). For Tversky and Kahneman, the heuristics are adaptations to these internal constraints. However, for Gigerenzer et al., heuristics are adaptations to ecological or problem constraints that allow satisfying solutions in spite of the information limits.

For Tversky and Kahneman, heuristics are violations of good thinking that are necessary due to information processing limitations. For Gigerenzer, heuristics are intelligent adaptations that often make the information processing limits irrelevant to the ultimate performance levels that can be achieved. And, in fact, they have suggested that some of the information processing limitations (e.g., short-term memory limits) may actually be well adapted to the demands of survival.

For example, Schooler, Herwig, and Herzog (2011) observe:

> Some researchers have suggested, however, that forgetting may be functional. One of the first to explore this possibility was James (1890), who wrote, "In the practical use of our intellect, forgetting is as important a function as recollecting" (p. 679). In his view, forgetting is the mental mechanism behind the selectivity of information processing, which in turn is "the very keel on which our mental ship is built."
>
> (p. 145)[15]

In essence, the claim is that working memory often functions as a selective filter that facilitates performance by narrowing attention to signals and thus minimizing the 'noise' associated with what would otherwise be a buzzing, booming confusion (i.e., data overload). In other words, the limitations on working memory reflect an adaptive tuning of the observer (Chapter 8) to reflect the demands for extracting the 'signal' (i.e., what matters) from the 'noisy input channel.'

Another important difference between these two approaches is the view of the decision-making process. For Tversky and Kahneman, the focus is on a specific choice (e.g., what option is more likely). In many of the experimental paradigms used by Tversky and Kahneman, people are given complete information (or at least, the problem is posed in a way that there is no opportunity to gather more information). However, for Todd and Gigerenzer the decision process is viewed as a search process. Thus, one of the important questions is the stopping rule. That is, at what point do you stop considering options and/or attributes and make a decision or act.

For Todd and Gigerenzer the process dynamic is more similar to the dynamic of the observer that we discussed in Chapter 8. As with the observer, there will typically be a speed-accuracy trade-off. Thus, the search process will always be judged relative to some value system (e.g., the costs of information, the costs of time, the costs of error, and the values associated with correct decisions or correct actions). The implication of this is that it becomes necessary to test the decision process against the pragmatics of the situation dynamics, rather than against some abstract mathematical or logical ideal.

Fault Diagnosis in Complex Systems

The classical information processing approach to human performance tends to significantly under-estimate the necessary 'loopiness' associated with adaptive control. This classical view is illustrated in Figure 9.3. This illustration is a closed-loop system, but it is typically treated as a logical pro-gression of independent information processing stages—from interpretation of the signs that acti-vate the system (up the left leg), to logic analysis of the situation and formulation of a goal (the apex), to development and implementation of a plan in terms of making specific actions (down the right leg).

In this conventional model, each of the boxes in Figure 10.1 represents a general-purpose pro-cessing module for accomplishing an information processing sub-task, and each of the circles rep-resents a transformation or recoding of information as a result of the operations of the preceding processing stage.

As a result of this view of information processing, researchers who take this perspective tend to focus on specific boxes, or subsets of boxes. For example, Gregory focused particularly on the left leg to understand how signs were processed to infer the state of the world. Kahneman and Tversky focused on the apex of this process to understand how the state of the world was interpreted and evaluated in order to generate a choice or make a decision.

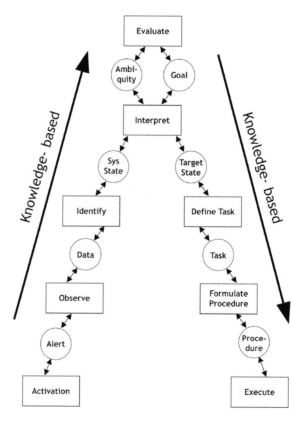

Figure 10.1 This diagram illustrates a view of information processing that is consistent with the 'rote instrument' view, where the Mind is viewed as a general-purpose computer.

In the classical approach, there is at least an implicit assumption that the operations of the individual modules within this process are generic and independent. With respect to our discussion of control and the crossover model earlier, this reflects an assumption that the transfer functions for the boxes are invariant.

In the 1970s and '80s, Jens Rasmussen was observing human performance in relation to fault diagnosis and general safety issues associated with the design and operation of nuclear power plants. For example, Rasmussen and Jensen examined information processing in the natural context of fault diagnosis in an electronic instrument repair shop.

They observed the testing process that the technicians followed when trying to diagnose problems with electronic instruments that were brought in for repair. They tried to map the observations onto classical models of information processing. However, the processes that they observed did not reflect a logical, orderly sequence of information processing stages as suggested by Figure 10.1.

First, they observed that the most common form of problem solving involved a topographic search. That is, the technicians tended to organize their search for the fault around the physical layout of the circuitry—tracing back from the fault and making good/bad judgments until they identified a problem. They noted that this process often involved many redundant tests. That is, the technicians did not take advantage of knowledge about the instruments that could have reduced the number of measures made.

Although not efficient in terms of minimizing the number of tests made, each measure only took a little time, and this process generally led quickly to a solution. The process also minimized the load on memory and the complexity of the reasoning involved. In other words, this process took advantage of the natural constraints (i.e., the wiring topography) to reduce the computational demands on the search process.

This was an example of what Runeson referred to as a smart instrument. A smart instrument is a solution designed around the constraints of a specific problem, as opposed to a solution that is designed around the generic internal constraints of a general information processing mechanism (i.e., a rote instrument).

Secondly, Rasmussen observed that the information processing did not map cleanly into the progression of information stages illustrated in Figure 10.1. That is, the search process seemed to be more opportunistic or heuristic than suggested by the classical model, as Rasmussen (1986) observed:

> Human data processes in real-life are extremely situation- and person-dependent, . . . the mental processes seem to follow the law of least resistance, and a shift between strategies will take place whenever a momentary difficulty is encountered in the current strategy or special information is recognized that makes another strategy look more promising.
>
> (p. 70–71)[16]

To illustrate the opportunistic nature of the search process, Rasmussen (1986) folded the classical information processing image to form the Decision Ladder. By folding the classical image, it was easier to show the opportunistic pattern of associations as arrows that cut across the stages of information processing.

These associations supported fast, frugal search processes that satisfied the pragmatic demands of discovering the fault and fixing the equipment, while minimizing the demands on components higher in the decision ladder.

Rasmussen (1986) wrote:

> immediate associations may lead directly from one state of knowledge to the next. Such direct associations between states of knowledge is the typical process in familiar situations and leads to very efficient bypassing of low-capacity, higher-level processes. Such associations do not follow logical rules; they are based on prior experience and can connect all categories of "states of knowledge."
>
> (p. 69)[17]

Thus, a technician might automatically associate an observation with a particular task or procedure, based on a simple association (availability)—"that's what worked yesterday"—without bothering to consider the logical relations that justified the procedure (e.g., a causal functional model of the equipment). The shunts or short cuts shown in Figure 10.2 illustrate just some of the many possible associations between knowledge states.

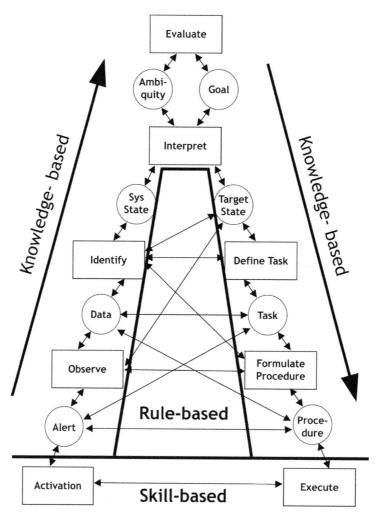

Figure 10.2 Rasmussen's Decision Ladder.

In principle, Rasmussen realized that any knowledge state can be associated with any other, and further these associations can go in any direction (e.g., in the process of formulating a procedure an observation may become more salient, or a hypothesis about the system state might be triggered). Thus, the Decision Ladder models the cognitive process as a richly connected associative network, rather than as a multi-stage communication channel.

In essence, the shunts across the Decision Ladder result from local mental models or schema that are built up through past experience. These models can be triggered both by specific properties of a problem (e.g., recognizing a familiar pattern) and by the broader context (e.g., proximity to another potentially unrelated event).

The 'higher' processes in the Decision Ladder (e.g., interpreting and evaluating) represent the most demanding mental operations from a computational point of view. In other words, the higher processes represent the processing bottleneck. Thus, the shortcuts across the Decision Ladder represent specific hypotheses about how experts can by-pass the limitations typically associated with logical computations. These shunts represent paths to fast, frugal solutions to the task.

The processes at the apex of the Decision Ladder represent what Piaget referred to as *Formal Thinking*. This formal thinking is typically associated with the normative logical procedures assumed by classical information processing theories.

The Decision Ladder represents a general hypothesis in line with Runeson's observations about smart instruments. This suggests that due to their extensive experience, experts have developed many associations (smart instruments or heuristics) that provide them with opportunities to by-pass the intensive analytical reasoning processes associated with the higher processes in the Decision Ladder.

These associations allow experts to 'recognize' solutions,[18] rather than analytically interpreting the situation and evaluating options (activities that may be necessary for novices, who haven't learned the shortcuts yet). This model provides an architecture for understanding the comments of Klein's firefighters. They "don't make decisions" (i.e., they by-pass the formal thinking processes typically associated with decision making).

Thus, the shortcuts across the decision ladder are the traces of *smart instruments*. In this case, the sources of the shortcuts are not associated with constraints internal to the information processing mechanism, but rather they are associated with constraints of the problem context. These leaps across the decision ladder reflect associations that have been reinforced by previous experience with the problem.

This possibility is reflected in Ericsson and Charness's[19] observations about expertise:

> acquired skill can allow experts to circumvent basic capacity limits of short-term memory and of the speed of basic reactions, making potential basic limits irrelevant. . . . the critical mechanisms [that mediate expert performance] reflect complex, domain-specific cognitive structures and skills that performers have acquired over extended periods of time. Hence, individuals do not achieve expert performance by gradually refining and extrapolating the performance they exhibited before starting to practice but instead by restructuring the performance and acquiring new methods and skills.
>
> (p. 731)

In order to explore this possibility further, it is necessary to ground the information processing mechanisms in the structure of the problem. That is, to move beyond the dyadic semiotic system that focuses exclusively on interpretive processing inside the head—to consider the structural links that anchor meaning in a triadic semiotic system that spans both awareness and situations.

In the Decision Ladder the shunts across the branches reflect the adaptations to the problem ecology. These adaptations will typically reflect improved fit (i.e., control efficiency and stability) based on leveraging task structure and minimizing computational demands.

Thus, the 'associations' represented by the shunts across the Decision Ladder will be constantly changing (adapting) as a result of the consequences of their applications. Shunts (heuristics or associations) that lead to success will be strengthened and shunts that lead to unsatisfying outcomes will be gradually extinguished.

With increasing experience in a stable ecology, the associations will become tuned to the ecological demands, providing an implicit mental model as the basis for smart intuitions. This tuning process only leads to skillful adaptation if the ecology is stable. When the ecology changes, the associations can be a source of error, because they may no longer reflect the situation demands.

The Semiotics of Smart Instruments

In Chapter 3, the dyadic and triadic approaches to the semiotic problem were contrasted. On one side of this dichotomy were the rationalists who view the mind as a symbol processing system. The rationalists modeled rationality as a dyadic semiotic system analogous to a computer program. And they typically look to normative models such as those championed by Kahneman and Tversky as prescriptions for how these programs should be structured.

Winograd and Flores[20] summarize the assumptions behind this approach:

> All cognitive systems are symbol systems. They achieve their intelligence by symbolizing external and internal situations and events, and by manipulating those symbols.
> All cognitive systems share a basic underlying set of symbol manipulation processes.[21]

A theory of cognition can be couched as a program in an appropriate symbolic formalism such that the program when run in the appropriate environment will produce the observed behavior.

Table 10.1 Three different semiotic modes in the Decision Ladder.

Processing	Sources of Structure or	Examples
Skill-based	Perception-Action Dynamic (Signals)	Optic flow relative to control of locomotion
Rule-based	Consistencies/Correlation/ Patterns in the Ecology (Signs)	Consistent mappings (e.g., in visual search experiments, in written and spoken languages, in HCI interfaces)
Knowledge-based	Formal Logical Processes (Symbols)	Scientific Method

Thus, the implication is that meaning is the product of symbolic computational processes (i.e., the programs). In contrast, ecological psychologists, such as J.J. Gibson, suggested that meaning was more directly grounded in the properties of the ecology, without the need for a mediating symbolic representation. Gibson's theory suggested a triadic semiotic system where the constraints in the ecology (i.e., affordances) were directly specified through patterns in the perceptual medium (e.g., optical invariants).

Rasmussen's model, however, suggested a resolution in which both sides in this dichotomy were right (i.e., an inclusional solution of the dialectic argument between the rationalists and the ecologists). He suggested that it was possible to identify qualitatively different styles of processing *(skill-, rule-, and knowledge-based)* associated with three different semiotic mappings to the problem ecology that he labeled: *signal, sign,* and *symbol.*

Figure 10.2 illustrates the three styles of processing within the decision ladder framework, and Table 10.1 illustrates the differential structure associated with the distinctions: signal, sign, and symbol.

As the different styles or modes of processing are briefly described, please note that each mode of processing involves a complete loop in which perception is coupled with action through the ecology. While the typical information processes are included in the Decision Ladder, all processes are not necessarily involved in all situations. The distinct loops are closed in ways that differentially tap into the information processing mechanisms. In particular, the mechanisms most closely associated with classical rationality (conventional or normative logic) are by-passed for skill- and rule-based processing.

Also, note that the processing modes are contingent on the mapping between the processing mechanisms in the head (constraints on awareness) and the structure in the problem ecology (constraints on situations). In essence, the three modes represent shifts in the degree to which the dynamics of processing leverage structure in the ecology. There is an assumption that with more structure in the ecology, the demands on formal symbolically based reasoning processes can be reduced.

In essence, consistent structures in the dynamics of perception and action and in the ecology allow the processing to become *smarter* (i.e., the computations become simpler or more direct) and thus, the thinking becomes more *productive* (a la Wertheimer[22]) or more *automatic* (a la Schneider & Shiffrin[23]) or more *intuitive* (a la Klein[24]).

Note, however, that this inverts classical ideas about what it means to be smarter. There has been an implicit notion that 'smart' means thinking like a computer; that is, algorithmically following the normative prescriptions of classical logic and mathematics (e.g., economic models of rationality).

In terms of the semiotics of the decision ladder and Runeson's construct of smart instrument, people are smartest when they leverage the natural constraints in the ecology to achieve their goals with minimal formal computations. Thus, the prototype for 'smart' shifts from the contemplative philosopher to the skillful athlete or artisan.

Signals: Skill-Based Processing

Rasmussen used the term *signal* to describe the semiotic relations underlying *skill-based* processing. Signal refers to situations where the structural constraints that specify important functional relations are intrinsic to the perception-action coupling.

Peirce used the term *indexical* for this type of mapping and used the example of a weather vane for specifying wind direction. The direction of the weather vane will *emerge* from the interactions with the wind. The direction of the wind is *directly* specified as a result of the physical interaction with the wind. Another physical example of an indexical relation is the height of mercury in a thermometer in relation to temperature. The height is a *direct index* of temperature.

Langewieshe's example of the horizon angle for specifying whether an airport is reachable in a glide is an example of a *signal* relation (i.e., there is a one-to-one mapping between the angular projection relative to the horizon and the affordances of the aircraft, the glide capability). The ability of experienced pilots to use this relation is an example of *skill-based processing*.

Experienced pilots can use the horizon constraint to by-pass any requirements to *calculate* or *logically infer* the reachability of an airport from symbolic data about distance and the aircraft's performance capability. Rather, the indexical relation between angular position with respect to the horizon and glide capability of the aircraft allow the pilot to directly *see* or *intuitively sense* the reachability of any location on the ground. Note that this suggests that intuition is grounded in structural properties of the perception/action coupling.

Gibson[25] (1958/1982) provides a more general description about how constraints in an optical flow field (essentially an angular coordinate system emphasizing invariant angular relations associated with the motion relative to surfaces) can be used to simplify the control of locomotion.

For example, here is Gibson's (1958/1982) explanation for steering and aiming:

> The center of the flow pattern during forward movement of the animal is the direction of movement. More exactly, the part of the structure of the array from which the flow radiates corresponds to that part of the solid environment toward which he is moving. If the direction of his movement changes, the center of flow shifts across the array, that is, the flow becomes centered on another element of the array corresponding to another part of the solid environment. The animal can thus, as we would say, 'see where he is going." The act of turning or steering is, therefore, a visual as well as a muscular event. To turn in a certain direction is to shift the center of flow in that direction relative to the fixed structure of the optic array. The amount of turn is exactly correlated with the angular degree of shift. The behavior of aiming at a goal object can now be specified (although the properties of a figure in the field of view which arouse this behavior have not yet been described). To aim locomotion at an object is to keep the center of flow of the optic array as close as possible to the form which the object projects.
>
> (p. 155)[26]

Gibson's general approach to optical control of locomotion provides a great illustration of skill-based processing. Gibson's optical invariants are structural constraints that emerge from the perception-action dynamics. That is, the optical flow invariants are created by the act of moving around in the world. Thus, they are being shaped by locomotion actions AND they are continuously feeding back as information that in turn shapes the control of locomotion action.

Note that *optical flow* cannot be found in light or eyes independently. Flow is created in the act of moving.

To briefly summarize qualities associated with skill-based forms of processing based on signals, there are three important characteristics of this form of processing:

Postulate 1. Skill-based processing will depend on learning by doing.

That is, the structure grounding for skill-based processing is a product of the perception-action coupling, and thus it must be discovered in the context of that coupling. Although good coaching may direct attention and facilitate discovery of the intrinsic structure, at the end of the day the only way to develop skill-based processes is through practice, practice, practice.

Postulate 2. Skill-based processing will be tightly coupled to the dynamics of action (i.e., the physical coupling between the body and the ecology), but loosely coupled to the dynamics of more abstract cognitive processes (i.e., language and formal logic).

Thus, skill-based processing will generally be difficult to articulate. This loose coupling has been recognized in classical research with terms such as *tacit knowledge, procedural knowledge, automatic processing,* or *intuitive decision making*. This dissociation between language and skill may explain why the best athletes are not always the best coaches.

Postulate 3. In some task situations, stable performance will be contingent on skill-based processing.

Generally, these situations will be ones where success depends on synchronizing actions with dynamically changing contexts. In these contexts, the efficiency of skill-based processing is essential to minimizing processing lags to avoid instability (e.g., pilot-induced oscillations). Remember that time delays set fundamental bounds that constrain the speed/accuracy trade-offs required for stability in closed-loop control systems (Chapter 7).

This is implicitly recognized in the Zen, "no-mind" approach to training skills (e.g., archery and swordsmanship) and may also be associated with the phenomenon of "choking" in sports or music performance. In high-risk or high-value contexts, people are tempted to "think too much" (in this context, to engage higher, knowledge-based or symbolic styles of reasoning that slow down the processes, leading to instability). The formal reasoning processes are simply too slow to meet the stability demands in many dynamic situations.

The key point is that skill-based processing is not a *lower* type of reasoning. It is a necessary adaptation to the demands of many dynamic situations (e.g., sports, music, skilled crafts). In these situations, *intuitive decision making* or *automatic processing* (i.e., fast or System 1 processes described by Kahneman[27]) will be far superior to alternative forms of processing that are too slow to allow

167

stable performance (e.g., formal, logical reasoning—slow or System 2 processes). For many situations, *skill-based processing* will be the smartest solution.

Signs: Rule-Based Processing

Rasmussen used the term *sign* to describe the semiotic relations underlying *rule-based processing*. Where the structure for *signals* is intrinsic to the perception-action dynamic, in contrast, the structure in *signs* tends to be associated with situational constraints grounded in the problem ecology. These include consistent social conventions (e.g., use of red to indicate stop) and other correlations among events or patterns in the task ecology that might provide a basis for predicting or anticipating future events.

In the context of the electronic repair shop, frequent types of problems in the past (e.g., bad power supplies) can suggest an initial first hypothesis to guide the diagnosis process. The key is that the hypothesis is not suggested by a causal analysis of the fault or an internal model of the specific failed instrument. Rather, it is stimulated simply by an association derived from past experience that may only be circumstantially related to the situation (e.g., prior frequency). This has the characteristics of an availability heuristic, since the first guess may be suggested by ease of recall (the memory of past events), rather than any logical link across these events.

The aiming off strategy[28] used by sailors and orienteers to solve navigation problems provides a good example of how structure inherent in a problem can provide the basis for rule-based solutions (i.e., heuristics) that greatly simplify computational demands. In the sailing context, consider the problem of navigating across the vast Atlantic Ocean from London to Charleston in the days before global positioning systems. The ship's pilot would need to frequently compute the position using whatever landmarks were available (e.g., the stars, the sun etc.). These computations can be very imprecise, and on a long trip errors can accumulate so that when the ship initially sights the North American continent, it may not be exactly where intended. In fact, Charleson may not be in sight.

A similar problem arises in orienteering, which involves a race across forested country from waypoint to waypoint using a compass and topographic map for navigation. When the next waypoint is a distant bridge across a river, because of the uncertainties associated with compass navigation, there is a high probability that due to accumulated errors, the orienteer will not be able to hit the river at exactly the location of the bridge. What does she do when she gets to the river and the bridge is not visible?

Skilled sailors and skilled orienteers use a strategy of *aiming off* to solve the problem of error in the *computational* approaches to navigation. That is, rather than setting their course to Charleston or to the bridge, they set their course for a point on the coast below Charleston or to the nearest point on the river below the bridge. That is, they purposely 'bias' their path to miss the ultimate target. Why? Is this an 'error'?

Using a computational solution, when you reach the coast or the river and the target is not in sight, which way do you go? If you use the aiming off strategy you know exactly which way to go. When you see the coast, you should be able to sail with the current, up the coast to Charleston. When you reach the river, you know which direction to follow the river in order to find the bridge. With the aiming off strategy, rough computations are used to get into a neighborhood of the goal (to reach the boundary constraint), and then, the local boundary constraint is used to zero in on the target using skill-based processes.

The *sign* relation is the structural association between the boundary (coast line or river) and the target (Charleston or bridge). Note that this is a consistency (i.e., pattern or constraint) within the task ecology that can be leveraged to avoid more formal analytical processes for navigating to the target. The consistency is extrinsic to the perception-action system (e.g., it exists independently from the ship or the orienteer), but it is intrinsic to the experience of the specific problem context.

Two examples from the experimental literature on human performance to illustrate the power of *signs* to support fast, frugal performance are the Stroop Task and Automatic Processing in visual and memory search.

In the Stroop Task[29] a conflict is created between two common associations with the same stimulus. For example, one variation uses color words that are presented in different ink colors. The task is to 'read' the color of the ink. This is difficult, however, because people tend to 'automatically' attend to the conflicting word. Thus, when the word 'red' is presented in blue ink—there is an automatic tendency to say "red," rather than the correct response "blue."

This tendency presumably is the result of a long history of experience with associating the letters r-e-d with the response "red." And in fact, this association is a very much more common situation than situations where you are asked to attend to the ink color of written words. Again, note the similarity with the availability heuristic, the strong association in memory (i.e., the word response) will, in this case, interfere with the task of naming the ink color.

In the case of visual and memory search, research by Schneider and Shiffrin (1977)[30] shows that when there is a consistent mapping between stimuli and responses (i.e., a target never appears as a distractor and vice versa), people will begin responding *automatically*—that is, the targets will eventually begin to "pop out" of the display, and response times will become independent from the numbers of items to be searched.

In a typical search experiment, a person might be presented from one to four target items to hold in memory. Then single or multiple display items are presented, and the person is to press a key if one of the display items is in the memory set and another key if the items are not in the memory set. The dependent measure is the response time. Under *variable mapping conditions*, the memory set items and distractors are drawn from a common set of letters, so that the memory targets on one trial may be used as distractors on other trials. Under this condition, response times tend to be proportional to the total number of comparisons (memory set x display set).

Under *consistent mapping conditions*, the memory items and distractors are drawn from disjoint sets of letters. So, the response to an item will be consistent throughout the experiment—once a target always a target (and vice versa). With extended practice under this condition, response times for the larger memory and display sets tend to be as fast as for the single comparison condition (memory set = 1 and display set = 1) under variable mapping conditions. Essentially, after sufficient practice the targets begin to "pop out" of the display—so that there is no need to search for them, and the result is fast response times that are independent of the number of comparisons.

The *automatic processing* exhibited in the Stroop task and the search task under consistent mapping conditions has many characteristics in common with skill-based processing. For example, performance takes on an almost reflexive characteristic. Also, like *skill-based behaviors*, development of automatic-like processing typically depends on extensive practice. However, from the triadic, semiotic perspective there is an important distinction between automatic processing in the Stroop and visual search task context and skill-based interactions such as the control of locomotion via optical flow.

In the Stroop and visual search contexts, the structure or consistencies are properties of the task. In some sense, this structure is imposed from without (as opposed to resulting from intrinsic properties of the perception-action dynamic). In the case of the Stroop task, it is mediated by the language culture that establishes the association between the letters r-e-d, the spoken word "red," and the color. In the case of the visual search task, the structure is imposed by the experimenter who constrains the mapping. Thus, performance in these tasks is mediated by well-learned associations or *signs*.

Within the local task contexts the structure or consistency in these experimental tasks is as reliable as any of the constraints that link invariants in optical flow fields to properties of locomotion. However, the consistencies between the optical array and motion can be discovered by moving around in the world. The consistencies between the optics and motion states are lawfully related to the physics of the perception-action dynamic. There is no need for mediation (although, again, discovery may be facilitated by good coaching). In contrast, there is no way to discover the association between the letters r-e-d and the word "red" or the color red through direct interactions with the letters themselves. The association is *mediated* by the larger social context that determines the rules.

Thus, Rasmussen used the term *signal* to describe semiotic relations that are grounded in the physical dynamics of perception-action coupling (e.g., associated with laws of optics and laws of motion). He used the term *sign* to describe semiotic relations that are grounded in the dynamics of the problem ecology.

Although *signal* and *sign* reflect different sources for grounding meaning in the constraints of experience, *skill-* and *rule-based* processes are both *smart instruments* in that they leverage the constraints (e.g., consistencies) to reduce uncertainty, and thus to simplify the information processing demands. The structure that underlies *signal* and *sign* relations might be what Wertheimer would refer to as the *deep structure* of a problem, and a good representation of the problem is one that takes advantage of this structure (makes it salient). The issue of 'deep structure' will be addressed more extensively in the next chapter.

Here are a few summary hypotheses about rule-based processing based on signs:

Postulate 4. Rule-based processes are organized to leverage the deep structure of problems, where deep structure reflects constraints or patterns embedded within the problem ecology that are independent from the perception-action constraints associated with any particular agent.

Independent in the sense that the pattern is an 'objective' feature of the problem, there will still be a dependency in terms of the observer's ability to detect the pattern (e.g., to see the coastline) in order for that pattern to be leveraged in problem solving.

> **Postulate 5.** The sign-based relations that are leveraged by rule-based processes are more likely to be based in explicit associations that can be articulated by the agent.

Thus, the rules can sometimes be expressed in explicit language as logical if-then conditionals. Thus, rule-based processing may sometimes be associated with what is classically referred to as *declarative forms of knowledge* (rather than procedural) and can be communicated in the form of explicit instructions. However, with continual use over extensive periods of time, rule-based associations can also fade from conscious awareness to become implicit habits—leading to Postulate 6.

> **Postulate 6.** In some cases, rule-based processing will result in efficiencies (in terms of reduced information processing demands and increased response speed and accuracy) that are comparable to those seen with skill-based processing (e.g., automatic processes); achieving these efficiencies will in some cases require the same levels of practice.

The result can be 'encapsulation' of the rule in ways that make it difficult for people to articulate. In this case the processing will appear like what has classically been referred to as *procedural forms of knowledge*. An important implication is that it is not possible to differentiate between skill- and rule-based processing simply by the qualities of the performance.

> **Postulate 7.** Sometimes the patterns experienced in task contexts will be circumstantial— that is, not grounded in the ecology or problem space, but rather resulting from serendipitous aspects of experience (e.g., a run of heads from random coin flips; a sample of only white swans).

It will often be difficult for an abduction system to distinguish between the consistencies or regularities grounded in the ecology and these circumstantial patterns. Sometimes the rule-based heuristics of an abduction system will reflect these circumstantial patterns. This can lead to errors or overgeneralizations (e.g., superstitious behavior).

Norman[31] and Reason[32] describe different types of errors that might typically be associated with skill- and rule-based forms of control. For example, a capture error where one passes too closely to a well-learned habit—and that habit captures performance.

Consider a time when you set off from the office with the intention to deviate from your normal route home to run an errand for your wife. However, when once you start on the familiar route home, you mindlessly follow that route home, forgetting to turn off at the point required for the errand. You only discover the error when your wife greets you at the door, reminding you of the intended errand. In essence, many human errors can potentially be explained in terms of overgeneralization of rules (i.e., applying associations that are appropriate in one context in a context where they are no longer appropriate).

Thus, as Simon observed, rationality based on smart mechanisms is 'bounded.' But the bounds are not necessarily linked to internal computational limits, but rather to the fact that structure in

the ecology is *situated*. A 'smart solution' in one situation may lead to difficulty if generalized to another situation.

Symbols: Knowledge-Based Processing (Formal Reasoning)

Rasmussen observed that in situations where the topographic search strategy exposed the technician to unpleasant or risky situations, (e.g., when working on components of the alarm system for the experimental nuclear reactor at Risø, where a test action might trigger alarms throughout the country), then the technicians adopted an alternative more deliberate, hypothetical-deductive strategy, where they were much more conservative about the tests that they made, basing the tests on careful, deliberate analyses of the system functions using abstract (e.g., symbolic) models of the processes involved (e.g., consulting manuals).

Thus, Rasmusssen observed that the rationality of the technician was highly context dependent. Rasmussen called the deliberate formal analytical process exhibited when working on the alarm system 'knowledge-based processing.'

Rasmussen used the term *symbol* to represent the semiotic structure underlying knowledge-based processing. Whereas signals are grounded in the dynamics of perception-action, and signs are grounded in the structure of the problem ecology, symbols are grounded in a representational system (e.g., a formal language).

Systematic application of an abstract representational system is what Piaget referred to as formal reasoning, and it is the same discipline that underlies scientific reasoning. This does not mean that symbols are meaningless, but rather it means that they are only indirectly related to the intrinsic constraints of perception-action or of the ecology. Rather, the structure emerges as a result of the imposition of some formal system (e.g., a grammar).

The mapping of the symbols to the dynamics of experience (e.g., the link between the speaker's intention and her words or the link between the words and the actual state of the world) depends on the mapping of structure in the representation to structure in the dynamic of experience (i.e., the correspondence problem).

In the context of experimental method, the quality of the inferences from an experiment about the effects of a particular variable depends on the scientist's ability to structure the experiment in a way that eliminates potential confounds with other variables. Thus, we might say that the grammar of the experiment plays an important role in determining the meaning of the result.

REFLECTIVE THINKING IS ALWAYS MORE OR LESS TROUBLESOME BECAUSE IT INVOLVES OVERCOMING INERTIA THAT INCLINES ONE TO ACCEPT SUGGESTIONS AT THEIR FACE VALUE; IT INVOLVES WILLINGNESS TO ENDURE A CONDITION OF MENTAL UNREST AND DISTURBANCE.

REFLECTIVE THINKING IN SHORT, MEANS JUDGMENT SUSPENDED DURING FURTHER INQUIRY; AND SUSPENSE IS LIKELY TO BE SOMEWHAT PAINFUL.

Dewey[33]

For example, mathematics can be a good model for representing many situations, if the numbers and operations chosen for the model are well mapped to the phenomenon being modeled. Bayes' theorem might be a good way for revising hypotheses based on multiple samples, if you can formalize the Prior Odds and Likelihood Ratio as numbers. If you can't enumerate the possibilities (or the denominators are essentially infinite), then you may not be able to map the phenomena into the representation in a meaningful way.

Thus, with *symbol* systems there are constraints (e.g., grammar and syntax) associated with the representation that may or may not align well with constraints in the situation being represented. With symbol systems the experience is mediated by the symbolic representation.

Ironically, Rasmussen chose the label *knowledge-based* for the processes that have the least concrete grounding in everyday experience. That is, knowledge-based processes become important when everyday experiences (in terms of knowledge about problem structure or the constraints on perception and action) are minimal. Thus, knowledge-based processes are most likely to be engaged when *smart instruments* or *heuristics fail*.

Knowledge-based processes are organized around the formalisms of the representation. Thus, effective application of knowledge-based processes requires education with respect to the formalism (e.g., formal grammar, classical logic and mathematics or formal scientific methods).

The formalisms will be most useful for dealing with novel contexts, where the consistent structures necessary for skill- and rule-based processing have yet to be discovered. Appropriately applied, knowledge-based processes can be very effective for dealing with novelty and for discovering structure in situations that might eventually support skill- and/or rule-based processing.

For example, the intrinsic constraints of perception and action (e.g., the horizon relation to glide angle) must be discovered through doing. Until this structure is discovered, skill-based processing will be an unrealized potential.

Formal reasoning provides a disciplined way to manage the search for that structure. Thus, the 'doing' can be a serendipitous, random search process which may never converge, or the search process can be a deliberate, disciplined search—such as might be conducted by a scientist (or supervised by a coach or teacher). Knowledge-based processing reflects the internal discipline for managing the search.

Knowledge-based processes will typically be associated with the outer loops in an adaptive control system. These outer loops represent disciplined approaches for evaluating and modifying the logic of inner loops in order to achieve stable control. For example, this process may involve pruning old associations (rules and/or skills) that are no longer valid as a result of changing situation dynamics and hypothesizing new associations as the basis for inner-loop control.

In Piagetian terms, skill- and rule-based processing reflect the dynamics of *assimilation*. That is, these forms of processing reflect our ability to generalize from past experience in order to respond in a smart, efficient way to future situations. In this context, the construct of *schema* simply reflects that the structures discovered through past experience (e.g., structural invariants or consistent mappings) shape or constrain how we respond to future situations. To the extent that these *schemata* reflect *signal* or *sign* relations that are relevant to the future situations, they will provide the basis for satisfying interactions. Thus, the shunts in the Decision Ladder reflect specific schema.

The schema underlying skill- and rule-based processing can be used generatively—that is, applied in new contexts. However, generalizations from experience are always bounded by the limits of our experience and the degree to which the future is similar to the past. Thus, we are constantly challenged to revise the schemas to incorporate new experiences or to adapt to a changing future. Piaget called this adaptive process *accommodation*. Knowledge-based processing may play a critical role in the accommodation process.

For knowledge-based processing, general strategies such as those suggested by normative logical models may be the most reliable. This is because knowledge-based processing is demanded in those situations where the structure needed for smart instruments has yet to be discovered.

That is, the *symbolic* semiotic relation reflects the world as described by Richard Gregory earlier, where the *symbol* is a clue that must be *interpreted*. Note that the classical approach to cognition assumes that this interpretation process is the fundamental basis for all processing. However, in an abduction system as represented by the Decision Ladder, knowledge-based processing is a very special form of processing that is reserved for novel situations (such as the puzzles typically used in laboratory experiments on cognition, perhaps).

The positive side of knowledge-based processing is that it is 'general purpose.' In other words, it can be applied in a wide range of situations. The down side of knowledge-based processing is that these types of processes are computationally most difficult. The *attention bottlenecks, resource limits,* or *working memory* limits that seem to constrain performance in many general laboratory tasks[30] are thought to reflect the computational costs associated with knowledge-based processing. Knowledge-based processing is simply hard work—it's difficult!

Here are a few hypotheses about knowledge-based processing based on symbols:

Postulate 8. Knowledge-based processing is mediated by formal (e.g., logic, scientific method) or informal (e.g., metaphors) representational systems.

The representational system imposes structure in novel situations where the semiotic relation demands interpretation (symbol).

Postulate 9. Knowledge-based processing is most closely related to the common notion of thinking as internal speech.

Thus, knowledge-based processing will be associated with declarative knowledge. This type of processing will be most apparent in verbal protocols when people are faced with novel situations (e.g., puzzle solving). The less familiar a task or situation is, the greater will be the reliance on knowledge-based processes.

Postulate 10. Knowledge-based processing will be where the conventional limitations on information processing will be most apparent.

Ideally, knowledge-based processing will take the form of formal reasoning (i.e., consistent with normative logic). However, knowledge-based processing is computationally demanding, and people will rarely meet these ideals—as reflected by extensive research that demonstrates information processing limitations when people are presented with novel puzzles in the experimental laboratory (like the Wason task form presented earlier). Ironically, while most of the empirical work on human cognition has focused on knowledge-based processes, these processes are probably the least common in terms of the everyday experiences of most people.

Situation Awareness

The three processing styles represent different couplings within the triadic abduction system, NOT different mechanisms in the head or brain. That is, the processes represent differential solutions to the semiotic problem involved with coupling situations and awareness in order to adapt to the pragmatic demands of life. These couplings, through structure intrinsic to the physics of the perception-action dynamic (signals), through consistencies in the problem ecology (signs), and imposed through formal reasoning (symbols) will often be operating in parallel.

Thus, the three types of processing don't represent discrete, either/or choices. Rather, these processes will typically all be operating in parallel and will be interacting so that associations of one type can be shaping and being shaped by associations of the other types as they all contribute to the overall perception-action dynamic to support skill-, rule-, and knowledge-based forms of interaction. In other words, the Decision Ladder represents a hierarchical, adaptive control system.

For example, in the context of the hierarchical control model for tennis presented in the previous chapter, diagnosing the weaknesses and strengths of an unfamiliar opponent may involve deliberate, knowledge-based problem solving, while decisions about when to come in to the net (game tactics) may reflect more rule-based reasoning (cue-action associations), and skill-based reasoning may be the primary mode for controlling the tennis racket to hit the ball. It could be hypothesized that the more the inner loops (tactics and motor control) take advantage of the constraints associated with signals and signs, the more resources are available for the hard work of diagnosing the capability of a new opponent.

This parallel operation of the three styles of processing is reflected in constructs such as *top-down* (knowledge-based) and *bottom-up* (skill- and rule-based) processing. In control theoretic terms, the different processes might be envisioned as nested control loops—with skill- and rule-based processes operating as inner control loops, and with knowledge-based processes operating as an adaptive outer loop—capable of tuning properties of the inner loops.

Also, terms such as *metacognition* might reflect the adaptive coupling across the different loops, with knowledge-based processing functioning to critique and tune smart mechanisms operating as inner loops.

Note that the labels *signal, sign*, and *symbol* are not 'objective' properties of stimuli. Rather, their meaning is derived from the role that they serve within the triadic semiotic system. Thus, a particular relation like the horizon ratio may change from being functionally a symbol, to sign, and finally to signal with increasing experience.

For someone without flying experience, the horizon angle can be a *symbol* (i.e., the significance is yet to be discovered relative to the problem of what is reachable). With more experience or as a result of instruction, the significance of this relation for a specific ship might be recognized as a *sign* (i.e., as a heuristic for judging reachability for a particular craft—e.g., a mark on the windscreen). Finally, with extensive experience the horizon angle may eventually function as a *signal* (i.e., as an optical invariant that directly specifies reachability across a broad range of situations).

Summary

One way to approach the design of human-machine systems is as if the goal is to create smart instruments. This goal requires that we explore opportunities to exploit the natural constraints of the triadic semiotic dynamic in smart ways.

Perhaps, this is a critical aspect of the success of the iPhone and iPad. These devices exploit natural constraints to allow people to directly manipulate and discover functions with minimal dependence on analytical (knowledge-based) forms of reasoning. This includes sensors in the device that close the loop to automatically adjust to situations (e.g., orientation of the image in relation to orientation of the device, utilization of information about the current location). It includes supporting topographical searches guided by the spatial layout of the applications. It includes consistent mappings within the various apps in terms of navigation and function.

Thus, the works of Rasmussen, Gigerenzer, and Klein are important counterweights to the trends of studying "errors" or "biases," rather than studying the dynamics of human experience. These research programs place a much stronger emphasis on how the underlying processes *work* to satisfy the demands of complex situations that require *fast, frugal decisions*. This approach is gradually influencing a growing field of *behavioral economics*, where there is evidence of a shift of focus from the "ought" (i.e., normative economic models of choice) to the "is" (i.e., descriptive models of choice and decision making in everyday contexts).[34]

Another issue with the Tversky and Kahneman program is the, at least implicit, assumption that the normative prescriptions of classical logical and mathematical models of decision making (such as Bayes' theorem) are appropriate for guiding decisions in everyday life. There is a very strong sense that the motive of their research program is to *correct* the weak reasoning of humans. There seems to be an implicit notion that a system that behaved in line with the prescriptions of logic and economic models would make *better* decisions.

However, Todd and Gigerenzer provide data that makes a plausible case that, at least in some natural contexts, simple heuristics may lead to better decisions:

> in comparing the performance of one-reason decision making heuristics against more
> traditionally rational mechanisms (including multiple regression and cue tallying) on

a set of 20 real-world data sets, it was found that the fast and frugal heuristics used less information (about a third the number of cues on average) and still came close to—and, in the case of generalizing to new data, even beat—the performance of the more information-hungry and computationally expensive standard benchmark algorithms.[35]

Thus, if the alternative version of the book bag and poker chip experiment is more representative of everyday situations, then normative models of logic may not be the best guides for decision making and problem solving. This was the core of Peirce's arguments for *Abduction* as a more representative model of how people make choices in everyday life. People are not logical engines in the classical sense; they are pragmatic engines designed to meet the practical demands of survival in a complex, uncertain world.

The Tversky and Kahneman approach, at least implicitly, suggests that the goal in designing decision support systems should be to turn people away from heuristic approaches. That is, to move them away from the "is" toward the "ought." Lindblom's suggestion to improve incrementalism suggests a different approach. Perhaps the information technologies should be designed to improve the skills of applying smart heuristics.

Thus, in designing technologies to aid human decision making, the conventional focus has been to supplement the limited capacities of human operators and to enforce more normative inferential processes. The focus of more ecologically motivated approaches based on a triadic semiotic model is to support the recognition processes.[36]

Rather than using technologies to 'compute' the right inference, perhaps the technologies can be used to help people to visualize the problem constraints in ways that effectively leverage them to simplify the problem demands in terms of efficient coding (i.e., chunking) and smart heuristics. Thus, the goal might be to help people to see the state of the world (i.e., the situation) relative to the field of possible actions and the potential consequences of those actions relative to functional goals.

In other words, the goals of design might be to support assimilation (to help people to make smart generalizations based on past experiences) and accommodation (to help people discover and tune to the constraints in new situations). Perhaps, the goal should be to make people better at muddling through, rather than to correct deviations from the prescriptions of conventional logic!

Notes

1. Simon, H.A. (1979). Rationality as process and product of thought. (p. 11). *The American Economic Review*, 68:2, 1–16.

2. (1989). Webster's Ninth New Collegiate Dictionary. Springfield, MA: Merriam-Webster, Inc.

3. Kahneman, D., Slovic, P., & Tversky, A. (Eds.). (1982) *Judgment under uncertainty: Heuristics and biases*. New York: Cambridge University Press.

4. Tversky, A. & Kahneman, D. (1974). Judgment under uncertainty: Heuristics and biases. *Science*, 185, 1124–1131.

5. Tversky, A. & Kahneman, D. (1971). The law of small numbers. Psychological Bulletin, 76, 105–110.
   Tversky, A. & Kahneman, D. (1974). Judgment under uncertainty: Heuristics and biases. *Science*, 185, 1124–1131.

6. Gilovich, T., Vallone, R., & Tversky, A. (1985). The hot hand in basketball: On misperceptions of random sequences. *Cognitive Psychology*, 17, 295–314.

7. Nickerson, R. (2002). The production and perception of randomness. *Psychological Review*, 109 (2), 330–357. This excellent review raises important concerns about whether the conclusions of Gillovich et al. are valid.

8. Kahneman, D. & Tversky, A. (1996). On the reality of cognitive illusions. *Psychological Review*, 103, 582–591.

9. Tversky, A. & Kahneman, D. (1971). The law of small numbers. *Psychological Bulletin*, 76, 105–110. (p. 110).

10. Kahneman & Tversky (1996). p. 582.

11. Gigerenzer, G. (2007). Gut feelings. The intelligence of the unconscious. New York: Viking Press.
    Gigerenzer, G., Todd, P.M. & the ABC Research Group. (1999). *Simple heuristics that make us smart*. New York: Oxford University Press.
    Todd, P.M., Gigerenzer, G., & the ABC Research Group (2012). *Ecological Rationality: Intelligence in the world*. New York: Oxford University Press.

12. Todd, P.M. & Gigerenzer, G. (2003). Bounding rationality to the world. *Journal of Economic Psychology*, 24, 143–165. (p. 147–148).

13. Goldstein, D.G. & Gigerenzer, G. (1999). The recognition heuristic: How ignorance makes us smart. In G. Gigerenzer, P.M. Todd, & the ABC Research Group (Eds.). Simple heuristics that make us smart. (p. 37–58). New York: Oxford University Press.
    Goldstein, D.G. & Gigerenzer, G. (2002). Models of ecological rationality. *Psychological Review*, 109, 75–90.
    Panchur, T., Todd, P.M., Gigerenzer, G., Schooler, L.J. & Goldstein, D.G. (2012). When is the recognition heuristic an adaptive tool. In P.M. Todd, G. Gigerenzer, & the ABC Research Group (Eds.). *Ecological Rationality*. (p. 113–143). New York: Oxford University Press.

14. Gigerenzer, G. Fiedler, K. & Olsson, H. (2012) Rethinking cognitive biases as environmental consequences. In P.M. Todd, G. Gigerenzer, & the ABC Research Group (Eds.). *Ecological Rationality*. (p. 80–110). New York: Oxford University Press.

15. Schooler, L.J., Herwig, R. & Herzog, S.M. (2011). How smart forgetting helps heuristic inference. In P.M. Todd, G. Gigerenzer, & the ABC Research Group (Eds.). Ecological Rationality. (p. 144–166). New York: Oxford University Press.

16. Rasmussen, J. (1986). *Information processing and human-machine interaction*. New York: North Holland. (p. 70–71).

17. Rasmussen, J. (1986). (p. 69).

18. Klein, G. (1989). Recognition-primed decisions. In W.B. Rouse (Ed.). *Advances in man-machine system research*, 5(47–92), Greenwich, CT: JAI Press.

19. Ericsson, K. A., & Charness, N. (1994). Expert performance: Its structure and acquisition. *American Psychologist*, 49(8), 725–747.

20. Winograd, T. & Flores, F. (1986). *Understanding computers and cognition. A new foundation for design*. Norwood, NJ: Ablex Publishing.

21. Winograd & Flores (1986). (p. 25).

22. Wertheimer, M. (1959). *Productive thinking*. Enlarged Addition. New York: Harper & Row.

23. Schneider, W. & Shiffrin, R.M. (1977). Controlled and automatic human information processing: 1. Detection, search, and attention. *Psychological Review*, 84, 1–66.

24. Klein, G. (2003). *Intuition at work: Why developing your gut instincts will make you better at what you do*. New York: Currency/Doubleday.

25. Gibson, J.J. (1958/1982). Visually controlled locomotion and visual orientation in animals. British Journal of Psychology, 49, 182–194. Reprinted in E. Reed & R. Jones (Eds.). *Reasons for realism: Selected essays of James J. Gibson*. (p. 148–163). Hillsdale, NJ: Erlbaum.

26. Gibson, J.J. (1958/1982). p. 155.

27. Kahneman, D. (2011). Thinking fast and slow. New York: Farrar, Straus and Giroux.

28. Whitaker, L.A. & CuQlock-Knopp, V.G. (1995). Human exploration and perception in off-road navigation. In P. Hancock, J. Flach, J. Caird & K. Vicente (eds.). *Local applications of the ecological approach to human-machine systems.* Hillsdale, NJ: Erlbaum.

29. Stroop, J.R. (1935). Studies of interference in serial verbal reactions. Journal of Experimental Psychology, 18, 643–662.

30. Schneider, W. & Shiffrin, R.M. (1977). Controlled and automatic human information processing: 1. Detection, search, and attention. *Psychological Review*, 84, 1–66.

31. Norman, D.A. (1981). Categorization of action slips. *Psychological Review*, 88, 1–15.

32. Reason, J. (1990). *Human error.* New York: Cambridge University Press.

33. Dewey, J. (1991). *How we think.* Amherst, NY: Prometheus Books. (p. 13).

34. Ariely, D. (2009). *Predictably irrational: The hidden forces that shape our decisions.* New York: Harper Collins.

    Ariely, D. (2010). *The upside of irrationality: The unexpected benefits of defying logic.* New York: Harper Collins.

35. Todd, P.M. & Gigerenzer, G. (2003). Bounding rationality to the world. *Journal of Economic Psychology*, 24, 143–165. (p. 151).

36. Bennett, K.B. & Flach, J.M. (2011). *Display and interface design: Subtle science, exact art.* Boca Raton, FL: CRC Press.

179

REMEMBER DUNKER'S TRAVELING MONK PUZZLE? I THINK IT APPLIES TO US AS WELL

A MONK TRAVELS UP A MOUNTAIN TO VISIT A TEMPLE. UPON DESCENDING, ASSUMING A DIFFERENT AVERAGE SPEED, HE WONDERS IF THERE EXISTS A SPOT WHERE HE WILL BE AT PRECISELY THE SAME TIME OF DAY AS DURING THE CLIMB...

THE CLUE IS IN REALIZING YOU WILL MEET YOURSELF CLIMBING UP, AT SOME POINT DURING THE JOURNEY DOWN

MEET YOURSELF?

OF COURSE! GOING DOWN, YOU WILL RUN INTO YOURSELF CLIMBING UP. THE POINT WHERE YOU MEET IS WHERE YOU WILL BE PRECISELY AT THE SAME TIME OF DAY CLIMBING UP AND DECENDING....

I THOUGHT WE COULD CHECK WHERE THAT IS DURING OUR MISSION...

WHAT DO YOU THINK?

WELL, I AM NOT SURE WHAT YOU EXPECT THIS SHIP CAN DO, BUT I ASSUME IT WILL NOT TRAVEL CLOSE TO, OR BEYOND THE SPEED OF LIGHT....

AND EVEN IF THE TIME-SPACE CONTINIUM IS WARPED, BEING AT TWO LOCATIONS AT THE SAME TIME POSES A LOGICAL PARADOX WE ARE NOT YET SURE IF IT CAN BE SOLVED. SO I DON'T SEE HOW WE CAN MEET OURSELVES..

OF COURSE I DO KNOW ALL THAT!

OH...

I MEANT TO DO A MENTAL EXPERIMENT

YES, 'MENTAL' IS WHAT CAME TO MIND

HOUSTON, COME IN HOUSTON, I THINK WE HAVE A PROBLEM...

11

DEEP STRUCTURE?

One morning, exactly at sunrise, a Buddhist monk began to climb a tall mountain. The narrow path, no more than a foot or two wide, spiraled around the mountain to a glittering temple at the summit. The monk ascended the path at varying rates of speed, stopping many times along the way to rest and eat the dried fruit he carried with him. He reached the temple shortly before sunset. After several days of fasting and meditation he began his journey back along the same path, starting at sunrise and again walking at variable speeds with many pauses along the way. His average speed descending was, of course, greater than his average climbing speed. Is there a spot along the path that the monk will occupy on both trips at precisely the same time of day? Yes or no? Prove your answer.

The Traveling Monk Puzzle was typical of the type of problem that Karl Duncker used to explore human problem solving.[1] The first time I (the first author) taught cognitive psychology at Wright State, I gave this problem to the undergraduate students and gave them a week to solve it.

Midway through the week an excited student came to my office to tell me how he suddenly discovered a solution. He began, "I had been working on this problem with no progress and finally gave up. But yesterday I was driving from my apartment to my parents' home, at the same time that my Dad was coming to see me. And suddenly I knew the answer!" What did the student know?

On the due date, I asked who could prove that the answer was yes. One woman said that she had proven it using a graph, and I invited her to show the class the graph that she had used. I was expecting her to draw the graph in Figure 11.1, which is a classical solution to this puzzle.

Figure 11.1 shows position on the mountain path on the vertical axis and time of day on the horizontal axis. Thus, any time history of a trip up the mountain starts at the bottom left corner of this space and ends at the top right corner of this space. Similarly, any time history of a trip down the mountains starts at the top left corner and ends near the bottom right corner. These time histories must cross, and the point of crossing is a point where the monk is at the same place at the same time on both trips—QED.

However, I was quite surprised, because the graph that the woman made did not look anything like Figure 11.1. Instead, she drew the graph shown at the top of Figure 11.2.

When I queried her about the graph, she explained, "Didn't you say that the path spiraled up the mountain?"

I replied, "Yes?"

She continued, "Well, the center of the spiral is the top of the mountain and the other end is the bottom."

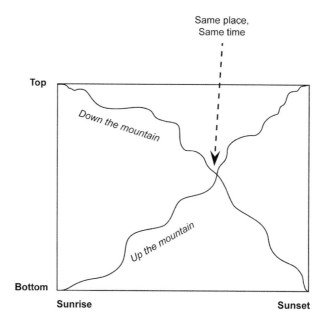

Figure 11.1 A solution to the Traveling Monk Problem showing that the paths must cross, proving that there is a point where the Monk must be at the same place at the same time on the two trips.

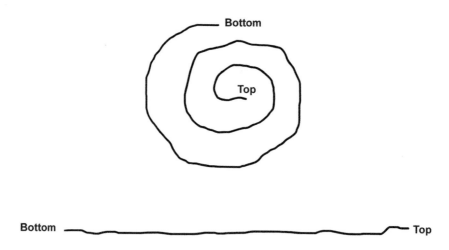

Figure 11.2 Alternative solutions to the Traveling Monk Problem.

To which I replied, "And how does this prove that the monk will be at the same time and place?"

She responded, "Well, I put one finger at the top and one finger at the bottom, and no matter what speeds I moved them, they always ran into each other."

I laughed; she had constructed a simulation, and indeed, she had proven the point!

Note that there was no need to draw the spiral. She could have also drawn a simple straight path with one Monk (or finger) on either end as shown in the bottom of Figure 11.2.

This leads to the other classical solution to the puzzle: to reframe the problem in terms of two Monks, both starting at sunrise, one from the bottom of the mountain and the other from the top. For most people, this shift in frame makes it obvious that if the two Monks take the same path, they must meet, no matter what their relative speeds! Q.E.D. This was the basis for the aha! moment experienced by the student who came to my office.

This puzzle is typical of the work of Gestalt psychologists on human problem solving. The Traveling Monk problem is often used to demonstrate that a shift in how a problem is represented can dramatically change the difficulty of a problem. In fact, problem solving is often characterized as searching for the 'right' representation, where the 'right' representation relates in some meaningful way to the deep structure of a problem.

Max Wertheimer illustrated this with the problem of computing the area of a parallelogram illustrated in Figure 11.3.[2] Once a student is taught the procedure for computing the area of a rectangle and then the area of a parallelogram, the question is what does the student learn?

In some cases, the student learns a procedure (e.g., a specific procedure or route to the solution). This learning generalizes poorly to other figures. Some students, however, learn something more fundamental than simply a rote procedure. They learn to look for ways to convert the

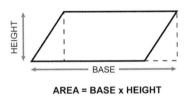

AREA = BASE x HEIGHT

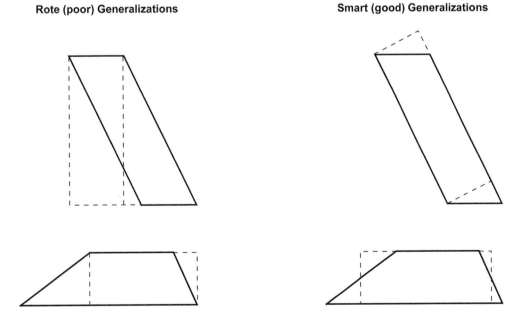

Figure 11.3 Wertheimer used the parallelogram problem to illustrate the difference between unproductive generalizations based on blindly applying a rote process and productive thinking based on an appreciation of the deep structure of a problem.

183

complex figure into a rectangle without altering the area. They gain a deeper understanding of structural relations that allows them to generalize more broadly (e.g., a kind of survey knowledge).

Wertheimer described the smart generalizations (i.e., productive thinking) as "realizing structural features and structural requirements: proceeding in accordance with and determined by these requirements."[3] He associated this process with a search for "structural" as opposed to "piecemeal" truth. Wertheimer was quite elegant in articulating why more classical approaches based on logic or association theory (e.g., behaviorism) fail to provide satisfactory explanations for the productive thinking:

> In their aim to get at the elements of thinking they cut to pieces living thinking processes, deal with them blind to structure, assuming that the process is an aggregate, a sum of those elements. In dealing with processes of our type they can do nothing but dissect them, and thus show a dead picture stripped of all that is alive in them. Steps, operations come into the picture externally: on the basis of recall, of some previous knowledge, general or analogical, of associations in connection with some items in the situation (or even with the sum of them all), or again, of mere chance. The items, the connections used, are blind or neutral to questions of their specific structural function in the process. Such are the classical associations between an a and some b, the blind connections between means and end; such is the way in which traditional logic deals with propositions of the form "all S are P," or "if A then B." The connections, the items, data, operations are structure-blind or structure-neutral, blind to their structural dynamic function with the whole, and blind to the structural requirements."[4]

Thus, the idea of "structural requirements" of a problem is a fundamental construct with regards to the Gestalt approach to problem solving. This construct has also been important in the literatures of linguistics and expertise, where distinctions have been made between 'surface structure' and 'deep structure.'[5]

Deep structure tends to be associated with 'meaningful' properties, and surface structure tends to be associated with more transient, insignificant changes. For example, here are two sentences with the same deep structure but different surface structures.

The dog chased the cat.
The cat was chased by the dog.

In the context of a classifying physics problem Chi, Feltovich, and Glaser suggested that experts grouped problems according to fundamental physical laws or principles (i.e., the deep structure), whereas novices grouped problems according to the physical configuration of objects involved (i.e., the surface structure).[6] Thus, experts were able to make 'smarter' generalizations than were novices.

Langewiesche's discussion of the pilot's way of judging distance (e.g., using an angular coordinate system anchored on the horizon) versus the passenger's way of judging distance (e.g., using a rectangular coordinate system) might be restated by saying that the pilot's representation was grounded in the 'deep structure' of the functional problem—leading to productive intuitions relative to flying (e.g., being able to 'see' reachability).

Similarly, one might say that the aiming off strategy used by expert navigators and orienteers reflects productive thinking in that they use 'deep structure' of the problem (e.g., boundaries like rivers and coastlines) in a very smart way, allowing them to use perceptual skills to meet what would otherwise be computational demands.

Also, consider the parallels with Tolman's studies of rats learning a maze. The behaviorists assumed that only route knowledge was learned, but Tolman's experiments demonstrated that a more general understanding of the layout (i.e., survey knowledge) was learned that allowed productive generalizations when the original route was blocked.

It could also be argued that the key distinction between the constructivist approach[7] to perception and the ecological approach[8] was that constructivists assumed that perception was based on 'surface structure' (e.g., piecemeal cues on the retina), while ecologists considered the possibility that perception was based on 'deep structure' (e.g., structures in optical flow field that were specific to affordances).

With regards to the variations of the Wason task, it might be argued that the key difference between the neutral original context (even numbers and vowels) and the permission context (i.e., legal table) is that the permission context provides deep structure (i.e., social constraints) that is not salient in the neutral context.

Finally, in the context of Rasmussen's decision ladder, the deep structure of a task (signal and sign relations) would be the basis for smart shunts at the skill- and rule-based levels.

Chunking

> It is a little dramatic to watch a person get 40 binary digits in a row and then repeat them back without error. However, if you think of this merely as a mnemonic trick for extending the memory span, you will miss the more important point that is implicit in nearly all such mnemonic devices. The point is that recoding is an extremely powerful weapon for increasing the amount of information that we can deal with. In one form or another we use recoding constantly in our daily behavior.[9]

The previous quote is from George Miller's classic paper, "The magical number seven, plus or minus two: Some limits on our capacity for processing information." Miller's work is typically cited as key evidence about the limits of human information processing (in particular, working memory). However, if you read the original paper carefully, a major insight is that due to the human's capacity to 'recode' information, there is NO effective information limit to working memory.

Yes, working memory is limited to about seven chunks, but "the span of immediate memory seems to be almost independent of the number of bits per chunk, at least over the range that has been examined to date" (p. 93).

Miller continues: "by organizing the stimulus input simultaneously into several dimensions and successively into a sequence of chunks, we manage to break (or at least stretch) this informational bottleneck" (p. 95).

The performance he is describing is the performance of Sidney Smith, who trained himself to recode five binary digits into single chunks (e.g., 10100 = 20). With this encoding, strings of about 40 binary digits were within the five- to nine-chunk capacity of working memory.

Miller's construct of chunking may perhaps be critical to linking the construct of smart heuristics with the earliest intuitions associated with Cybernetic models of cognition. Consider that the "recoding" that Miller refers to might be analogous to shifting coordinative systems to leverage task constraints in order to reduce the information processing demands (to break the "informational bottleneck"). The key to making this link is the hypothesis that the recoding seen in everyday situations is not arbitrary, but rather that it takes advantage of the constraints available in the ecology—that, is the consistencies that form the basis for Rasmussen's signal and sign relations.

One source of empirical support for this hypothesis comes from de Groot's observations of expert chess players that were confirmed by Chase and Simon.[10] Expert chess players are able to remember more information when presented with a configuration taken from a chess game for a brief period (on the order of a few seconds). This is typically attributed to the fact that experienced chess players are better able to integrate multiple pieces of information (or chess pieces) into larger coherent patterns or chunks, thus effectively extending the limits of working memory (e.g., recognizing a particular opening).

Chase and Simon included an important control condition. They showed that the advantage of experts over novices in remembering the placement of pieces was reduced (if not completely eliminated) when the configurations were random arrangements of pieces. Thus, it seems clear that the ability to extend the limits to working memory depends in part on the coherent structure of the game of chess that is eliminated in the random configurations.

This inference is strengthened by an experiment reported by Reynolds.[11] One aspect of the structure of the game of chess that appears to be important to experts is the distribution of pieces relative to attacking different areas of the board. Thus, for example, within the game there can be a functional 'center of mass' that reflects the focal point of attack.

Reynolds created three random arrangements that were systematically constrained with respect to the proximity of the pieces to a functional center of mass. The differences in recreating the arrangements from memory across skill levels increased as the configurations became more constrained relative to this functional center—with no differences at the low proximity condition and a more than two to one advantage for the highest-class players over the others in the high proximity condition. Again, this suggests that the improved performance is somehow linked to functional properties (i.e., deep structure) of the chess problem.

A conventional explanation of the improved expert performance in these experiments is that experts have a large bank of stored patterns that they can use to help recognize situations and chunk information. For example, it has been estimated that a master chess player would require storage of some 50,000 chess configurations.[12] However, Vicente and Wang (1998) offer an alternative explanation.[13] They suggest that the ability of experts is based on their experience with the constraints of the problem.

Vicente and Wang assume that the knowledge of the expert is not a collection of memorized patterns from specific games, but rather an implicit model of the domain constraints. These might include recognizing patterns that reflect the intention of an opponent; identifying offensive and/ or defensive strengths and weaknesses related to functional centers of mass; and identifying patterns related to distinct stages of the game, such as a generic opening; etc. Thus, rather than storing specific instances, they assume that memory is an integration that reflects 'invariant' functional properties suggested by such constructs as schema or prototype.

The general hypothesis of Vicente and Wang is that experts are more effectively tuned to the functional constraints than are less experienced players. Their knowledge of these constraints allows experts to chunk information into functionally relevant patterns, and thus to quickly zero in on good options. The violation of these constraints in the random conditions evens the playing field between experts and novices.

Vicente and Wang used Rasmussen's Abstraction Hierarchy[14] as an explicit, a priori way to differentiate 'deep structure' (e.g., more abstract constraints related to intentions and laws of the game) from 'surface structure' (e.g., more concrete constraints associated with physical properties of a situation).

Clearly, it takes experience with a domain to discover the deeper, more abstract constraints! But once discovered, there are dividends to be reaped with regard to the ability to organize information in ways that result in computational efficiencies. Thus, the ability to by-pass inherent information processing limitations is tied to the structure of the situation.

In this sense, expertise is the ability to utilize the natural constraints of situations to recode or chunk the stimuli in ways that enhance situation awareness and that effectively reduces the computational complexity related to the search for good solutions. In other words, experts are employing structure within the situation to reduce uncertainty.

The chunking observed by de Groot is not simply a memory gimmick; it has clear implications for the efficiency of processing. For example, the principal difference between stronger and weaker chess players that de Groot observed was the ability of experts to quickly grasp the situation, so that the first options that they considered turn out to be among the best choices.

De Groot writes that "within the very first five to ten seconds, the master subject is apt to have more relevant information about the positions available to him than the lesser player can accumulate in, say, a quarter of an hour of analysis."[15]

Dreyfus used the term "zeroing in" to characterize this ability of experts to quickly assess complex situations in order to make smart decisions. He contrasts this with more deliberate search processes that work systematically through the possibilities—"counting out." He writes that:

> The human player whose protocol we are examining is not aware of having explicitly considered or explicitly excluded from consideration any of the hundreds of possibilities that would have had to have been enumerated in order to arrive at a particular relevant area of the board by counting out. Nonetheless, the specific portion of the board which finally attracts the subject's attention depends on the overall position.[16]

Reynolds provides some insights into the zeroing-in process based on studies of the eye movements of chess players[17] and a reanalysis of some of de Groot's verbal protocols.

These studies show that weaker players tend to focus attention based on the distribution of pieces, but that stronger players tended to focus attention based on the distribution of spaces affected by those pieces.

Reynolds concluded that:

> The reanalysis of de Groot's protocols indicates that master and grandmaster chess players direct their attention to a different area of the board from that of players of lesser expertise. While the beginning tournament player is captivated by configurations of black and white pieces of wood, the masters and grandmasters center their attention on those squares affected by the pieces.[18]

Thus, rather than postulating thousands of past games stored in memory as the basis for expert-novice differences in chess, the hypothesis is that experts organize their sensemaking around a different coordinate system than that used by novices. The coordinate system of the expert is organized around functionally significant features of the situation (e.g., the strength of attack with

*) SOURCE: CHESSWEBSITE.COM

regards to spaces), whereas the coordinate system of the novice is organized around surface features of the situations (e.g., the pieces).

The "zeroing-in" process described by Dreyfus may reflect the operation of smart (skill- and rule-based) heuristics that support a recognition-primed selection of options, while the "counting-out" process may reflect more deliberate formal reasoning (e.g., what Klein[19] described as mental simulations) to evaluate the selected options.

Again, the parallels to Langewiesche's description of how pilots are able to see 'reach-ability' should be readily apparent. The key to both direct perception and to smart heuristics is to discover a coordinate system that reflects the 'deep structure' of the situation. In control theoretic terms, the point is to choose the correct coordinates for the functional state space (i.e., coordinates that organize the data to make the functional constraints salient).

Abstraction Hierarchy

As a result of the work of Wertheimer and others, there is a general hypothesis that access to the deep structure of a problem leads to more productive or smarter thinking (e.g., more effective chunking or parsing of the problem). However, this ends up not being of much value if the only way to differentiate a representation that reflects the deep structure from one that reflects the surface structure of a domain is the quality of thinking that results. Is it possible to frame the construct of deep structure independently from the quality of performance?

This will be particularly important for design in order to make at least tentative prescriptions for the content and organization of information in interface representations.[20] For example, in the design of safety-critical systems, it might be very important to start with a good understanding of the space of possibilities.

Kim Vicente observed that it is important to have a description of the work or problem demands (the possibilities) that is independent from the particulars of any previous design or the associated processes and/or activities.[21] He called such an approach a '*formative approach*,' and the idea echoes Marr's desire for a computational theory of perceptual systems.

While cognitive science abounds with normative approaches that prescribe what it means for a process to be rational and with descriptive approaches that describe the behaviors of particular people in particular situations, there is little discussion of the ecological demands that a cognitive system must satisfy in order to survive in complex problem domains.

Rasmussen's Abstraction Hierarchy represents an important attempt to provide a *formative approach* to ecologies (problem spaces or work domains). As leader of the Informatics research program at Riso Laboratory in Denmark, Jens Rasmussen, whose background was control engineering, was given the task of assessing the risks associated with nuclear power—did nuclear power offer a safe source of energy for Denmark? Could a safe system be designed?

Rasmussen quickly realized that safety of these complex systems depended on the cognitive abilities of the humans operating the plant. It depended on their ability to control the system under normal operating situations and on their ability to detect, diagnose, and correct the inevitable faults (what Perrow called normal accidents[22]) that were sure to arise in such a complex system. However, when he looked to cognitive science for guidance, he got little help:

> In the early 1960s, we realized from analyses of industrial accidents the need for an integrated approach to the design of human-machine systems. However, we very rapidly encountered great difficulties in our efforts to bridge the gap between the methodology and concepts of control engineering and those from various branches of psychology . . . because of the slow transition in psychological research away from behaviorism and the preoccupation of the early research in artificial intelligence with games and theorem proving, we found it impossible to wait for guidelines from such sources. It appeared to be necessary to start our own selective research program to find models useful for engineering design.[23]

One product of the research program that Rasmussen established was the Decision Ladder discussed in the previous chapter. Rasmussen used the decision ladder to represent the opportunistic (adaptive) thinking patterns he observed in verbal protocols from people doing fault diagnosis and troubleshooting in the context of industrial systems.

In addition to the decision ladder, Rasmussen realized that he also needed a language to describe the constraints that were shaping the adaptive behaviors. He needed a formative framework to describe the problem demands. He needed a way to integrate the third, ecological component into the semiotic system. He needed to identify the deep structure of the cognitive problems that operators would need to solve. For this, he chose an Abstraction Hierarchy in terms of means-ends relations.

Consistent with Gibson, Shannon and Weaver, Newell and Simon, and Marr, Rasmussen understood that it would be necessary to describe the problem space in a way that related the goals (ends) and the action capabilities (means, operators). However, unlike Newell and Simon, who could choose simple tasks (e.g., crypto-arithmetic, hobbits and orcs) where the state space could be easily enumerated, Rasmussen had the challenge of scaling up the means-ends analysis to a complex situation with a state space that could not be enumerated. Whereas Newell and Simon were dealing with closed-system problems, Rasmussen had the challenge of applying means-ends analysis to complex, open systems.

Remember the earlier discussion of open and closed systems (or well- and ill-defined problems) in relation to Bayes' theorem and computing probabilities? Note that the distinction between closed and open systems is different than the distinction between closed-loop and open-loop control.

In essence, a closed system is a well-defined problem that is completely isolated from its environment. All sources of variability (e.g., all possible legal moves) are accounted for in the problem description.

An open system is an ill-defined problem that is coupled to its environment, so that enumerable events in the environment (e.g., a tsunami, a terrorist, etc.) can have a potential impact on the system. Thus, in an open system there will be sources of variability that are not (and perhaps cannot be) specified.

In an open system it is in principle impossible to enumerate all the possibilities. So, rather than focus on the effectively infinite number of states, Rasmussen chose to describe the constraints that shaped the space of possibilities.

For example, to describe the field of possibilities for an aircraft, it would be impossible to enumerate all the possible positions and paths that an aircraft might take throughut the world, but it is possible to describe the constraints that shape those possibilities.

One constraint is where the pilot can go safely (e.g., places that are safe to land). Another constraint are the laws of aerodynamics—these laws will limit the potential paths that an aircraft of a particular form (e.g., type of wings and type of propulsion system) will be able to take given a specific initial condition. Additionally, the size of the fuel tank and the tolerances of the components (e.g., the g-tolerance of the pilot) will also set limits on where the aircraft can operate safely. And finally, there may be regulations that specify legal paths and values that specify desirable paths.

Rasmussen found that it would be useful to organize descriptions of the work domain constraints (i.e., the problem space) along two dimensions. One dimension reflected different levels of abstraction in terms of functional means-ends relations that addressed issues associated with why, what, and how. This dimension is consistent with Marr's analysis of different levels for describing an information processing system.

The other dimension reflected the level of aggregation in terms of part-whole relations. This dimension is consistent with the reductionist approaches that break down complex phenomenon into more elementary components.

Figure 11.4 illustrates a conceptual space formed from these two dimensions. The different regions in the Abstraction-Aggregation space reflect different ways to describe a problem (different perspectives), NOT different components of the work domain. The vertical and horizontal lines within the space illustrate different approaches to parsing the complexity of situations (through functional abstraction or through reduction, respectively). The significance of the diagonal line will hopefully become clear later.

The question that arises then is: of all the different ways to describe a work domain, is there one or a few types of description that will be particularly valuable for understanding the dynamics of abduction systems?

For example, is there a grain of analysis (level of aggregation) that might be privileged in terms of insights into the semiotics of meaning processing systems (elementary particles of cognition)?

Before addressing this question, let's step through the five levels of abstraction that Rasmussen proposed for decomposing the system with respect to means-ends relations and consider different

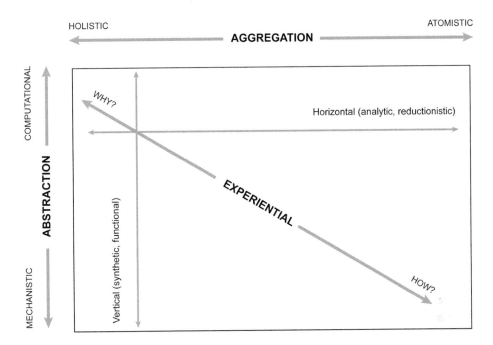

HOLISTIC | AGGREGATION | ATOMISTIC

COMPUTATIONAL

ABSTRACTION

MECHANISTIC

WHY?

Horizontal (analytic, reductionistic)

Vertical (synthetic, functional)

EXPERIENTIAL

HOW?

Figure 11.4 This space illustrates different perspectives and approaches for describing situations.

levels of decomposition within each level. These levels suggested by Rasmussen as the framework for decomposing problems to identify the deep structure provide an excellent place to start the search, but they should not define the search.

It is important to immerse yourself in the phenomena of interest (the work or problem domain) and to let the domain dictate the ultimate decomposition, but Rasmussen's hypotheses are a useful touchstone to keep you from getting completely overwhelmed by the complexity.

In our own applications of work analysis, we never start with the assumption that Rasmussen's levels are the 'right' way to decompose the deep structure, but we often end up with decompositions that match well with Rasmussen's categories.

Functional Purpose: Goals

The idea that behavior is organized with respect to the goal or ends to be achieved did not originate with the Cybernetic Hypothesis. In fact, this idea was central to behaviorist approaches that attributed behavior to the presence of rewards and punishment in the ecology. For example, the learning behavior of rats in a maze could be attributed to the acquisition of the reward in the "goal" box.

In fact, the idea that the goal or ends is fundamental to shaping cognitive activity was central to functionalist approaches to psychology. For example, Dewey wrote that "*the problem fixes the end of thought and the end controls the process of thinking.*"[24]

The impact of the Cybernetic Hypothesis, relative to the behaviorist paradigm, just shifted the locus of the goal from being a stimulus outside the head in the ecology (reward or reinforcement) to being a plan or intention inside the head.

Thus, many approaches agree that functional purpose is an important constraint shaping the activity of a cognitive system. For example, John Anderson writes:

> it seems that all cognitive activities are fundamentally problem solving in nature. The basic argument (Anderson, 1983; Newell, 1980; Tolman 1932) is that human cognition is always purposeful, directed to achieving goals, and to removing obstacles to those goals.[25]

In describing work domains, Rasmussen also suggested that *in order to ask the ultimate question of why an activity is performed it was essential to understand the functional purpose or goals of the system.* For example, to understand the operation of a nuclear power plant, it is important to understand the functional goals of that system—to safely and economically contribute toward meeting the energy demands for a region.

These functional ends will be important sources of constraint for shaping the cognitive activities of the plant operators. In contrast, a nuclear power plant may serve very different goals for a terrorist. It is the same plant, but the meaning of the deep structure will dramatically change with a change in the functional context.

Thus, the highest level in Rasmussen's Abstraction Hierarchy addresses the functional purpose of a problem or situation.

What is the objective to be satisfied? What are the rewards (or threats)? How will success be determined?

There is little controversy here—most paradigms include the functional purpose as an important constraint on cognition. However, the question is what is the appropriate level of decomposition for describing the purpose (i.e., goals, sub-goals, sub-sub-goals)? And more specifically, how do you link this level of description to the details of cognitive activity and/or behavior?

Behaviorism put its attention almost exclusively on this level of abstraction. In searching for explanations to behavior, behaviorists searched horizontally at this level by reducing the goals into smaller and smaller sub-goals and ultimately to elemental stimulus-response atoms.

This is most clearly seen in the construct of chaining.[26] Researchers such as Hull, Guthrie, and Skinner explained behaviors, such as maze learning, in terms of sequences of elemental pairs of stimulus-response associations—that when chained together (like a string of dominos) led to the acquisition of the ultimate goal. For the behaviorists, it seemed to be essential that the goal-based description be linked with the micro-structure of the behavior, so that every behavior could be linked to a comparable stimulus-response association.

On the other hand, Tolman took a different approach to explaining maze learning.[27] Rather than decomposing the purpose into finer and finer stimulus-response atoms, he shifted the level of abstraction to consider other dimensions of the problem or state space associated with maze learning. He considered different representational constraints (e.g., route versus survey knowledge) that might shape the problem-solving strategies.

This brings us to Rasmussen's next level of abstraction.

Abstract Functions and Priority Measures

In describing the problem of maze learning as a state space, what dimensions should be used to specify the states or the paths from the initial condition to the goal state? Perhaps, the states could be described in spatial terms. This might be done in terms of routes (that is, a linear sequence of turns) or it might be done in terms of a more abstract description—for example, in terms of cardinal directions.

As we discussed earlier, Tolman and others designed a number of clever experiments to assess whether the rats in the maze experiments might be organizing their activities with respect to spatial relations in the maze. Figure 11.5 illustrates the logic of one of these experiments. In this experiment, the rat was first trained to follow the path labeled B to attain the food reward. Once this behavior was acquired, the learned path was blocked.

From a strict behaviorist interpretation, the rat would have no basis to prefer the A path over the C path. However, if the rat learned something about the spatial relations in the maze, then one might suppose that the rat would be more likely to chose the C path than the A path (since this leads in the general direction of the reward). In fact, this is what happened.

There is much empirical data from maze experiments that suggest very strongly that rats are not simply learning chains of stimulus-response associations or routes, but rather they are learning about the spatial relations within the maze. In other words, they are acquiring survey knowledge. Thus, in describing the maze problem—in a way that will help understand the dynamic of learning—it seems essential to include spatial relations as part of that description.

At the Abstract Function level of description, the key question is what differences make a difference in terms of the problem space? In other words, what are the dimensions of the states? Three sources of constraint should be considered at this level: action, perception, and value.

As we noted earlier, the state space description should reflect the constraints on action—what actions are possible in terms of motions through the state space? This helps to specify the field of possibilities.

For example, in designing graphical decision support systems for nuclear power plant control, Vicente[28] found it was useful to organize the problem representation to make the mass and energy

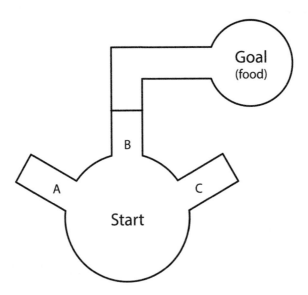

Figure 11.5 This illustrates the logic of experiments to assess whether rats are learning spatial relations when trained in a maze. After being trained to follow path B to attain food reward, that path is blocked. How do rats respond?

balances apparent. Thus, for controlling power generation processes, energy and mass levels are differences that make a difference.

For controlling motion of inertial systems, the laws of motion suggest that position and velocity will be important dimensions to consider. In both these cases, the physical laws (e.g., conservation of mass and energy and Newton's Second Law of motion) are the sources that suggest important dimensions to be included in the problem descriptions.

In addition to action constraints, perception constraints become important as potential feedback for assessing position in the state space relative to the goal—am I getting closer or farther from the goal? In the case of learning the maze, one might consider what sources of information are available to the rat with respect to spatial relations within the maze. In the case of the aviation example discussed earlier, the angular relations with the horizon may become important dimensions for differentiating potential landing sites.

Finally, there are often values associated with positions and paths through the state space, in addition to the final goal or ends that are important for differentiating the quality of performance. For example, these values may be associated with the costs of motion or the preferences among paths.

A trivial example would be the instructions in a simple manual target acquisition task (i.e., Fitts Law task) that asks the participant to move a cursor from a start position to a target position in minimum time. Thus, in addition to the position goal, time becomes an important measure for scoring behavior.

It might be debated whether this should be included in the Functional Purpose level or this level, but the main point is that any differences that make a difference should be reflected in the description of the state space at the Abstract Function level.

The Abstract Function level of description should provide a description of the situation as a functional problem. It should be based on fairly general constraints such as laws of motion (physical and/or legal) relative to the state space, information available relative to the goal, and values

J.J. Gibson[29]

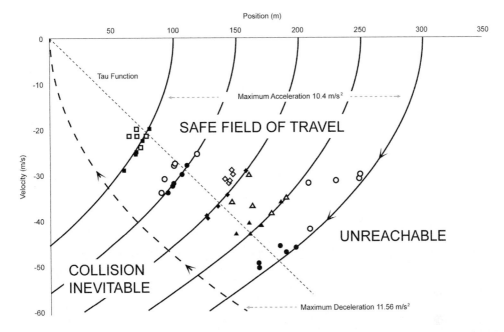

Figure 11.6 The 'state space' is one way to illustrate the constraints that partition the field of possibilities for a simple driving task. The points in the diagram illustrate the states at which participants released the accelerator, before breaking. Open symbols were from early trials and filled symbols are from later trials. The results suggest that participants were discovering the minimum time solution to this task—consistent with the instructions to reach the barrier as quickly as possible without crashing.[30]

associated with satisfying the function. These constraints should be general/abstract enough so that they can be applied to any mechanisms or processes that might be envisioned as potential solutions for achieving the functional purpose. *At this level the point is to visualize the field of possibilities.*

In control theory, state space representations are typically used to model the boundary conditions set by the physics of the situation, the initial state, and the goal state.

For example, Figure 11.6 illustrates a state space for a driving task where the different initial states of the car were at zero velocity at five different distances (300, 250, 200, 150, 100 m) from the target stopping state, which was a wall at the zero position.

The curves from these initial states represent maximal acceleration curves for the car. Thus, states below each of these curves are unreachable due to the physical constraints on motion. The car simply can't reach the combinations of position and velocity associated with these states from the initial condition due to the laws of motion.

The curve that intersects (0,0) represents maximal deceleration for the car in order to stop before crashing into the wall. For states below this curve, it is impossible to satisfy the goal to stop at the 0 position. That is, it will be impossible to achieve zero velocity at that position.

The states enclosed by the max acceleration and deceleration curves and the horizontal axis will be reachable from the initial condition, and it will also be possible to achieve the goal from those states. Thus, this region is one way to represent the field of safe travel for this particular driving task. The boundary of the field of safe travel represents the minimal time path from the initial state to the target state (i.e., full acceleration to the midpoint, then full deceleration).

The open symbols on the graph in Figure 11.6 show where people released the accelerator to begin breaking early in practice with this task. The filled symbols are after five hours of practice with this vehicle. Note that the participants seemed to learn to operate near the margins of the field of safe travel consistent with the instructions to approach the target position (a wall) as fast as possible without crashing into it.

In this case, plotting the performance relative to the physical motion constraints helps us to see the 'logic' of the participants' decisions about when to release the accelerator.

Computational Theory

These first two levels in Rasmussen's Abstraction Hierarchy are most closely associated to Marr's concept of a *Computational Theory*[31] of the function or to Vicente's Formative description of a problem. At this point, minimal consideration is given to the constraints of particular designs or mechanisms for solving the problem. For example, in the context of maze running, this level of description would be equally relevant both to understanding how rats learn to run mazes and to the design of autonomous robots that might be capable of solving this problem.

For Marr, the computational theory level of description is at a high level of abstraction. It does not specify a specific form of representation (e.g., decimal or binary numbers). It does not specify a specific algorithm or process, and it does not specify a specific mechanism. The computational theory is a description of the problem—or function, NOT a description of any specific device for solving it.

In fact, the computational theory provides the larger context that should encompass all the possible representations, algorithms, and devices. It provides the context for comparing one representation, algorithm, or device with another in terms of their ability to satisfy the function—to meet the demands of the what and why.

It is important to appreciate that almost universally when cognitive scientists describe themselves as computational theorists or modelers, it is because they are building processing programs—algorithms or mechanisms (e.g., ACT-R programs), NOT because they are wrestling with a deep-level description of the functional demands of an information processing problem.

Generally, computational modelers are filling in the boxes of the classical information processing model with input/output mechanisms or programs. Computational modelers typically define their work in opposition to Gibson's ecological approach.

However, Marr acknowledged that "in perception, perhaps the nearest anyone came to the level of computational theory was Gibson (1966)." He explains:

> Gibson's important contribution was to take the debate away from the philosophical considerations of sense-data and the affective qualities of sensation and to note instead that the important thing about the senses is that they are channels for perception of the real world outside or, in the case of vision, of the visible surfaces. He therefore asked the critically important question, How does one obtain constant perceptions in everyday life on the basis of continually changing sensations? This is exactly the right question, showing that Gibson correctly regarded the problem of perception as that of recovering from sensory information "valid" properties of the external world.[32]

BETTER THAN FOCUSSING ON THE WAY THINGS SHOULD BE (THE NORMATIVE APPROACH), OR ON THE WAY THINGS ARE (THE DESCRIPTIVE APPROACH), FORMATIVE APPROACHES FOCUS ON THE WAY THINGS COULD BE BY IDENTIFYING NOVEL POSSIBILITIES FOR PRODUCTIVE WORK

K. Vincente[33]

Thus, for Marr, the computational theory of vision was not a theory about a specific visual system (e.g., the human eye). Rather, it was a general theory of the problem of using light to guide interactions with the world.

The computational theory of vision should not presume anything about the type of eye or type of algorithms involved. The computational theory of vision would apply equally to natural vision systems and to engineered systems. It would apply equally to single-lens eyes (e.g., mammals) and multi-faceted eyes (e.g., some insects). The computational theory was a theory of the general function of vision apart from any specific realization of that function.

Vicente (1999) use the term 'formative model' to make the same point that Marr was making with the construct of computational theory.

Thus, the point of the two highest levels of abstraction is to visualize the field of possible solutions to a particular problem. The lower levels will then consider the particular constraints associated with specific mechanisms (strategies, tactics, algorithms, organizations) that might be used to achieve solutions to the computational problem.

In other words, the top two levels in Rasmussen's Abstraction Hierarchy (Functional Purpose and Abstract Function) represent the deep structure of a problem or work domain. The lower levels then begin to fill out the surface structure associated with particular solutions (designs, algorithms, organizations, etc.).

General Functions and Activities

In order to gain deeper insight into how the rat is able to learn about spatial relations within the maze, it might be useful to describe the general information processing functions that might be involved in the learning process. For example, somehow the rat must sense, interpret, and integrate the information about the spatial relations. This information then must be retrieved and used to guide decisions and actions in the maze.

The decomposition of a problem into a collection of general information processing sub-functions—typically represented as a flowchart where boxes represent different elemental functions—is the signature of the information processing approach to cognition.

In the same way that the behaviorist paradigm focused on a horizontal decomposition at the level of functional purpose or goals, the information processing approach tends to focus on a horizontal decomposition at the level of general function.

Thus, at the highest level of aggregation the system is modeled as an information channel with input and output. This channel is then decomposed in terms of more elemental stages (e.g., sensation, perception, decision, motor control), and then each of these stages can be further decomposed through research programs that focus exclusively on specific stages.

At this level of description, constraints associated with the organization (e.g., closed- or open-loop control) and with the flow of information (e.g., channel capacity) associated with solving a problem become important. These constraints can be described in terms of general constraints on control and information systems. Or these constraints can be linked to the structures of algorithms or particular mechanisms associated with particular approaches or strategies for solving the problem.

This level of description can be very important for understanding how a problem can be solved, but no matter what level of aggregation, you will have difficulty addressing the question of why at this level of description. Thus, the question of motivation has been largely defined out of the information processing approach.

Both theoretically and empirically, the information processing approach starts with the assumption of a well-motivated participant. It has no basis, however, for explaining the source of motivation. This is perhaps because these issues of 'why' require descriptions that include the higher levels of abstraction (i.e., functional purpose and/or abstract function) that are not well represented in terms of general functions in a flow diagram. For example, the cost function for a control system and the payoff matrix for a signal detection system are extrinsic to the processing mechanisms.

Note that a general information function like 'encoding' might be accomplished by many different mechanisms (e.g., eyes, ears, nose, etc.). This brings us to the next level of abstraction, which considers constraints associated with particular devices for accomplishing a general function.

Physical Processes and Activities

In digging deeper into the individual general information processing functions, it is typical for people to seek a grounding for the information processes in physical properties of either the information processor or of the stimuli being processed. For example, in visual perception, researchers differentiate between processing *where* (motion and orientation—magnocellular tracts) and processing *what* (form and detail—parvocellular tracts). Or at a more abstract level, research on attention has found it useful to distinguish different resources associated with how information is coded and responded to [e.g., different modalities (visual or auditory; manual or verbal) or different codes (spatial or verbal)].[34]

In the case of maze learning, the sensing function will be important, but the nature of the learning may be quite different depending on the modalities available for sensing. A blind rat will have different constraints on the types of information that will be available for learning about the spatial layout of the maze than would a rat with normal vision.

In designing safety-critical systems, an important distinction at this level of abstraction is the degree to which specific information processing stages are accomplished by humans or automation. For example, it is now possible to design aircraft that are pilotless (or more precisely, the pilot is on the ground). This has very important constraints on the ultimate design and operation of the vehicle (e.g., the size of the cockpit; the need for life support systems—relative to oxygen, operating temperatures, g-force tolerances, transmission delays).

Thus, at this level, the choice of a specific kind of physical system for a specific information processing function introduces other constraints associated with the requirements of that physical system (e.g., life support for humans; power for electrical systems; etc.). These constraints also will shape the potential form of problem solutions.

Physical Form and Configuration

For many, a full understanding of the rat learning the maze will depend on grounding the process in the micro-structure of the nervous system. For example, in specifying the specific brain processes in terms of regions, neurons, and/or connections that are involved and the specific synaptic changes that result from the learning process. This can be pushed to specific cellular pathways and perhaps even to micro-chemical changes at specific synapses. Here questions about how the physiology of the nervous system constrains how the rat learns become important.

For safety-critical systems, the detailed spatial configuration of a system introduces possibilities that may be difficult to appreciate from the more abstract representations. For example, different types of physical systems (e.g., hydraulic and electrical components) may interact as a consequence of spatial proximity (e.g., being located in the same conduit). In this case, understanding the spatial constraints among components may be critical (e.g., the potential for leaking hydraulics to short out electrical sensors will not typically be visible in any representation based on a decomposition illustrating more abstract, general functional relations).

In neuroscience much has been learned as a consequence of the different functional deficits associated with damage in specific spatial regions of the brain. This might be a bit of an exaggeration, but much of the current interest in neuro science today seems to be motivated by the hope that reduction at the physical form level will eventually provide the ultimate answers to the mystery of cognition. That is, once we have a completely detailed map of the nervous system (and/or the genome), we will be able to answer all the questions of psychology. That is, the hope is that the ultimate answer to what the rat learns in the maze will be found in the electro chemical processes of the nervous system. We are doubtful.

However, it is true that the understanding of the higher levels of abstraction have to be consistent with the capabilities of the basic physical components. A fundamental strategic question for cognitive science is: where to start the search?

Metaphysics of Situations

In essence, Rasmussen and Marr were attempting to define a metaphysical basis for describing the deep structure of situations. To make this more apparent, it might be useful to compare the Abstraction decomposition with Aristotle's four basic causes (final, efficient, formal, and material), as illustrated in Table 11.1.

Table 11.1 Three alternative ways to visualize the deep structure of situations.

Marr	Aristotle	Rasmussen
Computational Theory	Final constraints	Functional purpose
	Efficient constraints	Abstract function
Representation & Algorithmic	Formal constraints	General function
Hardware implementation	Material constraints	Physical function
		Physical form

The comparison becomes particularly striking if you substitute the word 'constraint' for the word 'cause' in Aristotle's framework, to avoid the entailment with agency that is typically associated with the construct of cause.

Thus, using Aristotle's system, cognitive or semiotic systems are constrained in four ways:

1. Semiotic systems are constrained by the purposes or intentions of the agents involved (i.e., final constraints). From the perspective of designers this could reflect a USE-centered perspective, where focus is on the functional objectives of the designers (i.e., what purposes they intend for their product). Or it could reflect a USER-centered perspective, where focus is on anticipating the goals of the consumers or operators who will use the product.
2. Semiotic systems are constrained by the physical and rational laws that bound the space of possibilities (i.e., efficient constraints). In the case of process control systems, physical laws (e.g., laws of motion) and rational laws (e.g., legal regulations) combine to determine the space of possibilities for the semiotic system.
3. Semiotic systems are constrained by the form or geometry of the system (i.e., formal constraints). This can include constraints associated with the structure of an organization (e.g., function allocation), the modularization of functions in software or hardware, or the organization of body components (e.g., the kinematic constraints on motion).
4. Finally, semiotic systems are constrained by the material properties of the components (i.e., material constraints). Here the underlying chemistry may become significant.

Multiple Perspectives: It's Turtles All the Way Down

Much of modern science is framed in terms of reductionism. In the context of Figure 11.4, this involves horizontal decompositions at a particular, privileged level of abstraction.

While different sciences such as psychology, biology, and physics may frame the problem at different levels of abstraction (e.g., general function, physical function, or physical form, respectively), each of the sciences tends to organize itself around horizontal analyses within the specific chosen level. That is, there seems to be a search for some single, privileged atomistic level of description that will provide the ultimate answers to the major questions (e.g., units of information, cells, molecules, or subatomic particles).

The problem with this approach is that there is no stopping rule. For example, in physics it seems that as the technology improves, we continue to break matter into smaller and smaller pieces. This problem is often illustrated with the turtle story that has been attributed to both Bertrand Russell and William James.

Here is one version:

> A well-known scientist (some say it was Bertrand Russell) once gave a public lecture on astronomy. He described how the earth orbits around the sun and how the sun, in turn, orbits around the center of a vast collection of stars called our galaxy. At the end of the lecture, a little old lady at the back of the room got up and said: "What you have told us is rubbish. The world is really a flat plate supported on the back of a giant tortoise." The scientist gave a superior smile before replying, "What is the tortoise standing on?" "You're very clever, young man, very clever," said the old lady. "But it's turtles all the way down!"[35]

In recognition of the turtle problem (no stopping rule) and inspired by observations of the behavior of expert fault diagnosis, Rasmussen's approach was to use interactions across levels of abstraction to guide decisions about the appropriate decomposition level. That is, rather than looking for a stopping rule within a level of abstraction (horizontal analysis), Rasmussen looked across levels (vertical analysis).

Figure 11.7 illustrates two different ways to visualize the interactions across levels of abstraction. In 11.7A the relations across levels of abstraction and level of aggregation are illustrated along a diagonal in the space.

In analyzing verbal protocols from observations of expert fault diagnosis, Rasmussen observed that these experts would often switch between different levels of abstraction—moving up to consider a particular fault in terms of more abstract functional relations and then moving down to link the functional organization with specific details of the system. Diagraming this search process in the abstraction-aggregation space often resulted in an iterative motion that tended to move up and down the diagonal—until eventually zeroing in on the precise location of a fault.

The implication of orienting the levels of abstraction along the diagonal in Figure 11.7A is that in moving down levels of abstraction, increasingly finer details become important. This suggests,

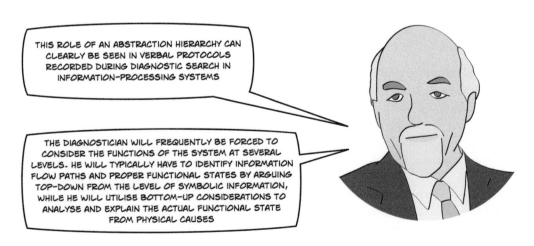

Jens Rasmussen[36]

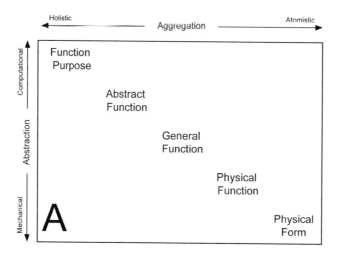

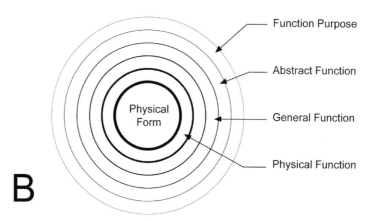

Figure 11.7 This illustration shows two ways to think about relations across levels of Abstraction: A—shows the levels as spanning the diagonal from holistic descriptions in terms of functional purpose to detailed descriptions of physical form; B—shows the levels as nested sets of constraints.

for example, that there will be little value in reducing the goal of attaining food—in the case of the rat in the maze—into finer and finer subgoals.

Rather, once you understand the motive that is organizing behavior, it will be more valuable to understand the problem of navigation in terms of spatial constraints on motion. Then it might be valuable to consider how this spatial information is processed in terms of general information processing functions. These in turn might be explored in terms of general physical constraints of the maze and the rat. Finally, these general physical constraints might eventually be linked to the specific layout of a particular maze or the neural anatomy of the rat.

The search will not necessarily move top-down across the diagonal, but rather discoveries at one level of analysis may motivate one to reassess the description at either higher or lower levels of analysis. However, in the end the ultimate description of a problem space will ground the functional description in the physical details—and will explicate the physical details in relation to satisfying certain functions.

In general, however, the point of the diagonal is that level of abstraction and level of aggregation will be at least loosely coupled in the dynamics of cognition—with the appropriate level of detail increasing as one moves down through levels of abstraction.

It is important not to take the 'diagonal' of this space too literally, but just to realize that in general, the higher levels of abstraction will get you to the 'ballpark' (provide general constraints) and the lower levels of abstraction will typically provide the details. Just as in a control system, the 'goal' accounts for the long-term steady state for a well-designed control system, but it will not specify the activities needed to get there.

Thus, abduction engines will tend to move (explore) along the diagonal in the Abstraction-Aggregation space. They will generate hypotheses top down—based on intentions and associated regularities (that provide the basis for anticipation/prediction), but they will test these hypotheses bottom-up in terms of the specific pragmatic consequences of action in the ecology—and thus, this structure needs to be captured in our theory of situations.

Figure 11.7B illustrates the Abstraction Hierarchy as a nesting of constraints. In this context, the Functional Purpose level of abstraction provides the context within which to understand constraints at lower levels of abstraction.

As Rasmussen (1986) notes:

> The way in which the functional properties of a system are perceived by a decision maker very much depends upon the goals and intentions of the person. In general, objects in the environment in fact only exist isolated from the background in the mind of a human, and the properties they are allocated depend on the actual intentions. A stone may disappear unrecognized into the general scenery; it may be recognized as a stone, maybe even a geologic specimen; it may be considered an item suitable to scare away a threatening dog; or it may be a useful weight that prevents manuscript sheets from being carried away by the wind—all depending on his immediate needs.[37]

The Abstract Function level focuses on the dimensions for describing possibilities relative to the functional purpose or intentions. Again, this reflects the possibilities in terms of constraints on action, perception, and value relative to the goal. At this level, one has the broadest picture of the field of possibilities for achieving the goal in terms of the opportunities for controlled action (maximal degrees of freedom).

At each successive level below the Abstract Function level, the degrees of freedom (the range of possibilities) become narrowed by further constraints in terms of the functional organization (General Function Level), the physical realization (Physical Function Level), and the detailed geometry (Physical Form Level).

Any problem—from the simplest laboratory puzzle to complex work domains such as operating a nuclear power plant—can be described in terms of nested levels of abstraction. And in fact, the problem must be described in terms of these multiple levels in order to appreciate the dynamics of cognition, where the subjective experience motivating behavior (the desire or intention; the why) must be linked to action in a physical ecology (the behavior; the consequence; the how).

In other words, the descriptions at multiple levels of abstraction are necessary in order to relate situations to awareness (or mind to matter) in order to appreciate what matters. Thus, the diagonal of the abstraction-decomposition space provides a framework for describing the 'deep structure' of a problem.

This is a pluralistic perspective in that each level of abstraction provides an alternative valid description of the semiotic problem. Each level of abstraction represents a different way to 'see' the system. Note that the different points along this diagonal are not 'parts' of the whole. Rather, each is a different view or way of looking at the whole.

The full abstraction-decomposition space represents many different valid ways to represent a functional problem, and the 'diagonal' is a subset of the many possible ways for viewing the semiotic system that may be particularly useful with respect to insights into the dynamics of pragmatic semiotic systems that are well grounded in the deep structure of the ecology or problem space.

Summary

In sum, the Abstraction Hierarchy is a multi-level description that spans both the functional and physical constraints in order to understand the deep structure that potentially shapes the activity of a triadic semiotic system (i.e., operating according to an abduction logic). The need for such a description was most clearly illustrated in Simon's oft-quoted analogy of the ant on the beach.[38]

In this analogy Simon noted that a description of the beach over which an ant travels—relative to the rewards, threats, and action capabilities of the ant—can be critical for explaining the behavior of the ant. The Abstraction Hierarchy offers a framework for describing the beach.

However, it is important to note that at the same time the beach is shaping the ant's behavior, the behavior of the ant is changing the landscape of the beach. Thus, the deep structure does not refer to an ecology that sits 'out there' apart from the ant. It is an ecology that is specific to the experiences of the ant (e.g., needs, desires, capabilities). The deep structure, thus, is a property of the full triadic semiotic dynamic.

A triadic approach to cognition demands that the dynamics of human experience be grounded both in the constraints on awareness and the constraints on situations. In the previous chapter, Rasmussen's Decision Ladder was introduced as a useful tool for visualizing the semiotic dynamics from the perspective of cognitive activity in searching for a solution. In this chapter Rasmussen's Abstraction Hierarchy was introduced as a useful tool for visualizing the abduction dynamics from the perspective of the ecology (situations).

Figure 11.8 illustrates how the two perspectives suggested by Rasmussen (the decision ladder and the abstraction hierarchy) fit into our image of the triadic semiotic system. Note that both perspectives are considering the entire dynamic, but the emphasis changes. It is important to avoid a dualism—where awareness and ecology are seen as separate realities. These are two perspectives on the single reality of experience. In linking these two perspectives, Rasmussen's distinction among signals, signs, and symbols can be very useful.

The fundamental lesson of Rasmussen's work on problem solving in the context of fault diagnosis is that the search to understand a complex process requires exploring at both different levels of detail and different levels of abstraction. In searching to understand a problem more fully, it is important to consider not only 'how' a problem is solved in terms of mechanisms (algorithms or particular solution paths), but also how this problem relates to the field of possibilities (i.e., alternative paths) in the state space and the goals and values of the semiotic system.

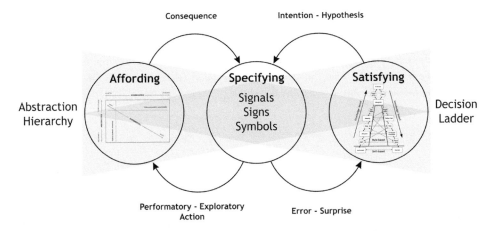

Figure 11.8 The Decision Ladder and the Abstraction Hierarchy offer two distinct perspectives on the dynamics of abduction.

It is impossible to compare alternative solutions or designs in terms of their quality (which solution is better) without this computational perspective.

At the end of the day, the goal is to construct a theoretical and empirical science that can embrace the full scope of human experience, including both that slice of reality that has been classically associated with the agent or ant (mental, subjective) AND that slice of reality that has been classically associated with the ecology or beach (physical, objective).

Thus, the Abstraction Hierarchy is designed to ground satisfying, specifying, and affording in the dynamics of the situation, and the Decision Ladder is designed to ground satisfying, specifying, and affording in the dynamics of awareness. But human experience is always an emergent property that reflects the coupling of constraints of awareness with constraints of situations. In searching for the emergent properties of semiotic systems, we need to explore both alternative levels of decomposition (essentially differentiation) and alternative levels of abstraction (essentially integration or categorization).

Notes

1. Dunker, K. (1945). *On problem solving*. Psychological Monographs, 58. American Psychological Association.
2. Wertheimer, M. (1959). *Productive thinking*. New York: Harper & Row.
3. Wertheimer (1959), p. 235.
4. Wertheimer (1959), p. 237.
5. Chomsky, N. (2006). *Language and mind*. 3rd ed. New York: Cambridge University Press.
6. Chi, M.T.H., Feltovich, P.J., & Glaser, R. (1981). Categorization and representation of physics problems by experts and novices. *Cognitive Science*, 5, 121–152.
7. Gregory, R.L. (1974). *Concepts and mechanisms of perception*. New York: Charles Schribner's Sons.
8. Gibson, J.J. (1979). *The ecological approach to visual perception*. Boston, MA: Houghton Mifflin Co.
9. Miller, G.A. (1956). The magic number seven, plus or minus two: Some limits on our capacity for processing information. *Psychological Review*, 63, 81–97. (pp. 94–95).
10. de Groot, A.D. (1965). *Thought and choice in chess*. The Hague: Mouton.

    Chase, W.G., & Simon, H.A. (1973). The mind's eye in chess. In W.G. Chase (Ed.). *Visual information processing*. New York: Academic Press.

11. Reynolds, R.I. (1982). Search heuristics of chess players of different calibers. *American Journal of Psychology*, 95, 373–392.
12. Simon, H.A., & Gilmartin, K. (1973). A simulation of memory for chess positions. *Cognitive Psychology*, 5, 29–46.
13. Vicente, K.J., & Wang, J.H. (1998). An ecological theory of expertise effects in memory recall. *Psychological Review*, 105, 33–57.
14. Rasmussen (1986).
15. de Groot (1965), p. 324.
16. Dreyfus, H.L. (1992). *What computers still can't do: A critique of artificial reason*. Cambridge, MA: MIT Press. (p. 103).
17. Tikhomirov, O.K., & Poznyanskaya, E.D. (1966). An investigation of visual search as a means of analyzing heuristics. *Soviet Psychology*, 5, 3–15.
18. Reynolds (1982), p. 391.
19. Klein, G. (2003). *Intuition at work*. New York: Doubleday.
20. Bennett, & Flach (2011).
21. Vicente, K.J. (1999). *Cognitive work analysis*. Mahwah, NJ: Erlbaum.
22. Perrow, C. (1984). *Normal accidents*. New York: Basic Books.
23. Rasmussen, J. (1986). *Information processing and human-machine interaction*. New York: North Holland. (p. ix).
24. Dewey, J. (1991). *How we think*. Amherst, NY: Prometheus Books. (p. 12).
25. Andersen, J. (1995). *Cognitive psychology and its implications* 4th ed. New York: W.H. Freeman and Company. (p. 237).
26. Skinner, B.F. (1953). *Science and human behavior*. New York: MacMillan.

    Hull, C.L. (1943). *Principles of behavior*. Englewood Cliffs: Prentice Hall.

    Gutherie, E.R. (1952). *The psychology of learning*. Rev. ed. New York: Harper & Row.

27. Tolman, E.C. (1932). *Purposive behavior in animals and men*. New York: Naiburg.
28. Vicente, K.J. (1999). *Cognitive work analysis*. Mahwah, NJ: Erlbaum.
29. Gibson, J.J., & Crooks, L.E. (1982). A theoretical field-analysis of automobile-driving. In E. Reed & R. Jones (Eds.). *Reasons for realism*. Hillsdale, NJ: Erlbaum. Originally published. (1938). *American Journal of Psychology*, 51, 453–471.
30. Flach, J.M., Jagacinski, R.J., Smith, M.R.H., & McKenna, B. (2011). Coupling perception, action, intention, and value: A control theoretic approach to driving performance. In D.L. Fisher, M. Rizzo, J.K. Caird, & J.D. Lee (Eds.). *Handbook of driving simulation for engineering, medicine and psychology* (pp. 43.1–43.16). Boca Raton, FL: Taylor & Francis, CRC Press.

31. Marr, D. (1966). *Vision*. New York: W. H. Freeman and Company.
32. Ibid. (p. 29)
33. Vicente (1999). (p. 110).
34. Wickens, C.D. (1984). *Engineering psychology and human performance*. Columbus, OH: Charles E. Merrill Publishing Co.
35. Hawking, S. (1988). *A brief history of time*. (10th Anniversary Edition). New York: Bantam Books.
36. Rasmussen, J. (1986). *Information processing and human-machine interaction*. New York: North Holland. (p. 121).
37. Rasmussen, J. (1986). *Information processing and human-machine interaction*. New York: North Holland. (p. 13).
38. Simon, H.A. (1969). *The Sciences of the Artificial*. Cambridge, MA: MIT Press.

THE TECHNIQUE OF BLASTING ROCK INVOLVED BORING A HOLE, ADDING BLASTING POWDER, A FUSE, AND SAND, AND THEN COMPACTING THIS CHARGE INTO THE HOLE USING THE TAMPING IRON. PROBABLY THE SAND WAS OMITTED, AND THE IRON SPARKING AGAINST THE ROCK MADE THE POWDER EXPLODE.

PHINEAS GAGE (1823 – 1860) SURVIVED THE ACCIDENT, EVEN THOUGH THE TAMPING IRON ROD WAS DRIVEN COMPLETELY THROUGH HIS HEAD, DESTROYING MUCH OF HIS BRAIN'S LEFT FRONTAL LOBE.

AFTER RECOVERY, IT WAS FOUND THAT THE ACCIDENT DID NOT IMPACT GAGE'S IQ OR COGNITIVE ABILITY. HOWEVER, IT DID IMPACT GAGE'S PERSONALITY; HIS FRIENDS SAW HIM NO LONGER AS GAGE, AND HE SEEMED TO BE LESS CAPABLE DEALING WITH SOCIAL LIFE

12

THE HEART OF THE MATTER?

> Any philosophic explanation of Quality is going to be both false and true precisely
> because it is a philosophic explanation. The process of philosophic explanation is an
> analytic process, a process of breaking something down into subjects and predicates.
> What I mean (and everybody else means) by the word 'quality' cannot be broken
> down into subjects and predicates. This is not because Quality is so mysterious but
> because Quality is so simple, immediate and direct.[1]

On first encounter with Rasmussen's Abstraction Hierarchy it seemed odd to have Functional
Purpose at the pinnacle, as the highest constraint. Certainly, the intentions (e.g., to create a safe,
clean, affordable source for electricity in the case of nuclear power) could not dominate the physical laws (e.g., thermodynamics). At first blush, it would seem that the physics must set the highest
constraint and that intentions must be framed in the context of these physical constraints.

In the context of process control, it seemed obvious that the physics of the process set the 'hard'
constraints, and that the intentions and values of the designers and operators were only 'soft'
constraints. However, we have come to conclude that for meaning processing semiotic systems,
Rasmussen got it exactly right. A cognitive system is defined by its 'desires' as the foundation for
everything else!

This is the difference between a rock and a piloted aircraft. The motion of the rock reflects a
passive reaction to the extrinsic forces applied in accord with the physical laws of motion. On the
other hand, while an aircraft may be subject to similar forces and it is subject to the same physical
laws, its motion is not determined by those laws. In fact, it might be fair to say that the aircraft's
motion path will be determined in spite of the extrinsic physical forces and laws, since the pilot
will actively null or counter the impact of any forces that result in deviations from her goal.

While the aircraft's motions are constrained by the physical laws, they are NOT determined by
those laws! It would be more accurate to say that the aircraft's motions are determined by the goals
and values of the pilot working in concert with the physical laws. Thus, in the cognitive system,
intentional constraints dominate physical constraints. While the pilot cannot violate the physical
laws, it is the pilot, not the physical laws that controls where the aircraft will go. But the pilot not
only thinks, she also feels.

This brings us to a fundamental question about the basic nature of goals and values, about
desire, or about quality. To what extent are goals and values associated with the head (i.e., mind),
as opposed to the heart (i.e., body/matter)?

In this case, we are not referring to anatomy, per se. The head is used to represent classically rational processes associated with planning and problem solving relative to satisfying some

objective. On the other hand, the heart is used to represent supposedly more primitive, 'bodily' processes associated with aesthetic sensibilities, passions, desires, or emotions.

Up to this point, we have looked at decision processes, like buying a house, through the lens of cold rationality. In that context, the debate has focused on various types of 'objective' reasoning processes (e.g., compensatory versus lexicographical processes or normative versus ecologically grounded models of choice) that are typically evaluated relative to some 'objective' criterion. But what role does passion or emotion play?

In my life, I have purchased two houses, and I can tell you that the choice process did not seem to fit with classical prescriptions for rationality. In both cases, my wife and I fell in love with the houses we bought first, and then we worked out a rational explanation to justify our choices (both to ourselves and to others). Consistent with Klein's RPD model, we immediately recognized the home we wanted when we saw it!

In fact, many of the important choices I have made in my life (e.g., a wife, a career, a car) seem more like falling in love than like deliberate problem solving. It is almost like the object chooses (or attracts) me, rather than the other way around. It doesn't seem like I add the data up to determine the choice, but rather it seems like I 'cook' the data to make the 'logic' consistent with what my heart (emotion) leads me to. In these cases, desire seems to set the target (i.e., makes the choice) and then the cognitive work seems to focus on overcoming any obstacles in the way (e.g., negotiating the price, finding the funds, etc.).

For the most part, the role of emotions in cognition has been ignored, or at worst emotion has been considered to be a primitive source of noise (or interference) to be filtered (or tamed) by the superior logical processes of mind.

This fits well with the computer metaphor of mind—that frames questions about thinking, decision making, and problem solving in the context of logic. The computer thinks, but it does not feel. In this context, emotions are typically seen as remnants of a more primitive stage of evolution that reflects lower forms of life. However, as we move away from the image of a logical engine and begin thinking more in terms of an abductive logic based on ecologically grounded heuristics, the door is open to consider plausible roles for emotions in connecting situations and awareness.

Embodied Cognition

In the dualistic ontology inherited from Descartes, emotions were associated with the body that was part of the physical world. This physical world was distinct from the world of thinking that was thought to function independently from the constraints of physical laws. In fact, that was the challenge for philosophy and psychology to discover the distinct laws of mental functioning.

This perspective set the frame for Saussure's dyadic semiotics that framed the semiotic problem in terms of the relations between signals and concepts, without consideration for how the signals were grounded in a physical ecology. This in turn became the foundation for Chomsky's approach to language in terms of a closed logical system. And this also fit with the computer metaphor of mind, which viewed the mind as a symbol processor. With the computer metaphor, the focus of psychology was on the logic of the software framed independently from any constraints of the hardware.

Although people realized that the software had to be implemented on a physical medium, attention was almost exclusively on brain function. Few appreciated the fact that the rest of the body, the face, hands, arms, legs, feet, and the physical constraints of the environment (e.g., gravitational

THROUGHOUT MOST OF THE TWENTIETH CENTURY, EMOTION WAS NOT TRUSTED IN THE LABORATORY. EMOTION WAS TOO SUBJECTIVE, IT WAS SAID. EMOTION WAS TOO ELUSIVE AND VAGUE.

EMOTION WAS AT THE OPPOSITE END FROM REASON, EASILY THE FINEST HUMAN ABILITY, AND REASON WAS PRESUMED TO BE ENTIRELY INDEPENDENT FROM EMOTION.

THIS WAS A PERVERSE TWIST ON THE ROMANTIC VIEW OF HUMANITY. ROMANTICS PLACED EMOTION IN THE BODY AND REASON IN THE BRAIN. TWENTIETH-CENTURY SCIENCE LEFT OUT THE BODY, MOVED EMOTION BACK INTO THE BRAIN, BUT RELEGATED IT TO THE LOWER NEURAL STRATA ASSOCIATED WITH ANCESTORS WHOM NO ONE WORSHIPPED.

IN THE END, NOT ONLY WAS EMOTION NOT RATIONAL, EVEN STUDYING IT WAS PROBABLY NOT RATIONAL

Antonio Damasio[2]

field, visual field, acoustic field) might be critical factors in shaping experience in general and cognition in particular.

Before we consider the roles of passion and emotion in shaping human experience, let's consider more generally the role of the physical body.

Two people who did appreciate the role of the body in shaping human experience were Jacob von Uexkül and James Gibson. Uexkül's construct of umwelt reflected the observation that 'meaning' was shaped by the physical relations between an animal and its ecology. The same object, for example a flower, will have different meanings for different animals as a function of body size and type. It might be a shelter for one insect, a source of nectar for another; it might be nutrition for a cow and a decoration for a child. These meanings are not arbitrary, but they are a natural consequence of the physical relations between the object and the animal.

Gibson recognized how the body shaped experience with the construct of affordance. The affordance construct recognized that the 'meaning' of an object was a function of the constraints and consequences of interacting with that object.

This was illustrated with the earlier example about how body size might be a factor in determining what is a safe distance from the edge of a cliff. Again, too close is not an absolute distance, but rather it might reflect a relation involving the height of the observer. Note that while the visual angle allows easy detection of too close, eye height per se is not the physical constraint that is important, but rather the height of the center of mass determines whether a slip forward might be catastrophic.

Similarly, Ester Thelen's work on the development of walking and more recent work on the development of walking robots based on passive computations demonstrates clearly the importance of taking physical constraints into account in order to understand motor coordination.

All this work seems to have direct relevance for perceptual-motor skill, but are there similar implications for other aspects of cognition?

Lakoff and Johnson[3] argue quite convincingly that the answer is "Yes!" They argue that the mind is 'embodied' such that language and, in fact, all of our conceptual experiences are grounded in our physical interactions with the world. They argue that the nature of our physical interactions with the world shapes the concepts and categories that we use to think.

For example, they argue that a fundamental concept like 'time' is based on generalizations of experiences with motion and physical change. They argue that a fundamental concept like 'cause' is based on generalizations of our experiences using our muscles to apply forces to initiate changes. Thus, for Lakoff and Johnson, physical experiences play a fundamental role with respect to "what matters" for cognitive systems.

Lakoff and Johnson suggest that a fundamental vehicle for constructing a rich mental life from basic physical experience is metaphor. That is, our physical experiences provide the conceptual sources that we then apply to more abstract experiences in order to make sense of them.

For example, anger is understood in relation to our experiences with heating of liquids (e.g., boiling, seething, build-up of pressure, explosions) and solids (e.g., burning and loss of functionality).

The important implication of the Lakoff and Johnson hypothesis is that the 'logic' of cognition is not based on disembodied mathematical constructs such as probability, but rather in the systems of metaphors that guide the sensemaking processes. Thus, in order to get insight into human rationality, it becomes necessary to probe the semantic entailments of the metaphors that shape our conceptual life.

For Lakoff and Johnson, the mind and body become integrated through metaphor, so that our mental life is essentially a metaphorical extension of our physical experiences. Figure 12.1 illustrates how this hypothesis fits with the underlying triadic dynamic of semiotics and abduction.

Given the dynamics illustrated in Figure 12.1, the metaphors that become engrained in common language that are described by Lakoff and Johnson would be ones that have been reinforced in

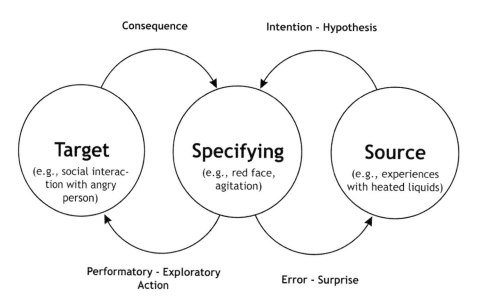

Figure 12.1 In this case, the experiences with a physical system (e.g., muscle control, heated liquids) become the 'sources' of expectations and hypotheses that link the medium (e.g., movement kinematics, red face, frantic motions) with an underlying functional process (e.g., cause or movement kinetics). Thus, our experiences with heated liquids may shape our understanding (e.g., in explaining why someone behaves the way they do) and our interactions with an angry person (e.g., stay clear to avoid getting scalded).

terms of leading to productive interactions with the ecology. In other words, enduring metaphors are ones that capture the 'deep structure' of the situations to which they are applied.

Although Lakoff and Johnson seem quite optimistic about the prospects that cognitive science will bring mind and body together into a 'philosophy of the flesh,' many of those who focus on the physiological basis for cognition continue to maintain a clear hierarchical separation between the 'higher' centers (e.g., neocortex) that are thought to govern the rational or logical aspects of our thinking and the 'lower' centers (e.g., brain stem) that are associated with the more primitive, emotional aspects of our thinking.

Phineas Gage

Antonio Damasio begins his book *Descartes' Error* with the remarkable story of Phineas Gage. This story is recounted in many introductions to Psychology as an important case study that led scientists to more fully appreciate the role of brain processes in shaping personality.

Phineas Gage had a severe brain injury as a result of an accident while tamping an explosive charge intended to clear rocks for a railroad bed. Although Phineas Gage survived the accident, changes in his personality were noted. In particular, Phineas seemed to change from a reliable worker to a drifter who seemed to have difficulty sustaining permanent employment or long-term relations.

The story of Phineas Gage seemed to fit the conventional narrative where higher/newer brain centers are thought to provide the higher cognitive abilities that differentiate humans from other animals. Thus, the damage to these brain centers (e.g., prefrontal cortex) are thought to be the reason for difficulty in controlling or inhibiting the more primitive (animalistic) impulses associated with lower brain centers. Thus, Phineas seemed to be less able to cope with the demands required for success in a more civilized (less animalistic) society, because he lacked the cognitive skills required for managing social life due to damage to the frontal cortex.

However, one aspect of this narrative puzzled Damasio. It seemed that with Phineas Gage (and similar contemporary cases that Damasio examined) the damage did not impact performance on standard measures of intelligence or cognition. Although the contemporary cases showed that, as with the Gage story, people with similar brain trauma had difficulty coping with the social demands of life after the trauma (e.g., losing jobs, failing marriages), these people tended to show no change in IQ or in other measures of cognitive ability.

So, if it is not a deficit in cognitive ability, how can we account for the poor social choices that these people make after the brain trauma?

The Iowa Gambling Task

Damasio eventually discovered a "cognitive" task that seemed to differentiate people such as Phineas Gage from people who have not suffered the same type of brain trauma.[4] The task is illustrated in Figure 12.2, and it is typically referred to as the *Iowa Gambling Task*.

The four decks for the Iowa Gambling Task are constructed so that two of the decks pay a fixed high value on each turn ($100) and the other two have a fixd low payoff on each turn ($50). The twist in the game is that the two decks with the high fixed values are associated with high risks— occasionally higher penalties, such that the expected value (over 10 turns) is negative.

In one of these decks (A/H5) there are five penalties of $250 per every 10 turns. In the other deck (B/H1) there is one penalty of $1250 per every 10 turns. For both of these decks the expected value is negative (i.e., on average there will be a loss of $250 over every 10 turns).

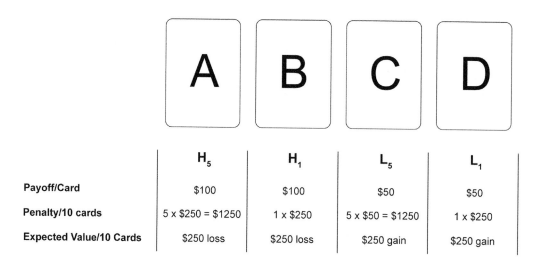

	H_5	H_1	L_5	L_1
Payoff/Card	$100	$100	$50	$50
Penalty/10 cards	5 x $250 = $1250	1 x $250	5 x $50 = $1250	1 x $250
Expected Value/10 Cards	$250 loss	$250 loss	$250 gain	$250 gain

Figure 12.2 In this task the participants are initially given a 'stake' of play money (e.g., $2000). They are then faced with an array of four decks of cards with neutral labels (e.g., A, B, C, D). They are instructed that they can choose cards from any of the four decks and that with each choice they will receive some money, but on some choices they will also be required to pay a penalty. They are instructed that the goal of the game is to make as much money as possible. They do not know how many choices they will get to make before the game ends.

The two decks with lower fixed payoffs are associated with lower risks. For one of these decks (C/L5) there are five penalties of $50 per every 10 turns and for the other deck (D/L1) there is one penalty of $250 per every 10 turns. For these two decks, the expected value is positive such that players can expect to win $250 per every 10 turns.

This game is designed to simulate some of the uncertainties associated with choices in everyday life—with no clear end and with uncertain risks.

In playing this game, most people show an early preference for the high payoff decks. However, they eventually move toward a more 'rational' strategy (i.e., consistent with expected value) in which preference is given to the lower payoff/risk decks. Although some people will occasionally make a choice from the high payoff decks, as the game progresses most people will have a strong preference for the more prudent choices associated with the low payoff/risk decks. This is the normatively better strategy, because it results in a positive outcome in the long run.

The interesting thing about the Iowa Gambling Task is that people with brain trauma similar to that experienced by Phineas Gage showed a different pattern of responding than most people.

As Damasio describes:

> the frontally damaged patients systematically turned more cards in the A and B decks, and fewer and fewer cards in the C and D decks. Despite the higher amount of money they received from turning the A and B cards, the penalties they kept having to pay were so high that halfway through the game they were bankrupt and needed to make extra loans from the experimenter.[5]

Some other interesting observations about the performance of the people with damage similar to Gage's:

> They appear to recognize the 'bad' decks.

They seem to react to the 'punishment' of big penalties by avoiding that deck for a short time after the penalty, but unlike most people, they soon returned to the bad deck.

Another difference was noted in later studies that measured peoples' skin conductance (GSR—galvanic skin response) while playing the game. The people with frontal lobe damage showed a similar response as everyone else to turning over the cards and learning of the result (payoff and/or penalty).

However, most people also developed an anticipatory response to choices from the bad deck that increased as the game progressed. That is, after a short time people typically showed a GSR response when they considered or decided to make a choice from one of the 'bad' decks, and the magnitude of this response tended to increase as the game continued. Note that this GSR response was anticipating the possibility of a large loss.

In contrast, the people with frontal lobe damage *showed no anticipatory response whatsoever, no sign that their brains were developing a prediction for a negative future outcome.*[6]

The Somatic-Marker Hypothesis

Damasio formulated the Somatic-Marker Hypothesis to account for these differences. This hypothesis suggests that with experience, choices that lead to very bad or very good outcomes become associated with an emotion that 'marks' that choice in terms of a 'gut' reaction that will be experienced when that choice is faced in the future. The consequence of this 'gut' reaction is that choices associated with a negative 'gut feeling' will be quickly eliminated from the set of potential options. Similarly options with a positive 'gut feeling' may be elevated or made more salient/attractive among the other potential options.

In the Iowa Gambling Task, the anticipative GSR response that most people experienced when considering the 'bad' decks would be evidence of this somatic marker that functions as an automated alarm signal warning of potential danger. The impact is to 'bias' these people toward the safer choices—in effect leading them to make choices that avoid the risks. In the particular case of the Iowa Gambling Task, this leads to more effective decision making (i.e., consistent with maximizing expected value). It seems that for patients with damage similar to Gage's, this alarm does not sound, allowing them to eventually be seduced by the larger immediate payoffs in the 'bad' decks. This in turn exposes them to the large risks that lead to calamitous results.

Damasio sums up the Somatic-Marker Hypothesis as follows:

> In short, somatic markers are a special instance of feeling generated from secondary emotions. Those emotions and feelings have been connected, by learning, to predicted future outcomes of certain scenarios. When a negative somatic marker is juxtaposed to a particular future outcome the combination functions as an alarm bell. When a positive somatic marker is juxtaposed instead it becomes a beacon of incentive.[7]

The Somatic-Marker Hypothesis puts the story of Phineas Gage in new light. Rather than his difficulties adjusting to social life following the accident being attributed to a failure of the 'higher' brain centers to inhibit the animalistic instincts associated with the 'lower' brain centers, the difficulties are attributed to a failure of the emotional components of lower brain centers to inform or shape the choices made by the higher brain centers.

This suggests that the brain damage that Gage experienced disrupted the communications or coordination between higher and lower centers of the brain—in effect, between head and heart.

Blaise Pascal

This challenges the conventional wisdom that separates the 'higher' logical aspects of mind from the 'lower' emotional aspects of matter/body. Once again there is a very clear implication that what matters involves a coordination between mind and body, between mind and matter. This challenges the conventional wisdom that puts 'logic' in a privileged position relative to 'emotion' in the hierarchy of rationality and control.

The Somantic-Marker Hypothesis emphasizes that rationality in everyday life may depend on coordination between logical and emotional components of experience.

Putting Emotion Into Control

In introducing the logic of control theory in Chapters 6 (Circles), 7 (Controlling), and 8 (Observing), the focus was on the dynamics of closed-loop systems in contrast to the billiard ball metaphors of causality that tend to guide experimental work inspired by information processing models of cognition. However, it is important to note that the block diagrams and the presence of 'feedback' are not unique to control systems.

There are many physical (e.g., springs), physiological (e.g., homeostasis), and social (e.g., prey-predator systems) systems that involve a similar circular coupling among variables as illustrated in the various block diagrams. These systems could be modeled using the same forms of differential equations used to model control systems. However, these systems would probably not be characterized as 'control' systems, at least in the engineering sense of the term. In effect, there is no 'pilot' or 'autopilot' controlling or directing action.

We suggest that the thing that differentiates control systems in the engineering sense from other closed-loop processes is the existence of a cost function. That is, in designing a control system an engineer is explicitly trying to optimize or at least satisfice with regards to some set of values that is typically operationalized as a cost function.

In manual control theory, the cost function is typically operationalized in terms of minimizing a joint function of error and effort (i.e., reducing error without expending too much effort). In

signal detection theory, the cost function is typically operationalized as a payoff matrix reflecting the value of correct actions (hits, correct rejections) relative to the costs of errors (misses, false alarms).

The quality of a controller and/or observer is determined relative to the cost function. That is, there is no such thing as an 'optimal' controller or 'ideal' observer without reference to the value system associated with the consequences of the choices that are made.

Also, note that the cost function is not represented in the block diagram of a control or observer system.

However, it is in reference to an implicit or explicit cost function that an engineer would make choices about the parameters associated with the control logic in the boxes (e.g., the gains). The cost function is the measure of quality or goodness with respect to the control system's function. Perhaps this fact, that the cost function is not explicitly represented in the 'images' of control systems, has led to its omission from consideration in models of information processing.

Here are ways that the cost function fits into the problem of what matters:

- the cost function corresponds with the highest constraint in Rasmussen's Abstraction Hierarchy;
- the cost function is intimately tied to rationality, particularly in relation to understanding 'why' a person is attracted to or repelled from some choices relative to others;
- the cost function is intimately tied to the emotional experiences associated with outcomes.

To emphasize the significance of emotion to control/observation, Figure 12.3 adds an emotion component to the triadic semiotic model. We want to emphasize that 'consequences' must be assessed relative to a value system and that this value system reflects both objective (e.g., practical) and subjective (e.g., emotional) facets of experience.

Another issue raised in connection with the observer problem was the common currency problem. In that context, the issue was how to compare an intention to land safely with the visual information associated with the current trajectory (e.g., optical flow field) in order to choose the appropriate actions on the stick, throttle, and rudders.

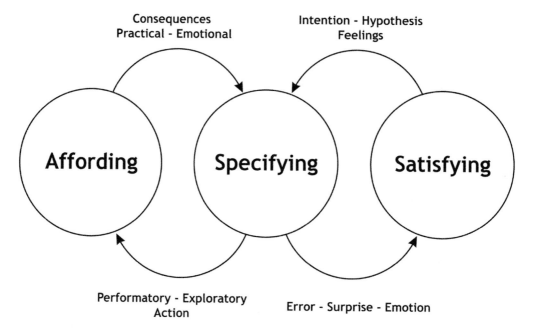

Figure 12.3 In addition, consistent with the spirit of Damasio's Somatic-Marker Hypothesis, it is important to realize that the emotions or feelings are integrated in our awareness and that the resultant feelings color our assessment of events and our expectations about the future.

However, Damasio raises a similar issue with respect to complex decisions. For example, he gives the example of a businessperson who is considering a possibly lucrative business deal with the archenemy of a dear friend. In deciding whether to pursue the deal, the businessperson must compare the potential benefits to his business against the potential impact on a valued relation.

How do you compare these very disparate things?

Damasio writes:

> You are, in fact, faced with a complex calculation, set at diverse imaginary epochs, and burdened with the need to compare results of a different nature which somehow must be translated into a common currency for the comparisons to make any sense at all.[8]

Damasio concludes that the cold analytic rationality associated with normative logical models will simply be overwhelmed by the complexity of this calculation.

> At best, your decision will take an inordinately long time, far more than acceptable if you are to get anything else done that day. At worst, you may not even end up with a decision at all because you will get lost in the byways of your calculation.[9]

Emotion may be the common currency that allows us to compare disparate alternatives. It may be the gut feeling driving some of our intuitive choices. It may be the sword that cuts the proverbial *Gordian knot* of complexity, by-passing the need to analytically compare options. Rather than analytically comparing alternatives, you go with your gut! In essence, you seek the more positive experiences. You buy the house that 'feels' like a good home.

Emotions vs. Complexity

The literature on leadership suggests that one of the characteristics of effective leaders is a bias toward action. In contrast, poor leadership is often associated with a 'paralysis of analysis' in which leaders are unable to act while they weigh all the variables and possibilities that will potentially impact the outcome of a choice. This paralysis often results in loss of opportunities in a dynamic environment where the windows of opportunity are opening and closing.

The penchant for action is illustrated in the legend of Alexander the Great and the *Gordian Knot*. The Gordian Knot is a metaphor for a complex problem that is intractable when approached by conventional analytical means (i.e., by disentangling it). However, the problem may be easily solved through decisive action (i.e., cutting the knot with a sword).

Many decisions that we make may be effectively Gordian Knots (e.g., buying a house, choosing a career, choosing a mate, deciding to have a family). There are so many factors to consider and the options are so disparate that making comparisons is extremely difficult, and there are often an uncountable number of options to consider (e.g, the perfect house may go on the market tomorrow, interest rates might change).

In addition, there are finite windows of opportunity for effective action (e.g., someone else might buy the house you wanted). Recognizing the challenge of these Gordian Knots, Walker Percy wrote *"Lucky is the man who does not secretly believe that every possibility is open to him."*[10] Percy knew that this secret belief could result in a 'paralysis of analysis' that would ensure a sad and difficult life.

In fact, this paralysis of analysis is exactly what Damasio observed with people with damage similar to Gage. For example, here is Damasio's description of one of his patients with ventromedial prefrontal lobe damage:

> I was discussing with the . . . patient when his next visit to the laboratory should take place. I suggested two alternative dates, both in the coming month and just a few days apart from each other. The patient pulled out his appointment book and began consulting his calendar. The behavior that ensued, which was witnessed by several investigators, was remarkable. For the better part of a half-hour, the patient enumerated reasons for and against each of the two dates: previous engagements, proximity to other engagements, possible meteorological conditions, virtually anything that one could reasonably think about concerning a simple date. . . . He was now walking us through a tiresome cost-benefit analysis, an endless and fruitless comparison of options and possible consequences. It took enormous discipline to listen to all of this without pounding on the table and telling him to stop, but we finally did tell him, quietly, that he should come on the second of the alternative dates. His response was equally calm and prompt. He simply said: "That's fine." Back the appointment book went into his pocket, and then he was off.[11]

This clearly illustrates the problem of conventional analytical models of rationality based in logic or normative economic models when faced with the complexities of everyday life. They lack a 'stopping rule.'

The analytic models provide a means for doing the computations, for processing the data, for making comparisons, but the computations will continue blindly as long as data is being fed in. Typically, there are no intrinsic criteria for terminating the computation in order to act.

In contrast, heuristics such as those described by Gigerenzer[12] typically have explicit stopping rules. Thus, one of the advantages of heuristics relative to more normative approaches is that heuristics are typically recipes for action, rather than processes for doing computations. This is emphasized in Rasmussen's Decision Ladder, which represents the heuristics as shortcuts that by-pass analytical processes to link perception and action.

Perhaps somatic markers are an important factor in reinforcing the heuristic shortcuts across the Decision Ladder as the basis for everyday human rationality. Thus, the gut emotions associated with heuristics are the reason why they 'feel' right, even when people recognize the limitations relative to normative logic.

We hypothesize that these 'feeling' primed heuristics are the foundations for common sense! They are the swords that allow us to solve the Gordian Knots of everyday life.

Beautiful Things Work Better!

This claim, typically associated with Don Norman,[13] reflects intuitions that have long been held by designers and artists. However, the statement can be somewhat puzzling in the context of the conventional dualistic view of mind and matter.

This is because it associates the practical objective property of 'working better' with the emotional subjective property of 'beauty.' Conventionally, these dimensions have been treated as if they were orthogonal (i.e., unrelated) dimensions. Yet the claim suggests that they are correlated!

One way that people have tried to make sense of this claim is to reconsider what it means to be 'beautiful.' Perhaps beauty is associated with function! So, that part of what makes something beautiful is the degree to which it satisfies its intended function. But of course, this blurs the lines between the objective functional value and the subjective emotional value, suggesting that the emotion is in part based in the functional value.

Alternatively, maybe the subjective emotional reactions that are typically associated with 'beauty' may in effect be somatic markers. These markers increase the attraction to the beautiful things, increasing the likelihood that they will be used. The consequence is that we are more likely to choose the beautiful things and make them work!

We suspect that both explanations are in part why the claim is true. The functional 'fit' of an object constitutes part of its beauty, and the subjective beauty of a thing constitutes part of our attraction to using it and making it work.

The net effect is that beautiful things often will work better! This is a key component of *Experience Design*. As Marc Hassenzahl observes:

> Usability Engineering . . . traditionally focuses on problems, frustration, stress and their removal. By restricting itself to the "what" and the "how"—levels of action . . . the field quite understandably became concerned with ensuring the potential instrumentality of interactive products. However, avoiding the bad experience due to lack of instrumentality does not necessarily equate with providing a positive experience.[14]

The block diagram representations of control systems focus on the 'what' and 'how.' However, to address the question of 'why' it is necessary to consider the cost function.

This is where questions of desire and motivation may be significant and where beauty might make a critical difference. Hassenzahl continues:

> the real advancement of an experiential approach is in understanding and focusing on what makes an experience positive, pleasurable, good. HCI already has a profound knowledge about avoiding the bad. What is needed is a science and practice of the positive.[15]

Closing the Loop on Emotion

It is tempting to invert the conventional wisdom that places the newer regions of the brain (neo-cortex) that are associated with analytical thinking at the pinnacle of the cognitive control system, with an alternative model that puts the older regions (mid and hind brain) that have endured through natural selection at the pinnacle. However, rather than framing this in the form of a classical either/or debate, frame it in terms of an inclusive (both/and) perspective where it is the intimate coupling of mind and body/matter that determines what matters!

The problem with conventional wisdom is that the emotional component of the coordination has been ignored or even vilified as a source of error or noise. Although cognitive researchers and theorists have recognized that value is subjective (e.g., subjective utility theory), the subjectivity has been operationalized in a very objective, unemotional way.

Prescriptions for effective decision making have focused on the process for integrating 'values,' not on the source of the values. The emphasis is on 'how' to perform the computations, not on 'why' some outcomes are more attractive than others.

One of the clear motivations of the classical work in decision making[16] (e.g., Kahneman and Tversky) has been to identify flaws in human rationality, so that these flaws can be corrected through training or through the use of more reliable automated decision tools. However, there is, in fact, very little evidence that decision making in complex domains can be improved through training in the conventional norms of decision making, or that automatons based on normative logic are better at making complex decisions than human experts.[17]

Perhaps one reason for this is that the conventional norms focus on the analytical processes. However, effectiveness may depend more on the actual values associated with alternatives than with the analytical processes.

For example, Kahneman writes:

> The objections to the principle of moderating intuitive predictions must be taken seriously, because absence of bias is not always what matters most. A preference for unbiased predictions is justified if all errors of prediction are treated alike, regardless of their direction. But there are situations in which one type of error is much worse than another. When a venture capitalist looks for "the next thing," the risk of missing the next Google or Facebook is far more important than the risk of making a modest investment in a start-up that ultimately fails.[18]

The point that we want to emphasize is that the quality of a decision may rest less on the process of choice and more on the process of assigning value. This is where experience in a domain becomes essential and where generic knowledge about analytic processes is impotent.

In everyday life, the consequences of errors are rarely symmetric or equal. The benefits of experience in a specific domain for effective decision making is learning about the values (i.e., the costs and benefits) associated with various options and consequences. In everyday life, effective decision making is measured relative to the cost function, and rarely does the quality of the decision depend on the processes used to make it.

For example, an accident or near miss when driving may result in an emotional shock that will mark similar situations and might lead to a safer, more cautious driving attitude. This emotional shock doesn't act directly on the decision or control process, but rather it acts on the cost function through a heightened awareness of the risks and dangers. The end result is a more cautious decision or control strategy consistent with the changed cost function.

Thus, the difference between an experienced and novice driver may not be in the 'analytic skill,' but in the calibration of value. An experienced driver is more in tune with the risks and opportunities associated with driving and thus is able to choose the safer path. In terms of the Iowa Gambling Task, the experienced driver is less likely to be seduced by the immediate rewards (e.g., getting to the destination quicker). The experienced driver will be biased toward choosing from the good (safe) decks.

Perhaps the only places where process matters is in the classroom, where you might be required to show your work or justify the logic of your choice, and in the courtroom, where you may have to defend the logic of a decision that resulted in a bad outcome (e.g., the decision to build a nuclear power plant on the coast of Japan).

In this light, the fixation of cognitive science on process may be the strongest evidence we have for hindsight bias. Process becomes important when trying to fix blame through causal analysis from the biased perspective of hindsight. However, everyday life is lived forward, not backward.

Escaping Dualism

As decision theorists like Gary Klein and Gerd Gigerenzer begin to look beyond the horizon of simple laboratory gambles, the appreciation for expertise and common sense that involves more intuitive approaches to decisions that integrate gut feelings into the process is growing.[19]

However, vestiges of Descartes' mind/body dualism remain in the tendency to pose two types of processes—analytic versus intuitive.

In his recent book, Kahneman[20] uses the distinction between System 1 (intuitive) and System 2 (analytic). This duality is also reflected in the distinction between right (intuitive/aesthetic) versus left (analytical/linguistic) brains. And in contemporary media this duality is reflected in the characters of Captain Kirk (intuitive/action bias) versus Spock (analytic/logic bias) or Dr. McCoy (analytic/conservative bias).

Be skeptical about this parsing of the cognitive system. On the one hand, recognize that the cognitive dynamic associated with problem solving and decision making can appear qualitatively different in different situations. The behaviors involved in solving simple gambles or puzzles that have been typically used in laboratory experiments (e.g., crypto-arithmetic) tends to be qualitatively different than the type of behavior observed in more naturalistic contexts (e.g., buying a home). On the other hand, do these qualitative differences reflect different internal mechanisms (System 1 vs System 2), or do the qualitative differences simply reflect the different situational demands?

Rasmussen's Decision Ladder suggests that there are many paths through the cognitive system and also suggests qualitative distinctions associated with different types of paths (i.e., skilled-, rule-, and knowledge-based). However, these qualitative distinctions in the decision ladder are a consequence of the situational grounding available for connecting perception and action (i.e., signals, signs, and symbols). They do not reflect different internal mechanisms.

Maybe there are not different mechanisms (e.g., different decision ladders), but rather there are many paths through a single mechanism (e.g., one decision ladder or a single neural or associative network). However, the patterns of behavior associated with different paths are qualitatively different as a consequence of the differential situations that the cognitive agent is adapting to.

Perhaps, the tendency to reify the qualitative distinctions in behavior as internal mechanisms reflects erroneous scientific reasoning (e.g., what James referred to as the Psychologist's Fallacy). More recently, Gigerenzer and colleagues have made a similar suggestion:

> the ecological analysis is a remedy against solely attributing behavior to internal factors— such as cognition, motivation, or affect—an explanatory strategy so prevalent that psychologists have labeled it the fundamental attribution error in their participants (Ross, 1977), while at the same time they often overlook it in their own theories.[21]

The alternative to committing the fundamental attribution error is to attend more carefully to the role of the situational demands in shaping the qualitative distinctions that are observed. Figure 12.4 suggests two dimensions of situations that may contribute to the qualitatively different kinds of strategies that emerge from the triadic semiotic dynamic.

We suggest that each of the four quadrants that results reflects demands for qualitatively different solutions.

The quadrant labeled 'Logic Puzzles' reflects the types of tasks that are typically used in laboratory experiments on problem solving and decision making. In these types of situations, analytical strategies will be the most successful. These are closed-system problems suited to normative decision models, and they are within the limited capacity (e.g., working memory) of humans.

The quadrant labeled 'Computational Complexity' also reflects stationary or closed systems, where the normative decision models should work well. However, they exceed the limited working memory capacity of humans. Thus, success depends either on access to computational tools

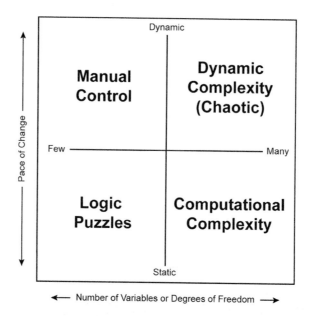

Figure 12.4 The horizontal dimension refers to the number of variables or degrees of freedom that are relevant to effective action. The vertical dimension refers to the pace of change in relation to effective action.

with higher capacity (e.g., pen and paper and unlimited time or computer-based decision aides) or on using heuristics that respect the bounded capacity while still being responsive to the situational demands (e.g., focusing on a few particularly important variables).

The somatic markers may be one aspect of the dynamic that helps us to satisfice. For example, the somatic markers may help us to focus on the important variables or heuristics that generally result in satisfactory, if not optimal solutions [e.g., to at least discriminate the 'good' (safer) decks from the 'bad' (riskier) decks].

The quadrant labeled 'Manual Control' reflects problems that are typically associated with perceptual motor skill, where people have to manage a few degrees of freedom in a dynamic situation (e.g., hitting a one-touch volley on goal or landing an aircraft). In this domain, the prescriptions of normative models of control will generally be appropriate. And, as some of the research cited in Chapter 7 suggests, with experience humans will typically converge on solutions that are consistent with the prescriptions of the normative (e.g., optimal) control models.

The last quadrant labeled 'dynamic complexity' is where intuitions based on conventional logic will often not be adequate. Yet, the situations in this quadrant are probably most typical of the problems and decisions that determine success in life. It is in this quadrant where the deficits from damage to the prefrontal cortex will be evident.

This quadrant is labeled chaotic to reflect the fact that conventional ways to decompose problems based on the intuitions of linear analytic techniques or traditional causal reasoning will fail. It is here where 'experience' and 'wisdom' are the best guides. It is here where Captain Kirk, Spock, and Dr. McCoy must work together to keep the boat stable amid the waves of epistemic uncertainty.

The Dynamic Complexity Quadrant is where the head and heart must trust each other and work together to muddle through. In this quadrant there is only the logic of survival—the right

choice is the one that works! And often the only reason it works will be that you did what was required to make it work!

This involves more than classical logic. It often requires going forward and following your intuitions, even when conventional logic says to turn back. It involves passion, persistence, and discipline. In this quadrant it is not about making the 'right choice.' It is about making your choices work! And typically, this will require the efforts of both head (mind) and heart (body).

Again, it is tempting to argue that the heart must take the lead in the Dynamic Complexity Quadrant, but we think this again reflects a dualistic trap based on either/or reasoning. We believe it is a matter of coordination between heart and head. It is not so much that the heart must lead, but rather that the heart is a necessary partner in the Dynamic Complexity Quadrant. Success depends on effective coordination between heart and head in order to make the choices work out right!

Without Captain Kirk, Spock and Dr. McCoy might get caught in infinite analytical loops and never pull the trigger, but without Spock and Dr. McCoy, Captain Kirk may not be able to make his choices work!

Notes

1. Pirsig, R.M. (1974). *Zen and the art of motorcycle maintenance*. New York: Perennial Classics. (p. 254).
2. Damasio, A. (1999). *The feeling of what happens*. Orlando, FL: Harcourt, Inc. (p. 39).
3. Lakoff, G. & Johnson, M. (1980). *Metaphors we live by*. Chicago, IL: University of Chicago Press.
4. Bechara, A., Tranel, D. & Damasio, H. (2000). Characterization of the decision-making deficit of patients ith ventromedial prefrontal cortex lesions, *Brain*, 123, 2189–2202.
5. Damasio, A. (1994). *Descartes' Error: Emotion, reason and the human brain*. New York: Penguin Books. (p. 214).
6. Damasio, A. (1994). p. 221.
7. Damasio, A. (1994). p. 174.

8. Damasio, A. (1994). p. 171.
9. Damasio, A. (1994). p. 172.
10. Percy, W. (1966). *The last gentleman*. New York: Picador.
11. Damasio, A. (1994). *Descartes' Error: Emotion, reason, and the human brain*. New York: Penguin Books. 12 p. 193–194).
12. Gigerenzer, G. (2007). *Gut feelings*. The intelligence of the unconscious. New York: Penguin Books.
13. Norman, D.A. (2005). *Emotional design*. New York: Basic Books.
14. Hassenzahl, M. (2010). *Experience design: Technology for all the right reasons*. Lexington, KY: Morgan & Claypool Publishers. (p. 27).
15. Hassenzahl, p. 28.
16. Fischhoff, B. (1982). Debiasing. In D. Kahneman, P. Slovic & A. Tversky (Eds.), *Judgment under uncertainty: Heuristics and biases* (pp. 422–444). New York: Cambridge University Press.
17. Billings, C. (1987). *Aviation Automation: The search for a human-centered approach*. Mahwah, NJ: Erlbaum.
18. Kahneman, D. (2011). Thinking, fast and slow. New York: Farrar, Straus and Giroux. (p. 192–193).
19. Gigerenzer, G. (2007). *Gut Feelings: The intelligence of the unconscious*. New York: Penguin.

    Klein, G. (2003). *Intuition at work*. New York: Doubleday.

20. Kahneman, D. (2011). *Thinking, fast and slow*. New York: Farrar, Straus and Giroux.
21. Gigerenzer, G., Fiedler, K., & Olsson, H. (2012). Rethinking cognitive biases as environmental consequences. In P. Todd and G. Gigerenzer (Eds.) *Ecological Rationality*. New York: Oxford University Press. (p. 91).

Part 4

BROADENING THE PERSPECTIVE

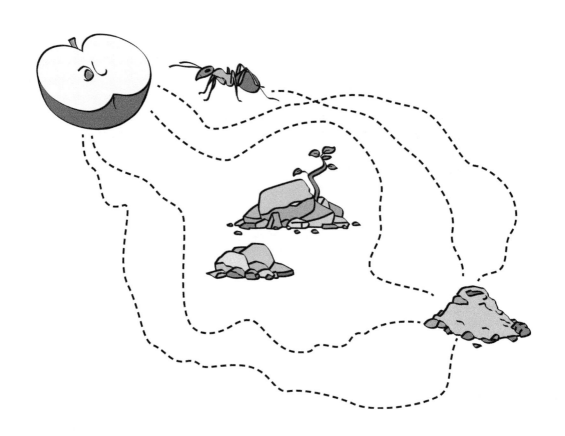

13

DYNAMICS MATTER

Dynamics is a formal branch of physics that deals with physical forces and their relation to motion. However, more generally, dynamics refers to patterns of change *over time*. In particular, we want to contrast this with the construct of cause, which is typically isolated as a particular point *in time* where a process is initiated (e.g., the root cause error that triggers a catastrophic accident).

These different relations to *time* have huge implications for how we think about phenomena— whether we visualize these phenomena as isolated elemental particles interacting like colliding billiard balls or cascading dominoes; or whether we visualize these phenomena as interacting patterns of constraint as in electromagnetic or gravitational fields.

The diagram on the opening plate to this chapter was inspired by Herbert Simon's parable of the ant on the beach. Simon writes that *"viewed as a geometric figure, the ant's path is irregular, complex, hard to describe. But its complexity is really a complexity of the surface of the beach, not a complexity in the ant."*[1] In this chapter we would like to take the parable of the ant on the beach as a common theme that can be used to explore ways to unpack behavior trajectories in order to make sense of the dynamics of human experience.

Time Histories

In the causal narrative, time is visualized as ticks of a clock or beats of a metronome with a clear ordering so that one beat precedes the other. This conventional view uses order in time as a critical index to the underlying causal dynamics.

Thus, to find 'causes' follow the path backwards in time. Figure 13.1 adds time signatures (t_n) to the path and a spatial grid (x-y coordinate system) so that we can better associate place and time. The spatial grid in Figure 13.1 is quite coarse, but both the tick tempo and spatial grid can be made as fine as necessary, depending on the scale of resolution that a researcher chooses.

It is now possible to associate position on the grid coordinates with time to create graphs of the time histories of the ant's movements. Figure 13.2 shows separate time histories for x and y. However, it is also possible to create a three-dimensional time history that shows x-y position as a function of time, although this can be difficult to represent on a two-dimensional page.

Because it is inconvenient to deal with the two-dimensional space of the beach, a researcher might choose to bring the ant into the laboratory, where behavior can be observed in an ecology with lower dimensionality.

For example, Figure 13.3 illustrates one possible configuration in which the ant is constrained to move along a restricted path, so that the activity space can be reduced to a single dimension

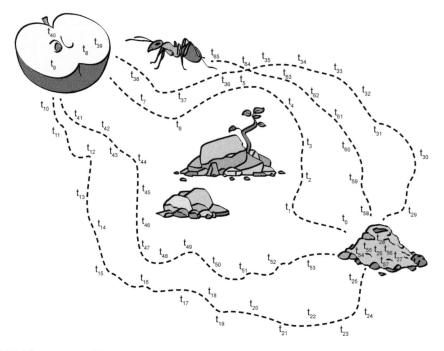

Figure 13.1 The trajectory of the ant can be quantified in terms of ticks on a clock (tn) and spatial coordinates (x,y) as illustrated here.

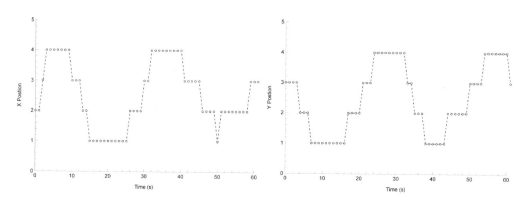

Figure 13.2 The trajectory of the ant can be represented as time histories for each of the two spatial dimensions (x on the left and y on the right).

Figure 13.3 To learn more about the capabilities of the ant, a researcher may observe behavior in a more constrained experiment that is more convenient for analytical purposes.

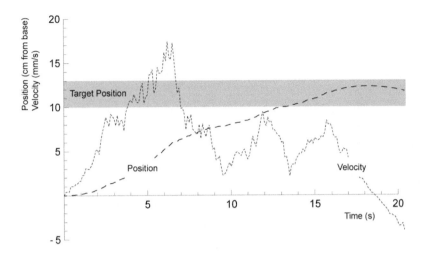

Figure 13.4 A sample time history of behavior in the experiment illustrated in Figure 13.3. Position and velocity relative to the initial home position are plotted as a function of time.

(i.e., distance from the home). This is somewhat analogous to the Fitts' Law paradigm for evaluating human motor control.[2]

Figure 13.4 shows what a sample time history for position and velocity relative to the initial home state might look like. The time history shows behavior over time. Examining behavior over time can be essential in order to discover the underlying dynamics of a system.

The graph of the time history allows us to 'see' important aspects of the ants' behavior (e.g., time to reach the target, peak velocity). It also allows us to make inferences about the organization of behavior. For example, inferences about component sub-movements can be made from the position and velocity patterns. The peaks and valleys in the velocity profile suggest possible places to partition the overall trajectory into components, where each component has an acceleration and a deceleration phase. The pattern in Figure 13.4 suggests two or three component sub-movements.

Dynamic Constraints in Space-Time

Note that in converting the behavior of the ant into a time history graph much information about both the ant and the beach are lost. Where is the meaning in this data? One way that physics has added some semantics to time histories is to consider the impact of absolute constraints—such as the speed of light. Thus, any objects that would require movements at speeds above the speed of light to reach are simply unreachable by the ant. They are outside of the ant's reality. Also, any events in the past that would require moving at the speed of light to reach the ant are also outside of its reality—they are not possible pasts or possible causes. They are not possible experiences.

Perhaps for biological and cognitive systems, we might modify this so that rather than using the speed of light as the critical constraint, we might use the maximum speed that the ant can travel

Richard Feynman[3]

(or for a cognitive system we might also be interested in the speed to process information). Thus, in Figure 13.5 we might use the top speed of the ant as a constraint to add some meaning to the time histories. This allows us to partition the space into possible pasts (where the ant could have been), possible futures (where the ant might go), and also to isolate space-time coordinates that are outside of the ant's reach. That is, the ant cannot get to (or have come from) those spaces due to constraints on how fast it can move. Although there may be things in the ant's ecology that can

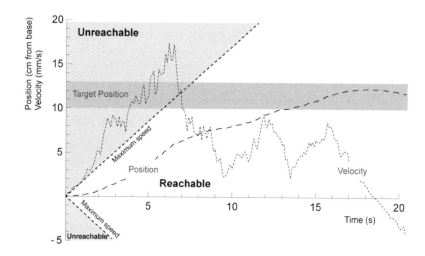

Figure 13.5 The dotted lines represent constraints on the ant's motion—maximum speed. This makes it possible to partition space-time into possible and impossible (unreachable) states relative to the initial condition.

Figure 13.6 Using Fourier Analysis the information in the time domain can be converted to the frequency domain, in which events are indexed relative to patterns over time (i.e., sine waves of different frequencies, amplitudes, and phases.

move faster than the ant, so we may want to consider other constraints (e.g., the speed of a predator) to use in partitioning space-time.

Remember in Chapter 7, we saw that it can be useful to examine performance of control systems with respect to the frequency domain. This might involve using a continuous tracking paradigm, where the ant might have to pursue a moving target or null a disturbance.

In the frequency domain, the time history is visualized relative to sinusoidal patterns, rather than relative to ticks on a clock. The sine waves are ordered in terms of frequency (rate of alternation) and the measure is the amplitude or power (i.e., strength) of the response and phase shift (e.g., time delays) at each frequency.

As was illustrated in Chapter 7, patterns in the frequency domain can be linked to properties of the system dynamics or transfer function (e.g., an integrator results in a decreasing amplitude response with increasing frequency and a quarter-cycle ($90°$) phase shift. Figure 13.6 illustrates that Fourier Analysis can be used to convert from the time domain (using ticks of the clock as the index of events in time) to the frequency domain (using sinusoidal frequencies as the index of events over time).

The frequency domain response can be used to make inferences about dynamic constraints within the ant, just as McRuer and Jex were able to use the frequency response in a compensatory tracking task to build a model of the human pilot. That is, the pattern of amplitudes and phases over frequency can be compared with the patterns of known systems (e.g., a mass-spring-dashpot system) to infer whether the response is similar to those systems.

For example, the frequency response might be characteristic of a second-order lag, suggesting that movements of the ant are constrained by Newton's Second Law of Motion. Thus, the limiting factor on motion may not be an absolute velocity, but rather the limiting factor may be more accurately specified in terms of possible accelerations. Figure 13.7 shows how this might impact the fields of possibility with respect to the ant's movement time history.

Once you have a model of the ant (based on a transfer function derived from the frequency characteristics or some other means), an alternative representation of the dynamics can be derived using model variables or states. For example, a model of the ant as an inertial system would be a second-order differential equation with two degrees of freedom (initial conditions) or states— position and velocity. Thus, it might be possible to visualize the ant's motion within a state space. That is, rather than x-y coordinates, the coordinates of the state space might be position and velocity, as we will see in Figure 13.8.

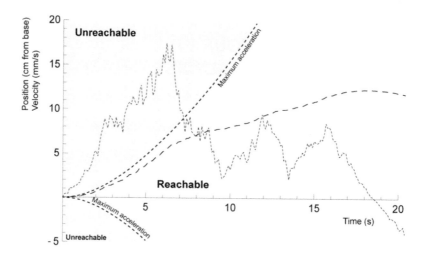

Figure 13.7 The dotted lines represent constraints on the ant's motion—in terms of a limiting acceleration. This makes it possible to partition space-time into now, potential pasts, potential futures, and impossible (unreachable) states based on the internal dynamics of the ant.

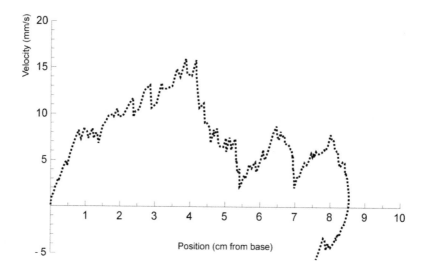

Figure 13.8 This 'state space' diagram shows the ant trajectory as a function of the two state variables: position and velocity.

Events in Space-Time

Once we know the dynamic limits on ant motion, we can apply these limits to where the ant is as in Figure 13.7, but we can also apply these limits to where the ant wants to be as in Figure 13.9. Figure 13.9 allows us to visualize an initial condition (where the ant is now) relative to some future goal or desirable path. In this example we used error relative to an optimal path as the index of position.

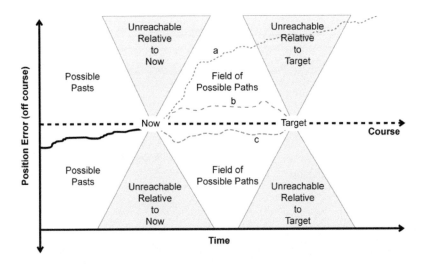

Figure 13.9 An 'event space' is one way to illustrate the constraints associated with both the initial condition (or state) and an intended target (or goal state).[5]

Note that the constraints on motion can be applied to both the initial and target states. Thus, the shaded fields represent states that can't be reached from the initial condition and states from which it would be impossible to reach the target. The remaining open space between the *now state* and the *target state* represents a field of possibilities, or in Gibson's terms a *field of safe travel*.[4] All possible paths for achieving the target will be within this space. An event space allows us to highlight intentional relations between where a system is and where a system might intend to go. The field relating the initial state to the goal state includes possible futures relative to the initial state and possible pasts with respect to the goal state. Note these possible futures and pasts are the result of motion constraints of the ant.

Within the space of possibilities, it would be possible to highlight specific paths of interest that link the initial and goal states. For example, the minimum distance, minimum time, and minimum effort paths might be of interest. In a flat, uncluttered space, these might all be the same straight line from target to goal. However, in a cluttered, undulating terrain these might be three different paths. If they were different, it would be interesting to see if the ant's path tended to be closer to one of these than to the others. This would provide some insight into the ant's value system (e.g., whether it was trying to save time or effort).

It is important to note that the dynamic limits to ant motion depicted in Figures 13.5, 13.7, and 13.9 are constraints *over time*. They apply to any space-time state that the ant might occupy or to any goal state that might be considered in relation to the ant. The motion constraints don't cause behavior. However, these constraints shape the field of possibilities from which the ant can choose. Applying the logic of field analysis, the field of possibilities becomes smaller and smaller as a function of the number of constraints. What are some additional constraints that might limit the field of possibilities for the ant?

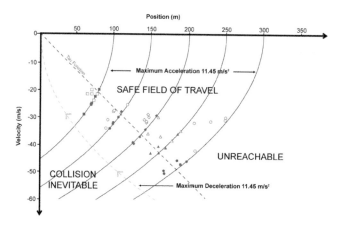

Figure 13.10 The 'state space' is one way to illustrate the constraints that partition the field of possibilities for a simple driving task. The points in the diagram illustrate the states at which participants released the accelerator, before braking. Open symbols were from early trials and filled symbols are from later trials. The results suggest that participants were discovering the minimum time solution to this task—consistent with the instructions to reach the barrier as quickly as possible without crashing.[6]

Figure 13.10 was first introduced in Chapter 11. This figure illustrates behavior (releasing the accelerator prior to braking) as a function of position (relative to a wall at position = 0) and velocity. The horizontal axis represents distance from a wall and the vertical axis represents velocity toward the wall (negative velocity indicates the direction toward the wall).

The five curves that intersect the horizontal axis on the right indicate maximum accelerations for each of five initial states (velocity = 0 at five different distances from the wall). These reflect constraints on the initial conditions for the different trials. The single curve that meets the horizontal axis at position = 0 represents maximum braking that leads to 0 velocity at the wall. This reflects a constraint associated with the goal to stop before reaching the wall, or more precisely to kiss the wall.

By mapping these dynamic constraints (maximum acceleration and maximum deceleration) on the state space, it is possible to partition the space to show the Field of Safe Travel. This Field of Safe Travel includes the states that can both be reached from the initial condition and that allow stopping without collision with the wall.

Outside of the Field of Safe Travel are states that are unreachable given the initial condition—the car cannot accelerate fast enough to get to those combinations of position and velocity—and states that will not allow approach without collision—from those positions and velocities it is impossible to brake hard enough to stop (achieve 0 velocity) before reaching the wall.

Visualizing behavior relative to the dynamic motion constraints, such as in Figure 13.7, allows us to interpret that behavior in terms of the internal constraints of the human-machine system, including constraints on motion and intentional constraints (to stop at the wall). This allows us to consider dynamic constraints (e.g., the car's motion capabilities) as well as environmental constraints (i.e., the position of the wall) in order to make sense of the driver's behavior. The state space representation helps us to see behavior in terms of *what matters*.

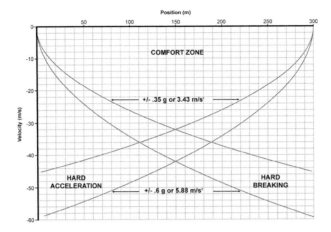

Figure 13.11 This 'state space' representation for a driving event shows boundaries associated with comfortable g-force limits (less than .35 g).

The pattern of behaviors in Figure 13.7 suggests that with practice participants adopted a bang-bang style of control in which they followed the maximum acceleration path to start and then released the accelerator in anticipation of the maximum braking limit. This suggests that the participants learned the dynamic limits of the simulated vehicle they were controlling. Note that this is very near to the optimal control in terms of getting from the initial positions to the wall in minimum time without collision, which is exactly what we asked participants to do.

We might typically say that the participants learned to brake at the "*right time*," but it might be more precise to say that they learned to brake at the "*right state*." In fact, we suspect that the information that supported this skill was optical correlates to the state variables—position (optical angles of the wall edges) and velocity (optical expansion rate of those edges).[7] Note that this study was done on a desktop simulator. Thus, the driver did not experience the g-forces associated with maximum accelerations and decelerations. In an actual driving situation, the g-forces that are comfortable may be important constraints that shape the driver's performance, as suggested in Figure 13.11.

Alternative Alphabets for Labeling States

What if there are dynamic constraints (e.g., preferences of the ant for a particular food) that might be difficult to model in terms of differential equations? Is it possible to derive a state space representation?

Figure 13.12 provides another way to partition the ant's activities in space-time. Rather than using x-y coordinates, the space is identified in terms of 'places,' and in this case the places are locations within the grid. However, the space could also be divided to reflect specific objects on the beach (e.g., home, food, rocks, etc.). The places then become a sort of alphabet for labeling the ant's behaviors.

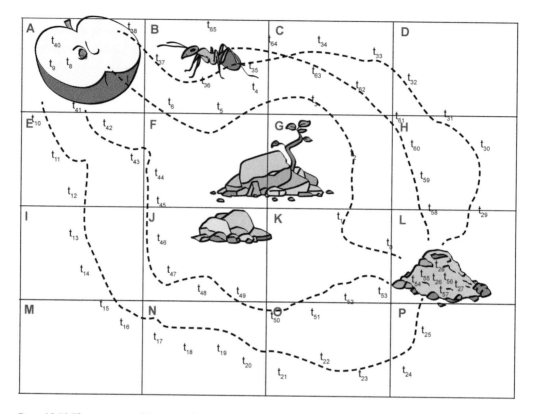

Figure 13.12 The trajectory of the ant can be quantified in terms of ticks on a clock (tn) and places or locations such as positions in the grid or positions defined relative to objects on the beach.

The location alphabet becomes the state description of the process, with each character in the alphabet (each place) corresponding to a different state. Figure 13.13 represents the behavior of the ant with respect to place as a state transition diagram in which the states are identified as nodes and arrows represent transitions from one node (i.e., state) to another. The numbers on the arrows indicate the frequency for each transition. The state transition diagram provides a conceptual map for visualizing the sequential relations among the states.

Given this state description, insights into the underlying dynamics of the ant-beach interaction can then be gained from examining the transitions between states. Figure 13.14 shows a *state transition matrix* (or return map) for the ant-beach interaction. The vertical axis of the matrix represents the state of the ant-beach system (i.e., position or place) at a time t, and the horizontal axis of the matrix represents the state of the ant-beach system at a time $t+1$. An entry in this matrix corresponds to a transition from one state to another in a single time step. For example, the '1' entry at K, K indicates that the first transition was from K to K (the ant was at place K on both P_0 and P_1). The next transition (2), the ant moves from K at P_1 to G at P_2, and so on.

The state transition matrix allows the behavior of the ant-beach system to be quantified using information statistics (based on a metaphor with entropy in physical systems). The information or entropy of the system reflects the degree to which the behavior 'fills' the state space or space of possibilities.

$$P_{t+1}$$

	A	B	C	D	E	F	G	H	I	J	K	L	M	N	O	P
A	8, 9, 39, 40				10, 41											
B	7, 38	5, 6, 36, 37														
C		4, 35, 6, 5	34, 63, 64													
D			33													
E					11, 12, 42, 43	44			13							
F						45				46						
G			3, 62													
H				32		61		31, 60								
I									14			15				
J										47, 48, 49						
K							2			52, 53	1	54				
L								30, 59				27, 28, 29, 55, 56, 57				
M													16	17		
N												18, 19, 20		21		
O										51				22, 23	24	
P												26				25

$$P_t$$

Figure 13.13 The state transition diagram provides a representation of the sequential relations among the states. Nodes represent states and arrows represent transitions between states.

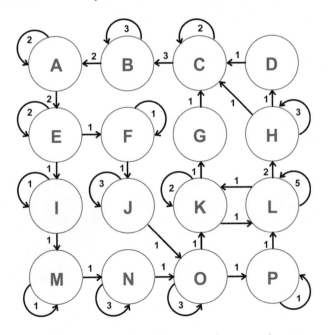

Figure 13.14 This state transition matrix or return map shows sequential transitions from one state (place on the grid in Figure 13.7) to another at each step along the behavioral trajectory of interactions between ant and beach.

If the behavior fills the space, so that entries are distributed evenly throughout the matrix, this would indicate that the behavior is unconstrained (maximum entropy or maximum information). In other words, all things (transitions) are possible!

If the distribution of the entries in the matrix is 'clumpy' (as it is), with some spaces having many entries and others being empty, then this would be evidence that the behavior is being constrained in some ways. In other words, this indicates that some relations are more likely, or happen more often than others. Events that happen very often might be identified as 'attractors' indicating that the system repeats these transitions over and over again. Other events that never happen or that happen only rarely might be identified as '*unattractive*' or maybe even '*repelling*.'

It is important to note that the technical use of the term *information*—a measure of uncertainty or degrees of freedom—can seem at odds with the way the term is used in common speech. The information statistic will be maximal when the state transition matrix is uniformly filled. This suggests that it is possible to move from any state to any other state in a single step. Thus, it is difficult to predict what will happen next—there is maximal uncertainty, maximal possibilities, or maximum information.

In everyday language, the term *information* is generally used in relation to messages or observations. If we actually look to see where the ant is, the amount of information in that observation typically refers to how much uncertainty was reduced as a result of that observation.

Thus, an observation (or message) is most informative when our prior uncertainty about the state of the system was greatest and is least informative when we have no uncertainty prior to the observation. If we already know where the ant is, then the observation does not reduce our uncertainty at all. The degree of information in a message reflects properties of the message in relation to properties of the source (the number of possibilities) and properties of the receiver (the amount of uncertainty about those possibilities).

Claude Shannon[8]

240

DYNAMICS MATTER

If the ant's behavior is highly constrained (i.e., it is clumpy with respect to the transition matrix), then it is relatively easier to predict where the ant might be. Thus, each observation is less 'informative.'

As Claude Shannon says in the previous quote, the information index itself was not designed to measure meaning. However, the fact that the distribution in the transition matrix does not fill the whole space (e.g., entropy or information is less than the maximum) suggests that the system is constrained, and these constraints are potentially meaningful. These constraints are the source of the patterns (e.g., melodies, see end quote from Eddington) that allow us to make predictions about the behavior of the system being examined. For example, we might start by considering the cells in the transition matrix in Figure 13.14 that get the most entries.

The cell in the transition matrix (Figure 13.14) with the most entries is L-L. This suggests that the ant spends a lot of time at the place corresponding to L. You might look at Figure 13.12 to see what could be significant about that place on the beach. Cells A-A, B-B, and E-E also have more entries than other cells. Again, look at Figure 13.12 to see why the ant might be attracted to those places.

It can also be useful to look at the cells with no entries. For example, consider the cells in the A row. There are transitions from A to A and from A to E, but there are no other transitions. For

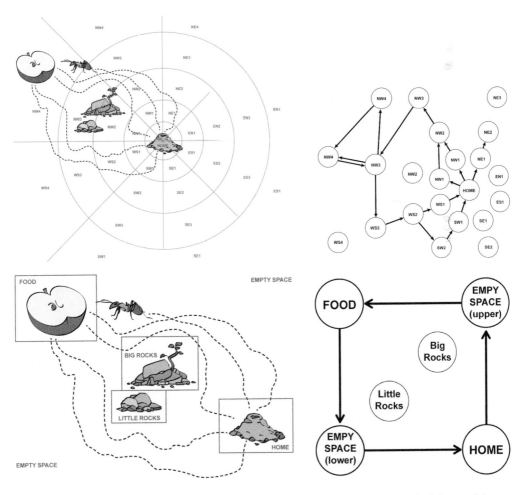

Figure 13.15 This figure illustrate two different 'alphabets' or coordinate systems for mapping the behavior of the ant-beach system. The system on the top-left uses a polar coordinate system centered on the home of the ant. The system on the bottom-left constructs an alphabet (labels) to reflect the different objects on the beach.

241

example, there are no transitions from A to L. This might reflect a constraint on how fast the ant can move relative to the measured time intervals. It may be impossible for the ant to get from A to L in a single time step. What is special about the transition from A to E? Aha, this transition is associated with the path from food to home!

Thus, while the information statistics don't provide meaning, they do allow us to quantify whether the phenomenon is constrained or not. If there are constraints, then the distribution in the transition matrix relative to its mapping on the phenomenon can inform our hypotheses about what these constraints might be. For example, is it due to a physical constraint on motion (e.g., how fast the ant can move or the presence of an impassable obstacle) or is it a value constraint (e.g., a nutritious food source). The quality of our hypothesis with respect to identifying meaningful constraints will depend in part on the *alphabet* we use in order to create the state transition matrix.

Figure 13.13 shows one alphabet. Figure 13.15 illustrates some alternative alphabets for mapping the space. The map on the top-left uses a polar coordinate system centered on the home. The map on the bottom-left identifies specific objects on the beach as the letters in the alphabet. A state transition matrix can be constructed from either of these maps. One can think of the different maps as coordinate transformations in mathematics or alternative projections in cartography.[9]

The art of discovery, particularly with respect to discovering *what matters*, can hinge on the choice of the right coordinate system for your map. Different coordinate systems will make different aspects of the functional dynamics more or less obvious.

Some things that might be considered when choosing this alphabet include: limits on affording (e.g., constraints on motion), limits on specifying (e.g., constraints relative to feedback with respect to progress toward some target), and limits on satisfying [e.g., goals or targets and criteria that might be minimized (time) or maximized (learning about the space) relative to the means for achieving those goals].

Perhaps, one of the obstacles that has made the problem of meaning so difficult for cognitive science is that the coordinate system that was inherited from Newton—fixed, absolute space and time coordinates—was accepted uncritically as the map for the ecology.

James J. Gibson[10]

A key insight that led to Einstein's alternative to Newton's physics was a change in the coordinate system—the realization that space and time were not absolute, that they varied as a function of motion of the observer. The implication of this is that an important step toward a science of what matters is to find the right coordinate systems for mapping the functional ecology. That is, to find coordinate systems that make the patterns associated with meaning most salient. As the quote from Gibson illustrates, we are not the first to suggest that cognitive science needs to explore alternatives to Newton and Euclid's coordinate systems.

Finding the Right Alphabet for a Science of What Matters

This is an alternative way to frame the central question of and motivation for this book. *What is the right state space or alphabet for applied cognitive science?* This is the question that justifies the excursions into metaphysics in the early chapters of the book. Choice of the alphabet is where the science starts. The alphabet sets the coordinates of our state spaces. It provides the set from which independent and dependent variables in our experiments are chosen. It provides the basis from which models and explanations are constructed.

A fundamental motivation for this book is a sense that the field of applied cognitive science has not yet settled on the right alphabet or alphabets; or at least that the conventional alphabets are not adequate, particularly when it comes to generalizing from cognitive science to design applications. *Is there an alternative alphabet that would help us to better appreciate what matters with respect to the dynamics of human experience?*

The first four chapters (1–4) of this book suggested that the alphabets should be chosen to reflect the functional couplings between the agent and the ecology. We suggest three dimensions of this coupling that we believe are critical to the functional ontology: affording, satisfying, and specifying.

Affording refers to constraints that limit what actions are possible (e.g., physical laws of motion). *Satisfying* refers to the value constraints that reflect what aspects of the ecology are desirable or undesirable (e.g., nutrition versus poison). *Specifying* refers to constraints associated with feedback relative to choosing actions that lead to satisfying consequences (e.g., optical invariants).

We don't expect that there is a single alphabet that can span all the constraints associated with these dimensions in all ecologies. In other words, we are not betting on any single alphabet to be privileged with respect to the dynamics of cognitive systems. We believe that a pluralistic episte-mology is necessary. This means that multiple perspectives (i.e., multiple alphabets) may be neces-sary to span the issues associated with what matters.

The next five chapters focused on the kinds of explanations that we believe will be most relevant to understanding the dynamics of cognitive systems. We argue that the classical causal explanations (i.e., the billiard ball model) are not adequate for explaining the behavior of cognitive systems. Rather, we argue that cognitive systems are inherently circular.

For example, the termite nest-building metaphor from Kugler and Turvey is used in Chapter 6 to illustrate how such a circular coupling might work. This coupling involves a dynamic in which the termites are shaping the ecological landscape (e.g., as a result of their deposits) and at the same time that ecological landscape (e.g., the pheromone distribution) is shaping the termite's behavior. This type of coupling illustrates the dynamics of self-organization in which the structure is not *caused* by factors that can be isolated in either the termites or in the ecology. However, behavior is constrained by properties of the functional coupling.

Chapter 5 considered the circular coupling relative to logic and suggests that the pragmatic logic of Peirce's *abduction* provides a more promising model for human rationality than the models associated with classical logic (*induction* and *deduction*). Abduction grounds rationality in the prag-matics associated with trial-and-error learning. With abduction a belief is evaluated relative to the consequences of acting on it. Beliefs that lead to satisfying outcomes are strengthened and beliefs that lead to unsatisfying outcomes are weakened.

Chapters 7 and 8 examined the circular coupling from the perspective of control theory. Chapter 7 explored the dynamics of control and considers the constraints associated with stability. Chapter 8 explored the dynamics of observation and considers the constraints associated with estimation.

Control theory provides an important context for considering the limits of stability for closed-loop systems. In particular, the adaptive control problem considers how the stability limitations can be negotiated in real time so that an agent can maintain stability in the context of changing ecologies.

Chapter 9 used the term *muddling through* to make the case that the dynamics of control systems are not only relevant to perceptual-motor skill (e.g., landing aircraft or driving), but these dynam-ics also reflect a very general aspect of cognitive decision making and problem solving.

Chapter 10 used alternative approaches to *heuristics* relative to decision making to emphasize the distinctions between a classical view in which heuristics are considered to reflect weaknesses of human rationality relative to more formal logical and/or mathematical prescriptions for reason-ing, and an alternative view in which heuristics are considered to reflect the strength of human rationality in terms of its ability to leverage ecological constraints to skillfully achieve satisfying outcomes in complex environments.

Note that in the classical view, heuristics are biases that *cause* errors in human decision mak-ing. However, in the alternative ecological rationality perspective, heuristics reflect sensitivity of humans to situated constraints in specific ecologies. From this perspective, utilizing the situated constraints provides a means to success, often in contexts where the assumptions underlying more formal analytic approaches are not met.

Chapter 11 connected the dots between the constraints that support heuristic decision making and the deep structure that has been long associated with productive thinking and problem solving.

The construct of *deep structure* is simply seen as a reference to constraints that are intrinsic to specific problems or ecologies. Rasmussen's Abstraction Hierarchy suggests that the deep structure of many problems can involve multiple layers of means-ends relations.

The Abstraction Hierarchy further suggests that different alphabets might be preferred for describing different layers in the means-end hierarchy. However, the layers are not completely independent, so it also becomes necessary to choose alphabets that enable linking constraints at one layer with constraints at other layers.

In Chapter 12 we emphasize one particular layer in the Abstraction Hierarchy, that is, the layer associated with value or quality of outcomes. This layer reflects the constraints associated with the dynamic of satisfying. The fundamental issue here is *goodness*. What is the cognitive system attracted to? What repels it?

While we don't want to go so far as arguing that this level of constraint is privileged, we do believe it is clear that the importance of constraints on satisfying have long been underappreciated. Due to the emphasis of classical logic on the *form* of arguments, cognitive science has emphasized quality of process over the pragmatics of quality outcomes. With the emphasis on process, classical cognitive science has lots to say about *how* to make proper decisions, but has little to offer about *why* cognitive systems might prefer one option to another. And more generally, classical science has been framed in a way that consciously excludes value as a dimension of interest.

In sum, a central goal for this book is to advocate for a field theoretic orientation to the dynamics of cognitive systems that focuses on identifying *constraints*, rather than *causes*. Further,

Arthur Eddington[11]

we believe that a first step toward a field theoretic orientation is to think critically about what type of alphabet will allow the best perspective for identifying the constraints associated with what matters.

Up to now, cognitive science has tended to look to the other sciences (e.g., physics and biology) for the dimensions of reality. On the one hand, we totally sympathize with James' desire for a singular science.[12] Thus, we feel that it is important to approach cognitive science from the shoulders of the other sciences. On the other hand, we believe it is a mistake to uncritically accept the dimensions that work best for physics or biology, as the best alphabet for gaining insights into cognitive systems. We argue that the maturity of cognitive science will depend on our ability to discover (or invent) alternative alphabets that better reflect the dynamics of meaning processing.

Thus, James' pursuit of a singular science is not about reducing human experience to physics or biology. Rather, the challenge is to elevate physics and biology to better reflect the constraints that are functionally relevant to the dynamics of experience.

An important aspect of a new active psychophysics will involve replacing the Newtonian constructs of absolute space and time with the construct of event. Where an event is a partitioning of time and space with respect to functionally relevant dimensions that reflect: satisfying (i.e., goals and values), affording (i.e., the constraints on action), and specifying (i.e., the constraints on information).

The key is to parse the problems into chunks that preserve functional meaning or significance with respect to the triadic whole. For example, the braking behavior of a driver can only be evaluated relative to the dynamics of the vehicle being controlled, the information feedback available to the driver, and the consequences that are being sought.

Notes

1. Simon, H.A. (1981). *The sciences of the artificial.* 2nd ed. Cambridge, MA: MIT Press. (p. 64).
2. Jagacinski, R.J. Flach, J.M. (2003). *Control theory for humans: Quantitative approaches to modeling performance.* Mahwah, NJ: Erlbaum.
3. Feynman, R.P., Leighton, R.B., & Sands, M. (1963). *The Feynman Lectures on Physics.* Reading, MA: Addison-Wesley. (pp. 17–14).
4. Gibson, J.J., & Crooks, L.E. (1938/1982). A theoretical field-analysis of automobile-driving. *American Journal of Psychology,* 51, 453–471. Reprinted in E. Reed & R. Jones (Eds.). *Reasons for realism: Selected essays of James J. Gibson* (pp. 119–136). Hillsdale, NJ: Erlbaum.
5. See Shaw, R., & Kinsella-Shaw, J. (1988). Ecological mechanics: A physical geometry of intentional constraints. In P. Kugler (Ed.). *Self-organization in biological workspaces.* Berlin: Springer-Verlag.
6. Flach, J.M., Jagacinski, R.J., Smith, M.R.H., & McKenna, B. (2011). Coupling perception, action, intention, and value: A control theoretic approach to driving performance. In D.L. Fisher, M. Rizzo, J.K. Caird, & J.D. Lee (Eds.). *Handbook of driving simulation for engineering, medicine and psychology* (pp. 43.1–43.16). Boca Raton, FL: Taylor & Francis, CRC Press.
7. Stanard, T., Flach, J.M., Smith, M.R.H., & Warren, R. (2012). Learning to avoid collisions: A functional state space approach. *Ecological Psychology,* 24(4), 328–360.

   McKenna, B., Bennett, A., & Flach, J.M. (2004). Using perceptual boundaries to control braking actions. Proceedings of the Human Factors and Ergonomics Society. New Orleans, Oct, 2004.

   Smith, M.R.H., Flach, J.M., Dittman, S.M., & Stanard, T.W. (2001). Monocular optical constraints on collision control. *Journal of Experimental Psychology: Human Perception & Performance,* 27(2), 395–410.
8. Shannon, C.E., & Weaver, W. (1963). *The mathematical theory of communication.* Urbana, IL: University of Illinois Press. (p. 31).
9. See Hutchins for an interesting discussion of alternative maps in the context of navigation: Hutchins, E. (1995). *Cognition in the wild.* Cambridge, MA: MIT Press.

10. Gibson, J.J. (1979). *The ecological approach to visual perception*. Boston, MA: Houghton Mifflin. (pp. 3 & 12).

11. Eddington, A. (1927). *The nature of the physical world*. New York: The MacMillan Company. (p. 105). Cited in Shannon, C.E., & Weaver, W. (1963). *The mathematical theory of communication* Urbana, IL: University of Illinois Press. (p. 28).

12. James, W. (1909). *Psychology*. New York: Henry Holt and Company. (p. 1). "Most thinkers have a faith that at bottom there is but one Science of all things, and that until all is known, no one thing can be completely known."

14

SOCIAL DYNAMICS

In Chapter 1 we made reference to the problem of measuring the length of a coastline to illustrate that the idea of an 'objective' length may be problematic for natural systems. The key issue is that due to the irregularities in the coastline, it may be impossible to specify the length, independently from the choice of a measuring instrument. This is because as the measuring instrument becomes more precise, more of the irregularities will be included in the measure, and thus, the length will increase.

This fractal property is illustrated in the Koch Curve shown in Figure 14.1. The Koch Curve is constructed by dividing a line of unit length into three segments and then replacing the middle segment with two segments connecting at an angle. The result is a line (the generator) that is now constructed of four segments, each of which is one-third the length of the initial line. So, the total length of the line is increased, but the positions of the ends have not changed. The shape created is then used to generate additional irregularities by shrinking it and replacing each of the four edges with four miniature copies of the generator.

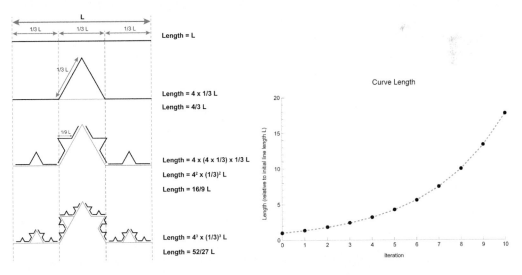

Figure 14.1 This figure shows the construction of a Koch Curve as an illustration of a fractal geometry. The length of the curve increases as irregularities at finer and finer grains are added.

249

Benoit Mandelbrot[1]

As this process is repeated, more irregularities are added and the actual length of the curve grows. In principle, this process can be repeated an infinite number of times, resulting in an infinite measure of length for a line of apparently finite length (contained in a finite area).

Thus, in reference to the earlier story, while it may not be 'turtles all the way down,' nature may have a fractal structure so that it is 'generators' all the way down. In other words, there may be properties of the geometry of the coast that are *scale independent*. The same pattern of irregularity will appear at every level of magnification.

The point for this chapter is to suggest that many of the properties that we have used to describe the dynamics of individual cognition might also be applied at other scales. For example, at a smaller scale it might be useful to think of subsystems within an individual (e.g., nervous system or individual nerves) as systems that must adapt to their ecology within the body, in many of the same ways that individual people adapt to their physical and social environments.

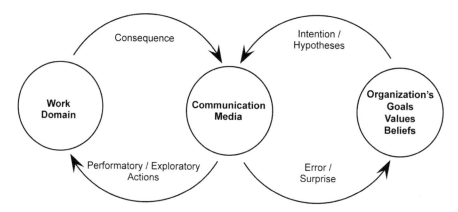

Figure 14.2 This figure illustrates the triadic semiotic dynamic of abduction as it relates to Organizational Sensemaking at the scale of a Sociotechnical System. This suggests that the principles of control and observation discussed in previous chapters can be applied at the organizational level.

However, rather than going down in scale we will go up in scale and suggest that most of the properties that we have discussed in the context of individuals can be applied at the larger scale of sociotechnical systems. We suggest that the dynamics of common sense and the dynamics of *organizational sensemaking* are very similar. An advantage of moving to a larger scale is that some of the common dynamics may be easier to observe and appreciate at the larger scale of organizations. Also, we hope that illustrating these patterns at multiple scales will help to emphasize the invariant properties of adaptive, abductive reasoning systems.

Organizational Sensemaking

Shotter (1993) likens managing to authoring a conversation and describes the manager's task as "not one of choosing but of generating, of generating a clear and adequate formulation of what the problem situation "is," of creating from a set of incoherent and disorderly events a coherent "structure" within which both current actualities and further possibilities can be given an intelligible "place"—and of doing all this, not alone, but in continual conversation with all the others who are involved."[2]

This quote is taken from Karl Weick's book on "*Sensemaking in Organizations.*"[3] Hopefully, the parallels between Shotter's description of the manager's task and the triadic dynamics of abduction described throughout this book are evident.

Up to this point, we have largely framed the triadic dynamic in terms of the experience of individuals. However, in this chapter we will explore this dynamic at the level of *organizational sensemaking*, as illustrated in Figure 14.2. In this context, the three components of the semiotic triad are considered in relation to a sociotechnical system. This allows us to consider the rationality behind the policies, decisions, and actions of organizations (e.g., families, teams, companies, political parties, armies, or countries).

In fact, we believe that human experiences are invariably social, so that the triadic dynamic is almost always situated in a larger social or organizational context. This context can be explicit (e.g., family or organizational decision making) or it can be implicit in the sense that family, organizations, and culture can be a primary source for the value systems that shape the experiences of individuals.

We believe that social cooperation has played a central role in the evolutionary development of humans. For example, the "permission schema" has been hypothesized to explain the disparate results found for isomorphic variations of the Wason task described in Chapter 5. Thus, it has long been an important dimension of the abduction dynamic. However, awareness of the importance of social/organizational dynamics to problem solving has been heightened by recent impacts of technology on the nature of collaborations.

The evolution of communication technologies has had dramatic effects on the field of possibilities with respect to coordinating human actions over space and time (e.g., the telegraph, the telephone, the internet, and the smart phone). This is perhaps most evident in the context of military operations, where coordination across space and time are essential to victory. The impact of recent innovations in information processing and communications on military operations has been described as a 'revolution in military affairs.' For example, Arquilla and Ronfeldt write that:

The most basic theme is that conflicts will increasingly depend on and revolve around, information and communications—"cyber" matters—broadly defined to include the related technological, organizational, and ideational structures of a society. Indeed, information-age modes of conflict (and crime) will be largely about "knowledge"—about who knows what, when, where, and why, and about how secure a society, military, or other actor feels about its knowledge of itself and its adversaries.[4]

An advantage of taking the sociotechnical perspective is that it can be easier to observe how the constraints on control and observation impact (and are impacted by) the patterns of communication among the elemental components inside the system. That is, at the organizational scale, we can observe how the component individuals coordinate their actions in order to adaptively solve ill-structured problems and to pursue common goals. Also, at the sociotechnical system level the time scale for events will be longer so that some patterns over time may be easier to follow. Of course, some aspects of the organizational dynamic might be more difficult to observe because they are distributed too widely and the changes happen too slowly.

Using Fractal Geometry as an analogy, we suggest that the triadic semiotic dynamic illustrated in Figure 14.2 and used throughout this book is a 'generator' for adaptive, cognitive systems. Thus, in cognitive systems this semiotic dynamic operates at multiple scales. For example, the economic system of a country can be viewed as a triadic semiotic system that must adapt to the international economic ecology. Industries within that country's economic system can be viewed as triadic semiotic systems that must adapt to the economic constraints of that country. Subunits and individuals can all be viewed as triadic semiotic systems adapting to the constraints of a specific industry. Again, it's 'turtles' all the way down.

Figure 14.3 provides an image for thinking about how individual triadic units might interact within a larger sensemaking organization. You should not think of these images as representing any specific type of existing organization. In fact, these images trivialize the complexity of natural systems. However, we hope that these images can help us to visualize the types of possible interactions, where actual interactions will typically involve some combination of these three basic types of interaction.

The three types of interaction shown in Figure 14.3 correspond roughly with three types of interdependence and coordination within organizations that Thompson[5] described: pooled (standardization), sequential (planning), and reciprocal (mutual adjustment).

Types of Interdependence and Coordination

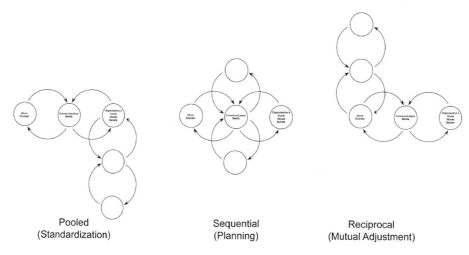

Pooled
(Standardization)

Sequential
(Planning)

Reciprocal
(Mutual Adjustment)

Figure 14.3 This figure illustrates three dimensions of interdependence and coordination within organizations.

Pooled interdependence refers to situations where each of the components within the organization operates with a high degree of autonomy, but the products must be combined to satisfy the organization's objectives. As shown in Figure 14.3, the components share a common goal, but there is little overlap in terms of a shared communication medium or a common work space. Since there is little active communication or interaction in the workspace, coordination is typically achieved through standardization.

For example, in the early days of scientific management, assembly work was decomposed into relatively independent component jobs with an explicit goal to minimize interactions among workers. In this system, the work and medium (e.g., tools and representations) could be optimized for each individual, independently from the work of other individuals. Coordination was accomplished by having the products of each individual worker comply with predetermined standards to ensure that the pieces produced would 'fit' together in the final assembly.

Assembly lines often included buffers of products from each worker, so that interruptions in the rate of production of one worker would not impact the rate of another worker. That is, one worker would not have to wait for another worker to finish something, before he could start. This way the assembly line would flow at a constant rate, independent of any local disturbances at an individual work station.

An advocate for the scientific management approach was heard to argue that there was no need for the workers to know what other workers were doing. In fact, he argued it was best if the workers could focus all their attention on doing their own job (i.e., meeting the standards that he had predetermined) and not worry about or be distracted by what the other workers were doing.

Sequential interdependence refers to situations where there are precedence relations among the components in the organization such that processes of one component depend on satisfactory completion of processes by another component. For example, there may be precedence relations such that one component can't start until another component finishes; or there may be shared resources that can only be used by one component at a time. In this case, not only do the shared functional goals require cooperation, but cooperation is also required in order to achieve local sub-goals. This type of interdependence requires some type of shared representation (e.g., a plan or schedule) to facilitate coordination.

With sequential interdependence, the function of the plan or schedule is to get the right people (or product) to the right place, at the right time. In very stable environments, the plan or schedule can be standardized ahead of time. However, in dynamic environments, disruptions are inevitable. Thus, the plans must be continually revised and updated in order to coordinate activities.

Figure 14.3 suggests that the 'plan' and/or the 're-planning' process requires a shared medium (e.g., a published schedule or a shared calendar) that allows people to 'see' what others are supposed to be doing and to 'tell' others whether they are on track and on schedule or not.

An example of the use of a shared representation to support planning, re-planning, and coordination is the 'status board' or 'white board' that historically were used in Hospital Emergency Departments (ED). These were typically large-format, dry erase boards that were posted in an easily accessible location. The boards generally had a grid-like organization where rows might represent treatment or patient locations in the ED, and columns represent aspects of the treatment process. Wears et al. write:

> Each column is contextually important to the group maintaining the status board. For example, such dimensions might include the patients' principal problem(s), identifiers for the staff assigned to the patient (nurses, physicians), time of arrival or length of stay

information, pending clinical activities (such as consultations or procedures), alerts and warnings (such as isolation, or name similarities). This information is typically densely encoded onto the status board in idiosyncratic but locally meaningful ways, and is continuously updated by the group during the course of their work.[6]

Wears et al. give specific examples of how the white board was used to facilitate coordination and efficiency in the ED. One instance involved the reporting of the results from electrocardiograms (ECGs). In the past, the results from the ECGs would be placed in the patients' charts. However, "this was inefficient for physicians, who had to repeatedly check the charts to see if ECGs were there, and for the ECG technicians, who had to search for charts and interrupt other workers to access them."[7] Now the ECG results are placed on the white board using a magnetic holder. Since the results were directly visible, the need for either the physician or the technicians to search for the charts was eliminated. An additional benefit was that "ECGs would be examined more quickly, since workers at the board for other reasons would quickly scan the ECGs placed there, even if they were not on their own patients, to be sure that major abnormalities were quickly noted."

In another study, Perry and Wears observed the consequences of attempts to replace the large physical boards with computerized status boards in two EDs. In one case, the staff refused to give up the physical white boards and the electronic status board was implemented in parallel. In the other case, the physical boards were replaced by the computerized boards. However, it was observed that the workers had to compensate for the loss of functionality and usability problems with the electronic system with paper notes and other workarounds. One worker commented that s/he felt "half as efficient" with the computer system.

This illustrates how important a representational medium can be for supporting cooperative work. Perry and Wears' observations indicate that "important functions of the status board—coordinating and providing a single overview of unit status—were degraded in the computerized board."[8]

In describing the use of 'white boards' in a surgical trauma unit, Xiao et al. noted that a key asset of the white boards is the flexibility to re-plan in response to unexpected events (e.g., an unscheduled emergency or a loss of equipment functionality in a scheduled operating room).[9] Xiao noted that this served both asynchronous and synchronous interactions among the staff to coordinate their work.

Typically, the construct of plan suggests asynchronous interactions. That is, the plan is created at one time for use at a later time. Also, in many cases the people making the plan are not the same people who will be carrying out the plan. For example, in military systems the plan may be generated by one set of officers in a remote central command center, but it may be executed by other field officers at the site of the battle. The white boards in medical settings served this type of planning in the sense that new shifts coming on will often start by observing the white board in order to see what is going on and what is planned for their shift.

However, Xiao et al. also observed the board being used to support synchronous re-planning in which people would huddle around the white board and manipulate the magnetic markers in order to cooperatively solve scheduling problems. For example, in one case it was necessary to open an additional operating room to accommodate a large caseload. Because this required both a room and resources (e.g., anesthesia), the charge nurse and the charge anesthesiologist jointly viewed the board to explore the various options together.

The example of synchronous re-planning leads naturally to the third type of coordination, *reciprocal interactions*, where the processes and functions of particular components must adapt in more or less real time based on how other components behave. In this case, there are not only sequential dependencies, but there are also process dependencies such that the processes within a component may need to change depending on actions of other components.

An example of a situation that depends heavily on reciprocal interactions is improvised musical performance. In this case, there is no predetermined plan or musical score. Rather, the music is created through the real-time interactions among the participants (including musician and audience). Borgo describes improvisation as 'form-making' music, to emphasize that the form emerges from the real-time interactions.[10]

The earlier example of the termites' nest building (Chapter 6) is also a good example of reciprocal interactions. In that example there is no plan to coordinate the actions. Rather, the coordination emerges as a result of continuous interactions among the moving insects and the flowing pheromone field. In that example, the actions of each insect are shaped in real time by the consequences of the actions of the other insects.

Thus, the three types of interdependence described by Thompson reflect the triadic partitioning of the semiotic dynamic. People in organizations interact through the common problem ecology (reciprocal interactions/mutual adjustment), such that co-workers are a part of the work ecology of an individual worker. Actions of co-workers change the field of possibilities or the affordances that are available to a worker. The interactions can expand the field of possibilities to the extent that the joint capabilities allow the team to accomplish things that cannot be achieved by an individual. The interactions can also restrict the field of possibilities in that limited resources used by one member of the team may not be available to other team members.

People in organizations also interact through shared interfaces/media/representations. Plans and schedules are examples of the kinds of representations that are used to coordinate team actions. When these representations are flexible enough to be modified in real time to reflect evolving contingencies (as with the white board in the ED), then they can facilitate mutual adjustments through

David Borgo[11]

255

reciprocal interactions mediated by the representations. In essence, this allows for continuous re-planning or re-scheduling to address evolving threats and opportunities.

People in organizations also interact in terms of shared values, beliefs, and expectations. Thompson's 'standardization' is particularly relevant to expectations. This is typically addressed in professional training in terms of standards of practice. These professional standards constrain performance in ways that allow workers to behave in ways that are predictable to their colleagues.

Within most organizations, all three types of interaction illustrated in Figure 14.3 will be simultaneously and continuously shaping the coordination among the individuals in the organization. However, from a design perspective, classical scientific management approaches tended to emphasize standardization and planning/scheduling as the primary interventions for achieving coordination. In other words, the design goal was to minimize the reciprocal interactions and the need for mutual adjustment. However, the consequence of this emphasis is that the organizations are ill-equipped to manage change and/or to innovate.

Today, emphasis is shifting to supporting mutual adjustment, with the goal of enhancing organizational flexibility and resilience. That is, by increasing the capability of companies to take full advantage of the capabilities of a diverse workforce in order to creatively respond to emerging opportunities and threats. In some respects, the example of the medical emergency department is becoming more typical of the type of ecologies that all organizations face. These systems can't count on the 'routine' or dictate the market. They have to be prepared for the unexpected. For example, in industry this reflects the accelerating demands of markets that are attempting to address diverse and changing customer preferences and demands. In ecologies with rapidly changing constraints, yesterday's standards and plans can quickly become obsolete.

Organizational Structure

Before we give further consideration to the semiotic or control dynamics of organizations, it may be useful to distinguish three aspects of structure within organizations: the control structure, the communication structure, and the authority structure.

The *control structure* refers to the functional relations between means (action) and ends (goals). It can be useful to describe this independently from the people who might specify the ends or who might carry out the actions. It will typically be useful to describe the control structure in terms of a hierarchical nesting, where outer loops specify the ultimate purposes or global values associated with the organization's primary function (e.g., to generate profit for shareholders, to provide safe and affordable energy, to provide safe and efficient transportation over long distances). In a sense this outer loop would reflect the most general or most dominant missions of the organization. This outer loop then would provide constraints (including targets/goals, regulations, resources, information) on inner loops within the organizations.

This type of hierarchical nesting was illustrated in Chapter 9 (Figure 9.3) in the context of tennis. Most organizations can be visualized in the same way. For example, in an air transportation system the outer loop might represent public policy that sets up the regulations on the industry. Inner loops might reflect regional airspaces, and nested within this might be air traffic control sectors, with the pilots as one of the innermost loops in this functional organization. In this structure, inner loops typically reflect the means for satisfying ends that are specified by outer loops.

In many respects the control structure is not a property of the organization *per se*, but rather the control structure is a property of the function or problem that the organization must solve, so it describes the structure of a work domain. Two properties of the organization, communication structure and authority structure, will have important implications for the success of an organization in managing the problems of a specific work domain.

The *communication structure* reflects constraints on who people can 'talk to,' 'see,' or 'pass information to.' The communication structure would typically be visualized as a network where the nodes would represent components in the organization (e.g., people or work units) and a link would represent a communication channel.

The communication structure can vary from being webs that are rich in connections (i.e., every component can communicate with any other component within the organization) or chains where the connections are very sparse. Historically, physical distance has been a major factor that limited the potential richness of communication networks. It simply was not possible for people who were separated by large distances to communicate directly. For example, it was difficult for military commanders to 'see' what all the units under their command were doing when the battle was spread over large areas. Or it was difficult for a CEO of a multinational company to directly observe the activities at all the operational units distributed around the globe.

With today's technologies (e.g., the internet, cell phones and other mobile communication devices, etc.) distance is less of a constraint on communications. Cairncross[12] has referred to the capacity for high-speed communication networks to link people in remote locations as the "death of distance," suggesting that distance is no longer a constraint on coordination within organizations.

In addition to the delays associated with communication chains or distance, the volume of communications can be another important factor. In a large organization a fully connected communication web may overwhelm people with too much information, much of which may have no local functional value (i.e., it is essentially noise). Thus, in some cases, by constraining who can talk to who within an organization it may be possible to enhance the effectiveness of communications so that people are able to pick up the important signals more quickly and reliably.

For example, Klinger and Klein[13] did an investigation of an Emergency Response Organization (ERO) within a nuclear power plant. This team had been under scrutiny by the Nuclear Regulatory Commission (NRC) for some weaknesses in the team work. One of the key findings of the investigation was poor communication. People did not know who the key decision makers were and they did not have a good sense of who needed what information. As a result there were unnecessary delays as information wormed its way through the system and there was unnecessary noise as people would 'spam' information across the team, rather than communicate directly with the appropriate people. Surprisingly, team performance was dramatically improved as a result of a recommendation to reduce the team size. At least one factor explaining this was the reduction in noise within the communication network.

Another factor in the improvements of the ERO was clarifying the lines of authority (i.e., identifying the key decision makers). In another instance, we observed a discussion during a regional emergency operations exercise in a midwestern city. One of the people in the emergency command center complained because the firemen and the police were on different radio frequency bands and thus could not talk to each other directly. Overhearing the complaint, the police commander observed that this was by design to preserve the lines of authority. That is, to avoid a situation where police or fire personnel were getting contradictory orders from different sources. The police commander thought the restrictions on communications were good because they helped to preserve unity of command.

This brings us naturally to the third aspect of organizational structure—the *authority structure*. This reflects who (what people or units) set the goals and constraints for others within the organization and who has the power to initiate action. It is this type of structure that is being referred to when people contrast hierarchical and flat organizations. To avoid confusion with the hierarchical control structure, however, we will frame the contrast between centralized authority versus distributed authority.

These contrasting authority structures can be seen in economic systems where socialist systems tend to adopt highly centralized authority structures. In these systems a governmental committee might dictate many of the economic decisions (e.g., what crops farmers can plant). In contrast, capitalist systems are characterized by distributed authority structures that allow individuals to make their own economic decisions (e.g., farmers decide for themselves what crops to plant). The economist F.A. Hayek was very interested in the implications of these contrasting authority structures for the stability of economic systems.

There are many possible variations between the extremes of a highly centralized and a highly distributed authority structure. Two intermediate examples are heterarchical authority structures and federalist authority structures. In a heterarchical structure, authority shifts from one unit in the organization to another as a function of changing circumstances (most notably access to information). For example, it has been observed that in dynamic, high-risk environments like landing operations on an aircraft carrier, authority might be shifted so that access to information temporarily trumps military rank in determining who has the authority to wave off an approaching aircraft. In such circumstances, it may take too long to go up the formal chain of command to get a decision in time to avert a potential disaster.[14]

Another variation on authority structure is Federalism.[15] A Federalist system is often described as a 'system of systems.' It is a collection of organizations, each with its own authority structure that might work together to achieve a common objective or to solve a common problem. The police commander's explanation of why it might be good for police and fire to each have their own communication frequencies suggests that he prefers a federalist authority structure.

In the federalist system, a joint operations center (emergency operations center or EOC) might mediate communications across multiple organizations (e.g., police, fire, hospitals). Each organization has its own specialized function and its own authority structure. However, the organizations join together to solve a common problem (a regional disaster). In this system, the authority is distributed across the loosely coupled subsystems, but may be highly centralized within some of the sub systems.

The distinctions among these three aspects of organizational structure can be very important for gaining insight into the triadic semiotic dynamics of organizations. The control structure reflects the functional problem or the control/observer demands on an organization. The communications structure reflects a major constraint on an organization's ability to address the problems associated with observation, and the authority structure reflects a major constraint on an organization's ability to address the demands on control. A central question in terms of the semiotic dynamics is how the communication and authority structures interact to determine the adaptive capacity, resilience, or stability of the organization.

Note that the distinction between the communication and the authority structure is not always made explicit. People will often talk about one or the other as THE structure of the organization. However, it is important that these are regarded as potentially (if not always practically) independent dimensions.

Gene Rochlin acknowledges the independence of these two types of structure in his book *Trapped in the Net*.[16] The book discusses alternative visions for authority structures as a function of information technologies that allow rich communication networks among components of an organization.

> IF WE CAN AGREE THAT THE ECONOMIC PROBLEM OF SOCIETY IS MAINLY ONE OF RAPID ADAPTATION TO CHANGES IN THE PARTICULAR CIRCUMSTANCES OF TIME AND PLACE, IT WOULD SEEM TO FOLLOW THAT THE ULTIMATE DECISIONS MUST BE LEFT TO PEOPLE WHO ARE FAMILIAR WITH THESE CIRCUMSTANCES, WHO KNOW DIRECTLY OF THE RELEVANT CHANGES AND OF THE RESOURCES IMMEDIATELY AVAILABLE TO MEET THEM.

> WE CANNOT EXPECT THAT THIS PROBLEM WILL BE SOLVED BY FIRST COMMUNICATING ALL THIS KNOWLEDGE TO A CENTRAL BOARD WHICH, AFTER INTEGRATING ALL KNOWLEDGE, ISSUES ITS ORDERS. WE MUST SOLVE IT BY SOME FORM OF DECENTRALISATION. BUT THIS ANSWERS ONLY PART OF OUR PROBLEM. WE NEED DECENTRALISATION BECAUSE ONLY THUS WE CAN ENSURE THAT THE KNOWLEDGE OF THE PARTICULAR CIRCUMSTANCES OF TIME AND PLACE WILL BE PROMPTLY USED.

> BUT THE 'MAN ON THE SPOT' CANNOT DECIDE SOLELY ON THE BASIS OF HIS LIMITED BUT INTIMATE KNOWLEDGE OF THE FACTS IN HIS IMMEDIATE SURROUNDINGS. THERE STILL REMAINS THE PROBLEM OF COMMUNICATING TO HIM SUCH FURTHER INFORMATION AS HE NEEDS TO FIT HIS DECISIONS INTO THE WHOLE PATTERN OF CHANGES OF THE LARGER ECONOMIC SYSTEM.

Friedrich Hayek[17]

One vision reflects a centralized authority structure, where the CEO or Commander can sit at the nerve center of the communication network where he can directly interact with every element of the organization, allowing him to micro-manage every decision. The contrasting vision is of a distributed authority structure or flat organization where each individual has access to the information resources that they need to act independently in response to their local preferences and circumstances, while coordinating with the larger organization. The point is that the 'network' communication capabilities of advanced information systems like the world wide web can be used to implement either a centralized or a distributed authority structure.

That brings us to the issue of stability in organizations. In the next section, the reasons why either extreme centralization or extreme distribution of authority may be undesirable in terms of system stability will be explored.

Stability in an Organizational Context

In examining the dynamics of observation and control and the implications for stability within organizations, four facets of the problem are particularly relevant to the triadic semiotic dynamic: the degrees of freedom problem, the time delay problem, the problem of essential friction, and the value of diversity.

The Degrees of Freedom Problem

The degrees of freedom is related to the flexibility within a process. On the positive side, many degrees of freedom mean that the same goal or end can be achieved in many different ways. On the negative side, many degrees of freedom increase the complexity of the observation and control problems, in terms of the number of variables that need to be attended and manipulated.

For example, the human body has many degrees of freedom. This makes it possible for a baseball short stop to throw the ball to first base in many different ways (i.e., from many different postures). For example, while running to his right, his left, or forward as a consequence of the actions required to first catch a grounder. However, Bernstein recognized that controlling all these degrees of freedom was computationally demanding, and he hypothesized that it would take too long for all the degrees of freedom to be observed and integrated into a stable central control solution.[18]

Remember that time is a major factor in terms of control stability. Bernstein was skeptical that consistently successful throws (i.e., accurate and fast enough to beat the runner) could be achieved via a central control system that had to continually take into account all the degrees of freedom simultaneously. Similarly, Hayek was skeptical about whether economies could be effectively managed via highly centralized organizations.

Bernstein suggested that a distributed style of control was necessary in which many of the degrees of freedom were locally constrained so that they did not have to be directly observed and controlled via control loops through the central processor. In this system, the central control mechanism would specify the general intention (e.g., to throw to first base), but many of the coordination details would be regulated through peripheral constraints.

The peripheral constraints would limit how different muscles and joints might move together, or they might lock out certain degrees of freedom all together. In both cases, the degrees of freedom or the range of possible movements would be constrained or reduced. This effectively makes the body a much simpler machine that is easier to control.

Now you might ask, "what is the advantage of having many degrees of freedom, if you're not going to use them?"

The idea is this: many degrees of freedom allows the body to become many different kinds of simple machines. For example, it can become different kinds of throwing machines—overhand or sidearm. It can be a catching machine. Or a hitting machine. In the context of golf, it can be a driving machine, a chipping machine, or a putting machine. Each machine is suited to a different type of situation so that the few degrees of freedom that are subject to central control are ones that are best suited to successfully doing the job that the machine was designed for.

For example, in order to drive a golf ball, a golfer locks the leading elbow and the head position and organizes the action around large muscle groups in the shoulders and trunk in order to generate a large force through a constrained arc. In order to chip or putt a golf ball, many of the larger muscles in the shoulders and trunk are constrained, and the action is controlled through smaller muscles in the arms and wrist. The result is that each action (e.g., driving or putting) involves a relatively low number of degrees of freedom (simplifying the real-time control problem), but they are degrees of freedom that are specifically suited to the particular demands of different situations.

The contrast to the coordinative structure or smart mechanism approach to managing movement is an engineering approach that simplifies control by reducing the degrees of freedom to a standard generic set of dimensions (e.g., x, y, z planes) that are used for all situations. Runeson[19] characterized these as 'rote' mechanisms. Such an approach results in the stereotypical clumsy motions associated with primitive robots, as opposed to the more elegant motions of biological systems that choose different dimensions or constraints for different situations.

One way to think about coordinative structures is that they are the complement of chunks. Earlier we suggested that a 'chunk' is an organization of information that typically is designed to take advantage of natural constraints of a situation. In essence, the process of chunking uses constraints on situations to reduce the possibilities that need to be considered (i.e., reduce the information demands). In a similar way, a coordinative structure sets up constraints on the action side, so that they align with the constraints of the situation to reduce the demands of the observation and control problems.

As with chunking, coordinative structures would be selected based on fitness relative to the functional dynamics of a task. For example, in learning to play guitar, a beginner may have to consciously direct individual fingers. With this type of centralized control, however, it is not possible to play at a fast tempo. With practice, picking patterns are learned. Within these patterns, the fingers become integrated within a coordinative structure so that the behavior of each finger is constrained by the behaviors of the other fingers. At that point, the central control system might be initiating the patterns and may be specifying parameters of the pattern (e.g., tempo), but the detailed movements of individual fingers are now subordinate to the global pattern. As players become more expert, the chunks may become larger (e.g., patterns nested within larger patterns).

The hypothesis that many skilled motor tasks depend on the development of coordinative structures is consistent with the Zen, "no mind" philosophy of training. With the development of coordinative structures, the mind becomes less and less involved in managing the details of the performance. This hypothesis would also explain why performance can sometimes deteriorate, when a young musician tries to bring the mind back in to micromanage performance (e.g., when under pressure to perform well for a teacher or audience). A positive benefit of coordinate structures is that since consciousness is freed from the demands of managing the details, it might devote its resources to more strategic or aesthetic properties of a performance.

In organizations, the subunits and individual people within subunits constitute potential degrees of freedom. The challenge in a large organization is how to manage the huge number of possibilities (i.e., the complexity) associated with a large number of degrees of freedom.

Federalism or 'systems of systems' approaches to large organizations can be seen as an analog to coordinative structures. In essence, the lower order systems (e.g., the police departments, the fire departments, and the hospitals) can be thought of as coordinative structures in relation to the larger coalition or system (e.g., the emergency response organization). In these systems, a central command center (EOC) might set up strategic goals and make general requests to the subsystems (e.g., to provide security to a particular region, or to help to evacuate casualties from a particular site). However, the details of how to accomplish a particular strategic goal or request (e.g., what specific people and equipment to send) might be left to the subsystems.

The key issue in managing a large number of degrees of freedom is how to distribute authority. When there are many degrees of freedom, it will typically be necessary to distribute or delegate some of the authority. This will be necessary due to the delays and noise that would be associated with communications from the sharp end of the organization (e.g., the emergency personnel on the ground—the first responders) to a centralized command center (e.g., the EOC). The delays and noise will make it impossible to achieve stable control (to keep pace with the demands of the situation) via a highly centralized authority structure. This leads naturally to a second important dimension impacting the functional dynamics of organizations—time delay.

Time Delays

As we saw in Chapter 7, time delays are an important factor in determining the stability of closed-loop systems. As time delays increase, the range of feasible control gains gets narrower. This results in a necessary speed-accuracy trade-off. If the gain is too high (i.e., the system responds too quickly given the time delays), then the system will become unstable. This property applies to any closed-loop system, whether it is an automatic control system, a pilot, a manufacturing company, or a national economy.

In organizations, two important sources of delay will be constraints on communications (i.e., transport delays) and constraints on information processing (i.e., reflecting the complexity of the problem, the number of possibilities/degrees of freedom, or the signal to noise ratio). As noted earlier, historically distance has been an important constraint on the communication rate; the greater the physical distance or the practical distance (e.g., the number of links in the chain), the longer would be the transport delays within the control loop.

Thus, Hayek's skepticism about the ability of highly centralized organizations to manage economies is well founded. Simply collecting the information that is distributed over a large area will take time, and then it will take additional time to make sense of what the information means (i.e., pulling out the signal from the noise). Due to these delays, organizations with highly centralized organization structures will often be severely limited in their ability to respond to rapid changes.

Just as Bernstein understood that the delays in the human nervous system were too long to allow central control of all the degrees of freedom involved in many complex motor skills, Hayek hypothesized that the complexity of the economic problems would limit the potential for highly centralized authority structures to respond quickly enough to keep up with the pace of changing opportunities and threats with respect to a large economy.

The implication of this is that in designing organizations it will be important to consider ways to reduce time delays. With shorter time delays, the speed at which an organization can respond or adapt to changes in the environment will increase. Particularly in competitive environments, speed may be critical for survival. For example, military theorists partially attribute the success of the Mongols in the 14th century to their dominance of battlefield information. Arquilla and Ronfelt observe that the Mongols' "'Arrow Riders' kept field commanders, often separated by hundreds of miles, in daily communication. Even the great Khan, sometimes thousands of miles away, was aware of developments in the field within days of their occurrence."[20]

Today, communications are supported by elaborate networks of information technologies. For example, in a military context, Rochlin quotes a Department of Defense source that claimed that: "The services put more electronics communications connectivity into the Gulf in 90 days than we put in Europe in 40 years."[21] As noted previously, distance is no longer an obstacle to quick communications. Today, commanders on one continent can directly communicate through voice and video with troops fighting on the other side of the globe. Thus, the transport lags are often not the limiting factor on stability.

However, despite the 'death of distance,' it still takes time to process the information. As noted by Rochlin, it can take significant time to process and make sense of the increasing amounts of data that are now available to commanders as the result of advanced communications systems.

The other significant factor with regards to the lags in the semiotic control loop will be the information processing demands. The key here will be to reduce the problem to a minimally valid set of possibilities (i.e., the signals) relative to the functional goals. This means to focus attention or filter the variability that is inconsequential in relation to the functional goals. This will depend on how we code, represent, chunk, or parse the problem. As discussed in the context of representations and chunking, the key is to parse the problem to reflect the functional constraints. Or in the context of coordinative structures, the key is to design simple special-purposes devices for specific tasks.

THE DEMAND FOR INTELLIGENCE DATA, PARTICULARLY SATELLITE AND RECONNAISSANCE IMAGERY, FOR TARGETING PRECISION-GUIDED MUNITIONS, WAS INSATIABLE, AND SIMPLY COULD NOT BE MET EVEN BY THE COMMITMENT OF AS MANY U.S. RESOURCES AS COULD BE MADE AVAILABLE.

NOR WERE THE SERVICES ABLE TO ORGANISE, PROCESS, AND COORDINATE EFFICIENTLY. THE VOLUME OF DATA SIMPLY SWAMPED THE TACTICAL INTELLIGENCE SYSTEM, AND CAME NEAR TO PARALYSING OTHER SYSTEMS FOR ELECTRONIC INTEGRATIONS AND COMMAND AND CONTROL.

Gene Rochlin in reference to the 1991 Gulf War[22]

From the organizational perspective, an effective way to parse the problem will be by distributing authority within the organization. In essence, the information processing delays can be reduced by distributing the decision load across the organization. For example, in a military context, it is useful to think about the distribution of authority between central command and field officers. For example, a conclusion from the Vietnam War was that the US military did not distribute authority in a way that would facilitate quick responses to changing contingencies on the ground. In assessing the impact of technology on that war, Rochlin writes, "Perhaps most damaging of all, command and communications technologies had far outstripped other aspects of military technology, not only enabling but fostering the constant intervention of remote commanders into even the smallest details of battles on the ground."[23]

Sage and Cuppan suggest that one of the dimensions that is important for effective coordination within systems of systems is *subsidiarity*.[24] Subsidiarity means that authority for solving problems should be distributed to the lowest level in the organization consistent with a solution. Or conversely, it means that a central authority should deal with only those decisions that cannot be made effectively at a local level. In other words, the role of the central authority becomes more supportive and less authoritative with respect to subsystems in the organization.

For example, in managing regional disasters, EOCs typically take the role of distributing information and resources to the cooperating emergency agencies, rather than 'commanding' those agencies.[25] Thus, much of the authority remains with each of the cooperating agencies, as suggested by the comments of the police commander discussed earlier. In essence, he is the authority with respect to police operations, not the EOC.

In military systems, the need for subsidiarity is reflected in the construct of 'command intent.' This suggests that commanders should leave sufficient discretion to junior-level officers so that the system can adapt to changing contingencies that could not be anticipated in a fixed formal plan. Commanders should specify a general 'intent,' but they should trust local subordinates to work out the details of implementing that intent based on local contingencies. Thus, one of the failures of the Vietnam War may have been a failure of the military to achieve the right level of subsidiarity.

The key point is that organizations can often increase their ability to respond quickly to changing situations (i.e., their efficiency) by effectively distributing authority. The concept of subsidiarity suggests that centralized authorities should not micromanage. Rather, subsystems should have the authority to make local decisions, whenever this is feasible. In assessing this feasibility, access to information will typically be a critical factor. In many cases, subsystems (e.g., local farmers, or field commanders) will have direct access to much of the information that is necessary in order to make smart choices (e.g., about what crops to plant, or about tactical maneuvers).

One aspect of the Scientific Management approach to work design (i.e., Taylorism) was determining the appropriate distribution or partitioning of the work. By parsing the work into component tasks and distributing those tasks among people, who were specially trained for each specific task, overall efficiency could be increased.

The risks of subsidarity is that the subsystems may sometimes be working at cross purposes. Subsidarity does not eliminate the need for coordination. Coordination within a federation of systems depends on shared commitment to a common goal (often including a willingness to compromise local self-interest for the good of the global system mission). It also requires information coupling between subsystems (so that the right hand knows what the left hand is doing) and information coupling relative to the goals and values of the Federation (so that local situations can be seen in the context of organizational goals).

Not all the information necessary for stable control with respect to organizational goals may be available locally. Sometimes, access to valuable information requires integration over time and space. In other words, local subsystems may lose sight of the 'big picture' necessary for them to adequately cooperate or contribute toward the larger functional goals of the organization. Without the 'big picture' it is likely that in the process of satisfying local problem constraints, subsystems may end up working at cross-purposes with respect to the overall organizational goals.

For example, without a shared global vision of quality, a well-partitioned manufacturing system may produce poor quality or defective cars very efficiently. Or in the context of military

Lawrence Shattuck[26]

operations, without 'common ground' or 'top site,' the subunits will not be able to achieve the level of coordination required to achieve global objectives. This introduces the issue of *essential friction*.

Essential Friction

Consider the second-order (inertial) system that we discussed in Chapter 8 (Figures 8.1 and 8.2). If you remember, the system in Figure 8.1 was a closed-loop system, but there was no convergence to a steady state goal in response to a step input—the output was an oscillation. However, stable convergence could be achieved when velocity feedback was added, in Figure 8.2. This circuit is analogous to a spring, and the velocity feedback represents friction or damping. An important implication of that example is that friction is essential to stability of inertial systems.

The generalization to organizational sensemaking can be quite straightforward. The inertial process in the model system (two integrations) introduces phase lags. Similarly, the integration of information in order to assess the state with respect to organizational goals will generally take time (create lags). The model system in Figure 8.2 requires feedback of two variables that need to be considered in determining an appropriate control action. Organizational problems typically involve many state variables that need to be 'integrated' in order to assess the 'big picture' with respect to organizational goals.

Gene Rochlin has hypothesized that just as friction is necessary for stability in physical or mechanical inertial systems, social friction may be necessary for stability in organizations.[27] He contrasts this hypothesis with conventional approaches to work design (e.g., Taylorism) that typically focus exclusively on efficiency. In these conventional approaches, friction is typically seen as wasted energy to be eliminated.

Rochlin argues that in a complex system, where errors (e.g., wrong hypotheses) are inevitable, friction can help to damp out the impact of an error before it has significant consequences with respect to the organizational goals. This can be particularly important for a muddling through process, where errors are a necessary part of the learning process. Social friction has the potential to catch errors or poor decisions and to damp them out before they propagate to the point of catastrophe.

Rochlin concludes that:

> For most of this century what has been at stake in the search for organizational efficiency and administrative control is command—who has the power to say 'yes' and to what, who has the power and authority to rule. What must be recognized in the modern era is that it is at least as important to consider who retains the power to negate, to dissipate and to terminate. Friction is essential in organizations because it provides space for the exercise of the ultimate human responsibility—the power to say 'no,' and to enforce it.[28]

Taiichi Ohno has made a similar point with the contrast between *automation* and *autonomation*.[29] He used the example of a loom. An automated loom runs as long as the motor is running. If a thread breaks, the automated loom will continue to run, producing defective cloth. However, an autonomous loom has sensors to detect when the thread breaks. The autonomous loom will stop when the thread breaks.

Thus, the automation/autonomation distinction recognizes the difference between useless or counterproductive motion (e.g., generating defective products) and productive motion or work. In generalizing to human organizations, the autonomation concept suggests a potential value of adding social friction to an assembly line, so that any worker has the authority to shut down the process, if they discover a potential defect.

This contrasts with the Scientific Management approach, where the assembly workers were typically isolated with regards to both the information necessary to appreciate the 'big picture' and any authority beyond the limits of their elemental tasks. In conventional Ford-style assembly lines, workers may not have had the information to detect potential design problems, and even if they were to detect them, they would not typically have the authority to stop production—only management had the authority to shut down the line. The emphasis was on continuous motion (keeping the assembly line moving), rather than on the quality of the product.

Based on observations of high-risk operations (e.g., aircraft carrier landings), Rochlin hypothesized that distributing the responsibility to detect threats to system safety AND the authority to act in response to those threats (e.g., issue a command to abort a landing) broadly (e.g., without respect to rank) may be essential for high reliability.

Taiichi Ohno[30]

The estimation problem discussed in Chapter 8 (Figure 8.6) is also relevant to the issue of essential friction. Remember that the observer gain can be thought of as determining the speed of response to the difference (error or surprise) between the current observation and the expectation based on all previous samples. In the context of organizational friction, it might be thought of as the relative weights given to the current momentary impulse and to the long-term plan (which reflects the integration of all past observations). A high gain is an organization that acts quickly on the current impulse. This is analogous to a system with low friction. An observer with high gain (low friction) will be quick to take advantage of new opportunities. However, it will also tend to follow the noise down blind alleys.

Thus, an organization with low friction will be able to act quickly to implement good hypotheses, but it will also act quickly to implement poor hypotheses. A high-gain/low-friction system will have a high *hit rate* with regards to acting on good hypotheses, but the price for this will be a high *false alarm rate* where the system acts quickly on bad hypotheses.

An observer with low gain is one that gives heavier weight to the conventional wisdom based on the learning history of the system. This is analogous to having high friction. This system will be sluggish (or conservative) in responding to emerging new opportunities, but will have a low false-alarm rate. That is, bad ideas will rarely get through. Of course, the price that this organization will pay is a high *miss rate*—some good hypotheses will be rejected and opportunities will be missed.

As with the ideal observer problem, determination of the right gain or the right amount of friction depends on the payoff matrix—the costs and benefits associated with the various outcomes (hits, false alarms, misses, and correct rejections). As has been emphasized throughout the book—*Context Matters!*

In a high-risk environment, like managing a nuclear power plant or landing on an aircraft carrier, there can be high costs associated with going too far down a wrong path. In these ecologies a high amount of social friction is essential to safety. If anyone in the organization senses a problem, they should have the authority to say "No!" (i.e., shut the plant down, or abort the landing and order a fly around).

However, in other contexts such as the high-technology business—the costs of a false alarm may be relatively modest compared to the payoffs associated with being the creator of the next hot technology product (e.g., the ipod or the iphone). In this context, some friction will be warranted, but it will be important to keep friction low in order to be competitive in a rapidly changing business landscape.

With regards to economic systems, Hayek's observations reflect these kinds of systems' intuitions. He hypothesized that economies where the authority structure was highly centralized (e.g., socialism) would have too much friction. In essence, this kind of organization would be too conservative to keep pace with important changes in the economic ecology. On the other hand, Hayek observed that some degree of friction, in terms of regulated markets and public information sources, was necessary for stability in economies where authority was broadly distributed (e.g., capitalism).

In the simple observers from Chapter 8, the predictions were based on integrating information over time. However, in complex organizations information has to be integrated over both time and space. That is, an organization has an opportunity to tap into the unique perspectives of people in many different places, each with perhaps unique insights and also unique biases. This brings us to the last consideration relative to the semiotic dynamics of organizations—the challenges and opportunities associated with diversity.

Diversity

There is a well-known African proverb:

> If you want to go fast, go alone. If you want to go far, go together.

This reflects a contradiction or tension between two visions of organizational effectiveness. On the one hand, there is the vision that focuses on the leaders, as heroic experts who ignore the conventional wisdom of the crowd. Typically, this person has a 'Damn the torpedoes, full speed ahead' attitude with a penchant for action. This is a common theme in our history books that tend to fixate on the 'great' men (and women) who have the *confidence* to go against the current in order to lead their organizations to accomplish great things.

On the other hand, there is the vision of the participatory leaders who listen to and empower the people in their organizations in order to harness the wisdom of the crowd.[31] In this vision, the collective wisdom of the organization (the crowd) is considered to be smarter than any single expert. Thus, the success of the leader is attributed to the *humility* required to defer to the collective voice and to leverage the collective skills of the people in the organization.

The African proverb suggests that the first vision will be quick to seize opportunities when they arise. While this strategy may be good in the short run, it will not take an organization far, because this strategy increases the probability of taking a wrong turn, of getting lost. No matter how intelligent the heroic leader, he will not have all the information that is available to the crowd. This is a high-gain or low-friction system, quick to respond to change (whether its source is signal or noise).

The second vision will be slow or sluggish. It typically takes time to build consensus and to get a crowd moving toward a common goal. The consequence is that the organization with a participatory leader will often miss opportunities that require quick responses. However, the crowd is less likely to take a wrong turn! This is a low-gain or high-friction system, slow to respond to change, but a system that takes full advantage of the information available, and thus, more consistently moving in a positive direction.

Which vision of leadership is correct? You should be catching on by now—this is another situation where it is not a question of *either-or*, but rather *both-and*. The wise leader has to be confident enough to pull the trigger (i.e., to act in pursuit of a goal) in order to avoid the paralysis of analysis; AND the wise leader has to be humble enough to know that he can only see part of the whole problem (i.e., to value the opinions of others and to delegate authority).

In this context, confident or humble is not a contradiction, but rather a question of balance in a circular dynamic that has to meet the joint constraints of the control and observation problems in order to adapt to the functional stability requirements. In semiotic terms, the organization has to find a balance that allows it to converge on the 'meaning' relative to satisfying its functional objectives. Different functional situations will require different balances. There are no absolute solutions to effective leadership—there is only better or worse solutions to the functional situational demands. In high-tempo environments, the participatory leader may simply be too slow to act. In complex, high-risk environments, the heroic leader may be too quick to act.

One factor to consider when searching for the right balance between trusting the wisdom of heroic leaders or the wisdom of crowds is to consider what are the right conditions for making crowds smart? This is where the issue of diversity may be very important.

Hung and Plott explored the dynamic of group decision making using a variation of the book bag and poker chips experiment described in Chapter 8.[32] In their experiment, there were two urns: one (RED) urn contained two red balls and one white ball and the other (WHITE) urn contained two white balls and one red ball. Groups of ten people participated in the experiment. Each person would make one private draw from the urn (i.e., only they saw what color was drawn), then the person would make a public guess about whether the urn was RED or WHITE. Thus, each person had two sources of information to use: 1) their private observation and 2) the responses of everyone who had drawn before.

How should these two pieces of information be weighted? Should you go with your unique observation? Or should you trust the crowd?

Again, it is impossible to answer these questions without knowing the reward structure or payoff matrix. The experiment used three different payoff structures. In one condition, people were awarded for the accuracy of their own guess about the urn. In another condition, people were awarded based on whether the group vote (majority) was correct. In a third condition, people were awarded based on conformity to the group choice (whether accurate or not).

The pattern of responding was quite different for the three reward conditions. In the first condition (reward contingent on individual accuracy), there was a tendency for people to discount their own observation relative to the choices of a prior majority. This turns out to be a fairly smart strategy, since the choices of others can be valid information about the true state of the world. This results in a *cascade* so that eventually people fall in line with the majority, even when it is not consistent with their unique pieces of evidence.

In the second condition (reward contingent on the majority vote), people would report their unique observations. There was little evidence of cascading. This turns out to be a very smart strategy. This is a clear case where the group can be smarter than any individual, because each individual contributes a unique piece of evidence.

In the third condition (reward contingent on agreement with the majority), there was a very strong tendency to cascade—people had a strong tendency to follow the crowd. This, of course, was the least effective strategy for accurately determining the urn color.

This study illustrates the potential value of diversity. In condition two, where each person contributed a unique and independent perspective, the group was smarter than any individual and smarter than the other groups. In condition one, the group was not quite as smart as the majority, since once a cascade began the unique observations of those individuals would be lost, but individuals could improve their performance by taking advantage of the information from others. However, in a condition where there was strong pressure to conform, the group was not much smarter than any individual. In this last condition, the value of diversity was lost.

Another study gave groups of 2 to 5 people a series of problems to solve in an attempt to measure group IQ. The results showed that there did seem to be a group IQ, such that groups that were good at some problems also tended to be good at the other problems—suggesting a general quality of intelligence for groups.

The interesting result from this study was that there was not a strong correlation between the group IQ and either the average of the individual IQs or the highest individual IQ in the group. It turns out that the measure that was most strongly related to group IQ was the average social sensitivity of group members. Another significant factor was turn taking in the group interactions. "Groups where a few people dominated the conversation were less collectively intelligent than those with a more equal distribution of conversational turn-taking."[33]

The importance of social sensitivity for group success supports the hypothesis that success in muddling through life depends on both the heart and the head. It is important to remember also that for a group, success in muddling through will not simply be a function of making the 'right' choice, but it will also be a function of making the choice 'right.' In other words, ultimate success of group muddling also requires coordinating (e.g., sharing information and adjusting behaviors to synchronize with the actions of others) and cooperating (e.g., compromising self-interest in order to satisfy the group interest). It is likely that social sensitivity will be even more important to sustaining coordination and cooperation as it was to solving the cognitive problem reflected in the group IQ study.

Sensemaking

In Chapter 9 (Figure 9.3), we presented the example of tennis as a hierarchical nesting of control loops. This type of image can be adapted to any functional problem. Figure 14.4 illustrates the multiple loops that might be involved in a larger organizational control problem, like managing a nuclear power plant. Within this hierarchy of control loops, outer or higher loops tend to set the constraints on inner or lower loops. Also, inner loops will tend to involve smaller time constants and faster operational tempos than outer loops.

Figure 14.4 shows the functional dynamics of the problem, but the organization structure reflects the communication links and distribution of authority over these functional constraints.

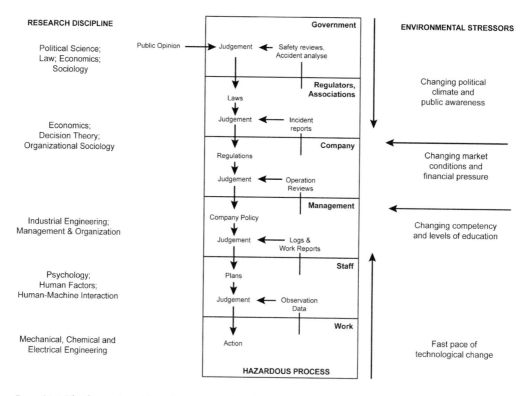

Figure 14.4 This figure adapted from Rasmussen and Svedung (2000) illustrates the multiple social layers that shape the behavior of sociotechnical systems. Such couplings have important implication for the breadth of analysis and for the range of disciplines that must collaborate to fully understand these complex systems. [34]

All the constraints on stability that we discussed in earlier chapters apply to this multi-loop system. Thus, a key to the quality of performance of the organization will be whether the communication links and distribution of authority match well to the functional demands.

From the perspective of observability, the question is whether the loops at different levels have timely access to the information necessary to accurately assess the relevant 'states' of the organization with respect to the relevant functional goals. Note that different 'states' of a work domain will be accessible and relevant at different levels within the functional dynamic. For example, it may be important for an air traffic control center to consider the volume of traffic relative to multiple runways over an extended time period, in order to set up a proper landing sequence. However, a pilot might focus on where his plane fits within the sequence for a single runway within a much shorter period of time.

Also, while individuals (e.g., pilots and physicians) might have timely information for a small subset of situations (e.g., landing approaches or patients), they may not have access to information about the overall safety of the industry, which requires integration of observations over many individuals for longer periods of time. This kind of information is only accessible to regulatory agencies who have access to distributed information (e.g., error reporting systems) and have the analytical resources to integrate the data in order to observe industry-level patterns and trends.

From the perspective of control, the tempo of operations that determines the windows of opportunity for responding to situations will be critical to decisions about the distribution of authority. In high-pace environments, the time to pass information up the chain of command and to pass instructions back down may simply be too long for stable control. In these situations, stability will demand that authority be distributed to lower levels of the organization.

In very high-pace ecologies, it will be necessary to distribute authority to the sharp end of the organization (i.e., flatten the organization). In these ecologies, the higher levels will be less involved in control. However, they may play a very important role with respect to observation. That is, the higher levels may be an important and/or necessary source of information about global states, trends, or patterns that people at the sharp end of the organization need in order to make consistently smart choices.

Due to the joint impact of the availability of high-speed communication networks and of ecologies with fast tempos of change due to competitive pressures, there is much enthusiasm for *flattening* organizations (i.e., distributing authority). However, it is important that in pursuing the benefits of distributed authority structures, we do not lose sight of the value that centralization can have for integrating information over time and space in order to 'see' the big picture with respect to organizational goals.

Predicting the future may be essential if an organization wants to go 'far.' While those at the sharp end of the system may be better coupled with the short-time demands, they may not have the capacity to do the integration of information that is necessary to see very far down the road. Thus, for organizations that want to go 'fast' and 'far' it will be necessary to empower both those at the sharp end (e.g., the boots on the ground) to act in response to local disturbances and those at the blunt end (e.g., central headquarters) to listen in order to detect global patterns and to provide 'top view' or 'common ground' to facilitate coordination at the sharp end. In this vision, the role of higher levels in the organization changes from being the *central command* (emphasis on greasing the wheels to facilitate participation in action) to being the *central intelligence* (emphasis on providing the essential friction to avoid catastrophic mistakes).

Concluding Remarks

It is impossible to do full justice to the dynamics of sensemaking in organizations and groups in a single chapter. The goal here was to provide a second perspective on the semiotic triad to emphasize that this dynamic is not a unique property of individual people. The control and observer problems reflect general properties of functional systems, whether they are cells, people, robots, or organizations.

We chose the organizational perspective because this perspective is particularly important for those interested in designing more effective work systems. Work is seldom a solitary activity. Work is accomplished by sociotechnical systems that include multiple people using a variety of technical tools.

The organizational perspective was also chosen for pedagogical reasons. By scaling up the semiotic problem to the organizational level, we hope that some aspects of the muddling process may be more salient. For example, the problem of coordinating multiple degrees of freedom and the value of organizing those degrees of freedom into coordinative structures might be more obvious when the degrees of freedom are distinct people in an organization, rather than individual muscles in a body.

Finally, we would like to comment on a trend toward 'systems thinking' in the social sciences. People are becoming increasingly aware of the organizational context of work. This awareness is often broadcast as a 'general systems approach' to work. The emphasis is on *systems* and the term emphasizes that relative to former approaches that might have focused on the human-machine interaction, the new approaches are taking into account the larger 'whole' or system that includes organizational constraints.

However, we think that these approaches are often missing an important element of 'general systems thinking.' General systems thinking is not just about making the field of view bigger—looking at more things. General systems thinking involves understanding dynamics that generalize broadly across levels and across domains. We would like to see greater emphasis on the term *general*.

Thus, the key point from a general systems thinking perspective is that the dynamics of circular systems apply generally. They apply to any system where perception and action is coupled. As in the cognitive literature, in the broader literature on social and organizational dynamics there are often references to control theory, and the box diagrams typically illustrate the presence of feedback. However, the generalizations rarely go beyond the diagrams and trivial metaphors.

One of our goals is to convince social scientists to take the rich literature on systems dynamics a bit more seriously, so that both research and design will be guided by theories of dynamic systems.

While it is encouraging that social scientists are beginning to appreciate the circular dynamics of cognition and sensemaking, it often feels like they are reinventing wheels that have long been available in the broader fields of communication, control, and system dynamics.

Notes

1. Mandelbrot, B.B. (1983). *The fractal geometry of nature*. New York: Freeman. (p. 27).
2. Cited in Weick (1995, p. 9). Shotter, J. (1993). *Conversational realities: Constructing life through language*. London: Sage.
3. Weick, K.E. (1995). *Sensemaking in Organizations*. Thousand Oaks, CA: Sage Publications.
4. Arquilla, J., & Ronfeldt, D. (1997). *In Athena's camp: Preparing for conflict in the information age*. Santa Monica, CA: RAND. (pp. 4–5).
5. Thompson, J. (1967). *Organizations in action*. New York: McGraw-Hill.
6. Wears, R.L., Perry, S.J., Wilson, S., Galliers, J., & Fone, J. (2007). Emergency department status boards: User-evolved artefacts for inter- and intra-group coordination. *Cognitive Technology & Work*, 9, 163–170. (pp. 163–164).
7. Wears, et al. (2007), p. 167.
8. Perry, S.J., & Wears, R.L. (2012). Underground adaptations: case studies from health care. *Cognitive Technology & Work*, 14, 253–260. (p. 287).
9. Xiao, Y., Kiesler, S., Mackenzie, C.F., et al. (2007). Negotiation and conflict in large scale collaboration: A preliminary field study. *Cognition Technology & Work*, 9, 171–176.
10. Borgo, D. (2005). *Sync or swarm: Improvising music in a complex age*. New York: Continuum.
11. Borgo (2005), p. 26.
12. Cairncross, F. (2001). *The death of distance: How the communications revolution is changing our lives*. Boston: Harvard Business Press.
13. Klinger, D., & Klein, G. (1999). An accident waiting to happen. *Ergonomics in Design*, 7(3), 20–25.
14. Rochlin, G.I., La Porte, T.R., & Roberts, K.H. (1987). The self-designing high reliability organization: Aircraft carrier flight operations at sea. *Naval War College Review*, 40(4), 76–90.
15. Sage, A.P., & Cuppan, C.D. (2001). On the systems engineering and management of systems of systems and federations of systems. *Information, Knowledge Systems Management*, 2(4), 325–245.
16. Rochlin, G.I. (1997). *Trapped in the net: The unanticipated consequences of computerization*. Princeton, NJ: Princeton University Press.
17. Hayek, F.A. (1945). The use of knowledge in society. *The American Economic Review*, 35(4), 519–530. (pp. 524 525).
18. Bernstein, N.A. (1967). *The co-ordination and regulation of movements*. Oxford: Pergamon Press.
19. Runeson, S. (1977). On the possibility of "smart" perceptual mechanisms. *Scandinavian Journal of Psychology*, 18(1), 172–179. DOI: 10.1111/j.1467-9450.1977.tb00274.x
20. Arquilla, J. & Ronfeldt, D. (1997). *In Athena's Camp: Preparing for war in the information age*. Santa Monica, CA: Rand. (p. 24).
21. Rochlin, G.I. (1997). *Trapped in the net. The unanticipated consequences of computerization*. Princeton, NJ: Princeton University Press. (p. 180).
22. Rochlin, G.I. (1997). p. 180–181.
23. Rochlin, G.I. (1997). p. 139.
24. Sage, A.P. and Cuppan, C.D. (2001). On the systems engineering and management of systems of systems and federations of systems. Information, *Knowledge Systems Management* 2, 4, p. 325–245.
25. Flach, J.M., Steele-Johnson, D., Shalin, V.L., Hamilton, G.C. (2014). Coordination and control in emergency response. In A. Badiru & L. Racz (Eds.). *Handbook of Emergency Response: Human Factors and Systems Engineering Approach*, (p. 533–548). CRC Press.
26. Shattuck, L. (2000) Communicating intent and imparting presence. *Military Review*, Mar–Apr, 66–72.
27. Rochlin, G.L. (1998). *Essential friction: Error-control in organizational behavior*. In Akerman, N. (ed.) The necessity of friction. (p. 132–163). Boulder, CO: Westview Press.
28. Rochlin, G.L. (1998). P. 160.
29. Ohno, T. (1988). *Workplace management*. Cambridge, MA: Productivity Press.
30. Ohno, T. (1988). p. 91.
31. Surowiecki, J. (2005). *The wisdom of crowds*. New York: Anchor Books.
32. Hung, A.A. & Plott, C.R. (2001). Information cascades: Replication and an extension to majority rule and conformity regarding institutions. *The American Economic Review*, 91(5), 1508–1520.
33. Woolley, A.W., Chabris, C.F., Pentland, A. Hashmi, N., & Malone, T.W. (2010). Evidence for a collective intelligence factor in the performance of human groups, *Science*, 330(6004), 686–688.
34. Rasmussen, J. & Svedung, I. (2000). *Proactive risk management in a dynamic society*. Karlstad, Sweden: Swedish Rescue Services Agency.

15

PUTTING EXPERIENCE TO WORK

As Lindblom[1] has pointed out there is little disagreement with respect to the heuristic nature of either human rationality or organizational sensemaking. The source of disagreement arises with regards to the 'ought' or the norms for human rationality. The conventional approach has looked to mathematics (e.g., deductive logic, probability theory, statistics) and economics (e.g., utility theory) to provide the 'benchmarks' for rationality.

As Lopes[2] has observed, this approach tends to 'score' human performance relative to the metrics suggested by the mathematical and economic models. When human performance deviates from the prescriptions of these models, it is labeled an error or irrational, and it is typically attributed to 'weaknesses' or 'limitations' inherent to humans (e.g., limited memory or attention).

The motive driving the conventional research programs in perception and cognition is the idea that through observing where the human fails, we will be able to gain insights into the nature of the internal mechanisms. The ultimate goal is to learn how the human mind works, but the assumption is that a critical first step to learning how it works is to discover where it fails.

These research programs can be very seductive. The first step is to define a specific problem. For example, consider the problem described in Chapter 5: to discover the rule for generating strings of three numbers, where 2, 4, 6 is given as an exemplar that is consistent with the rule. Key criteria for choosing a problem are that it fits the assumption of a specific model of rationality and that it has a well-defined 'right' answer.

An additional criterion is that a significant portion of people will get it wrong! If most people get it right, it is generally considered a trivial problem, and it will get little attention from conventional researchers.

Thus, the typical research narrative proceeds: 1) choose a problem that is well-defined with respect to your model; 2) collect empirical data demonstrating that many people get it *wrong*; 3) demonstrate using the model what is the *right* answer; and 4) suggest hypotheses about the internal limitations, weaknesses, or biases to account for the deviation.

The applied implication of this research program is that *humans are irrational*. Thus, it is important that designers compensate for this irrationality through either training or automation or both. That is, we need to train people to better conform with the mathematical model used to define the right answer and/or we need to replace the human with a computer program that will reliably conform to the mathematical model.

This conclusion that humans are irrational can be reinforced by observations of humans at work. Jens Rasmussen[3] has observed that when observing experts in their natural domains, many of their choices appear irrational relative to the normative conventions. Note also that experts are often

prone to the same errors and biases reflected in the general population when tested using the typical laboratory puzzles.

However, Rasmussen continues that as he learns more about the particulars of an expert's
domain, he typically discovers that the behavior that appeared irrational at first often reflects the
expert's deeper understanding of the domain constraints. Typically, these apparently irrational
strategies are adaptive responses to the constraints of the situated dynamics. For example, remember the example of *aiming off*. The tendency to always miss the bridge to the near side might appear
to be a *bias* to a naive observer who does not understand the implications of missing the bridge and
not knowing its relative direction along the river.

The other insidious aspect of observations of people at work is ironically associated with a *bias*
that has been well documented in the conventional literature—that is, the hindsight bias. However, in this case, the bias applies to researchers, not to the human operators being observed.
When an accident or disaster happens (e.g., a loss of coolant accident in a nuclear power plant or
an airplane crash), it is typical for researchers to trace backwards along the events leading up to
the accident in search of the *root cause*.

Rasmussen observes that with respect to this approach to explaining accidents, the human operators are in a very unfortunate position. This is because it will almost always be possible to find a
point on the event trajectory where a human did something that contributed to the accident or
failed to do something that would have prevented the accident. Thus, researchers conclude that a
very large portion of industrial accidents are *caused* by human error!

In more sophisticated approaches to accident investigations, the search for an explanation may
not stop with the first human error. These approaches search further to discover that there may
be failures at higher levels in the organization (i.e., failures in organizational sensemaking, patho-
gens[4]) that contributed to the human error (e.g., inadequate staffing or resources, or pressures to
increase efficiency/profits at the cost of increased risks). However, the bottom line typically boils
down to the fact that someone at some level of the organization made an irrational decision. It is
defined as irrational because there was an accident (i.e., based on hindsight). Further, no one is
surprised that this irrationality would result from human decision making, since we have so many
clear demonstrations in the laboratory that prove humans are irrational.

What's wrong with this narrative of the irrational human? How on earth have these irrational, weak-minded animals survived? Lopes suggests that if humans consistently deviate from our

models of rationality, then maybe the *errors* or *weaknesses* are not attributes of humans but attributes of our models:

> Although it is common in the sciences for the achievements of one model to serve as a benchmark against which to evaluate the achievements of another model, it makes no sense to say that a model of behavior can serve as a benchmark for the behavior it is modeling. If there are disparities between the behavior and the model, then it is the model that has failed to measure up, not the other way around.[5]

The implication is that maybe the models that are held up as the norms for rationality are not appropriate! Perhaps, mathematical/logical prescriptions provide the wrong benchmarks or ideals for scoring performance. So, where do we look for guides with respect to a rationality that will lead to success in everyday life and in the workplace.

The hypothesis that we will suggest is that, *rather than looking to mathematicians and economists for our standards of rationality, perhaps we should look to our elders.* That is, we should measure rationality relative to the successes of those who have gone before. For general benchmarks with respect to a successful life, we should look to the wise men and women who have preceded us (e.g., the sages and/or perhaps our parents and grandparents). For benchmarks with respect to specific work or problem domains, we should look to the experts within those domains. Just as in athletics, we look to the achievements (records) of the best athletes as the standards against which to measure performance, so too in other domains we should start with the assumption that the appropriate standard for quality is the level of accomplishment of the 'best' people.

The key to this approach to rationality is that the rational person learns from the successes and failures of those who have gone before. And of course, the converse of this is that the irrational person is the person who doesn't benefit from the experience of others and insists on making every mistake themselves!

Experience in Context

Underlying the conventional approach to cognition that holds the ideals of mathematics and logic as standards for rationality is the dyadic semiotic model of cognition and the dualistic ontology where mind and matter are distinct. Note that the conventional approach assumes that there are 'mechanisms' of mind! The implication is that mind has a structure (i.e., a mechanism) that can be understood independently from its function with respect to survival in an ecology. Thus, context doesn't matter. Any stimulus or puzzle is potentially as good as any other with regards to revealing that underlying structure, since it will be the same structures (same head) in the work ecologies as in the laboratory puzzle ecologies.

Of course, a fundamental premise of the triadic model that underlies an ecological alternative to the conventional approach is that context does indeed matter! Klayman and Ha's review of the 2, 4, 6 puzzle described earlier (originally introduced in Chapter 5) provides an excellent case for how context does matter for this particular task.[6]

Klayman and Ha note that Wason (1962)[7] picked this particular task specifically to demonstrate "the pitfalls of confirmation bias." In this case, the typical Hypothesis suggested by the initial example is 'increasing by 2.' This hypothesis is a subset of the True Rule, which is 'any three increasing numbers.' As illustrated in Figure 15.1, in this particular case, if people only test the rule by

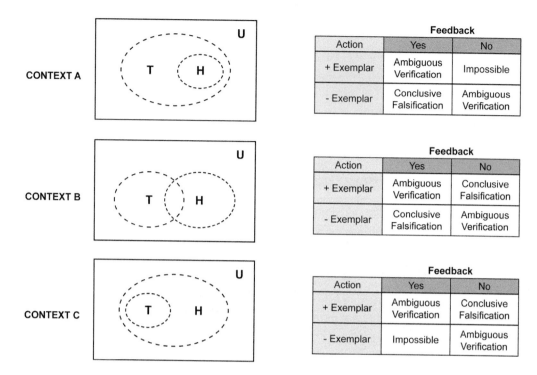

Figure 15.1 This figure shows Wason's (1960)[8] rule discovery task. In the context of three different relations between the True Rule (T) and the Hypothesis (H) being evaluated (after Klayman & Ha, 1987).

making positive tests (i.e., testing exemplars that are consistent with their hypothesis), then they will never get a 'No' response, and the 'Yes' responses provide only ambiguous verification of their hypothesis. Participants using this strategy typically become increasingly confident in their hypothesis, however, they are unlikely to discover the True Rule.

Also note that consistent with the prescriptions of inductive logic, the only conclusive or diagnostic feedback results from using an exemplar from outside the Hypothesis Set. An exemplar from outside the hypothesis set (a negative test), such as '5, 10, 30,' will provide conclusive falsification. That is, it will reveal that the hypothesis of 'increasing by 2' is too narrow. Note that using a different negative test, such as '6, 4, 2' results in ambiguous verification that the 'increasing by 2' hypothesis is correct.

However, Klayman and Ha observe that the relation between the common hypothesis and the True Rule is one of many contexts that participants might encounter in everyday life. For example, suppose the True Rule was 'three even numbers.' In this case, there is overlap between the common hypothesis (increasing by 2) and the True Rule. Thus, a positive exemplar (1, 3, 5) could result in a 'No' response, which would conclusively falsify the hypothesis of increasing by two.

A third context is also illustrated in Figure 15.1. In this context, the True Rule (i.e., 3 consecutive even numbers) is a subset of the common hypothesis (increasing by 2). In this context, a 'No' response to a positive exemplar (e.g., 1, 3, 5) is the only conclusive feedback. No conclusive feedback will result from using negative exemplars (i.e., using the prescribe disconfirmation strategy).

Note that the positive test strategy is not perfect. It will not work in all contexts. It is a heuristic (or bias). However, Klayman and Ha avoid the conventional inclination to conclude that humans are irrational, because they adopt a strategy that does not work in all situations. They observe that "under some very common conditions, the probability of receiving falsification with +Htests could be much greater than with -Htests." They conclude:

> Our review suggests that people use the +test strategy as a general default heuristic. That is, this strategy is one that people use in the absence of specific information that identifies some test as more relevant than others, or when the cognitive demands of the task preclude a more carefully designed strategy. Our theoretical analyses indicate that, as an all-purpose heuristic, +testing often serves the hypothesis tester well. That is probably why it persists, despite its shortcomings. For example, if the target phenomenon is relatively rare, and the hypothesis roughly matches this base rate, you are probably better off testing where you expect the phenomenon to occur rather than the opposite. This situation characterizes many real-world problems. Moreover, +tests may be less costly or less risky than -tests when real world consequences are involved.
>
> (Einhorn & Hogarth, 1978; Tschirgi, 1980).[9]

In a world where context matters, it is always risky to generalize a procedure that works in one context to another context. A procedure that works perfectly in one context may lead to catastrophic results in another context. However, the conventional decision literature is very prone to this error. Large generalizations are made about the nature of human rationality, based on a very narrow set of contexts, all of which tend to be motivated by a commitment to mathematical norms as the standards of rationality.

Brunswik[10] has long argued that our experimental contexts have to be 'representative' of the contexts to which we want to generalize. If we want to make a broad statement about human rationality, then this should be based on a broad sampling of contexts.

Conventionally, psychologists have recognized the need to appropriately sample the subject population, when making broad generalizations. However, since the 'situation' is not included as a factor within the dyadic semiotic, they have conventionally not recognized the need to sample situations or contexts.

Klayman and Ha illustrate why it is essential to sample various contexts, before drawing the conclusion that humans are irrational or that they are poor decision makers. In fact, Klayman and Ha suggest just the opposite. When performance is viewed through a triadic semiotic lens that considers the impact of context, it seems that the general strategy that people use is one that may be very well tuned to the general demands of making decisions in complex contexts.

The Bounds of Experience

Simon's construct of *bounded rationality* fits very well within the conventional narrative about human decision making. In the context of the underlying dyadic semiotic, the bounds on rationality reflect properties of the internal thinking mechanisms or the internal programs. As noted earlier, these bounds are typically attributed to information processing limitations (e.g., limited channel capacity, limited memory, limits on computational capacity). From the perspective of a triadic semiotic model, the construct of bounded rationality remains important. However, it shifts the focus from the internal mechanisms to the experiences of the humans.

To fully appreciate this shift in perspective, it is important to realize that *all models, whether internal cognitive strategies or computational models implemented on the highest-speed super computers available,*

are **bounded**! The internal models or strategies that humans use to make decisions and solve problems are bounded by their experiences, which determine what they pay attention to and how they integrate the available information to make sense of the situation and guide action.

However, this is also true of every computational model implemented in any form of hardware. Every model is bounded by the assumptions that guided its design, which determines what data the model *attends* to and determines how the data are *integrated* to form conclusions or guide actions.[11]

Thus, there is no *super observer* that we can hold up as a gold standard for rationality. When human decision making deviates from the behavior of a particular computational model, the best we can conclude is that the bounds or constraints on the two different strategies are different. Thus, we propose that the only basis for comparing the quality of two alternative rational processes is pragmatic and local! Does one work better than the other in a specific context?

Note that it is likely that this will vary with situations—one model might be better than another in any specific situation—but we can also score the models in terms of their robustness. A more robust model is one that works over a broader range of situations. Thus, a way to restate the conclusions of Klayman and Ha is that humans are biased to apply the more robust strategy to the Rule Finding task, rather than one that is specifically designed for that task. While a robust solution (or control system) may be capable of achieving satisfying levels of performance in a wide range of situations, it may not be optimal for any specific situation.

In the context of the triadic semiotic model, rationality will always be bounded by experience or learning. Thus, the 'error' illustrated in Wason's particular variation of the rule discovery task is a problem of transfer of learning, not a symptom of a flawed internal mechanism (or flawed rationality). In essence, people tend to apply a strategy that has worked generally in the past to a novel situation, where in this particular case it happens not to fit well.

This is necessarily the case for all observers, as discussed in Chapter 8. The estimation of the true state of the world for an observer is always a joint function of the current observation (e.g., the puzzle presented to the participant in the Wason experiment) and the expectation based on an integration of all prior observations (e.g., prior experience in trying to discover rules or patterns). The gain of the observer determines the relative weight given to these two sources of information.

An observer with a low gain gives more weight to or is more tightly bound by past experience. For example, the participant in the rule discovery experiment trusts a strategy that has been reliable in the past. An observer with a high gain is less constrained by experience, putting more weight on the specifics of the particular situation.

It is important to understand that there is no absolutely perfect solution to the observer problem. Lower gain will be less likely to follow the noise, but it will also be sluggish or conservative in detecting real change. In decision terms the low-gain observer will tend to overgeneralize—depending heavily on strategies that worked in the past—and it will be slow to adapt new strategies when faced with novel or unfamiliar situations.

The high-gain observer will be quick to detect real change, but it will also tend to chase the noise. In decision terms, the high-gain observer will tend to be reactive to situations, not fully taking advantage of learning to develop generally robust strategies.

To put this in practical terms, consider the decision problem in a hospital emergency department. In observing emergency physicians, Feufel[12] found that two heuristics were very important in shaping their decisions. The first heuristic is "Common things are common." In the context of observer theory, this heuristic suggests that the physician's gains should be low. That is, they should give heavy weight to experience, which is the basis for identifying something as 'common' (i.e., it has been seen frequently in the past).

The second heuristic is "Worst Thing." That is, rule out any potentially hazardous condition that might be consistent with the symptoms, even if it is low probability. In the context of observer theory, this heuristic suggests that the physicians' gains should be somewhat higher. That is, they should give heavy weight to anything that might result in serious harm, even if it is not consistent with expectations based on what is common.

Figure 15.2 illustrates the situation of the emergency department physician as an adaptive observer/control system embedded in a larger sociotechnical system. In this illustration the two

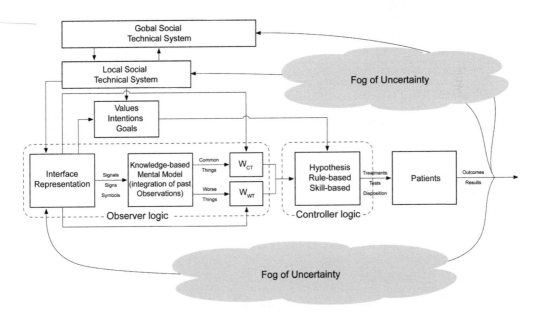

Figure 15.2 This figure illustrates the task of an emergency room physician as an observer/control system. In this system, choice of action is contingent on a weighted function of two heuristics: "Common Things" and "Worse Things." The values that constitute the payoff matrix or cost function for the observation/control system are constantly being negotiated within the larger sociotechnical system.

heuristics are represented as outputs of the physician's *mental model* showing the possibility set being considered. The illustration suggests that these two heuristics are weighted and combined in order to select the next set of actions.

If physicians lean too heavily on the "Common Thing" heuristic, there is a risk that they might miss a less common, but potentially critical problem, which could result in serious consequences for the patient. If physicians lean too heavily on the "Worst Thing" heuristic, they may expend expensive resources unnecessarily. In contexts where resources are scarce, this could have potentially serious consequences for other patients who need those resources.

The million-dollar question is what is the right balance or optimal weighting for these two heuristics? In essence, the question is what is the ideal gain for the observer? This brings us to another construct that Simon introduced in the context of human rationality—*satisficing*.

The Experience of Value

Of course, there is no perfect solution to the question about the right balance between the two heuristics guiding the physicians' choice of action—to the extent that 'perfect' means that errors are completely eliminated. It is a matter of which kind of errors to reduce or eliminate (see Figure 15.3).

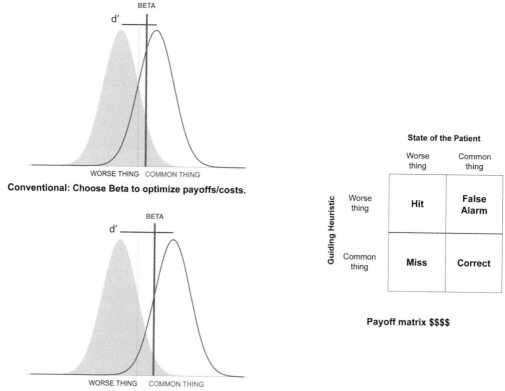

Figure 15.3 This figure illustrates the signal detection trade-offs. The parameter Beta is linked to the control problem, where optimal control involves setting the Beta to maximize the payoff. The parameter d' is linked to the observer problem, where an ideal observer is one that fully utilizes the available information to discriminate the signal from the noise (maximizing d').

If expense and availability of resources is not an issue, then it is possible to do exotic tests to rule out the 'Worst Thing,' minimizing the chances of missing a potentially critical disease. However, if expense and resources are limited, then the 'best' solution will focus on treating the 'Common Thing.' The consequence would be that there will be occasions where a potentially dangerous condition might be missed.

So, a perfect solution is not possible, but what about an 'optimal' solution? The first step in addressing optimality would require specification of the different errors on a comparable scale (e.g., missing a dangerous condition, wasting valuable resources). One possible scale is money ($). What is the cost of a test? What is the cost of time? What is the cost of an injury or of a life?

Some of these questions are very difficult, emotional, subjective, and situated. Does it make a difference if the ED is located in a poor inner city or a wealthy suburb? Does it make a difference if the patient is a wealthy celebrity, a close friend, a family member, or an indigent stranger? Who decides the value of a life? This is one of the bounds on many of the normative models. For example, in order to maximize the expected value, it is necessary to quantify the various possible outcomes on a common scale. It is necessary to specify the value of a life in terms that are comparable or commensurate with the value of the time, effort, and resources involved with the various medical tests and treatments.

Note that in the conventional research program on human biases, the values of different responses relative to the effort of the experimental participants is rarely part of the narrative. Performance is often evaluated on an absolute scale. There is an absolutely right answer specified by the guiding normative model, and any deviation from this norm is considered to be simply and absolutely wrong!

This suggests an additional hypothesis to account for some of the deviations from the standards that the experimenters have conventionally use to 'score' behavior. Perhaps the values of some of the participants (i.e., the payoff matrix, or cost function) are different than that assumed by the experimenters. Perhaps all of the participants are not interested in identifying an absolutely right answer, but only one good enough to merit credit from the experimenter for participation in the experiment.

In the conventional dyadic semiotic narrative, *satisficing* typically refers to deviations from a normatively optimal choice (i.e., the 'best' option). These deviations are often associated with compromises that reflect the internal constraints on human information processing. However, other constraints like time and effort are also typically acknowledged as contributing factors.

From a pragmatic perspective, the critical question is whether the internal values shaping the decisions and actions of the human are consistent with the functional demands of the work or problem domain. Thus, satisficing plays a much richer role in the triadic semiotic narrative. In this context, satisficing can reflect both the desire for a robust solution across multiple contexts and the real ambiguities associated with the values that determine whether an outcome is satisfying.

It is likely that the value systems that are used to score performance in many complex systems like the ED are somewhat ambiguous and quite controversial. Thus, it may be difficult to fix a system for 'scoring' performance in terms of optimality, since the values themselves are constantly changing as a result of negotiations within the larger sociotechnical system.

This is where emotions may play a very critical role. Emotions may play an important role in tuning the internal value system (i.e., the payoff matrix shaping the agent's actions and expectations) and the ecological value system (i.e., the payoff matrix that determines success with regards to the functional demands of survival).

Consider the physician's dilemma again. What is a satisfactory balance between the two heuristics: Common Thing or Worst Thing? Perhaps the best standard available is an expert physician. That is, a physician who has achieved long-term success in the particular domain (e.g., emergency medicine) and who is regarded highly by peers.

It is unlikely that the balance that guides the expert physician after many years of experience is the same as at the start of her career. How was that balance achieved? And what makes that balance the right balance?

Here is a narrative that fits with the dynamics of triadic semiotic systems. At the start a novice physician might be expected to be out of balance with regards to overemphasizing one heuristic or the other. For example, a novice physician might not be cognizant of the costs of many of the tests, both in dollars and in the availability of the resources for treating other patients. And she might be eager to prove her cleverness by searching diligently for that 'worst thing' that her colleagues might miss. Alternatively, she may have been trained in a way that emphasized the 'common things' and may not have the experience to anticipate low probability, but potentially hazardous 'worst things.'

How will she discover that she is out of balance? In a triadic dynamic, the tuning is expected to change as a result of feedback. On the one hand, finding a worst thing that colleagues overlooked and saving a patient will result in praise and positive emotions. On the other hand, missing a worst thing that leads to harm to a patient or even death will open the physician to blame (perhaps even a lawsuit) and negative emotional experiences. There will also be additional feedback from colleagues and hospital administrators that make the physician aware of the costs of tests and procedures. The physician who orders many tests creates more work for her colleagues and cuts into the financial goals of the hospital administrators. She will get subtle and sometimes explicit feedback if her payoff matrix is out of line with that of her colleagues or the administrators.

Does that suggest that the colleagues and the hospital administrators determine what the right payoff matrix is? No! The point is that the 'right' balance cannot be specified objectively or independently from the semiotic dynamic. For example, a physician with many years of experience in a hospital in a wealthy suburb may discover that her internal payoff matrix (which is well-aligned with her previous colleagues) is completely out of line with her new colleagues when she moves to another hospital in a poor inner-city ecology.

The 'right' value system or the standards for a rationality that will lead to satisfying results can only be realized as an emergent property of the circular dynamics of the triadic system. In other words, the value system underlying satisfying is in continuous negotiation. It is being negotiated in the legislatures as they debate the government's role in healthcare. It is being negotiated in the hospital boardrooms as financial officers consider the economic viability of their organizations. It is being negotiated in the courtrooms as judges and juries make decisions about awards in malpractice cases. It is being negotiated among doctors, nurses, and other staff in the process of coordinating their day-to-day interactions. And increasingly, the patients are gaining a voice in these negotiations.

These debates at all levels are emotional. One tragic case that elicits a broad and strong emotional reaction from the public can have a very strong impact on the negotiations, although that impact may be transient. For example, consider the impact of an expensive speeding ticket on your driving behavior. Most people will be much more conservative in their driving behavior for a short period following the ticket. However, over time the memory of the pain fades and other factors, such as the value of minimizing your commute time, may have more weight in shaping your driving behavior.

However, learning is an integral process, and even the transient impacts eventually accumulate to influence the payoff matrix. For circular dynamics, the expectation is that systems that endure for long periods will have internal payoff matrices that have become aligned with the demands of their ecologies, so that there is a satisfactory (not necessarily optimal) fit. This is analogous to the dynamics of natural selection.

Thus, in searching for an authoritative standard for scoring rationality, the triadic model looks to experience. The triadic model puts its faith with the experts within a domain as the authorities of rationality. In contrast, the conventional model trusts mathematics. It puts its trust in the authority of the spreadsheet and in doing so, undermines faith in the authority of experience.

John Ralston Saul has written a very important book titled *Voltaire's Bastards*[13] that suggests that faith in spreadsheet models associated with the conventional perspective of the Harvard Business School is leading society down a garden path to catastrophe.

Voltaire played a significant role in moving society from a value system based on the divine authority of kings to a value system based on reason. At the beginning of the Age of Reason, reason was understood to reflect consensus among people as reflected in democratic or parliamentary forms of government. Reason was the product of negotiations and arguments among groups of people. Thus, to a large extent reason was grounded in the experiences of the people participating in the debate.

Saul's thesis is that increasingly the authority has shifted from the experience of people to the computations of spreadsheets. In other words, the authority has now been invested in the formal logic and mathematics that underlie the spreadsheet calculations. The arguments have been reduced to dueling spreadsheets. And any experiences that cannot be quantified in terms commensurate with the spreadsheets are ignored. Today, authority often rests with the people who own the spreadsheets.

Saul refers to the people who own the spreadsheets as Voltaire's bastards, because he argues that the spreadsheets are often as disconnected from the pragmatic realities of everyday life as were the kings that ruled prior to the Age of Reason. Saul suggests that putting trust in the spreadsheets is as irrational as putting trust in the divine authority of kings. He provides compelling examples of how Voltaire's bastards are undermining the quality and ultimately the stability of many social systems.

The Voltaire's bastards narrative goes like this: a person starts a company to produce high-quality running shoes, because he simply can't find any shoes on the market that satisfy his needs. The company becomes successful and too big for the founder to manage, so he hires skilled managers to take care of the business side of the company.

These managers begin examining the company through their spreadsheets and discover that they can dramatically increase profits if they use cheaper materials and labor. The company founder objects because the changes are undermining the quality of the shoes and violating his sense of responsibility to the skilled workers who made important contributions to building the company. These objections are dismissed as (irrational), since the quality of shoes and the ethical responsibility to the workforce are not factors in the business spreadsheet.

Profits go up, the founder retires because the work is no longer satisfying, and the manager takes a much higher offer to manage a new computer startup after an article is published in a business magazine praising his role in increasing profits. Finally, the customers' loyalty to the company gradually erodes, because the quality of shoes no longer meets their expectations, beginning a slow descent into mediocrity or complete collapse.

The most insidious aspect of the authority of spreadsheets is that the social evaluation or scoring of people is determined by the spreadsheets, so that the same people who are undermining the quality and stability of institutions are being celebrated and rewarded as 'heros' or 'geniuses.' While the people who actually care about things that are not commensurate with the spreadsheets (e.g., the quality of shoes or of a patient's life) are ignored or sidetracked.

The faith in the spreadsheet computations has become heavily ingrained in Western culture. The participants who deviate from the prescriptions of the mathematical norms for rationality when faced with the conventional research puzzles, such as Wason's tasks, are easily convinced that they are wrong when the experimenter or teacher demonstrates the 'right' answer using the spreadsheet computations. The underlying theme of the conventional decision paradigm has been don't trust yourself or other humans—trust spreadsheets! The conventional decision research program has been a clear winner, because it is well aligned with the authority of the spreadsheet.

Integrating Experience Across the Ages

Someone who is committed to the conventional dyadic view of cognition and decision making might raise a potentially serious challenge to Saul's thesis with respect to Voltaire's bastards: "Doesn't mathematics, logic, and economics reflect the cumulative experience of humans? In trusting the authority of the spreadsheets, aren't we in fact leveraging the experiences of many generations?"

However, these questions miss the point. The problem is not the mathematics or the computations behind the spreadsheets. The problem is that the spreadsheets often do not align with the functional values that determine long-term success in an ecology or domain. The problem is when the spreadsheet logic that led to a profitable automobile business is applied uncritically to managing a hospital or a university. The problem comes when the authority is given to people who are skilled at managing the spreadsheets (the Harvard MBA), even when they have no experience in the domain to which the spreadsheet is being applied (e.g., making quality running shoes).

The problem is when the authority for determining the 'right' decisions with respect to health-care is taken from the healthcare professionals and the patients and given to the MBAs. The problem comes when the healthcare professionals are serving the spreadsheets, rather than when the spreadsheets are the tools of those whose experiences are grounded in the healthcare domain. If Saul's thesis is correct, then Western society is heading on a dangerous path where instability and collapse is very likely. How did we come to be traveling this wrong path?

Pirsig[14] suggests that Aristotle and Plato are in large part responsible for setting Western society on this wrong path. Obviously, Plato's *Myth of the Cave* aligns well with the conventional dyadic narrative. Unaided, humans only have access to the shadows on the wall. The only path to truth is through mathematics! Don't trust your senses; put your faith in the computations of the geometers and other mathematicians. Aristotle, on the other hand, put his faith in the systematic processes of empirical science. Trust the analytical methods of experimentation and statistics to pull out the truth from the noisy data.

Thus, the spreadsheet plays a very important role for both Plato (who focuses on the purity of the computations) and Aristotle (who focuses on integration of the accumulated noisy data). In essence, Pirsig has nominated Plato and Aristotle as the progenitors of Voltaire's bastards. Or in other words, he is suggesting that the irrationality of a world dominated by Voltaire's bastards is an inevitable result of taking the path set by Plato and Aristotle.

What's the alternative? Where do we look to find an alternative to Plato and Aristotle? Pirsig suggests that rather than look to Plato and Aristotle, who are the winners on a scorecard aligned with the logic of spreadsheets, we might consider the losers. The common enemy of Plato and Aristotle were the Sophists. They were the big losers! In the world of Voltaire's bastards, the Sophists are vilified. Their name has become intimately associated with irrationality (sophistry—the use of fallacious arguments, especially with the intention of deception).

Why were the Sophists such a threat to Plato and Aristotle? Why have they been vilified in the world of Voltaire's bastards? Reconsider this quote from the noted sophist, Protagoras:

Man is the measure of all things!

The Sophists taught rhetoric. For the Sophists the path to truth was debate and argument. The test was consensus! Rationality was associated with the ability to convince other people. Thus, rationality was grounded in the experiences of the people participating in the debate or the vote and their ability to eloquently and convincingly express those experiences.

For the Sophists, the ideal was *arete*, where *arete* reflects excellence in achieving or fulfilling a purpose or function. This fulfillment of purpose reflected both skill and character or virtue. A person with arete was an expert within some domain (e.g., he was an excellent farmer, or an excellent warrior, or an excellent artist). This is the guy or gal whose judgment can be trusted!

The person with arete knows how to do things right and knows what the right or moral/ethical things to do are. Thus, the standard of rationality for the Sophists was the GOOD MAN (the person with arete). It is important to note that the 'good' here is not an absolute. Arete refers to a situated good. One person could have arete due to her skill and wisdom as a physician, another person could have arete due to his skill and wisdom as a nurse, and other people could have arete due to their skill and wisdom in other domains. In today's world, one of the skills might include being able to manipulate the spreadsheets. However, arete is only present when the skill is complemented by the wisdom to know what goes into the spreadsheet and what the output means with respect to doing the right thing in a specific domain of application.

Perhaps the closest contemporary construct to arete is 'wisdom.' Stephen Hall writes of wisdom:

> One of the hallmarks of wisdom, what distinguishes it so sharply from 'mere' intelligence, is ability to exercise good judgment in the face of imperfect knowledge. In short, do the right thing—ethically, socially, familiarly, personally.[15]

> Many definitions of wisdom converge on recurrent and common elements: humility, patience, and a clear-eyed, dispassionate view of human nature and the human predicament, as well as emotional resilience, an ability to cope with adversity, and an almost philosophical acknowledgement of ambiguity and the limitations of knowledge. Like many big ideas, it's also nettled with contradictions. Wisdom is based upon knowledge, but part of the physics of wisdom is shaped by uncertainty. Action is important, but so is judicious inaction. Emotion is central to wisdom, yet emotional detachment is indispensable. A wise act in one context may be sheer folly in another.[16]

The Sophists looked to the domain experts as the authorities for a rationality where knowing how and knowing why were intimately linked. Pirsig faults Plato and Aristotle for splitting the how from the why! They linked truth with the 'how' as reflected in mathematics and scientific method. In doing so, they objectified truth in terms of cold, hard facts that fit the logic of the spreadsheet. In doing so, they undermined confidence in everyday human experiences. They undermined confidence in common sense—in human wisdom.

Plato and Aristotle set a path toward a 'pure' science that was not contaminated by common practical, ethical, or aesthetic concerns. These subjective contaminants or obstacles to truth were relegated to the 'arts.' Thus, we have the gap between science and art in Western society. Science equals truth. Art equals fiction. Science is objective. Art is subjective. Science is based in logic. Art is based in emotion. Science is rational. Art is irrational. Science tells us how. Art tells us why.

Plato and Aristotle paved a path to knowledge, but perhaps at the cost of common-sense wisdom.

Peter Hancock[17]

The influence of Plato and Aristotle has shaped Western approaches to education. In the world of Voltaire's bastards, the goal is to distill the objective facts away from the subjective context. Thus, we get texts that focus on de-contextualized, concrete/quantitative facts (e.g., bullet points) and formal methods (i.e., rules and procedures). Evaluation has tended to focus on the ability to recite the facts and rigorous adherence to the methods and procedures. The universities provide knowledge about how to achieve our goals, but they are often silent with respect to suggesting what goals are worth pursuing. They offer knowledge for the sake of knowledge alone!

This is the type of education system that led to Pirsig's existential crisis. Pirsig began to realize that the facts were accumulating, but they were not adding up; and that adherence to the rules and procedures did not guarantee the quality of the output. Something was missing: Quality? Arete? As Hancock notes: you can't fully appreciate the *how* without consideration of *why*! The cold science of Voltaire's bastards is excellent at addressing the question of how to get somewhere, but it is impotent when it comes to deciding where we 'ought' to go!

One alternative to the 'textbook' approach to learning is a case-based approach to education. Here, the vehicle for passing on accumulated experience is the story. Unlike the conventional textbooks, good stories integrate the objective and the subjective, the facts and the ethics, the logic and emotions. A good story can simultaneously draw attention to facts, illustrate methods, engage emotions, and convey a moral.

Appreciation for the power of stories, both for eliciting expertise from experienced people and for communicating that expertise to inexperienced novices, is growing. For example, Gary Klein[18] suggests that 'lessons learned' from employees' concrete experiences with specific problems is critical for effective 'corporate memory.' He suggests that these "lessons learned are best transmitted through stories."

Klein has found that by probing stories that experts tell about critical incidents, he has been able to discover cues to the rationality underlying the ability to make good decisions. In many cases, the experts themselves are unaware of the factors shaping their decisions until they are explicated through the critical incident interview.

For example, Klein[19] describes the case of the fire commander who 'intuitively' decided to order his men to leave a burning building moments before the floor collapses. Although the commander originally attributed his intuitive decision to ESP, in the process of evaluating the account using the critical incident technique, Klein and the commander discovered the cues (e.g., the unexpected response of the fire to the actions of directing the hoses, the sounds, and the direction of the radiant heat) that caused the commander to reevaluate his hypothesis that the fire was above them and to decide to vacate the room.

Klein and others focus on the value of stories for eliciting and communicating the specific experiences of domain experts. However, an implication of their success is that those seeking more general norms or guides for rationality might look to the stories that endure across the ages—classic literature, histories, biographies, fables, parables, koans, nursery rhymes, and tribal/family lore.

With respect to these potential sources of norms to guide decision making in a complex world, John Sumida's[20] thesis on Clauswitz provides an interesting perspective on history as a source for teaching military leadership and decision making. Conventionally, the role of the historian has often been seen as that of explaining great events. In essence, this typically boils down to elucidating the causes of success or failure based on extensive analysis to distill out the historical 'facts' or 'truths' (i.e., based on hindsight).

In contrast, Sumida suggests that the point of Clauswitz's 'theory' was to capture the full experience of the uncertainties and emotions that commanders inevitably faced, not to extract away the booming, buzzing confusion, but to authentically simulate that confusion. The goal of history should not be to explain from hindsight, but to help in the development of foresight.

In this context, Clauswitz's construct of 'genius' had much in common with the Greek term *arete*. Genius was not simply a reference to superior tactical skill, but rather it reflected "the will of the commander to make decisions in the face of incomplete and misleading information, fear of failure, and the unpredictable major and minor difficulties that could arise in any military operation."[21]

Sumida suggests three factors that led Clauswitz to conclude that a "positive doctrine," or a normative procedural or rule-based approach to training command decision making, was futile:

- the role of moral force—that is, emotion;
- that war consisted of a series of actions and reactions by two or more adversaries, whose course was inherently unpredictable;
- the fact that the information upon which both sides based action was bound to be uncertain.

In place of a positive theory, Sumida suggested that Clauswitz was suggesting that history focus on going deep into a few events for which there was adequate information to fully recreate the uncertainties of the situation and to create empathy for the emotional experiences of the commander. The goal is not to isolate the objective facts from the subjective experience, but rather to link the objective with the subjective in order to simulate an authentic experience of the complex situation faced by the genius or expert.

> This constructed truth, moreover, was a thing that had to be felt as much as thought—it was addressed to the subconscious as well as conscious mind. The goal of intensive engagement through study and reflection with a combination of fact and surmise, in other words, was not erudition, but the experience of replicating certain aspects of actual experience.[22]

It seems that the lessons that Clauswitz was seeking from history are exactly the kind of lessons that Klein was seeking in his critical incident interviews with domain experts. The goal was to discover the deeper aspects of experience that are not easily captured in objective descriptions of events. These deeper aspects of experience that include morality, uncertainty, and emotion are not easily captured in abstract bullet points, and they are often trivialized in causal narratives constructed from the perspective of hindsight.

Clauswitz seems to be suggesting that capturing this deeper insight requires a kind of reliving or simulation of the experience. This is true for both the person who experienced the original event and for others who hope to learn vicariously from the successes and failures of others. Thus, Clauswitz was very skeptical of normative models as standards for decision making, preferring the example of experienced, successful people. He writes that what "genius does is the best rule, and that theory can do no better than show how and why this should be the case."[23]

"ACTION" HE HAD OBSERVED, COULD NEVER BE BASED ON ANYTHING FIRMER THAN INSTINCT, A SENSING OF THE TRUTH" THUS "THE MAN RESPONSIBLE FOR EVALUATING THE WHOLE MUST BRING TO HIS TASK THE QUALITY OF INTUITION THAT PERCEIVES THE TRUTH AT EVERY POINT."

BUT BECAUSE "TRUTH IN ITSELF IS RARELY SUFFICIENT TO MAKE MEN ACT," THE COMMANDER HAD TO AMPLIFY THE PROMPTING OF INTUITION WITH AN EMOTIONAL IMPULSE.

THE COMBINATION OF INTUITION AND DETERMINATION – THAT IS, A SYNTHESIS OF SUB RATIONAL INTELLIGENCE AND EMOTION – CONSTITUTED THE BASIS OF EFFECTIVE SUPREME COMMAND THAT COULD BE CALLED THE PRODUCT OF GENIUS.

Sumida[24]

Designing Experiences

When the problem of improving the design of 'cognitive systems' is framed in the context of the triadic semiotic system (Figure 15.4) or in terms of an adaptive control system (15.2), a guiding assumption is that the internal logic will tend to naturally converge onto robust, common-sense solutions to complex problems, given sufficient experience. In other words, it is assumed that given time, the semiotic system will learn to manage the complexity—it will gradually select the skills, rules, and knowledge that are necessary for success.

There are two important qualifications, suggesting ways that these systems can fail. The first is that learning takes time, and in high-risk environments adaptive systems may not survive long enough to develop the expertise needed for robust performance. For example, in World War I more pilots were killed learning to fly the Sopwith Camel aircraft than were killed in combat.

Additionally, for very complex domains, it might take a very long time to reach expertise. A heuristic from the expertise literature is that it takes about 10 years of deliberate practice to reach top performance levels in domains like competitive chess. So, one important factor for developing effective cognitive systems is to make sure that the system has the time needed to learn the appropriate skills, rules, and knowledge.

The second qualification is that these types of systems will become unstable and fail catastrophically if the gains are too high, as we saw in previous chapters. The implication is that these systems should have a somewhat conservative bias. That is, there should be a relatively strong tendency to stay with things that have worked in the past. This reflects a common saying in aviation: "There are bold pilots and old pilots, but there are no old, bold pilots."

Another facet of the story of the Wright brothers' success in discovering the keys to flight is the way they managed risk. The choice of the sand dunes at Kitty Hawk was partly motivated by the fact that the relatively soft sand reduced the danger of crashes. In the beginning, the brothers avoided flying together—so that if one died in an accident, the other would be able to carry

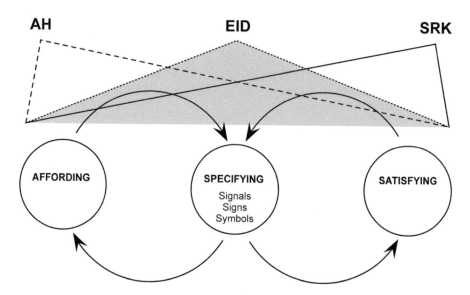

Figure 15.4 This figure illustrates three perspectives on the triadic semiotic dynamic. The Abstraction Hierarchy (AH) emphasizes the possibilities (i.e., affordances) relative to the functional goals (i.e., satisfying). The SRK Model emphasizes the goals and strategies (i.e., satisfying) relative to different forms of representation (i.e., specifying). Ecological Interface Design (EID) considers alternative forms of representation (i.e., signals, signs, and symbols) relative to both the possibilities (i.e., affordances) and the functional goals and strategies (i.e., satisfying).

the work forward. For the brothers spreadsheet computations (i.e., analysis) were important for discovering the correct lift coefficients. However, an equally important aspect of success was their appreciation of the uncertainties and dangers associated with flight and their wisdom in managing the associated risks.[25]

Thus, in more colloquial terms a high gain reflects a tendency for people to overreach their skill level. That is, to take on risks and challenges that they are not ready for. It is said that one of the important aspects of developing high-level boxers (fighters) is to make sure that they don't face competitors that are too strong early in their career. The ideal is to have them face gradually increasing competition, so that they learn from each bout without suffering a bad defeat along the way.

Another important implication of the fact that the tuning of the adaptive system happens over time is that an important attribute that can be necessary for achieving expertise in complex domains is persistence. Mistakes can be an important source of information that will guide the tuning process. Achieving expertise will typically require that the system persist in spite of mistakes and errors. In some domains, failures are necessary stepping stones along the path to genius. Thus, a key to persistence might include managing the emotional and motivational impact of these mistakes, as well as the skills, rules, and knowledge. Failure was also an important facet of the Wright brothers' story. Their ability to persist despite significant failures and discouragement was another important factor in their success.

A final thing to appreciate as you consider the implications of the triadic semiotic perspective for improving performance is that the target for your designs will often be complex, open systems, where no single algorithm or procedure will consistently produce satisfying results. The goal of designing systems to cope with complexity cannot be to constrain the system to follow a single, predetermined 'best way.' But rather, the goal will be to prepare the system to muddle through to satisfying solutions to ill-defined problems that are impossible to fully anticipate in foresight.

From the perspective of designing sociotechnical systems that are effective, robust adaptive control systems, two important ways that the cognitive performance can be enhanced are through training and interface design. Let's briefly consider these two means for tuning the semiotic dynamic from the perspective of Rasmussen's Cognitive System Engineering framework.

Figure 15.4 shows the three components of Rasmussen's framework as different perspectives on the semiotic dynamic. The Abstraction Hierarchy examines the semiotic triad from the perspective of the possibilities offered by the environment—the affordances. The SRK Model or Decision Ladder examines the semiotic triad from the perspective of the strategies and heuristics that experts might use to satisfy their functional goals. The construct of Ecological Interface Design (EID) examines the semiotic triad from the perspective of alternative representations for specifying the affordances relative to the functional goals that need to be satisfied.

Ecological perspectives on both training and interface design have tended to emphasize perceptual, rather than logical aspects of cognitive performance. Focus has been on the education of attention, rather than on fixing aspects of rationality. There is an implicit assumption that if the system is picking up the right information relative to the affordances and the values (satisficing), then the system will naturally converge on the most effective skills, rules, and knowledge. In essence, the emphasis is on helping people to 'see' better, rather than helping them to 'think' better. But in fact, in the closed-loop dynamic, 'seeing' and 'thinking' are best treated as integral rather than separate processes.

Figure 15.2 illustrates the semiotic dynamic as an observer/control system. In this context, a useful simplification is to relate the observer function to the system's ability to discriminate signal (meaning) from noise (d-prime), and to relate the control function to the response criterion (Beta), as illustrated in Figure 15.3. With this heuristic simplification, the design problem can be framed in terms of improving control/decision and improving observation.

Hopefully, it is becoming clear that the quality of control in a closed-loop system can be significantly constrained by the quality of information. This includes information about values and it includes feedback (i.e., information about the current situation) and prediction (i.e., information about the future).

The d-prime parameter in Figure 15.3 is used to represent the quality of the observer process—the ability to estimate current and future states of the system. This reflects the perceptual tuning or the perspicacity of the system. The Beta parameter is used to represent the control or decision process. That is, it reflects the criterion for choosing one action or another (e.g., pursuing the Common or Worst Thing).

Note that whereas shifts in the Beta parameter result in trading off one source of error (e.g., misses) for another (e.g., false alarms), changes in d-prime can reduce both misses and false alarms. That is, a design change that increases the ability of a physician to discriminate between a Worst Thing and a Common Thing will make it easier to detect Worst Things AND will reduce the number of resources spent looking for the Worst Thing when the patient has the Common Thing. So, improvements in the observer process can have high potential payoffs, independent of the particular control strategy (i.e., the Beta). In this sense, Beta reflects an EITHER-OR choice, but d-prime can lead to a BOTH-AND solution.

Improving Control

Improving control involves choosing the right Beta for a given d-prime. This will generally involve trading off one source of error for another to yield a generally satisfactory result. Using the ED example, shifting the Beta one direction will increase the number of Worst Things detected (hits), but this will be at the expense of more resources expended on Common Things (false alarms). Or conversely, shifting the Beta in the other direction will reduce the amount of resources expended on Common Things, at the cost of sometimes missing a Worst Thing.

The optimal control problem involves setting the Beta to get the best 'payoff,' where the payoff reflects some value system. In situations where the values are constant and quantifiable, then it may be possible to identify an 'optimal' control strategy that might be coded into an automatic control system. However, in a context like the ED, where values may be difficult to quantify and may change as a function of context, it is unlikely that any automatic control system would be able to achieve the same levels of satisfaction that is generally achieved by human experts.

Thus, with respect to the control problem, one important role of design can be to support the negotiation process that determines the values in the payoff matrix. This involves facilitating communications across levels within the sociotechnical system. For example, helping the physicians to get a better sense of the economic constraints associated with hospital resources and helping the hospital administrators to get a better sense of the uncertainties and risks that the physician is facing in the ED.

One of the critical sources of difficulties with respect to sensemaking within complex sociotechnical systems, such as the healthcare system, is the fact that different values are salient at different levels within the system. The hospital CFO is struggling with balancing the financial spreadsheets, while the ED physician is struggling with people and families who are in pain. Thus, a Beta that is satisfactory with respect to the values that are salient at one level may be very unsatisfactory with respect to the values that are salient at another level.

In this context, a solution that is optimal at any one level may be catastrophic at another level. For example, optimizing around patient care to minimize missed Worst Cases may lead to financial collapse of the hospital. Thus, satisficing across levels may be the only viable solution. In these complex systems, satisficing is likely to reflect a dynamic equilibrium that varies continuously as a result of negotiations across levels. In this context, the counter-arguments at the different levels provide the 'friction'[26] that keeps the system from becoming unstable as a result of chasing any particular unattainable 'optimum.'

For example, a physician who is always looking for Worst Things will get 'friction' or pushback from hospital administrators or other colleagues who must shoulder the expense or the additional workload of doing many extra tests and procedures. On the other hand, a hospital that misses too many Worst Things may get 'friction' or pushback from the larger community in terms of lawsuits or increased regulatory scrutiny.

Thus, from the perspective of the control problem, a focus of design should be to facilitate the negotiations across levels in the sociotechnical system. By facilitating communications across levels within the system, it is possible to have a system that is 'smarter' than any of its components. That is, a system that stays within satisfactory bounds. The criterion is not perfect, or zero error. The criterion is stability over time—in other words, 'survival' (e.g., stability, anti-fragility, resilience, robustness).

The key point is that the quality of control strategies can only be assessed relative to a payoff matrix/cost function (i.e., a value system). One goal of a good design is to ensure that the functional values are communicated clearly. A fundamental design hypothesis is that if the values are clearly specified, then smart humans can generally be trusted to eventually adjust their behavior to achieve satisfactory performance relative to those values (e.g., discover the optimal beta).

Thus, the problem in most complex systems is not the control 'logic' (i.e., flawed rationality). Rather, the problem is that the values are not clearly specified. In very complex domains, specifying the values may be extremely difficult due to the fact that the value space has high dimensionality (i.e., multiple goals), that the dimensions may not be stationary (e.g., moving targets), and the dimensions may not be commensurate (e.g., involve different units of measurement). In these cases, a design goal should be to help make the values explicit and to facilitate the ongoing debate about these values.

Improving Observation

With respect to improving observation, the design challenge is to provide the best information possible about the current and future states of the process. Woods[27] framed this as the representation design problem, and Rasmussen and Vicente framed this problem as the problem of Ecological Interface Design.[28]

A first step to addressing this challenge is to determine what the information needs are (i.e., what is the best information?). In the triadic semiotic dynamic, this requires consideration of both the situation dynamics (e.g., what are the affordances? how do the processes work? what are the preconditions and consequences of actions?) and the awareness dynamics (e.g., what are the intentions, skills, rules, and knowledge available to the operators?).

With respect to the design of representations, it is critical to appreciate a distinction between 'data' and 'information.' In the formal sense, information reflects not simply the 'value' of a variable (e.g., a quantitative measurement), but the value relative to the possible intentions or relative to the constraints on the source of the information (i.e., the meaning). For example, the speed of an aircraft is a piece of data. However, the aircraft's speed relative to a normal cruise speed, a stall boundary (i.e., the speed necessary to keep the aircraft from losing lift), a maximum relative to the integrity of aircraft structures (e.g., above which damaging the wings is likely), or relative to a prescribed arrival time at a particular destination is information.

Similarly, medical information such as temperature, blood pressure, cholesterol levels, cardiac rhythms is only information when seen relative to constraints (e.g., population norms or patients' recent past history).[29] Unfortunately, this has not been well recognized in the design of most modern healthcare information technologies (HIT). Too often, these technologies are designed around spreadsheets of data, with very little effort to help physicians to 'see' the constraints associated with health. There is genuine concern that by focusing on convenient ways to manage data, the HIT designs have made access to information much more difficult for physicians—thus, undermining the physician's ability to judge the state of the patient's health or to anticipate changes in that state.[30] In essence, the HIT systems have been designed to meet the needs of Voltaire's bastards, but not to meet the needs of the ED physician.

The key to effective observer performance is to understand how the feedback in terms of signals, signs, and symbols specifies the actions that will best satisfy the functional objectives. To do this it is necessary to consider the sources of the values and affordances (e.g., using the Abstraction Hierarchy) and to consider the skills, rules, and knowledge of the agents (including people and algorithms) that will be making the decisions and selecting the actions.

Thus, an important goal for design is to construct representations that help to specify smart actions with respect to the functional objectives of the work domain. This can be done through training (i.e., constructing internal representations) and through interface design (i.e., constructing displays) that make the functionally significant relations salient.

Training

Most everyone has had the experience of entering a new field of endeavor (e.g., beginning driving, learning a new sport, learning a new video game) and experiencing a buzzing, booming confusion that at first seems impossible to grasp. However, after extensive experience, the confusion begins to make sense, and eventually they are able to master the confusion and, in fact, it may eventually be difficult for them to understand how anyone could be confused—it now seems to be a simple matter of common sense.

A fundamental goal of training is to expose people to a series of experiences (e.g., exemplars) that get them from the naive confused state (e.g, an undifferentiated neural network) to the mastery state (e.g., a well-tuned neural net) as efficiently as possible. And the fundamental question will be, what training experiences (e.g., what exemplars) will be most beneficial or meaningful?

Within the training literature, many different aspects (e.g., fidelity) and techniques (e.g., whole-task, part-task, backward chaining, etc.) for training are discussed. In fact, the literature tends to be organized around techniques (e.g., part vs. whole task) to determine which is best.[31] However, the answer almost always turns out to be that—"It depends." This suggests that all the techniques can be used effectively in some contexts. Thus, the important question for designing training systems is—"What does it depend on?"

Figure 15.5 suggests that two important dimensions to consider when designing training systems are the domain fidelity and the degree of challenge or cognitive manageability of the experience.

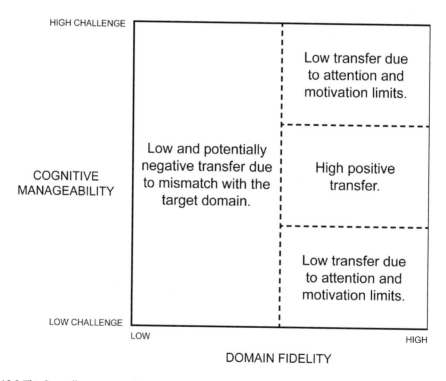

Figure 15.5 This figure illustrates two dimensions to consider in the design of training systems. Domain Fidelity reflects the degree to which the training experience is representative or authentic relative to the target domain. The Cognitive Manageability dimension reflects the degree of challenge or difficulty with respect to the capabilities of the trainees.

As illustrated in Figure 15.5, there is typically a sweet spot, such that experiences that are both high in fidelity and at an intermediate level of challenge will typically provide the highest levels of positive transfer. That is, the experiences in training will help to 'tune' the abduction system in ways that will lead to improved performance in the target domain.

The dimension of domain fidelity focuses on the degree to which the training experiences are representative of experiences in the target domain. One aspect of this involves the fidelity of the devices used in training. For example, in the aviation domain there has been much discussion of the extent to which the dynamic response of flight simulators (e.g., the flight equations) are equivalent to the dynamics of the actual aircraft. This is important, but domain fidelity is a much broader concern. In addition to the devices, domain fidelity considers whether the situations or problems faced in the training context are similar to the situations or problems faced in the actual domain.

However, high domain fidelity does not necessarily mean that every aspect of the target domain be involved in each training experience. For example, in order to satisfy the Cognitive Manageability dimension in Figure 15.5, it may be beneficial to reduce a complex domain into components that are better scaled to a trainee's current ability levels. In parsing the domain into part tasks, there will be partitions that preserve meaningful domain relations and partitions that break these relations. The key to achieving high domain fidelity is to use partitions that preserve relations that are meaningful to domain success.

The Abstraction Hierarchy analysis can be very useful in making decisions about how to parse work domains into meaningful training experiences. Each level within the hierarchy suggests different dimensions for partitioning the work (e.g., goals/values; functional constraints/affordances; organizational components; component physical systems). Relations across levels in the abstraction hierarchy suggest important aspects of meaning that may be important to preserve in the training experience.

In addition to the Abstraction Hierarchy, a consideration of the skills, rules/heuristics, and knowledge that domain experts employ can provide important insight into how to partition the work in meaningful ways. However, direct presentation or description of the skills, rules/heuristics, and knowledge to novices will rarely be effective. A fundamental goal of training abduction systems should be to create experiences that allow the trainees to discover the skills, rules/heuristics, and knowledge through active engagement with problems. For example, rather than telling people the 'moral' or 'rule' as a bullet point, telling a story and allowing the trainees to discover the moral in the context of the story will generally be more effective.

The key consideration with regards to Domain Fidelity is that once again "Context Matters!" In general, the goal is that meaningful dimensions of the target domain be well represented within the training experience—understanding the limitation that in complex domains it will not be either feasible or desirable to cram all the meanings into any single training experience.

Figure 15.5 suggests that there is an optimal level of challenge with respect to Cognitive Manageability. If the challenge is too great, then the trainees will be overwhelmed with the complexity and will have difficulty discriminating signal (meaning) from noise. This will often lead to disappointing outcomes for the trainees and may undermine their determination to persist long enough for the training to have a positive impact on performance. If the challenge is too low, then the trainees may get little benefit beyond what skills, rules, and knowledge they already have. And here too, determination to persist may be undermined due to boredom or lack of engagement.

In sum, the key to effective training interventions will be to have experiences that are authentic with respect to the work domain and that are challenging enough to stretch trainees beyond their current capabilities, but not so far that they are overwhelmed. In simple terms, training should be designed so that people are making mistakes that they can learn from. If there are no mistakes, then the challenge is too low. If the mistakes are large and catastrophic, then the feedback may not be informative with respect to educating attention and may undermine the persistence that is necessary for mastery.

Interface Design

As illustrated in Figure 15.2, the interface representation is an important component of the observer function. The design of the interface will determine what feedback is salient—what is figure and what is ground. In terms of Figure 15.3, the objective is to increase the d-prime—to improve the ability to discriminate signal from noise. This will have a major impact on the evidence that guides both action and learning (e.g., the adjustment of the internal associative weights).

Here the distinction between data and information becomes very important. In many instances, maximizing information will be achieved by reducing the amount of data in the interface. It has been rumored that a major function of the interface designers at Google is to make sure that nothing other than the title and entry box is displayed on the opening screen. The result is that the primary function of search is made salient—there is nothing to distract from this function.

A major misconception influencing many designs is that adding 'data' to the interface is equivalent to increasing information. This is patently false. Whether an additional piece of data increases the discriminability of the signal from the noise (i.e., reduces uncertainty) will depend on its relation to the other data. For example, consider that each data element may be a function of both signal and noise. Depending on whether the noise is independent or correlated, averaging these two pieces of data may either strengthen the signal or reinforce the noise (increase the bias). It is for this reason that decisions based on a single piece of highly diagnostic evidence may actually be better than a decision that is based on an integration of all the available evidence, as suggested by the work of Gigerenzer on One Shot decision making.[32]

Thus, the design of an interface representation is analogous to tuning a filter to discriminate signal from noise. The representation will determine what signals will be picked up. Of course, a fundamental question that must be addressed in designing this filter is: What are the properties that distinguish the signal from the noise?

Again, Rasmussen's Abstraction Hierarchy and SRK model were developed explicitly to help address this question. The Abstraction Hierarchy focuses on the signal source—to determine what are the important distinctions relative to the constraints relating the ends (i.e., functional values) to the means (i.e., affordances). An important implication of the Abstraction Hierarchy is that meaning may involve many dimensions and levels of abstraction, and different distinctions may be meaningful at different levels of abstraction.

When meaning is a function of layers of abstraction and multiple dimensions, making the signal salient will often depend on the organization of the data (or chunking). Good organization of the data can make meaningful relations among the different dimensions salient as patterns in the representation.[33]

The SRK Model focuses on the receiver to identify the important distinctions relative to the capabilities and expectations of the humans. For example, it is important to understand how people will naturally parse a representation in terms of foreground and background. What are people looking for or what aspects of a representation will attract attention?

In building interfaces, it has been found that analogical representations have been particularly useful for linking constraints associated with physical laws (e.g., thermodynamics or aerodynamics) to human skills and rules. Geometric relations on the interface are typically used to reflect lawful interactions (constraints) among multiple physical state variables, and motion typically reflects change over time. These types of representations allow people to transfer skills developed through common physical experiences (e.g., moving and manipulating physical objects) to managing more abstract or complex processes (e.g., keeping a thermodynamic process within safe limits).

Metaphorical representations have also been found to be useful in helping people to map skills, rules, and knowledge from familiar domains (e.g., managing files in your office) to less familiar domains (e.g., managing data structures in a computer). The key in using both analog and metaphorical representations is to make the meaningful distinctions as explicit as possible so that they guide both action and learning.

Emotion and Design

Remember Don Norman's claim that "Beautiful things work better"?[34] What is the role of beauty in enhancing performance of cognitive systems? Certainly, industrial designers have embraced social and emotional components as significant factors that impact the quality of consumer products (e.g., the iPhone).[35] But in the design of safety-critical systems such as commercial aviation systems or process control plants, should we be concerned about the operators' emotions? Should the pilots' or plant operators' happiness be a design consideration?

In Damasio's[36] work with people with brain injuries similar to that of Phineas Gage, he found that many of these people had a very hard time coping with life (e.g., keeping a job or maintaining family relations). It is interesting that these people did not show any deficits with respect to IQ tests or most other classical tests of cognitive ability. This led Damasio to conclude that the difficulties were not associated with 'thinking' in the classical sense (e.g., cold, objective, logical reasoning). Rather, Damasio hypothesized that the deficits were a function of an inability to coordinate logical and emotional processes.

The implication of Damasio's work is that emotions may play a very important role in the dynamics of the abduction process (i.e., the adaptive observer/control system). There are at least four aspects of the processes illustrated in Figure 15.2 where emotions may play a critical role.

First, the values and goals that provide the references for evaluating feedback are not simply 'intentions' in the mind of a single individual. Rather, these properties emerge due to interactions within the larger sociotechnical system. For example, the values that shape performance in the ED are influenced by cultural factors (e.g., sacredness of life), professional factors (e.g., ethical standards, credentialing), political factors (e.g., legal standards), economic factors (e.g., healthcare financing), and local social factors (e.g., the expectations of co-workers) to name just a few. This means that social intelligence and the emotional components of this (e.g., empathy, humility, integrity) will play an important role in determining how well the system is tuned to the 'intentional constraints' that emerge from the sociocultural context.

Damasio also suggests that emotions may function as a kind of 'common currency' that allows us to compare or trade off dimensions of values that are otherwise incommensurate. For example, "gut feelings" may be the thing that allows a medical professional to trade off the health risk to a patient versus the financial costs of a particular diagnostic or treatment.

299

A second way that emotions will influence the muddling dynamic of the abduction process is that emotions will have an important impact on the salience of information. Damasio's hypothesis that the strong emotions 'mark' the consequences or situations associated with them suggests that emotions are a strong influence on what will be figure and ground with respect to internal representations.

For example, it is expected that a missed Worst Thing that has tragic consequences (e.g., the unexpected death of a young person) will have a strong emotional impact—and thus, will have a marked impact on how evidence is weighted in the future. In essence, strong emotions help to ensure that people do not repeat errors that are associated with costly negative consequences, and strong positive emotions may reinforce actions that lead to success.

A third way that emotions may play an important role in performance of the muddling dynamic is that they may be the criterion for triggering action. One of the observations that Damasio makes about his patients is that they can sometimes deliberate endlessly over even trivial decisions. They don't seem to have a well-tuned stopping rule for transitioning from observing (analyzing the problem) to controlling (initiating action).

A final aspect of emotions that may be critical for muddling performance is the emotional engagement that a person has with the work domain. In essence, the hypothesis is that people who love or care about the work are more likely to put in the time and effort that it takes to 'tune' the system to the complexities of the domain. In the early stages of professional development, people will get knocked down (i.e., will experience failures). Those who don't love their work eventually stop getting up and start looking for another domain that is more satisfying.

In sum, Damasio's work provides strong grounds for hypothesizing that 'beauty' is not just important for consumer products. Beautiful things will work better, because people will persevere and learn what it takes to make them work. Classically, emotions have been considered to be noise with respect to cognitive work. However, it seems clear that emotion can be an important factor shaping the salience of information and the persistence of people and thereby impacting whether the muddling process converges on skills, rules, and knowledge that will lead to generally satisfying performance.

The emotional satisfaction of the people in a system may be a very important metric for assessing the quality of a design. For example, if technology interventions in healthcare and aviation begin to have adverse impact on the happiness, pride, and sense of satisfaction of the physicians and pilots, then this may be an indication that the technology is undermining stability (e.g., safety), rather than making things better.

Conclusions

This chapter considers the standards or norms of rationality and the implications for designing systems that can effectively deal with the ambiguities and irreducible uncertainties of complex work, such as in emergency medicine. The thesis is aligned with Lindlum's observations about muddling. The conventional view has been to 'fix' or 'tame' the muddling process, so that it conforms with formal logical or mathematical models. An implication of this is that we need better 'spreadsheets' to aide the thinking process.

The alternative view that Lindblum advocated was that we need to get better at muddling. This means that we need to facilitate the learning or adaptation process so that the closed-loop observer/control process converges onto smart solutions. The design implication is that we need better representations (e.g., interfaces). Here the emphasis is on making sure that the right things are going into the spreadsheet. Making sure that the spreadsheets conform with the pragmatic demands of the situations and with the values of the people at all levels within the sociotechnical system.

In line with Clauswitz's commentary with respect to the role of 'genius' in military systems, this view suggests that the best benchmarks for assessing the quality of performance are the systems that have endured over time. We should look to the people who have had enduring success in a domain as the standards for quality, rather than to logical or mathematical abstractions.

Following from the Sophists, this suggests that the 'good man/woman' (arete) is the highest standard of quality. In this sense, good reflects both virtue and skill. It reflects a system that is tuned emotionally, socially, and cognitively to the situation—so that it is possible to judge both the ends (why? goals/values) and the means (how? skills, rules, and knowledge) with respect to surviving in an uncertain world.

In this view, constructs like bounded rationality and satisficing take on new connotations. The limiting bounds of rationality are framed in terms of experience (e.g., transfer of learning) rather than in terms of mechanism (e.g., channel capacity). Satisficing reflects the fact that robustness becomes more valuable than optimality for surviving in domains where the demands are changing and uncertain.

With respect to design, this suggests that it is important to frame the problem in ways that recognize the need to coordinate cognitive, social, and emotional skills in order to facilitate learning. There is no easy path to genius—it takes a long history of learning and overcoming the mistakes and errors that are inevitable in any complex domain.

Finally, although the discussion in this chapter has been very critical of rationality based exclusively on 'spreadsheets' and/or normative analytical models, it is important not to lose sight of the important role that mathematics and analytical thinking play in adaptive systems. Because of the power of analytical thinking, today we are able to observe or 'see' things (e.g., models of chaotic systems) and control things and go places (e.g., exploring the solar system) that were not possible for previous generations.

Mathematics and normative logic are important tools for cognitive systems. These tools provide a means to ends that were not possible before. However, there remains the question of which of these new possibilities should we pursue. In the medical context, how much resources should be expended looking for Worst Things? In a larger sociotechnical context, we have to wrestle with the ultimate value of a life and the responsibilities of a government in terms of providing access to healthcare.

The key point is that no amount of computational power can compensate for a lack of wisdom. The mathematical tools are somewhat analogous to the engine of an automobile. With a more powerful engine the car can go faster, further, and climb steeper slopes. In some respects this makes the car safer (e.g., in merging onto expressways) and more reliable, but in other ways it increases the potential for catastrophic accidents (e.g., high-speed collisions). Ultimately, the safety of the car will depend on the wisdom of the driver.

No amount of power can compensate for a lack of wisdom or driving experience. In fact, it is more likely that the opposite is true. The more powerful the car, the more important it will be to have a driver with experience at the wheel. Thus, constructs like wisdom and arete reflect an integration of power with values.

The person with arete has the power to do things that others cannot and the values to know what things are worth doing. This reflects an integration of thinking and emotion. An experienced

driver is able to discern what risks to take and what risks to avoid. This is likely the product of many mistakes that have helped to calibrate both knowledge (e.g., understanding of the car's limitations, ability to anticipate behaviors of other drivers) and emotion (e.g., appropriate levels of fear, confidence, and humility).

Thus, the spreadsheets provide increasingly more powerful engines for cognitive systems. The challenge is to make sure that we do not let these engines drive us quickly over a cliff. The emotional and social constraints associated with muddling through may be the necessary friction that helps us to keep on the road to success, rather than sliding into catastrophe.

Notes

1. Lindblom, C.E. (1979). Still muddling, not yet through. *Public Administration Review*, 39(6), 517–526.
2. Lopes, L.L. (1986). Aesthetics and the decision sciences. *IEEE Transactions on Systems, Man, and Cybernetics*, 16(3), 434–438.
3. Personal communication.
4. Reason, J. (1990). *Human error.* Cambridge, UK: Cambridge University Press.
5. Lopes (1986), pp. 434–438. (p. 436).
6. Klayman, J., & Ha, Y.-W. (1987). Confirmation, disconfirmation, and information in hypothesis testing. *Psychological Review*, 94(2), 211–228.
7. Wason, P.C. (1967). Reply to Wetherick. *Quarterly Journal of Experimental Psychology*, 15, 250.
8. Wason, P.C. (1960). On the failure to eliminate hypotheses in a conceptual task. *Quarterly Journal of Experimental Psychology*, 12, 129–150.
9. Klayman, & Ha (1987), p. 225.
10. Brunswik, E. (1956). *Perception and representative design of experiments.* Berkeley, CA: University of California Press.
11. Brill, E.D. Jr., Flach, J.M., Hopkins, L.D., & Ranjithan, S. (1990). *MGA: A decision support system for complex, incompletely defined problems.* IEEE Transactions on Systems, Man, and Cybernetics, 20(4), 745–757.
12. Feufel, M.A. (2009). *Bounded rationality in the Emergency Department.* Doctoral dissertation, Wright State University, Dayton, Ohio, USA.
13. Saul, J.R. (1993). *Voltaire's bastards.* New York: Vintage Books.
14. Pirsig, R.M. (1974). *Zen and the art of motorcycle maintenance.* New York: Harper Collins.
15. Hall, S.S. (2010). *Wisdom: From philosophy to neuroscience.* New York: Knopf. p. 4.
16. Hall, S.S. (2010). p. 11.
17. Hancock, P.A. (1997). *Essays on the future of human-machine systems.* Minneapolis: Human Factors Research Laboratory.
18. Klein, G.A. (1992). Using knowledge engineering to preserve corporate memory. In R.R. Hoffman (ed.) *The psychology of expertise.* (p. 170–187). New York: Springer-Verlag.

19. Klein, G.A. (2005). The power of intuition: How to use your gut feelings to make better decisions at work. New York, NY: Knopf Doubleday.

20. Sumida, J.T. (2008). *Decoding Clausewitz: A new approach to On War*. Lawrence, KA: University of Kansas Press.

21. Sumida, J.T. (2001). The relationship of history and theory in On War: The Clauswitzian ideal and its implications. *The Journal of Military History*, 65(2), 333–354. (p. 337).

22. Sumida, J.T. (2001) p. 346.

23. Sumida, J.T. (2001) p. 338.

24. Sumida, J.T. (2001). p. 338.

25. McCullough, D. (2015). *The Wright Brothers*. New York: Simon and Schuster.

26. Akerman, N. (Ed.) (1998). *The necessity of friction*. Boulder, CO: Westview Press.

27. Woods, D.D. (1995). *Toward a Theoretical Base for Representation Design in the Computer Medium: Ecological Perception and Aiding Human Cognition*. (p. 157–188).

    In Flach, J.M., Hancock P.A., Caird K., & Vicente K.J. (eds.). *An Ecological Approach to Human Machine Systems I: A Global Perspective*. Hillsdale, N.J.: Erlbaum.

28. Rasmussen, J. & Vicente, K.J. (1989). Coping with human errors through system design: Implications for ecological interface design. *International Journal of Man-Machine Studies*, 31, 517–534.

29. McEwen, T., Flach, J.M. & Elder, N.C. (2014). *Interfaces to medical information systems: Supporting evidence-based practice*. IEEE: Systems, Man, & Cybernetics Annual Meeting, 341–346. San Diego, CA. (Oct 5–8).

30. McEwen, T.R., Flach, J.M., & Elder, N.C. (2012). *Ecological interface for assessing cardiac disease*. Proceedings of the ASME 2012 11th Biennial Conference on Engineering Systems Design and Analysis, ESDA2012, July 2–4, Nantes, France. ASME ESDA2012-82974.

    Wears, R.L. (2014). *Health Information Technology and Victory. Annals of Emergency Medicine*. http://dx.doi.org/10.1016/j.annemergmed.2014.08.024

31. Flach, J.M., Lintern, G., & Larish, J.F. (1990). *Perceptual motor skill: A theoretical framework*.

    In R. Warren & A.H. Wertheim (Eds.). *Perception & Control of Self-Motion*. (pp. 327–355). Hillsdale, NJ: Erlbaum.

32. Todd, P.M. & Gigerenzer, G. (2012). *Ecological rationality*. New York: Oxford University Press.

33. Bennett, K.B. & Flach, J.M. (2011). *Display and Interface Design: Subtle Science, Exact Art*. London: Taylor & Francis. ISBN-13: 978-1520064384

34. Norman, D.A. (2004). *Emotional design. Why we love (or hate) everyday things*. New York: Basic Books.

35. Hassenzahl, M. (2010). *Experience design: Technology for all the right reasons*. Morgan & Claypool Publishers. www.morganclaypool.com.

    Sanders, E. & Stappers, P.J. (2012). *Convivial Toolbox: Generative research for the front end of design*. Amsterdam: BIS Publishers.

36. Damasio, A. (1999). *The feeling of what happens: Body and emotion in the making of consciousness*. Orlando, FL: Harcourt.

16

CLOSING THE CIRCLE

The goal of this final chapter is to summarize and emphasize the main points that we hoped to communicate with this book.

1. The first point is a metaphysical point about the reality of experience or cognitive systems. *The key point is that experience involves the coupling or integration of mind and matter as a unified real semiotic system that can be viewed from many valid perspectives, no single one of which is privileged.*
2. The second point has to do with the nature of the dynamics of experience. *The claim is that the dynamics of experience are inherently circular. Thus, it is very important for those interested in achieving a deeper understanding of experience to develop intuitions consistent with theories of closed-loop systems (e.g., control theory, observer theory, Self-Organizing Systems theory).*
3. The third point has to do with the nature of rationality. *The claim is that rationality involves a muddling through process that can only be evaluated pragmatically.* Does it eventually converge on stable, satisfying solutions? Does it survive?
4. The final point has to do with the implications for design. *The claim is that humans are uniquely capable of muddling through complex problems. Thus, the ultimate goal of design should be to engage humans more effectively in order to facilitate better muddling.*

Metaphysics

The claim that 'experience' is the fundamental grounds for reality is very difficult for many people, particularly in Western cultures, to grasp. This is partly because they instinctively assume experience to be *mental* and don't fully appreciate the role of the ecological niche or context in shaping experience. Thus, for many people in the West it is difficult to discriminate Radical Empiricism (i.e., James' claim that experience is the basis for reality) from Idealism or Mentalism.

A common challenge from skeptics is the "Tree Problem." It goes like this: "So, if my experience of the tree is reality, and I die (or if all humans die), you are saying that the tree will no longer exist."

Of course, this is NOT what we are saying. But what we are saying is that if there were no humans, then the reality of trees will be different than when there are humans. If there are no humans, then all the affordances that are unique to humans (e.g., refining lumber for building purposes) will also disappear. The tree's existence does not depend on humans, but the tree's reality does! A tree in a world without humans exists in a different reality than a tree in a world with humans. Similarly, a human in a world without trees exists in a different reality than one in a world with trees.

The key point is that the relations between humans and trees are real. And these relations exist in a single reality that includes both subjective and objective dimensions of experience.

Similarly, the same can be said for the relations between birds and trees; and squirrels and trees; etc. Some experiences of trees may be different for different animals, because the semiotic elements of affording, specifying, and satisfying are different. However, the experience of birds is not less real than the experience of humans. Different humans may experience trees differently. A lumberjack might focus on one set of affordances, while a child playing in the forest might focus on another set of affordances. The experiences may be different, but one experience is not less real than the others.

The ontological claim is that all the different experiences are part of a unified reality. The tree doesn't exist in one reality, while a person's idea of a tree exists in another reality.

This ontological position leads to a pluralistic epistemology, which suggests that there are many valid ways of knowing a tree! To know the tree through the experiences of a human is different than to know the tree through the experiences of a bird, but neither experience is privileged with respect to reality. Similarly, to know the tree through the experiences of a scientist or biologist is different than knowing the tree through the experiences of a child playing in the forest, but neither is less real.

The graspability of a limb or the climb-ability of a tree is not less real than its molecular structure. The reality of graspability or climb-ability reflects properties of both the child and the tree, while the molecular structure reflects properties that are important to the biologist, chemist, or paper manufacturer. While classical science has tended to search for attributes that are observer-independent, observations at the quantum level suggest that this search may be futile (e.g., remember Wheeler's surprise version of the 20 Questions Game). Regardless of the goals for the physical sciences, it is essential that a cognitive science expands the focus to include the reality of observer-dependent properties.

The practical implication of this for both a basic and an applied science of cognition is that the fundamental unit of analysis must span mind and matter. This is reflected in the triadic semiotic model (Figure 16.1). Breaking the triad into elements or into dyads destroys the relations that constitute experience (e.g., cognition). The claim is that breaking this triad changes the reality, eliminating the relations that are fundamental to the phenomenon of cognition. The claim is that the pieces, while perhaps interesting in their own right, will not add up to a complete understanding of cognition. You won't find graspability or climb-ability in the molecular structure of the tree or in the biology/physiology of the child.

The image in Figure 16.1 is a variation on our earlier representations of the triadic semiotic dynamic. As you can see, we are still exploring alternative ways to represent this. In Figure 16.1, rather than associating affording, specifying, and satisfying with objects within the representation, we suggest that it might be better to consider these as three different perspectives on the total triadic dynamic. We have faded the objects in the image in order to emphasize that we want to focus on the 'dynamic relations.'

The labels in the objects in Figure 16.1 are intended to make explicit the mapping to Peirce's triadic semiotics (i.e., referent/object, representamen/specifier, interpretent/specified) and to Wiener's Cybernetics (process, comparator, control/observer logic).

Thus, the critical ontological point is that the elements that make up the semiotic/cybernetic system are all essential components of a cognitive system. To dissect any of these components from the field of observation is to destroy or kill the phenomenon of cognition or experience.

In contrast to some contemporary trends associated with neuroscience or brain science, the claim is that cognition/experience does not happen in brains. It happens in the functional

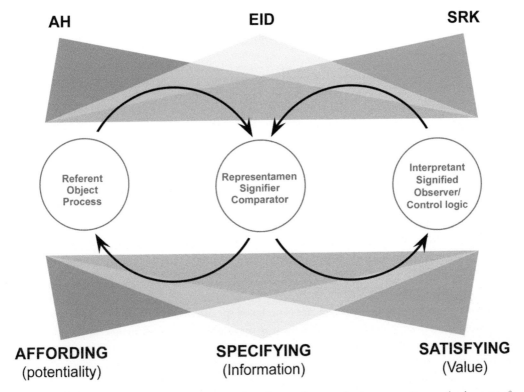

AH   **EID**   **SRK**

Referent
Object
Process

Representamen
Signifier
Comparator

Interpretant
Signified
Observer/
Control logic

AFFORDING   **SPECIFYING**   **SATISFYING**
(potentiality)   (Information)   (Value)

Figure 16.1 This figure shows affording, specifying, and satisfying as three overlapping perspectives on the dynamics of the semiotic triad. The objects are faded to emphasize that the dynamics (i.e., represented by arrows) are the objects of study. Labels on the objects illustrate the isomorphisms with Peirce's Semiotics and with Wiener's Cybernetics.

interactions involved in coping with the complexities of day-to-day living (and working). Certainly, the brain is an important component of the dynamic of experience, but an exclusive focus on the brain biology/physiology will never add up to an understanding of experience. However, a brain science framed in the context of the triadic semiotic dynamic will be better positioned to ask smart questions and to parse the complexities of brain biology/physiology in ways that might illuminate the larger whole of experience.

The triadic perspective has important theoretical and methodological implications. While the contrast with some contemporary neuroscience trends may seem to be anti-reductionist, the point is more subtle than that. Reductionism will always be essential to scientific reasoning. The point is that some reductions (some ways of parsing the phenomenon) will be useful (will add up), and other ways of parsing the problem will destroy the phenomenon of interest.

We suggest that the partitioning in terms of affording, specifying, and satisfying and the associated methodological frames reflected in the abstraction hierarchy, ecological interface design, and the SRK model provide promising directions for further exploration.

The motivating concern is that theories and methodological approaches that are predicated on separating *Mind* and *Matter* will never add up to a satisfying understanding of *What Matters*. Ultimately, we are not making a claim about an absolutely RIGHT perspective, but rather for one

NECESSARY perspective with respect to cognitive science and experience design. We allow that this perspective may not be sufficient, but we claim that our understanding of cognition and experience cannot be complete if this perspective is not considered.

Circular Dynamics

A salient feature of the triadic system illustrated in Figure 16.1 is the circular couplings among the components. This reflects an abduction, learning, or adaptive process where the consequences of action feed back as information. This circular flow of information means that actions both shape consequences and are shaped by consequences. Thus, no absolute temporal precedence allows any component to be unambiguously isolated as either 'cause' or 'effect.'

This dynamic is analogous to the dynamics of natural selection. Just as it would be a mistake to say that either genetic variation or ecological forces 'cause' the speciation of life forms, it would be a mistake to say that either mental or environmental forces cause behavior or experience. Experience emerges from the interplay of the multiple sources of constraints. Mental aspects of experience (e.g., beliefs, hypotheses, heuristics) are selected or reinforced as a function of the degree to which they satisfy the functional demands of an ecology. Experience emerges as a property of the coupling between Mind and Matter.

Fortunately, a growing body of theories is designed specifically to address the dynamics of systems with circular couplings. Unfortunately, it is very difficult for most people in the social sciences to access the literature associated with these theories, because few academic programs in the social sciences offer either courses associated with dynamic systems or the prerequisites required for the courses offered in other disciplines.

We first learned about the dynamics of circular systems through early exposure to control theory and observer theory, in the context of the design of engineering control systems. However, developments in nonlinear dynamics and theories of self-organization were very important to us for expanding the intuitions developed from analysis of simple linear systems to more complex natural systems.

Although the literature on self-organization and complexity reveals many of the limitations of classical linear systems theories for modeling many natural systems, our experiences lead us to believe that there is great pedagogical value from the study of simple linear systems (e.g., control systems and observers) that will generalize toward insights into the dynamics of more complex, natural systems. Thus, we are troubled by current tendencies to completely dismiss linear control theory in the process of embracing nonlinear dynamics. We are convinced that both linear and nonlinear dynamics should be basic elements in social science curricula.

When evaluating the performance of circular systems, it is essential to consider alternatives to the conventional concept of time, as discrete positions (ticks) on a directed line. One important alternative is the frequency domain, where time is indexed by sine wave patterns. The frequency and amplitude of sine waves provides an important alternative to ticks on a clock/metronome, as a means for characterizing flow. Whereas the conventional image provides a useful perspective for isolating events *in time*, the sinusoidal image provides a useful perspective for isolating relations and patterns *over time* (e.g., synchrony, rhythm, melody).

Again, the point is NOT that one representation of time is right and the other is wrong. Rather, the point is that both perspectives are bounded with respect to the real complexities of experience. The conventional view emphasizes the 'notes' and the temporal relations within a line of

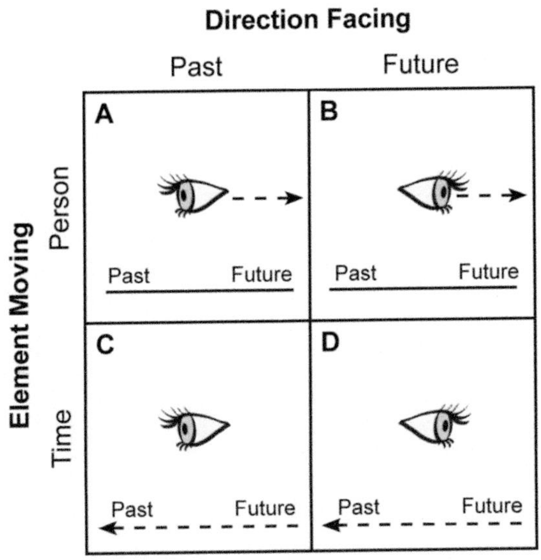

Direction Facing

Figure 16.2 Four alternative perspectives for conceptualizing time.

music (e.g., precedence), but obscures the rhythms and melodies that span lines of music (e.g., invariance across scales). The frequency domain emphasizes the melodies and relations across scales, but can obscure the notes and relations within scales. By considering both perspectives for representing temporal relations, it is possible to get a richer understanding than is possible from either perspective alone. The combination of perspectives makes it possible to see the notes in the context of the melody and vice versa.

In addition to the different analytical ways of looking at experience in and over time, it is important to consider the foundational metaphors that shape our concepts of time. Figure 16.2 illustrates four different ways to conceive of time as a function of the direction the observer is facing and the element that is moving.[1]

In Western cultures our construct of time is generally based on the assumption that we are facing the future (Quadrants B & D). Within this framework, we tend to be comfortable with either motion of the observer (e.g., we are moving through time) or with motion of time (e.g., time is flowing past). With this image the past is behind us and thus invisible. This leads to a construct of memory where the past must be 'stored' so that it can be available to us in the present and future.

However, a few cultures take a different orientation. In their metaphor, the observer is facing the past (Quadrants A & C). In this metaphor, the past is visible and the future is obscured or uncertain. Perhaps, this provides a better context for thinking about the closed-loop, abduction dynamic of adaptive systems. In the closed-loop system, feedback resulting from past actions is the input (i.e., what the observer is looking at). This feedback is the basis for both observation and control. Observation involves integration of feedback over time to determine the current state and to predict future states. Control involves integration of feedback to guide action. Further, learning means integrating over past mistakes and successes in order to better tune to the demands of the future.

This shift in orientation with regard to past and future has significant implications for the construct of memory. Since we are looking at the past, storage is not so important. Rather, the function of memory is to integrate over past experiences in order to extract the patterns (e.g., schema) that will facilitate anticipation of the future in order to guide actions that will ultimately satisfy aspirations.

In essence, an abduction logic involves integrating what one has seen over the past in order to make smart guesses and choices with respect to an uncertain future. For everyday life, the future lies out of sight. However, because there are constraints, such as physical laws and social conventions, it is sometimes possible to predict the future, by carefully examining (integrating) the past.

The idea of integration emphasizes that it is insufficient to think about experience as being *in time*. It is also necessary to consider experience as being *over time*. In other words, experience is not necessarily punctate or discrete, such as frames of a movie. Rather, experience is extended over time as nested patterns of flow. This suggests for example that the coupling between notes and melody in a song are bi-directional. In a circle, the notes shape the experience of the melody, while simultaneously the melody is shaping the experience of the notes. It also suggests that perception of the melody allows us to generalize learning to new contexts (e.g., a different scale).

As both James and Gibson have remarked, there is no absolute present—no clear divide between past and future. Gibson writes:

> The stream of experience does not consist of an instantaneous present and a linear past receding into the distance; it is not a 'traveling razor's edge' dividing the past from the future. . . . A special sense impression clearly ceases when the sensory excitation ends, but a perception does not. It does not become a memory after a certain length of time. A perception, in fact, does not have an end. Perceiving goes on.[2]

To continue our musical metaphor, a perception of a note is co-extensive with the perception of a melody, and more globally the perception of a melody is co-extensive with the cultural experience of music. It is a fractal type of structure, where there is an infinite nesting of parts and wholes.

Again, it is important to appreciate that the conventional view of time and the associated images of causation are not necessarily wrong. However, they are incomplete or insufficient to fully appreciate the dynamics of experience. The consequence of reducing closed-loop systems using only causal models is to trivialize important dimensions of experience.

The main point is that circular dynamics cannot be described or understood fully using models based on conventional images of cause-effect or stimulus-response. Conventional analyses and conventional logic break down for systems that are circular, iterative, or self-referencing. A classical example that illustrates this breakdown is the famous Liar's Paradox.

"This sentence is false."

If this sentence is true, then it must be false. This is a contradiction. Circular systems that feed back to reference themselves are tricky. As we have seen, they lead to coastlines of infinite length contained within finite spaces (another apparent contradiction). Circular systems challenge many of the assumptions at the basis of conventional Western scientific thought. In particular, circular systems require a BOTH-AND perspective, where context matters. Such an approach may provide a path toward resolving the many contradictions that arise in the conventional EITHER-OR search for absolute truths.

310

THE ERROR LIES, IT SEEMS TO ME, IN ASSUMING THAT EITHER INNATE IDEAS OR ACQUIRED IDEAS MUST BE APPLIED TO BARE SENSORY INPUTS FOR PERCEIVING TO OCCUR. THE FALLACY IS TO ASSUME THAT BECAUSE INPUTS CONVEY NO KNOWLEDGE THEY CAN SOMEHOW BE MADE TO YIELD KNOWLEDGE BY "PROCESSING" THEM.... KNOWLEDGE OF THE WORLD CANNOT BE EXPLAINED BY SUPPOSING THAT KNOWLEDGE OF THE WORLD ALREADY EXISTS. ALL FORMS OF COGNITIVE PROCESSING IMPLY COGNITION SO AS TO ACCOUNT FOR COGNITION.

KNOWLEDGE OF THE ENVIRONMENT, SURELY, DEVELOPS AS PERCEPTION DEVELOPS, EXTENDS AS THE OBSERVER TRAVELS, GETS FINER AS THEY LEARN TO SCRUTINIZE, GETS LONGER AS THEY APPREHEND MORE EVENTS, AND GETS RICHER AS THEY NOTICE MORE AFFORDANCES. KNOWLEDGE OF THIS SORT DOES NOT "COME FROM" ANYWHERE; IT IS GOT BY LOOKING, ALONG WITH LISTENING, FEELING, SMELLING, AND TASTING.

J.J. Gibson[3]

Rationality

Perhaps the ability to specify a single *a priori* Truth or Validity value to a particular choice or to a process for making a choice based on formal analysis is what makes classical logic and mathematical analysis so attractive as potential benchmarks for scoring rationality? Establishing extrinsic standards for measuring (e.g., the meter) has been an important and useful step in the development of an objective experimental science. It is not surprising that people have attempted to use the same strategy to build a science of Mind. Thus, mathematical reasoning and logic were chosen as potential standards for measurement.

But perhaps in attempting to emulate the successes of the physical sciences, the social sciences have missed something important? Feynman hints at this possibility when he points to psychology as a 'cargo cult' science.[4] That is, he suggests that while social sciences go through the surface actions associated with doing science, they often fail to grasp the deeper meaning of these actions.

It is a question of precedence. Measurement is important, but there is a very important decision that must precede the choice of measures. That is, the decision about what dimensions of the phenomenon (e.g., position, velocity, mass, energy) to measure. Is it possible that in their rush to achieve credibility relative to more mature sciences, social sciences have defined their phenomena around their measures, rather than choosing their measures to reflect the phenomenon?

Have the social sciences organized their experimental programs around the things that are easiest to count/evaluate (e.g., reaction time, percent correct, grammar/syntax)? And in doing this, have they missed essential properties of experience (e.g., meaning, emotion, creativity)?

Whenever you examine decision making and problem solving in complex ecologies like a hospital emergency department, it quickly becomes obvious that the process is often a very messy kind of muddling through that reflects competing values and agendas, fuzzy fields of ill-defined possibilities, and ambiguous information.

The fundamental question is: Is the messiness noise that hides the phenomena of interest or is the messiness an essential feature of the phenomena of experience? Conventionally, the messiness

IN THE SOUTH SEAS THERE IS A CARGO CULT OF PEOPLE. DURING THE WAR THEY SAW AIRPLANES LAND WITH LOTS OF GOOD MATERIALS, AND THEY WANT THE SAME THING TO HAPPEN NOW. SO THEY'VE ARRANGED TO MAKE THINGS LIKE RUNWAYS, TO PUT FIRES ALONG THE SIDES OF RUNWAYS, TO MAKE A WOODEN HUT FOR A MAN TO SIT IN, WITH TWO WOODEN PIECES ON HIS HEAD LIKE HEADPHONES AND BARS OF BAMBOO STICKING OUT LIKE ANTENNAS — HE'S THE CONTROLLER — AND THEY WAIT FOR AIRPLANES TO LAND.

I THINK THE EDUCATIONAL AND PSYCHOLOGICAL STUDIES I MENTIONED ARE EXAMPLES OF WHAT I LIKE TO CALL CARGO CULT SCIENCE.

THEY'VE DONE EVERYTHING RIGHT. THE FORM IS PERFECT. IT LOOKS EXACTLY THE WAY IT LOOKED BEFORE. BUT IT DOESN'T WORK. NO AIRPLANES LAND. SO, I CALL THESE THINGS CARGO CULT SCIENCE, BECAUSE THEY FOLLOW ALL THE APPARENT PERCEPTS AND FORMS OF SCIENTIFIC INVESTIGATION, BUT THEY'RE MISSING SOMETHING ESSENTIAL, BECAUSE THE PLANES DO NOT LAND.

Richard Feynman[5]

has been treated as noise. This leads to an experimental strategy of choosing more controlled laboratory puzzles, in order to reduce the noise and reveal the deeper phenomenon. And it naturally leads to the conclusion that deviations from the prescriptive standards reflect weaknesses or limitations of human rationality.

Note that an important side effect of this conventional view is that the weaknesses and limitations of the 'standards' (e.g., the analytical computations) tend to get overlooked. Thus, the standards become idealized, which can lead to the conclusion that the solution to many problems in complex environments is to replace the humans with automated technologies designed to conform with the analytical ideals. Thus, automatic pilots, electronic healthcare systems, and driverless cars have often been advocated as 'solutions' that will make these systems safer and more efficient (i.e., more nearly optimal).

One of the implications of the Liar's Paradox is that it demonstrates a potential fundamental limitation of formal, analytical approaches to rationality. Practically, the limitations of analytical approaches have become increasingly obvious as automation has been integrated into work domains, such as aviation and healthcare. Again, the power of computation can increase the field of possibilities and expand access to information, but this does not necessarily lead to either increased safety or efficiency.

Ultimately, the impacts on efficiency and safety depend on value judgments made by people in the sociotechnical systems. For example, Perrow describes how accidents remain 'normal' in domains, where the technology advances are primarily applied to increasing efficiency (e.g., faster aircraft and denser airspaces).[6]

Although some types of errors are reduced through the application of computational technologies, other classes of errors increase (e.g., mode errors). The reality is that ANY computation is bounded with respect to the real complexities of domains such as aviation and healthcare. There is no single best way, no absolute recipe for success, no *a priori* optimal solution.

Since there is no *a priori* solution to many of life's problems, it often becomes necessary to create a solution through active, real-time engagement with the problems. It becomes necessary *to make the decision right*. This typically reflects a trial-and-error learning process. It involves muddling through. Far from being noise, the muddling observed in complex work domains is in fact the essence of rationality. Thus, the fundamental question with respect to rationality is to understand the muddling process, and the practical question with respect to design is how technologies can be used to improve or facilitate the muddling process.

This perspective puts heuristics in a different light. In this context it is not at all surprising that heuristics, like any computation, tactic, or strategy, are bounded with respect to their applicability. However, now the bounds are attributed to the 'fit' between the situation and awareness, rather than exclusively to human information processing limitations. For heuristics that are applied broadly, an important facet of the question becomes why are these heuristics selected? What makes them generally useful? In this context, heuristics are evaluated as *smart mechanisms* that are bounded in terms of situations, rather than *biases* that reflect internal limitations or weaknesses.

This approach does not deny the limitations on human information processing (e.g, limited working memory). However, it recognizes that these limitations rarely place hard limits on what smart people can do. In fact, that is what makes heuristics (e.g., skills and rules) so interesting. These smart mechanisms often reflect very intelligent strategies for working around the intrinsic limitations, in order to meet the demands of complex situations. Thus, the limitations that are apparent when people confront novel situations are rarely apparent after extensive experience with a situation.

So, the main point is that the fundamental question with regards to rationality focuses on learning. The index of quality of rationality then focuses on how efficiently the system converges on a satisfying solution to a situation. This is fundamentally a question of stability. Does the circular dynamic converge on a stable relation or does it diverge into extinction?

In this context, a rational system is one that learns from its mistakes and adapts toward increasingly stable relations with its ecology. An irrational system is one that fails to adapt, by either making the same mistakes over and over again or by overcorrecting (not tuning appropriately to the feedback). Damasio's work (described in Chapter 12) suggests that human emotions may play an important role in our ability to learn from our mistakes.

Metaphorically, the conventional approach to rationality suggests that *the proof of the pudding is in the recipe*. That is, the test of rationality is conformity to *a priori* prescriptions or rules derived from mathematics and logic. In contrast, the circular dynamic of abduction suggests that *the proof of the pudding is in the eating*. That is, the test of an idea can only be determined in relation to a context of use—it is an emergent property of interactions. It suggests that rationality can only be evaluated pragmatically. Does it work in practice? Does it eventually lead to satisfying consequences? Does the pudding actually taste good?

Design

As suggested by the earlier Feynman quote and consistent with the dynamics of abduction, the ultimate question for a science is "Do the planes land?" That is, can we apply our theories of experience to solve relevant practical problems, such as improving outcomes, efficiency, and safety in the emergency department? Can our theories of cognition and learning lead to designs that actually improve performance in complex work domains?

The ideas in this book reflect more than 60 years of combined experience in trying to apply cognitive science in order to design more effective sociotechnical systems. These experiences have forced us to re-evaluate that cognitive science. The experiences have caused us to question many of the things that we were taught and many of the things that we once firmly believed.

As a result of these experiences, we have gained a deep appreciation of the quote from William James in the first chapter that "the metaphysical puzzles become the most urgent of all." Unfortunately, we have also learned that most of the people responsible for designing many of our technologies have little patience for metaphysics, much less theory. We have been directly told that we are "far too theoretical to contribute anything useful for most engineering problems."

Most designers are not interested in philosophy or science. What they want is a design procedure or process (e.g., Vicente's Work Domain analysis[7] or Leveson's Systems Theoretic Process Analysis—STPA[8]) that they can follow step-by-step to a satisfying design solution. We believe that Work Domain Analysis and the STPA process are very powerful tools for evaluating and discovering meaning and potential hazards in sociotechnical systems, and that the systems perspective that they are based on is very compatible with the general orientation of the triadic semiotic model. However, we are skeptical whether these processes can be successfully applied, unless the people using them have an appreciation for the underlying theoretical and metaphysical properties of human experience. No matter how high the quality of a tool (e.g., chisel), it will not compensate for a lack of skill (e.g., ability of the sculptor). We believe that the skill in applying tools like Work Domain Analysis and STPA depends on a deep understanding of the triadic semiotic dynamic.

We are hopeful that this is changing. We see evidence for this hope in growing interest among designers in Cognitive Systems Engineering (CSE) and user experience (UX Design). Although the labels are not always a reliable basis for this hope, since some people embrace the labels without fully appreciating the theoretical and metaphysical implications. Unfortunately, there are many cargo cults.

The main point we want to make with respect to design is that the unit of analysis MUST be the triadic semiotic system! That is, we are not designing technologies (e.g., machines or interfaces), we are designing experiences! This is emphasized in Figure 16.1 by suggesting that each of the components of Rasmussen's Cognitive Systems Engineering approach reflects alternative complementary perspectives on the entire semiotic dynamic.

With respect to triadic semiotic systems, we believe that humans have unique capabilities when it comes to learning and meaning processing. These capabilities reflect the ability to integrate logic and emotion in order to discern *what can be done* and *what should be done*. This integration of logic and emotion allows a flexibility in adapting to changing situations that is not easily achieved with rule-based, logical systems. This flexibility allows the triadic system to create solutions to a wide range of situations that, while seldom optimal, are generally satisfying. That is, the flexibility allows the system to be robust in the face of ambiguity and rapidly changing ecologies.

The practical implication of this belief in human capabilities is that we believe that a primary goal for design should be to heighten engagement of humans with the problem domains. This involves enhancing perspicacity, biasing people toward those heuristics and strategies that are most likely to succeed, and in increasing peoples' emotional investment in wanting the system to work.

This approach contrasts with some previous trends in design that have been predicated on the idea that humans are a weak link or a source of error and that the ultimate solution will be to eventually replace the human with increasingly capable automated systems. We fully appreciate the power that increasingly capable technologies offer for improving the performance of triadic systems, but this power will be most effective when it is put into the hands of smart humans. As illustrated in the example of the Wright Brothers presented earlier, we believe that the ultimate solution for improved muddling is to use technology to put control into the hands of humans.

An irony of technological and scientific progress with respect to cognitive processes is that it adds to the complexity, rather than reducing it. It increases the number of possibilities, for both good and ill. It increases the amount of available data, for both enhancing signals and adding noise. Thus, the advance of technology will not reduce the cognitive demands, but rather it will only increase them!

With respect to design, our goal is not to provide an answer or a process that will simplify the designer's task. Rather, our goal is to provide an antidote against potential trivializations of phenomena of cognition and the uncritical adoption of simple, easy-to-understand (and market) wrong design solutions. Our goal is to help designers to more fully appreciate the real complexities of experience. We hope that this deeper appreciation might be a seed for discoveries and innovations that are beyond our capacities to anticipate.

We believe that the critical first step to innovation is to ask interesting questions. Perhaps, the contribution of philosophy and basic science (theory) is not to provide answers to design questions, but to shape the questions that designers ask. In essence, science helps to map the 'space' of inquiry. It is up to designers to decide specifically where to go in that space. But it can often be a long and difficult journey, and there are no guarantees for a satisfying result in the end. However, if scientists and designers collaborate, both the successes and failures can reflect back to further refine the conceptual map that will guide the next iteration of theory and design. By bridging or narrowing the gaps between science and design, theory and practice, art and technology, we improve both science and design.

THERE IS NOTHING SO PRACTICAL AS A GOOD THEORY

Kurt Lewin[9]

The Sound of One Hand Clapping

This book has been a long and difficult, but rewarding journey of discovery that has taken over 10 years. At the start we had a collection of threads (Pragmatism, Functionalism, Gestalt Psychology, Ecological Psychology, Semiotics, Control Theory, Complexity Theory, Cognitive Systems Engineering) and a very rough sense that it might be possible to weave these threads together in an interesting and aesthetically pleasing way. We were hopeful that the final tapestry might be of interest to anyone who was wondering about the nature of human experience and the implications for design.

Though we had a rough vision at the start, we are a bit surprised at the final result. At some point on the journey, the creation process shifted from trying to MAKE the arrow hit the target, to LETTING the arrow hit the target. At the start we thought we had answers to important questions. The original title was: "The Abduction Engine." We had a sense that Peirce's constructs of Abduction and Triadic Semiotics provided solutions to many important contemporary questions about cognitive systems.

Still thinking we had the answer, but wanting to engage a wider audience, we changed the title to: "What Matters." However, at the end we realized that the title was misleading. What had looked to us to be the peak of the mountain at the start turned out to be just a foothill at the end. We realized that we had not reached an answer. We had just reformulated the question. Thus, for our next title we added a question mark:

"What Matters?"

Perhaps, this is consistent with the logic of circles. In walking around the circle, the farther you go from the start, the closer you get to the start. The circle has no end, only an infinite number of starting/stopping positions. Perhaps, the idea that there is an ultimate answer to the complexity is an illusion. Perhaps, it really is turtles all the way down—each question sitting on the back of other bigger questions?

Perhaps, the fundamental challenge of science, design, and life in general is not to find the answers (e.g., 42), but to refine the questions? We create temporary solutions, but these solutions open up new opportunities, new threats, and new questions. As with the fractal coastline, the deeper we probe, the more wiggles we find.

In the end, we decided that 'what matters' is *meaning*. That is, what matters is our ability to resonate to the meaningful properties of our experience. The key conclusion is that meaning is not 'in our heads' and it is not 'in the world.' Rather, meaning emerges from the coupling of agents and ecologies.

We expect that this book was a difficult read for many, and even at the end many readers may be skeptical that the threads have been integrated into a coherent picture. We thought we had answers when we began writing, and we expect that it was a search for answers that motivated many people to take this journey with us. For some it will be frustrating to find that we don't have the answers to give them.

Those who are determined to get to the ultimate mountain peak are likely to be disappointed by this book. But a few will simply enjoy the hike and the changing vistas along the way. In fact, they might be happy to discover that the journey is not over and thrilled at the prospect that even more satisfying vistas lie ahead of them. They may be excited and eager to discover that it is up to them to create their own answers, or to further refine the questions.

Human experience is all around us. And yet, it can be hard to see, particularly if our focus is on an extrinsic ideal, a distant peak. A focus on the wrong thing or at the wrong distance may occlude the very things we are looking for. For us, this book is an exercise of changing focus, searching for a deeper appreciation of common sense and for better ways to frame the question: What Matters?

Notes

1. See Lakoff, G., & Johnson, M. (1999). *Philosophy in the flesh: The embodied mind and its challenge to western thought.* New York: Basic Books.
2. Gibson, J.J. (1979). *The ecological approach to visual perception.* Boston, MA: Houghton Mifflin. (p. 253).
3. Gibson (1979), p. 253.
4. Feynman, R.P. (1985). *Surely you're joking Mr. Feynman.* Toronto, Canada: Bantam Books.
5. Feynman (1985), pp. 310–311.
6. Perrow, C. (1984). *Normal accidents.* New York: Basic Books.
7. Vicente, K.J. (1999). *Cognitive work analysis.* Mahwah, NJ: Erlbaum.
8. Leveson, N.G. (2011). *Engineering a safer world.* Cambridge, MA: MIT Press.
9. Lewin, K. (1951). *Field theory in social science: Selected theoretical papers.* New York: Harper.

DURING A HIKE IN THE MOUNTAINS, ROBERT PIRSIG REFLECTS ON WHAT HE TERMS 'EGO CLIMBING.' WHILE ROBERT FOCUSES ON THE JOURNEY, ENJOYING THE FOREST AND THE OCCASIONAL VISTAS, CHRIS IS FOCUSING ON THE MOUNTAIN TOP, EXPERIENCING FRUSTRATION WHEN THE NEXT CREST REVEALS A STILL DISTANT PEAK AND EXPERIENCING THE FEAR OF NOT HAVING THE STRENGTH TO SCALE THE NEXT SLOPE. PIRSIG ASSOCIATED THIS FIXATION ON THE MOUNTAIN PEAK WITH "EGO CLIMBING."

NOW THAT YOU ARE AT THE END OF THE BOOK, YOU MAY WELL BE DISAPPOINTED TO FIND OUT THAT YOU ARE NOT AT THE FINAL PEAK. MANY QUESTIONS REMAIN WITH RESPECT TO THE QUESTION: 'WHAT MATTERS?'

FOR US, THE JOURNEY OF THIS BOOK HAS BEEN A SATISFYING CLIMB. ALTHOUGH WE WERE NAÏVE ENOUGH TO THINK WE KNEW THE ROUTE AND WE STARTED WITH THE INTENTION OF REACHING THE PEAK, WE ARE NOT UNSATISFIED TO END THE BOOK WITHOUT A FINAL ANSWER.

THE THINGS THAT MAKE THE JOURNEY SATISFYING ARE THE QUESTIONS BEING ASKED, NOT THE ANSWERS. AS PIRSIG DISCOVERED EARLY IN HIS CAREER AS A SCIENTIST, SUCCESSFUL EXPERIMENTS GENERALLY PRODUCED MORE QUESTIONS THAN ANSWERS. IF YOU SEE HUMAN EXPERIENCE AS A DYNAMIC THAT IS EVOLVING - THEN THERE IS NO FIXED PEAK - NO FINAL ABSOLUTE ANSWER OR 'TRUTH' TO BE DISCOVERED.

PERHAPS, THE POINT OF SCIENCE IS NOT TO GENERATE ANSWERS, BUT TO REFINE THE QUESTIONS. NEW QUESTIONS ALLOW US TO SEE IN NEW WAYS, TO ENJOY NEW VISTAS, AND TO EXPERIENCE THE WORLD IN INCREASING SATISFYING WAYS. THE PEAK IS NOT A FIXED POINT SOMEWHERE OUT THERE INDEPENDENT FROM US. RATHER, IT IS A DYNAMIC TARGET THAT WE ARE BOTH PURSUING AND CREATING.

SO, THIS IS WHERE WE LEAVE YOU - TO PURSUE STILL HIGHER PEAKS, TO ASK STILL DEEPER QUESTIONS. BUT WE IMPLORE YOU TO NOT FIXATE ON REACHING AN ULTIMATE ANSWER; BUT RATHER TO ENJOY THE JOURNEY TO PLACES THAT GERDA, FRED AND I MAY NEVER SEE.

INDEX

Page numbers in italics indicate figures and in bold indicate tables on the corresponding pages.